27
AVI
CES

CÉSAR FRANK
AND HIS CIRCLE

THE MONUMENT TO CÉSAR FRANCK
Alfred Lenoir, sculptor

LAURENCE DAVIES

CÉSAR FRANCK
AND
HIS CIRCLE

BARRIE & JENKINS
LONDON

© 1970 BY LAURENCE DAVIES
FIRST PUBLISHED 1970 BY
BARRIE & JENKINS LTD
2 CLEMENT'S INN, LONDON WC2
SBN 214 65085 5
PRINTED AND BOUND IN GREAT BRITAIN BY
W & J MACKAY & CO LTD, CHATHAM

CONTENTS

ILLUSTRATIONS

ACKNOWLEDGEMENTS

As may be assumed, this book poses a variety of obligations, both with respect to writing and production. My first duty must accordingly be to discharge these obligations as best I can.

In the matter of sources, I am clearly indebted to a great many French publishers, of whom Messrs Durand, Salabert, Hamelle, Heugel and Leduc are the most important. My gratitude to these takes account, not merely of special courtesies shown to me on visits I have paid to them, but also of permission to reprint brief musical examples from works listed in their catalogues. UMP, the chief agency for French music in London, has likewise assisted me in importing scores from its headquarters in Montague Street.

Some of my research in writing the book was carried out at the Bibliothèque de l'Opéra in the Rue Scribe, Paris, and I should like to proclaim my sincere thanks to M. André Ménétrat, the Librarian, for allowing me to make use of his facilities. A similar acknowledgement is extended to the clergy at the Church of Sainte-Clotilde, who answered queries I put to them about César Franck's work as an organist there; to the registrar of the Schola Cantorum for supplying me with information about Vincent d'Indy and the school's history; and to the librarian and staff of the Paris Conservatoire, where so many of Franck's pupils received their formal training.

Nearer home, I must say how much I have appreciated the criticisms and comments of eminent authorities on French music, some of whom have helped me by writing constructive reviews of my previous book in this field, and others by their kindly interest. In particular, I should like to name Rollo Myers, Edward Lockspeiser, G. W. Hopkins, and Felix Aprahamian, the last of whom laboured hardest on my behalf by giving up his valuable time to reading the complete manuscript. For further observations on my style and presentation of the subject, I owe much to Robert Layton, Music Talks Producer for the B.B.C., for whom I did a series of talks on French music during the summer of 1969.

Coming to the question of production, the staff of Messrs Barrie & Jenkins merit individual and collective acknowledgement. Mr John Bunting, and his colleague Mr John Pattisson, have each lent me the warmest encouragement, while I remain much indebted to Mr Paul Courtenay for his meticulous copying of the music examples and Miss Deborah Carswell for patient editorial assistance. The production department, too, is entitled to my thanks for its contribution. Most of all, however, I am grateful to the firm's former Music Editor, Mr David Sharp, who not only corrected all manner of niggling errors in the text, but whose trust and belief in the value of my work leave me without words to express what I feel. For me, he has been the kind of Editor every author looks forward to having, but seldom if ever encounters.

Lastly, I should like to pay tribute to my wife once again, who has smoothed out countless practical obstacles with an altruism of which no one else would have been capable.

Introduction

The world of César Franck and his pupils, though less than a century away from us in time, has already come to seem so remote in its tastes that we can only marvel, in our present age of licence, at the strength of the chains that bound it. A lofty and intimidating emplacement set in the most insecure soil, it was essentially an invention of the Second Empire, to the unheedful corruption of which it provided the perfect complement. Drenched in the odour of sanctity, yet always managing to exude a whiff of sensuality, it was a world fit only for moral heroes, men able to combine in judicious proportions the extremes of passion and self-control. True to its principles, its denizens sought to be loyal and devout, even though each exhibited some subtle creative blemish. Like the sober universe of Dr Arnold—which it very much resembles—it had its roster of successes and failures, only the founder contriving to escape classification.

To those who are intent on resurrecting this world, the obvious step must be to avoid prejudice. It would be simple enough to bypass controversy by falling back on the judgements of a more trusting age, but to take this option would probably be to forfeit the curiosity of today's readers. Our contemporary biographers, as sceptical as they are inquisitive, tend to reject all limitations placed upon their powers, upholding the doctrine that nothing has the right to remain 'in camera'. Adopting their cue from Lytton Strachey, they are disposed to echo: 'Je ne propose rien, je n'impose rien, j'expose.' Armed with such a bleak philosophy, all we can do when writing about César Franck and his followers is to begin by rehearsing the difficulties. For like most nineteenth-century worthies, Franck endeavoured to hide his doubts beneath a rigorously moral exterior, giving the world little cause to question the propriety of his sentiments. When we take into account the unpsychological nature of the age in which he lived and died, the wisdom of resorting to complex explanations may be freely challenged. In the absence of properly constituted case-study, the use of clinical tools becomes still more dubious. Yet it is surely true that modern methods, employed with the right degree of scrupulousness, can shed light on every stage of our history. It is hoped that by tempering these methods with the composer's own virtues of tolerance and charity we shall be allowed to uncover things our predecessors have neglected or ignored.

Let us start by asking some of the really puzzling questions. How is it, for instance, that a Belgian, unencumbered by any of the fads of the Gallic sensibility, was invited to become the defender of French musical culture? And why, when it was in the opera-house and not the organ-loft that reputations were sought and won, did it take a failed pianist, immured in churchly obscurity at Sainte-Clotilde, to awaken the talents of an entire generation of French musicians? To what special mystique did Franck owe those loyalties upon which he was to draw so heavily for his renown? What part did the composer's German ancestry play in things? These are all questions every reader will want to see answered; though not everyone is likely to be convinced by the evidence we shall bring. What makes them so daunting is that the Franck circle was limited by just that intense musicality that has so persistently been ascribed to it, rendering it unusually restricted in the material it can hope to yield the biographer. Compared with Ravel's band of 'apaches', or the more cosmopolitan 'Les Six', its exigencies are at once apparent. To assign its members to a plane of widest cultural significance—a natural procedure when considering the 'fin-de-siècle' group and its successor—would accordingly seem a risky and even spurious course to pursue. Morally and spiritually, the circle exhibited a fascinating range of symptoms; but there is a temptation to represent these as the product of some deliberate *kitsch*. One of the most taxing issues to confront the writer is therefore that of deciding upon what is a right and proper perspective. To throw open the door too wide would be to exaggerate the circle's powers of self-consciousness, while to narrow the approach might be to pass up valuable insights.

At this point, it is time my own aims were made clear. I did not wish to embark on a fully comprehensive study, partly because this would have required virtually unlimited documentary resources, certain of which do not yet aspire to be common property. Neither did it seem feasible to analyse the full corpus of music written by both Franck and his various associates. Such a labour of Hercules would have precluded attention being paid to other, less technical, matters. Contrary to either of these aims, my object was to focus the reader's interest on the nature of the circle itself, to inquire into the existence of what after all seemed a very remarkable gathering of artists; and to try and appraise, in musical terms, the contribution which they made to the life of their times. From the moment of setting out on the project, it struck me as curious that a haphazard assembly of students, more used to busying themselves with the theory than the practice of their art, should have come together in Paris at a time when military service beckoned fiercely to all below a certain age, and created an enclave in the founding of which they achieved, not merely a compelling musical aesthetic, but a degree of self-realization as complete as it was unlooked for. Such a happening seemed sufficiently unusual to constitute its own justification. Throughout this book, my role will consequently be that of chronicler of an artistic enterprise. That this enterprise was not destined to win great fame for its architects is a fact that need not deter us. It should be enough that it acted as a landmark in the musical history of the nation, and paved the way for the more exciting developments associated with Debussy and his colleagues. If its tenets are no longer fashionable today, this should not blind us into supposing them feeble or contemptible. Sympathy with the subject is desirable in both the writer and his reader, and neither should feel ashamed at seeing the ideas for which the Franck circle stood presented in a decently favourable light.

My contention is that the men discussed in this book all merit our respectful interest and attention. Though not universal geniuses, they were far from being negligible in their attainments. Perhaps we are too much at fault today in reserving all our praise for the mighty, not appreciating how much solid effort went into the careers of artists who belonged to the second rank. Unfortunately, it is only too easy to patronize such figures with a condescending attitude, bred of a mixture of topicality and hindsight. What is far harder is to learn how to suspend judgement until we have been able to recapture the historical frame of mind, to invoke what Lionel Trilling has aptly called 'the image of the other culture'. Molière complacently set the tone for every subsequent generation when he remarked: 'The ancients were the ancients, but we are the people of today.' It is only by rejecting such specious appeals to modernism that we may hope to avoid the charge of crassness in our dealings with those who have preceded us to the tomb. If further justification is needed for this collective biography, it would be necessary to point to the special fascination which cliques of all kinds have always exerted for the bystander. Civilization has thrown up a magnificent variety of these, most of them having regarded it as their aim to turn back the clock, to deny the 'Zeitgeist' in each of its tiresome postures. Such departures from the norm tend to alert us in the way the physical mutation alerts the biologist, or the circus freak the crowd. Uncertain what they may portend for our own obscure destinies, we attend to them with all the curiosity and compulsion of our race. In that band of musicians which assembled at the church of Sainte-Clotilde during the 1860s —and later at the famous apartment on the Boulevard St Michel— we encounter a clique as united as any in the history of art.

Although the personality of Franck offers itself as the obvious focal point of the book, certain preliminaries cannot be dispensed with. For example, it would not do to skirt the problem of whether his influence was something that emerged *sui generis*. Even cliques do not remain intact without being borne up by the tide of events, so that we ought to be under a strong obligation to examine the musical environment from which he and his disciples sprang. As Taine was at pains to make clear, the *milieu* can be as relevant as the men who occupy it. The unfolding of a panorama depicting musical conditions under the Second Empire must therefore seem a first step in understanding the issues before us. In particular, we need to be told how far Franck and his pupils were reacting, not against a book of rules invented by their predecessors, but against lax and corrupt standards within the metropolis. It scarcely requires a Marxist to observe that political events in nineteenth-century France helped to trigger off some of the age's most disturbing aesthetic phenomena. The red-vested 'claques' at the opening night of *Hernani*; the feelings unleashed at the trial of Flaubert and his alter-ego, Madame Bovary; Manet's scandalous exhibiting of *Déjeuner sur l'herbe*; above all, the attempts of Zola and Proust to rally literary support over the Dreyfus affair—these were not accidental happenings in some aesthete's demi-world. Neither can they be attributed to the bohemian excesses ushered in by Murger's famous play in 1849, and adumbrated in the behaviour of many before that date. On the contrary, they were blows delivered by acknowledged adversaries, mortal skirmishes in the struggle between the artist and his increasingly estranged society. While debating the moral of such events, it would seem almost perverse to look upon the Franck circle as an ill-equipped outpost, some annexe entirely remote from the splendours and miseries of the contemporary scene.

The obstacles which stand in the way of portraying César Franck the man are already somewhat notorious. They refer not only to his retiring disposition, but to the unduly apologetic dispositions of his admirers. It is a fact that those who have written about him most vividly also happen to be those least likely to have resorted to impartiality. As with many a great mentor, Franck did not have to wait long before falling victim to the eulogizing of his principal followers, men whose writings came to have the effect of directing indignation back on to the person of their idol. In this sense, Franck has had the worst of both worlds. Modern critics, on the other hand, rarely stand in the same need of inoculation against enthusiasm. What they do have to suffer is the task of disentangling truth from hagiography. In being obliged to rebut the slanders of the composer's enemies, they also have to be on their guard against over-dramatizing a man who in essence was a singularly undramatic figure—whatever influences it may be possible to credit him with. Such perplexities combine to render the main protagonist of our book more than ordinarily inaccessible. Franck's disciples, though they are less well documented, show a tendency to emerge as more sharply defined individuals, their features lit up by the polemical ripostes their positions elicited. Much can be inferred about these men from examining the kind of music they wrote, not all of it charged with those over-laden expressions of piety which seem characteristic of Franck at his worst. A good proportion of this music actually reflects that metropolitan taste which we shall begin by deploring. Moreover, it is possible to claim that not even the most hero-worshipping of the composer's acolytes was quite without his own title to originality. Hence the temptation to brand all the pupils undeviating Franckists is one that we must resist from the outset. The chief points to remember in assessing the capabilities of the various members of Franck's school are that they differed enormously in age and background, and that they were often inclined to think of themselves as independent agents. This is particularly true of the later careers of those pupils who lived on after the master's death.

The sources it is necessary to consult in order to become familiar with the aims and objects of the circle are similarly varied. Documents begin with the middle years of the century, when Franck's earliest compositions attracted notice, and reach a flood around the 'fin-de-siècle', when the composer died and acquired a somewhat inflated posthumous reputation. Another spate of literature then appears between the wars, when survivors of the circle like Pierre de Bréville were impelled to contribute their reminiscences. Memoirs and letters in fact form a steady trickle from the time of Coquard's tremulous obituary right down to the 1930s and beyond. For external assessment of the work done by Franck and company, we must turn to the comprehensive studies of Maurice Kunel, Norbert Dufourcq, Léon Vallas, Norman Demuth and Jean Gallois, all appearing after the Second World War; or else to historical surveys beginning with Julien Tiersot's pioneer *Un demi-siècle de Musique Francaise* and ending with Robert Pitrou's stimulating *De Gounod à Debussy*. Meantime, the more famous pupils had attracted their own champions, Dr Oulmont having written movingly on Duparc and Gustave Samazeuilh on Chausson. Each of these disciples was treated to an English biography in the course of time, Dr Sydney Northcote's account of Duparc appearing in 1949 and the centenary tribute to Chausson by the two Americans, Professors Barricelli and Weinstein, in 1955. Some of the best criticism has been presented in the form of periodical articles, such as that of M. Sonneck on Lekeu, which goes back to one of the first issues of *The Musical Quarterly*. Material dealing with other members of the group, like Alexis de Castillon, and Augusta Holmès for instance, has proved somewhat more scarce. Perhaps the most encouraging sign of the past year has been the publication of Emmanuel Buenzod's long awaited study of Franck in the *Musiciens de tous les temps* series.

But by far the most authentic book ever written about the composer continues to be that by Vincent d'Indy. Translated into English by Rosa Newmarch in 1910, this labour of love is greatly marred by the impression of special pleading which it conveys. Free with unconsciously comical flights of praise, it now seems exactly the sort of book we might have expected from Franck's advocate-in-chief. D'Indy falls into the habit of protesting too much so that to rely on his as the standard source would be to commit ourselves to an exceptionally narrow body of insights. That he fancied himself as something of a *littérateur* is proved by his having written, not simply his own libretti, but the histories of practically every institution to which he belonged, from his old regiment down to the Schola Cantorum. Despite this, his prose remains turgid and unenlivened by those shafts of opinion which are said to have characterized the man himself. Among other Franck pupils, Coquard, Bordes, Chausson, Guy Ropartz and Paul de Wailly all wrote memoirs dealing with experiences arising out of their pupilship; but these tend to appear amateurish when set beside the heavy artillery of modern criticism. Their chief value resides in the glimpses they offer of the circle's working habits. More importance attaches to Alfred Cortot's thorough monograph on the piano music and Robert Jardillier's excellent essay on the chamber works—both commentaries on aspects of great significance to the composer's admirers. For those who consider Franck's stage works worth the trouble of detailed investigation, there is M. Destranges's early study *L'Oeuvre lyrique de César Franck* and M. Van de Borren's complementary *L'Oeuvre dramatique de César Franck*—neither account very up to date in its terminology. The mystical side to the composer's nature is explored in Gustave Derepas's book, but the reader is warned against taking its insights too literally. Except for the passing analyses contained in these studies—and Norman Demuth's have been found particularly useful—there seems a dearth of recent criticism of Franck's music, especially the large-scale choral works upon which he set so much store.

Of livelier interest to the general reader must be the uncensored comments of the composer's relatives, some of which have been preserved intact. Franck's wife was remarkably outspoken about his art. Her shrewish dislike of all his more erotic-sounding works was coupled with the most ungullible conviction that it was her husband's pupils who had done worst damage to his cause. Despite Professor Wilfrid Mellers's comment to the effect that Félicité wanted Franck to write nothing but 'hymn-book insipidities', it may be said that her real wish was to wrest him from the clutches of his followers, whom she suspected of harbouring selfish designs. If true, this suspicion sheds a new light on the atmosphere of bliss in which the circle is always thought to have moved. Yet another domestic perspective may be had from the composer's son Georges, a pompous university lecturer who subjected his father to an unsolicited extra-mural course in the stiffer classics of philosophy. Neither of these intimates presents Franck as a little deity, after the fashion of certain of the pupils. On the contrary, they tend to expose his weaknesses quite unmercifully.

Once we turn to the pupils themselves, there is no such central enigma to resolve. That they were an exceptionally gifted group has already been argued. A list of their names reads very like a dossier on French musicians of the Third Republic. To begin, there was Henri Duparc, so silent about his master as he was about his own voluptuous music. He was accompanied by Arthur Coquard and Alfred Cahen as the original pilgrims to the shrine. Their pupilship dated from the middle of the 1860s. Afterwards came the brilliant Alexis de Castillon, cruelly fated to fall victim to the Franco-Prussion War, of 1871. He was followed by the grim and redoubtable d'Indy, pedagogue supreme of the tradition that was to build itself around Franck's teaching in later years. Belonging to a slightly younger generation was Ernest Chausson, a wealthy dilettante who enhanced the literature of French song with his rich settings of the Parnassian poets, and who was destined to die in a mysterious bicycle accident on his country estate when only forty-four. Camille Benôit, curator at the Louvre and spare-time composer, was a further addition to the band. But much the most turbulent of the pupils was the Irish beauty, Augusta Holmès, who aroused in Franck emotions too torrid to be ascribed to the forces of religious communion. Indeed, the entire group seems to have been temporarily struck off balance by this engagingly nubile bohemian, whose behaviour was the chief cause of Mme Franck's unease. After her, the remainder cannot help seeming lustreless. Yet we should honour Pierre de Bréville, a worthy successor to his teacher in the

sphere of piano writing; Louis de Serres, who removed himself
with the surviving Schola pupils of 1932 in order to found the Ecole
César Franck, where he continued to spread the gospel; the versa-
tile and industrious Guy Ropartz, renowned for his work as
Director of the Nancy and Strasbourg Conservatoires; Charles
Bordes, co-founder of the Schola and instigator of the French
polyphonic revival; Dynam-Victor Fumet, night-club entertainer,
spiritualist and manufacturer of bombs; the indefatigable Gabriel
Pierné and the gentle Charles Tournemire, each destined to follow
Franck in the organ-loft of Sainte-Clotilde; Paul de Wailly and
Sylvio Lazzari, both faithful guardians of their teacher's memory;
and finally the precocious Guillaume Lekeu, another Belgian
whose life was tragically cut short by typhoid at the early age of
twenty-four. This does not by any means complete the list of
Franck's pupils—his tenure at the Paris Conservatoire helped to
extend it to almost unmanageable lengths. But it does contain the
names of those who were most active in support of the cause, and
who are most likely to be remembered for their own music as well as
their connection with the master.

Inevitably there were some musicians who expressed sincere
regard for Franck without finding it necessary or possible to register
as pupils. Their presence often proved of immense encouragement to the others. One such figure was Emmanuel Chabrier,
lover of Spain and breaker of pianos, whose gusty personality
could never have been accommodated within the restrained precincts of the circle. Like Lekeu and Duparc, Chabrier was prominent among the French Wagnerians. Indeed, it is not too much to
say that each of these three composers discovered in Bayreuth the
most shattering experience of his life, Lekeu having to be hauled
out of the Festspielhaus unconscious, leaving Chabrier to be rendered an object of tearful commiseration. Nevertheless, it was the
over-ardent composer of *Gwendoline* who was called upon to
deliver Franck's funeral oration, a task he performed with the utmost solemnity and good will. His remarks on that occasion stand
testimony to the gratitude which he bore his friend and the high
esteem which he placed upon his music. Camille Saint-Saëns was
another French musician who had links with the circle, but of a
distinctly less amiable kind. The prodigious success he had won for
himself as an artist meant that he stood in no need of anyone's
advice, least of all Franck's. But the concern he felt for the new
forms—including the symphonic poem and the experimental
piano piece—was such that he thought it essential to keep an eye on
his rival's charges, and as time progressed certain jealousies and
intrigues were allowed to spring up. Deeply proud of his Jewish-
ness, Saint-Saëns profoundly suspected the pro-German bias

César Franck—A Daguerreotype
taken at the time of his engagement to
Félicité Desmousseaux

The Church of Sainte-Clotilde
circa 1860

A view of Paris after the bombardment of 1870–71.
The twin spires of Sainte-Clotilde are just visible

A caricature of César Franck and
his pupils at the Conservatoire by Engel
(the pupil being chastized is Chausson)

Ernest Chausson, aged about thirty-five

Ernest Chausson (left) astride the bicycle on which he
was later killed. The cycling cult was one that swept
Paris in the 1890s, including among its devotees both
Emile Zola and Tristan Bernard

Franck seated at the organ
Portrait by Rongier

Henri Duparc   Vincent d'Indy

Le Journal illustré

VINGT-SIXIÈME ANNÉE — N° 39   DIMANCHE 22 SEPTEMBRE 1889   PRIX DU NUMÉRO : 15 CENTIMES

LES ANNONCES SONT REÇUES AU BUREAU DU JOURNAL, 61, RUE LAFAYETTE
ET 16, RUE GRANGE-BATELIÈRE.

Mᵐᵉ AUGUSTA HOLMÈS

Auteur de l'Ode triomphale exécutée au Palais de l'Industrie.

Dessin d'après nature, par Henri Meyer. — Gravure de Navellier. — Voir l'article, page 26.

Augusta Holmès—A sketch done at the time of
writing the Ode Triomphale

Vincent d'Indy around 1920

shown by Franck and his associates, and was incensed at the anti-
Semitism revealed by d'Indy and his friends. The sniping and
grousing indulged in by the composer of the 'Danse Macabre' became a familiar accompaniment to much of the circle's work,
particularly after 1870. By comparison, the presence of Paul
Dukas on the periphery was wholly congenial. The fact that he too
wrote symphonic poems has led many people to convict him of
having been a Franck pupil, but this was not actually the case. The
habits of gentle self-effacement which the two men practised in
common rather created a bond of friendship which endured
throughout the painful years in which the nation was re-making
itself anew. Perhaps it is worth stressing, in view of the large
number of fellow-travellers Franck enlisted, that none of these
men wrote music so obviously akin to his own as to justify the
tracing of an influence. At least, it is quite clear that neither Chabrier nor Saint-Saëns was more than very slightly influenced by
Franck, if at all. It is therefore best to think of them as interested
spectators, men whose *amour propre* was already too well formed to
respond to pressure.

Far more pungently affected by the composer's ideas were those
pupils of the second generation who emerged from beneath
d'Indy's stern tutorship at the Schola Cantorum. This was the
sober academy of music which came into being a few years after
Franck's death. Starting as a school for the revival of Gregorian
chant, it soon aspired to become a second Conservatoire, out-
pacing the first in the attention it paid to pre-classical music.
Offering a thorough training in harmony, counterpoint and composition, the Schola led the way in re-discovering the opera-ballets of
Rameau and re-establishing the status of old masters like Palestrina. The equally obscure Lalande and Marc-Antoine Charpentier
were others whose works were given a much-needed airing on its
premises; indeed it was at the Schola's instigation that Monteverdi's *Orfeo* was at last dredged up from its resting place. Since
d'Indy was the first Director, it was only natural that he should
have chosen the institution as a repository for Franckist teachings.
It was due to his superior energy that these teachings eventually
spread to the provinces, to Lyons and Marseilles, Bordeaux and
Avignon, Nancy and Montpellier. In all this, Franck's music
did not play an important part, nor was there a recrudescence of
that intense spirituality which had marked the original dispensa-
tion. Rather the emphasis fell on technicalities, on a particular
range of models. The notorious *Cours de Composition Musicale*,
which was d'Indy's contribution to the theoretical side of his art,
became the key document in accelerating the changes. Ultimately,
Franck's principal disciple acquired his own aura of authority and

attracted to himself a fresh batch of disciples, thus duplicating the situation in which he had received his early commission. When this happened the movement of ideas we have set out to describe took on a new and different aspect.

My concern in the later stages of this book will be to trace the achievements of the Schola in some detail. In so doing I shall be accused of having extended the term 'Franck circle' beyond the literal limits laid down. On reflection, however, I do not feel that my course really calls for an apology, since the connections tend to pose a strong justification. While it cannot be argued that everything which happened at the Schola was traceable to Franck's influence, it can certainly be claimed that several of d'Indy's more prominent pupils have almost come to seem pupils of Franck, so rigid was the line of descent. At any rate, they were beneficiaries of the Franckist inheritance, and accordingly should not be omitted from our survey. To this one may add that it was only within the Schola that Franck's teachings ever secured an official outlet, for they were reviled at the Conservatoire amid whose petty regulations the composer was forced to thread his way for the last twenty years of his life. Viewed from this angle, the Schola can be considered the culminating bulwark in a long chain of fortifications which members of the circle had been obliged to erect during the period of their martyrdom. Of course, it was also something more, being a corrective to the sloppy standards set by independent music teachers and a rebuke to those reared on the fatuities of Auber and Ambroise Thomas. It was in the sense of mission which it exuded that Franck's presence stood to be most readily detected. Among the institution's staff and students there were many who were later to gain the widest renown. These men helped to indemnify the school against factionalism and illiberalism. Aside from the founders, some of the most prominent figures were Albeniz, author of the suite *Iberia* and one of the greatest of all Spanish composers; his countryman Turina and the Cuban exile, Joaquin Nin; that delightful writer of piano miniatures and former Fauré pupil, Gabriel Grovlez; the much-lamented Albert Roussel, whose ballets *Le Festin de l'Araignée* and *Bacchus et Ariadne* deserve to be reckoned among the crowning glories of the entire French tradition; the eminent musicologist Maurice Emmanuel, known for the thoroughness of his Burgundian researches and for a brief but penetrating biography of Franck; the lovable Déodat de Sévérac, musician of Languedoc and composer of gaily coloured suites for the keyboard; the respected teacher and theorist Blanche Selva; and, not least among the institution's more unconventional products, that incomparable *fumiste* and hoaxer, Erik Satie, collaborator of Diaghilev and Picasso and self-styled gadfly of the modern musical move-

ment. Nor must we forget d'Indy's private pupils, several of whom
attained real distinction. The heroic Magnard, whose career was
brought to an end by the 1914–18 War, merits a tribute to himself
in that connection.

Each of these distinguished figures brought with him to the
Schola traces of his own individual outlook; so that if, taken
together, they can be said to have digested all that Franck taught,
then it follows that it was they who were responsible for dissipating
the exclusiveness of his teachings. Although d'Indy's efforts to
keep alive Franck's principles were crowned with a good measure of
success, it would be too much to claim that a recognizable school
of Franckist composers persisted long after the First World War.
The select band who had known Franck personally continued to
take pride in the bonds which united them; but those younger
musicians who had merely experienced his teachings at second-
hand were increasingly prone to assert their independence. The
turn-of-the-century revolutions—including both the Debussyiste
movement and the experiments proceeding from the Schoenberg
school—were instrumental in checking whatever vogue Franck's
followers might have created for the music they wrote under his
aegis. When, some years later, French music fell prey to that combination of violence and neo-classicism which we find celebrated
in Stravinsky and the early Poulenc, it became apparent that
Franck's hour had come and gone. As in the case of those similarly
academic English composers, Stanford and Parry, his appeal was
transitory, and derived as much from the eminence of his pupils as
from any artistic supremacy of his own. Unlike these counterparts
across the channel, however, Franck never altogether disappeared
from the lists, enjoying periodic returns to favour, many of which
were spurred on by the acclaim he won in other lands. For the
purposes of our study, it will be convenient to view the activities
of the d'Indyists as marking the sunset of the Franck era. After
their time, the composer's reputation began to depend more on
the usual factors, and hence took its place in the lottery of posterity.

Enthusiasts who read this book may regret that many bypaths
of the subject will have been left unexplored. They may likewise
feel that there has been insufficient analysis of important Franckist
masterpieces. I can only retort that I thought it best not to impede
the narrative with too much digression, whether of the technical
or historical kind, but to permit the steady play of events to build up
towards a composite portrait of the circle in action, and to document briefly the ways in which it achieved ultimate recognition. I
hoped that by lengthening the panorama a little at both ends I
should be successful in placing the circle's activities within the

context of modern music as a whole. To have divorced the analytical from the biographical would surely have been to deny the link which exists between a composer's life and his work—a link signally evident in the case of Franck himself and scarcely less apparent in the case of his disciples. It would have been possible to have divided the book into two parts—one to deal with the life and the other the works—but I could not escape the conviction that to have taken this course would have been to destroy what unity was offered by the subject. For the truth is that a good portion of our interest in any artist's work stems from our awareness of the circumstances under which it came to be written; while even the most cursory account of an artistic personality must lead us to inquire more closely into the nature of its products. Hence the paradox that it is only by recourse to the complete *Gestalt* that we can ever hope to comprehend the workings of the culture we have set out to study.

It remains to draw attention to the peculiarly ambiguous position Franck continues to occupy in the history books. Is he a late Romantic composer, as he is usually portrayed, or ought he to be seen as a precursor of the modern movement? It would be deceptively easy, using the evidence of the works, to make out a strong case for either of these assumptions; or even both of them. Moreover, the baroque strain—manifested in the composer's love of fugue and counterpoint—adds the confusing possibility that he might have been simply a throwback, a German *Kapellmeister* mistakenly strayed into the age of Edison. Stranger accidents have happened, and Franck's consistent ill-luck contributes a doubt as to whether he may not have deliberately cultivated the role of misfit. It will be one of my contentions that part of the difficulty we experience in classifying the composer stems from historical uncertainty. After all, is it not equally difficult to classify some of his disciples, and one is not thinking only of those who most resemble their master? Should d'Indy, for example, be counted a typical French Wagnerian, and hence a child of the later nineteenth century; or must we acknowledge him as a forerunner of the dodecaphonists? Did Chausson reach the limits of his talent in expressing a faded end-of-the-century charm, or would he have gone on to become a second Ravel, perhaps a second Honegger? We have no sure way of answering such questions, since they demand from the observer an ideal perspective which he is forever prevented from attaining. But merely to propound them is instructive in drawing attention to the transitional age with which we have to deal.

As he was among the first to suffer the effects of transition, Franck was prone to display these irritating ambiguities with great consistency. We can take the measure of the changes he witnessed if we recall that as a boy he learned to play Hummel's piano concerto while that most accomplished of Beethoven's rivals was still alive; yet as a veteran of sixty-eight he survived to see Debussy publish his *Cinq Poèmes de Baudelaire* and Richard Strauss launch his *Tod und Verklärung* at Eisenach. Only to recognize the welter of styles in force between these two epochs is to be made aware of the enormous obstacles which were placed in the way of the composer's originality. Still more discouraging was the savage factionalism that persisted throughout the remainder of the century into which he was born, making it virtually impossible for him to have been guaranteed fair play. To have lived through the corrupt years of Napoleon III, when charlatanism abounded and the première of each new work was attended by months of intrigue, was penance enough for the most facile musician. Unhappily for Franck, he was made to suffer the full complement of indignities on this count, so that it has become increasingly useless to speculate on how his music might have turned out had he been accorded the warm public patronage of a later day. His decision to follow the solitary and unprofitable life at Sainte-Clotilde was in one sense extremely beneficial, in that it provided him with the peace and security he needed to go about his tasks unhampered. But at the same time it must be said that this decision helped to deprive the composer of that sophisticated and fully social criticism which every artist requires if his work is to escape the taint of provincialism.

Implicit in all these observations is the conviction that Franck's status as a musician cannot be casually reckoned. There are good reasons why he continues to be a problem to critics and tastemakers. For one thing, his influence seems to have been strong enough to lay the claims of greatness without it being quite so pervasive as to make us feel justified in granting these claims. If we are foolish enough to think of him as having unleashed a major musical revolution—comparable to the cataclysms wrought by Beethoven and Wagner—it becomes only too easy to discredit him for having failed to create the taste of his age. On the other hand, if we are content to describe him as nothing more than a gifted teacher, the writer of a small handful of masterpieces, we risk ignoring the sly, almost hidden, authority which he commanded. In order to assess any artist's claims, it is perhaps necessary to take into account the nature of his endowments. Calling on our portrayal of French musical life in the 1850s, it is evident that only a man of boundless strength and cunning could have restored the nation's standards at that point in time. Even Wagner, an experienced publicist who was not short on either of these qualities, failed to win a sympathetic hearing for himself in Paris, his music having to await a succession of later propagandists. By comparison

Franck was a thoroughly timid supplicant, honestly bewildered by the jostle and glitter of his more worldly contemporaries. Patience was about the only weapon by which he could have hoped to succeed, and it is worth remembering this fact when judging both the man and his achievement.

PART ONE

I

Phantoms at the opera

It has often been remarked that the French musical genius finds its highest expression in the theatre, yet an intelligent visitor to Paris in 1851, the year of Louis Napoleon's *coup d'état,* would have found it hard to concur in this verdict. For although it was a time of clamorous activity at the principal centres of opera and drama, the radical creative impulse, like its political counterpart, had already disappeared underground, emasculated by the philistinism of a victorious bourgeoisie. The brutalization of taste which had accompanied this repression had also been quick to bring about a schism in French culture that has persisted without interruption to the present day. Artistic attitudes having aligned themselves along the plane of class rather than sentiment, it was only natural that the middle classes should have been observed celebrating their triumph by indulging in an orgy of pretence. Perceiving that among all the art-forms at their disposal opera offered the fullest opportunities for aggrandisment, they began by soliciting its claims in terms calculated to advance the most flamboyant mediocrity.

Even during the decades leading up to the revolution of 1848, the musical life of the capital had tended to centre almost exclusively on the succession of spectacular productions held at the theatre to which Méhul and Spontini had made their respective pilgrimages.[1] The differences which were presently to emerge related more to matters of scale than intention. That is to say, opera was rapidly reaching the stage at which money and pageantry had

[1] This was the old Opéra. The new *grand palais*—the corner stone of which was laid in 1862—was not officially opened until January 1875. No expense was spared on this later building, which remains the largest theatre in the world in terms of acreage if not seating capacity. Its architect, Charles Garnier, was said to have used more than twenty miles of drawing-paper in planning its construction.

begun to count for something, and the possession of genius for hardly anything. Certainly there was very little that was magical about the quality of inspiration shown by composers of the Second Empire. If anything, their works marked a definite step down in artistic ambition. Whereas the older masters had been determined to preserve the classical decorum of the first Napoleonic régime, their successors relapsed into an increasingly grandiose torpor, relying on the ingenuities of the stage designer and costumier to help bolster their sagging talents. The 1830s had witnessed the premières of *Robert le Diable* and *Les Huguenots, La Juive* and *Guido e Ginevra, Le Philtre* and *Gustav III*—all conspiring to provide an impressive prototype of the cinema epic of modern times. The citizen-kings who composed these harrowing dramas— Meyerbeer, Halévy, Auber—were fêted throughout the length and breadth of the land, mistakenly compared to Shakespeare and Racine, toasted by foreign royalty, and finally ousted by the impossibility of repeating their own unhealthy successes. At the time of Napoleon III's rise to power, their popularity was still at its height, and the public had become sufficiently comatose to cease petitioning for any but their acknowledged, money-spinning favourites.

At the Opéra itself, only a handful of new productions emerged during the first few years of the administration, and even these offered little incentive to the composer who wished to depart from accepted formulas. The situation at Paris's other opera-house, the lighter Opéra-Comique, was in some respects worse, with Hérold's *Zampa* and the ubiquitous Auber's *Fra Diavolo* comprising an unbeatable pair of trumps at the box-office.[1] At both institutions, the cult of Italianate music was beginning to have a discouraging effect on native musicians. The spectre of Rossini was a particularly inhibiting influence, since it was he who had set the cult in motion. To an unbiased observer, it seemed outrageous that so much of France's glory was having to depend on the foreigner. Unable to point to a musical equivalent of Delacroix or Flaubert, patriots were reduced to vague and embarrassed gestures.

Not that the experience of being dominated from without was altogether novel. The eighteenth-century *Guerre des Bouffons* offered a curious parallel. What served to distinguish the present situation was the fact that the chief protagonists did not long remain alien. It had only been a short while before that Berlioz had issued

---

[1] The Opéra-Comique was also an old-established institution, having been founded as far back as 1715. Its earlier function had been to parody the tragic drama, offering *spectacles de la foire*. Later on, it provided light entertainment for the bourgeois family, and came to be inseparably linked with the works of Offenbach.

his famous threat to blow up the Italian Theatre during a performance of *La Gazza Ladra,* a threat some of his younger colleagues
were to regret he never managed to put into execution. Perhaps the
composer of *The Damnation of Faust* was too conscious of the pen-
alties of omniscience to have experienced a sufficiently acute attack
of jealousy. Yet his patience had been sorely tried. In him, we
encounter France's greatest musical chauvinist—paradoxically cosmopolitan in outlook—reacting against over-exposure to the
Southern temperament, and speaking out fearlessly in the name of
his own Gothic imagination. Berlioz was never opposed to the
classical qualities of the Italian mind—the qualities residing in his
beloved Virgil—but he believed the epic was becoming a debased
form, dependent more on special effects than on a genuine sense of
grandeur.

To read this composer's sensation-packed memoirs is to be made
rapidly aware of the frustrations imposed on native talent during
his lifetime. Not unjustifiably, he presents himself as the victim of
heartless intruders upon his nation's ways of thought, a man driven
into the position of heroically defending his culture. It is a position
we find later taken up by Debussy in quite another context, and
one that French artists periodically seek to embrace—much to the
amusement or consternation of outsiders. While he was a student
at the Conservatoire, Berlioz fell foul of old Cherubini, the institution's foreign-born director. He appears as a dessicated survivor
from a more pedantic age, who had so traded on his acquaintance
with Beethoven as to set himself up as judge and pontiff over all
who aspired to the title of composer in his adopted country. The
story, as Berlioz gloatingly relates it, concerned the occasion when
he broke into the conservatoire's library in order to study the scores
of Gluck, at that time his chief model and exemplar. Having acted
in defiance of his principal's wishes, he was unlucky enough to be
confronted by the old man immediately on entering the building,
finding himself in the position of a burglar face-to-face with the
prefect of police. After this episode, Cherubini came to regard him
with a kind of apoplectic fury, seeing in the young rebel all those
qualities he detested in the rising generation placed under his
charge. As for poor Berlioz, his relationship with the Italians—
whom he took to be an unmusical people—received a second jolt
when he was introduced to the composer of *Guillaume Tell,* an
opera he began by admiring and ended by vilifying. It is small
wonder, given these provocations, that France's most notable
romantic should have spent the greater part of his life harbouring
thoughts of revenge.

It would be a mistake, however, to interpret Berlioz's intransig-
ence entirely in the light of his personal situation. His feelings were

to be shared by an astonishingly large number of younger compatriots. Many years later, the middle-aged Saint-Saëns was to inveigh grimly on the conditions which had obtained in his youth, when Beethoven's Eighth Symphony had been dismissed as 'algebra in Music' and his own early chamber-works cast aside as incomprehensible. From these and similar occurrences, we may infer that the prospect facing the instrumental composer was very little better than that which confronted his opposite number in the opera-house across the street. Indeed, it was to be another twenty years before the Société Nationale led its successful crusade for the appreciation of chamber music in France. In the meantime, there were several lesser societies devoted to the performance of trios and quartets, but these were quite moribund when it came to bringing out new and challenging compositions. Even the standard works in the repertory—those by Haydn, Mozart and Beethoven —had a hard time winning a hearing, eliciting only an antiquarian interest from the more fulsome critics, who dared not proclaim too openly their attachment to so rarified an art. Gossec had formally introduced the symphony into France a couple of generations previously, but it had never properly taken root there. Nor was it to do so in the years ahead.[1] Admittedly, the Conservatoire continued to give impeccable accounts of the Beethoven symphonies—the Ninth was heard there by Wagner with what effect the world was soon to learn—but the ambitions of the typical French musician were irretrievably linked to the theatre, there to remain for the duration of the Empire.

Likewise, the salons of Paris, those genteel feminine abodes where the bejewelled matrons wept crocodile tears to the strains of Liszt and Thalberg, could scarcely be regarded as places for the promotion of new music. It was symptomatic that Chopin, riddled with disenchantment and disease, had preferred to die rather than endure their indignities for another season. Taken in all, the situation which presented itself to the earnest young composer was bleak in the extreme. He could either signify his acquiescence in this complacent blend of commercialism and snobbery—in which case his standards quickly plummeted to the ground—or else he could go his own way, as Berlioz had tried to do, inviting the opprobrium of the masses and their betters alike. In neither case could the choice be thought uplifting. It can scarcely be wondered why César Franck, embarking on a career in the middle

---

[1] The struggle which Franck himself had to establish the symphony in France was only partially successful. It took the concerted efforts of men like Saint-Saëns, d'Indy, Chausson, Dukas and Roussel to give the form anything like the hallowed respectability it had possessed from the beginning in Germany.

years of the century, should have found himself in such a pitiable quandary.

The source of corruption in all the various sectors of music was actually the same. It consisted of the desire to embellish musical ideas with the superfluities of the singer; to gild the lily in such a way as to appease a bloated and undiscriminating public. This betrayal began, as may be imagined, in the opera-house, and only gradually spread to include music being written for instruments. The original exponents of the *bel canto* style—composers such as Bellini and Donizetti—were not guilty of the sin of excess. They endeavoured to make decoration subservient to the equities of phrasing, being constantly strict in their emotional fidelity to the situation they wished to convey. The same could be said, *mutatis mutandis*, about those instrumental composers, such as Field and Chopin, who appropriated the Italian *cantilena* and techniques of ornamentation, either directly from Bellini himself, or at second-hand from men like Spohr. Chopin is actually something of a test-case in this matter, since he was always at pains to restrain his pupils from the casual borrowing of coloratura devices. It is true that he was more responsible than anyone else for adapting such devices to the idiom of the piano, but the manner in which he performed this task reflects no discredit upon him. As Dr Gerald Abraham has observed, in his illuminating book on the composer, Chopin's melody is essentially a stylization rather than an imitation of the *bel canto*. Moreover, there is evidence that the composer of the Nocturnes was harshly critical of singers' exaggerations, preferring Cinti to Malibran for this very reason. By contrast, the tragedy of an artist like Rossini, who also shared in the work of pioneering the new style, was that he failed to adopt the right degree of scrupulousness in his dealings with the public. Realizing that he had stumbled on a stock means of inducing certain emotional responses, he lacked the integrity necessary to take the next step and renounce his discovery. By adopting the lazy way out, Rossini furnished both himself and his imitators with a recipe for dispensing stock drama.

Welcomed with open arms in France, this untroubled musical tycoon was allowed to pour forth his florid 'roulades' and 'fioritures' to his heart's content. Not surprisingly, perhaps, his later works came to have the effect of merely titillating his audiences. Though he did not scruple to make further use of his formula, Rossini was fated to see his creative impulse wither like a branch in a storm. Unfortunately, the tricks and flourishes he perfected persisted to putrify the talents of a young generation. As had been the case with Handel, they bred a whole school of imitation composers bent on the search for effects. To saddle Rossini with all the blame would, of course, be manifestly unfair. His disciples, particularly musicians like Boieldieu and Adolphe Adam, had their own equally flimsy legacy to bequeath. The real failure can be traced to the fact that no one wished to offer himself as an example of better things, to prescribe more rigorously the pattern to be followed by his juniors. The music of each of these composers seems less at fault than their philosophy, and in Rossini's case one cannot help feeling it a pity that so facile an artist should have descended to becoming such an ambitious and commonplace man.

Reasons for the dazzling impact made by his work are not difficult to unearth. Most listeners fell upon it as a form of light relief after the heady classicism of the years before Waterloo. Comedy had been frowned upon in the opening decades of the century, and the people, tiring of the imperial vestments at last, showed themselves only too glad to be able to slip into something more comfortable. With the emergence of a strongly articulate middle-class, smugly dedicated to the improvement of its status, tastes underwent yet another change.[1] This began to become apparent from the 1830s onward, though it did not express itself fully until much later. The Second Empire witnessed the fruits of change at their most disturbing, giving rise to a whole range of retrograde art-forms. It is not true that there was a serious attempt to revive the ponderous mythological plots of the early period, but the reading of the new proclamation certainly produced a mood of musical euphoria which resulted in something equally tendentious. The spirit of bluster emanating from business and political circles was such that Rossini's comic exuberance quickly became a thing of the past, being replaced by a fresh style of operatic production in which the element of spectacle was brought to the fore. The succeeding decade was accordingly that in which the apotheosis of 'grand opera' took place, and in which efforts were made to elevate yet another foreigner, this time a Jewish banker's son from Berlin.

Typically precocious in his gifts, Meyerbeer—for that was the name which henceforth began to hang from everyone's lips—had been a pupil of Browning's Abbé Vogler. It proved a good indication of his astuteness, as well as his lack of scruples, that he wasted no time before arriving in Italy to absorb the music of Rossini at the source, and to change his name from Jacob to Giacomo. 'I was involuntarily drawn into that delicious maze of tones,' he disingenuously recalled much later, 'and bewitched in a magic garden from which I could not escape.' At thirty-five, responding to the

[1] To observe these subtle fluctuations of taste at their clearest, the reader is recommended to study the career of Victor Hugo who, after fighting the battle of *Hernani* in 1830, went on to become a fossilized bourgeois under Napoleon III and even ended up in the Pantheon.

bewitchment of a more jingling range of sounds, he nevertheless did escape to Paris, where it did not take him long to set the city on fire with his glib melodies and winning sense of instrumentation. Balzac was one of the first to be bowled over by his work, recognizing in the composer qualities not unlike those which had accompanied his own rise to fame. *Robert le Diable*—which was Meyerbeer's first big success—appeared in 1831, and the popularity which it conferred lasted for more than thirty years. At the première of *Robert*, the cast experienced several mishaps leading to disasters that would have deterred a less resilient artist. These must have been hilarious in view of the horrifying nature of the plot. A classic piece of *grand guignol*, the opera began to look like misfiring when the tenor fell through a trap-door intended for one of the other characters. Things were scarcely improved by the chorus getting itself caught in a gauze curtain which had been erected to suggest a passing bank of cloud. Fortunately, the audience seemed oblivious of these impediments, even going on to give the work a tremendous ovation. From that moment on, Meyerbeer's fame seemed assured, and it was only a matter of discovering fresh, and equally bloodthirsty, plots on order to repeat his various triumphs.[1]

Probably we cannot visualize the coruscating power these unpromising dramas exuded for the citizens of their own day. Men whose judgement we should otherwise be inclined to trust went almost berserk in their praise of them. Even the jaundiced Berlioz was utterly swept off his feet—at least to begin with. Writing of the famous 'Benediction des Poignards' scene—one of the extravagant set pieces from *Les Huguenots*—he resorted to the following piece of hyperbole:

> The effervescence of the emotions excited by this masterpiece makes one desire to be a great man in order to place one's glory and one's genius at the feet of Meyerbeer.

Such language nowadays seems hollow, but there can be no doubt that it was sincerely meant at the time. Indeed it by no means exhausted the range of superlatives showered on the work of this Goliath among composers. The novelist George Sand, not in the least notable for being gullible, was moved to describe him as 'the greatest poet of us all'—an incredible judgement considering her catholic circle of friends. In much the same way, Goethe considered Meyerbeer the only musician to whom he could entrust the setting

---

[1] This rule seems scarcely less valid today than in 1831 to judge from the response to Peter Hall's production of Schoenberg's *Moses and Aaron*. The late Sir Victor Gollancz was only one among many to comment on the gloating attitudes displayed by audiences in the face of the overdone orgy scenes.

of *Faust*, while Bizet went as far as to dub him 'the Michelangelo of music'. It is a well-known, and perhaps slightly less surprising, fact that Wagner retained a ruinous penchant for Meyerbeer's music, which it was said could reduce him to tears even as an old man. Viewing these opinions alongside the commonly held conviction that Rossini was the superior of Mozart, it is difficult to credit the age with the sense and taste normally ascribed to it.

Our faith in the judgements of its more redoubtable figures is restored somewhat when we turn to examine what sort of reaction was aroused by the later career of this astonishing man. Always ready to accommodate himself to the demands of his interpreters, Meyerbeer slipped into the habit of inserting fanciful cadenzas, additional grace-notes and other inessentials into his scores. This practice seemed innocent enough at first, but soon earned him a host of brickbats from the critics. Some had suspected from the beginning that this was how the composer would end up, and it is interesting to note that George Sand's early letters of praise had not entirely glossed over the composer's failings in this respect. After having acclaimed him a universal genius, she went on to warn him of the temptations which would accrue to his position, temptations he evidently did his utmost to ignore:

> Why these used-up and monotonous forms which destroy the effect of the most beautiful phrases? You have not yet altogether disburdened yourself from the ignorance of the vulgar public and from the demands of unintelligent vocalists. You cannot do it, I suppose! Perhaps even you have only succeeded in making your most beautiful ideas acceptable by employing obligatory formulas.

Mme Sand's reservations were to be echoed in time by almost all of the artist's admirers, including some who had once exceeded the limits of conventional adulation. Berlioz, angrily unblinkered at last, repeated the *volte-face* he had indulged in over Rossini, writing that he wished he could now bite the hand he had formerly kissed.

The operas Meyerbeer wrote towards the end of his long reign, chiefly *Le Prophète* and the posthumously produced *L'Africaine*, failed to equal his earlier works in stagecraft or musical panache.[1]

[1] One wonders what the composer would have made of Herlischka's anti-illusionist production of *Le Prophète* given in Berlin in 1966. Dividing the action between the Anabaptist Middle Ages and the French Second Empire, this producer's version ended with a fantastic bacchanal in which, as one critic put it, 'Offenbachian can-can girls and big-breasted Maenads joined in an explosive death'. This production incidentally seems to have sparked off a renewal of interest in Meyerbeer's work, since there have been various attempts to revive him, including a concert performance of *Les Huguenots*, in London in recent years.

By the time the Empire staggered to its end, the demise of the genre he had so showily created was also in sight. The man himself suffered from absurd apprehensions about his fate, seeming to arrogate to his own situation most of the fears and compulsions he had lavished on his dramatic menagerie. On his deathbed he was said to have ordered his hands and feet to be bound with miniature bells so that he could be hastily disinterred at the slightest sound of respiring life. In the event, nothing more was heard from him once the shroud was pulled over his head. His career remained in the memory, however, serving as a vivid reminder of the ease by which a nation's tastes had been traduced, of the rapidity with which a set of artistic trappings had been allowed to outweigh the principles of truth and consistency. Not until Hollywood took over the job of producing mammoth musical spectacles for the consumption of a war-weary public in the 1920s was there a return to such obviously false standards.

In underlining the cautionary aspects of the tale we should remind ourselves that some of the elements of Meyerbeer's aesthetic were common to all romantic composers. His devils, in addition to being colourful stage properties, may thus be regarded as one expression of that picturesque urge associated with writers like Hoffmann and Jean-Paul, an urge said to contain the essence of the romantic philosophy. It had already found an echo in Schumann's piano pieces, like those comprising the 'Kreisleriana' suite, in which a whole dictionary of fantastic metaphors is left open to be catalogued. What is interesting to note is the way in which such gentle veins of introspection were transformed, via Meyerbeer's epics, into the diablerie of the Faust Symphony and similar works of Liszt. It is clear that Berlioz had his part to play in this progression, though his 'Witches' Sabbath' was written long before the influence of Meyerbeer began to be felt.[1] No doubt the excessively revolutionary temper of public events had a still greater significance, since the artist was no longer encouraged to regard himself as the idle dreamer of, say, Eichendorff's 'In der fremde', but rather as a rebel affronted by the horrors of a war with society. In this new and more hostile context, it was only natural that he should have singled out the more demonic components of romanticism to serve as the basis of his work.

[1] Neville Cardus, in his essay on Franck, nevertheless denies French musicians a place in the cult of diabolism which reached fruition during the middle of the nineteenth century. He states: 'There is no demonism in French music; the diablerie of Berlioz is a dramatic affair, almost a "coup-de-théâtre".' Even so, he concedes that Franck introduced an element of the grotesque in works like *Le Chasseur Maudit* and the other tone-poems of the later period. (See *Ten Composers*, Jonathan Cape, 1945.)

How ironical it seems to us today that, despite their violently opposed aims, the artist and his bourgeois enemy should have arrived at common ground in this fashion. Each was attracted to the bizarre and terrifying for what looked like entirely different reasons. For the artist, these things were the means of signifying his awareness of the thin protection afforded by a rapacious society, of the callous and brutal behaviour in which his betters were prone to indulge given the minimum of provocation. To the bourgeois, on the contrary, spectacle offered itself as an antidote to the humdrum nature of his bureaucratic existence, and perhaps as a sop to the illusion he cherished of living in an age of splendid anarchy. Thus each settled down to a long run of sadistic epics which did not lose their hold until the Commune intervened with a bout of direct action in 1871. The extent of the absorption in these heroics may be gauged from the fact that even at the least pretentious level of taste—as symbolized by the frothy inventions of the Opéra-Comique—patrons were regaled with the deeds of Achilles and Menelaus in comic parody, their guide being the irrepressible Offenbach. Indeed, the circle reaches completion when we discover that the favourite author of this supreme entertainer—the man who wrote the *Contes* by which their two names are indissolubly joined—was none other than E. T. A. Hoffmann himself.

Knowing these facts, we can no longer think it a coincidence that some of the younger composers who took part in the Franckist reaction also betrayed lapses in the direction of hyper-romanticism. In the popular symphonic poems of Franck himself, both the style and the subject-matter hark back unmistakably to Liszt, and through him to the extravagant gestures of his operatic forerunners. Similarly, the themes chosen for operatic treatment by several of the 'progressive' musicians of the earlier twentieth century (and one is thinking of examples like the *Ariane et Barbe-bleue* of Dukas) suggest a surviving preoccupation with grisliness, with what Jung has called the 'shadow-side' of human life and personality. It is worth stressing how powerless academic and ecclesiastical barriers were to prevent this side from getting expressed, even after all romantic associations had been forgotten. It re-emerges, not simply in the repressed disciple of Franck, but in such an independent figure as Debussy, whose unfinished opera based on Poe's *The Fall of the House of Usher* forms clinching testimony to its influence. Hence, if Bach and Beethoven were eventually restored to their rightful place, becoming a focus of ritual to the musicians of the Third Republic, Meyerbeer and company were still to be found hovering in the background like spectres at some premature thanksgiving.

Meantime, French opera had reason to be grateful for enlisting the talents of at least one genuine reforming spirit, a man who shunned the exhibitionism of the Italian school and yet was much more amenable to reason than the intractable Berlioz had been. This saviour was Gounod, a musician whose gifts were so apportioned that he had no difficulty in satisfying both the purist and the public at one and the same time. His obvious flair for melody, the subtle habit he developed of underplaying the emotional aspects of his situations, his clarity of orchestration and general grace of movement—all these things combined to single him out as the only French composer to be equipped with the full complement of national virtues. Today, we are inclined to judge him on the basis of a few mawkish scenes from *Faust*, by no means his most typical work. To appreciate this underrated artist at his true worth, it is necessary to compare the taste and restraint shown in a score like *Philemon et Baucis*—first produced at the Théâtre Lyrique in 1860—with the bombast emanating from the average piece of dramatic writing of the day. In an age when so few were doing anything to uphold France's workmanlike tradition of writing for the stage, Gounod was a godsend—a progressive in intention if not invariably in terms of execution. The late Sir Thomas Beecham was not the only conductor of his generation to record his gratitude to the composer for having saved the art of opera from succumbing to the worst and most melodramatic excesses, and for having kept alive the habit of creating buoyant and tuneful music.

Gounod's impact on the climate of taste in Paris was among the most considerable exercised by any composer of the century. Reaching maturity at about the same time as Franck (he was actually born a few years earlier than César in 1818) he evolved a complex set of ideals that put him somewhere between the dramatic cliques and the more sober-minded academics. Brought up to revere Bach and Palestrina, his early training equipped him with far greater integrity than most theatrical musicians. Though he won the Prix de Rome in 1839, he did not think of the Villa Medici as a sophisticated potting-shed for future Rossinis; nor did he simply idle away his time there by engaging in insults, as Debussy was to do. Instead, he broadened the direction of his sensibilities by interesting himself in the painter Ingres, and by seeking out the friendship of those literary ladies of the musical world, Pauline Viardot and Fanny Mendelssohn. Women were never to stray very far from Gounod's thoughts, and his revulsion against the melodramatic excesses of his countrymen had something to do with the tenderness and beguilment which he learnt in their company. Indeed the attributes of his famous heroine Marguerite were in many respects those of Gounod himself; and if they were responsible for infusing a weak and feminine strain into French music (notably in the work of his imitator Massenet) they must also be seen as a welcome change from the doleful heroics of his predecessors.

Back in Paris after having done the grand tour to Leipzig and Vienna, Gounod began by attempting to preserve a long flirtation with the church. Taking a post as organist at the Missions Etrangères, he almost allowed himself to be inveigled into the priesthood. What held him back was the sense of doubt he developed as to whether he could uphold the vow of chastity, a doubt he was wise never to put to the test. For all that, he continued for a long time to sign himself Abbé Gounod and to preface his letters with the sign of the cross. Such harmless conceits evidently gave him an inordinate amount of satisfaction, for it was part of his vanity to believe that he had almost renounced the world and its pleasures. Like that other priest-manqué, Frederick Rolfe (otherwise known as Baron Corvo), he was actually the victim of a superbly contradictory temperament which propelled him on the one hand towards sensuality and on the other to an unctuousness that was worthy of any *curé de campagne*. When the musical life finally imposed itself on his ambitions, it was not without certain constraints which he carried over from his clerical ethics, and which served to modify the consumer-based dictates of his profession.

At the beginning of his career, these constraints guided him well. Putting aside the larger forces of grand opera, the composer had no compunction about reverting to the chamber-opera style made popular by ancient French musicians. That is to say, he modelled himself, whether deliberately or accidentally, more on Rameau than Meyerbeer. His first work for the theatre, *Sapho*, was produced in 1851, and its lack of 'sciences des planches' resulted in its being taken off after only nine performances. Even the vocal talents of a Viardot had been unable to save it from being a failure. Gounod's friends attributed the disaster to the action of the censor (references to Phaon were interpreted by the commissioner as a threat to the new Emperor) but the real reasons were less flattering. They may be sought in that stylistic inconsistency which the composer was never altogether successful in rectifying even in his best period. Elements of the *a capella* style were found to consort oddly with music intended to excite amorous feelings, and the opera still gives the impression of having been something of a 'sport'. As Théophile Gautier cruelly put it at the time of the première:

> Gounod's score seems comparable to a beautiful woman whose body and face were painted by Ingres, her legs and arms by Delacroix.

Sapho nevertheless became the means by which the composer earned a second chance with managements and the public, and it was not long before he made another bid for fame with his *Ulysse*. Unfortunately, this opera met with no better a reception when it was mounted in the following year.

As may be imagined, it was *Faust* that put the seal on the composer's reputation, and that work did not appear until the close of the decade during which he had occupied himself in the theatre. Though not a roaring success at first—it antagonized too many German critics to whom it continues to seem a desecration of one of their national treasures—the opera won plenty of adherents wherever it was played.[1] Unlike its predecessors, it found room for spectacle (a wise precaution on the composer's part in view of the débâcle caused by the postponed ballet in *Tannhäuser* a few years later) and included enough in the way of action to satisfy the crudest bourgeois taste. During the period between *Ulysse* and *Faust* Gounod's reputation had wavered rather disconcertingly and he had suffered a certain amount of ill-health in consequence. He was relieved to receive the plaudits of Berlioz, who generously forgave him for pirating the libretto of *La Nonne Sanglante*, yet remained tense and anxious. A nervous breakdown almost put an end to his career in 1857, but once he had recovered he seemed to display even greater assurance than before. The turning point in his life came when the critic Scudo, writing in the *Revue des Deux Mondes*, chided him for a lack of colour in his treatment of dramatic subjects. This attack decided the composer to renounce a good measure of his fastidiousness and accept more of the operatic conventions—in the words of Martin Cooper 'to go whoring after the strange gods of Meyerbeer'.

The effect of this move was to enthrone the worst aspects of Gounod's musical *persona*, and incidentally slow down the development of French music by a good many years. The later operas—and the composer continued to draw on this rich vein of melodrama right up to the time of writing *Le Tribut de Zamora* in 1881—did nothing to increase his popularity with the general public, while contributing significantly to the odium in which he was held by the

---

[1] The German response to *Faust* was first made explicit by Wagner, who referred to Gounod's opera as 'a sugary, vulgar, nauseating, bungling piece of work'. A similar point of view was much later expressed by the musicologist Alfred Einstein, who stigmatized it as 'a string of salon songs'. The mistake each of these critics makes is to assume that Gounod viewed his work as a literal transformation of Goethe's play. The fact is that he abstracted what he thought to be a suitably poignant episode and enlarged it; possibly the episode's sentimental implications have been too much insisted upon by its interpreters.

forward-looking musicians who were to belong to the Third Republic. Like his protégé Bizet, who was to inherit a great deal of his promise, Gounod was fated to live on through the one work that sprang to everyone's lips at the mention of his name. That he was still capable of writing fresh and charming music in middle age is evidenced by the delectable *Mireille* which first appeared in 1863. For the most part, however, the later works merely revealed what critics knew from experience—namely that the composer suffered too obviously from eclecticism and from the vagaries of an unstable temperamant. Despite the temporary *réclame* secured by *Roméo et Juliette*, nothing among the final group has succeeded in shattering the fustian image which comes to mind at the thought of his theatre music, which is hardly nearer complete acclaim today than it was in Gounod's own day.

Realizing that a chain of triumphs in the opera-house would elude him, the composer spent his last years trying to recover some of that high-mindedness which had deserted him in France's hour of greatest need. Part of his new austerity sprang from a sojourn in England, where he fled on sensing that Paris was about to be invaded by the Prussians. The thought of working in conditions of war was far too distasteful to this squeamish artist, and he did not see anything odd about continuing to make his protests from a vantage point across the sea. Finding Victorian London very much to his liking, he stayed for four contented years. While there, he discovered, much as Saint-Saëns was to do on the occasion of his receiving a Cambridge doctorate in 1893, that the English were far from being monsters of philistinism. On the contrary, their skill and dedication in the field of choral singing could not but seem admirable. A pleasant attachment accordingly sprang up between the ageing Frenchman and the various choirs he heard perform. Also of some importance to him was the English fondness for drawing-room ballads, an interest that held the promise of consoling advantages. Quick to avail himself of all forms of hospitality, Gounod was able to use his stay in England to re-kindle a number of early enthusiasms, luxuriating in a show of nostalgia which his hosts found touching. His stirring cantata *Gallia* expressed the anguish he felt at his country's humiliations, and no one doubted the sincerity which lay behind the work.[1] Possibly because he had stayed such a long time abroad, Gounod had difficulty in adapting himself to French ways again when he

[1] Also written during his stay in London—and presumably with similar motives at heart—was the lesser-known *Jeanne d'Arc* (1873). Neither this nor *Gallia* has withstood the test of time as well as the very late *Mors et Vita* (1884) in which the composer managed to recover a measure of his best manner.

returned from exile in 1874. A number of annoying habits which he had contracted soon got in the way of his relations with his fellow-countrymen. The most pronounced of these was his habit of delivering gnomic utterances on the more imponderable problems of life. Like Hugo before him, and Gide after him, Gounod took great care to unburden himself of these sayings only when he was certain that a disciple was at hand to jot them down. On one famous occasion his pretensions were neatly punctured by Mme Bizet, widow of the composer of *Carmen*. It seems that a group of musicians had been to the theatre to hear the première of Massenet's *Herodiade*. When the performance was over, Gounod was anxiously solicited for his opinion of the new work. 'C'est rhomboidal!' exclaimed the old man with a knowing air. 'Ah! cher maître,' cried Mme Bizet cuttingly in reply, 'j'allais le dire.'

The extent of Gounod's influence must be sought, not so much in the lead which he gave to operatic composers—which in all conscience was rather slight—but in the habits of renunciation which he strove to pass on. His reversion to sacred themes set an important precedent for composers like Fauré—whose submissive Requiem did not appear until 1887—and the later Franck.[1] It should nevertheless be remembered that Gounod's setting of *Rédemption* followed Franck's by an interval of more than ten years. Of greater significance than any influence which he may have exerted on the Franck school was the effort at rapprochement which arose out of his attempt to bridge the two worlds of pulpit and opera stage. In this respect it is not too fanciful to liken Gounod's role to that pursued in more recent times by Francis Poulenc. The latter's *Gloria* and *Stabat Mater* betray clear debts to the composer of the *Messe Solennelle*, and all three of these works helped to prove that it was still possible for Frenchmen to write religious music of a pleasing and unpretentious kind. If we are still disposed to think of Gounod as a musician who ended by forfeiting his trust— coming to ally himself more with Meyerbeer than Palestrina after all—it should not be forgotten that his was the only church music, apart from Franck's, which made any sort of acknowledgement of the nation's heritage. Added to this is the fact that it was Gounod who did most to inspire the art of the *mélodie*, that subtle and far-reaching means of communication favoured by composers of the

---

[1] It should be recalled that the period 1880–90 witnessed a huge upsurge of scepticism in France. Romain Rolland has recorded the extent of the unbelief at the Ecole Normale, where Renan's influence was particularly strong. That this attitude went far towards destroying the fabric of French religious thought goes without saying; more significant here is the fact that it also helped to deprive composers of their motive for writing sacred music.

calibre of Fauré, Duparc, Debussy and Ravel. Whatever we may
think of his music today—and to many it has almost become a
synonym for triviality—the position he occupied as an innovator
can hardly be denied. He did as much as anyone to provide France
with art-forms which possessed a distinct appearance of national
identity.

The important events of the 1860s amounted to a consolidation
of interest in the art—as opposed to the profession—of music.
This was something a variety of people had helped to bring about.
Bizet, a typical representative of the younger generation, wrote
with a confident despair that seems almost modern in tone. His
disdain for the products of the market-place was both lofty and far-
seeing. Comparing the composer's lot with that of the pariah in
former societies, he flaunted an aggressive spirit of alienation that
would have been unknown, because unexperienced, among his predecessors. His shouts of defiance appear more provocative, less
claustrophobic, than the trapped animal cries of a Berlioz. Our
contemporary composers, Bizet grandly declaimed, 'cry as they
fall, like the gladiators of old, "Salve, popule! te morituri
salutant!"' Sadly though his own career was to turn out (his
masterpiece *Carmen* proved a flop, and was not revived until eight
years after the composer's death), Bizet can be recognized as the
product of a more conscience-stricken age, still lacking enlightenment, but much less hopelessly intolerant than any which had
recently preceded it. As a student at the Conservatoire, he had
found himself greeted, not by another irate Cherubini, but by the
gentle and good-humoured Halévy, whose daughter Geneviève he
was destined to marry. His style, marked by a refreshing absence
of frills, could only have been learnt from Gounod, and was perfectly formed from an early stage. Thus whatever troubles he was
fated to endure as a composer, his principal assets—those things it
had taken Gounod so long to discover in himself—were never in
serious doubt. Like Saint-Saëns, whose facility he came near to
sharing, Bizet's struggles were not really artistic and were certainly
not inner-inspired. They resulted from the factional disturbances
which threatened his society, and from the purely practical
difficulties of getting his music performed.

In comparison with the earlier situation, even the day-to-day
problems confronting the musician were becoming less daunting.
For it can hardly be contested that by the time Bizet approached
maturity Paris had shed most of her slothful musical practices and
a more enterprising attitude was discernible. In 1860, Pasdeloup
had begun his famous series of Sunday concerts, a boon for which
all orchestral composers were to become increasingly thankful.
Not only were the works of younger musicians allowed to appear

on his programmes, but a generous proportion of the time was allotted to the symphonies of Berlioz, Schumann and Mendelssohn, at that stage still the property of the *avant-garde*. As early as 1863 Pasdeloup had been able to include a Scherzo by Bizet at one of these concerts, the piece receiving favourable notices in both the *Revue Musicale* and *Le Menestrel*. At its second performance—a luxury earlier composers would have envied—the twenty-five-year-old prodigy was accorded the honour of directing his own work. Saint-Saëns, it may be noted, was given a similar opportunity at the very same concert. Later on, Bizet had yet another work performed at the Cirque d'Hiver (which was the venue for the Concerts Populaires, as they had become known). This was his *Souvenir de Rome*, written to commemorate his prize-winning stay in the Eternal City.

Pasdeloup's concerts had grown out of the work of an organization known as the Société des Jeunes Artistes, a fairly small body used to giving a maximum of six or seven concerts a year. The bias, even after the society's ambitions had been taken over, was therefore towards living rather than dead composers. Bigots continued to protest at the inclusion of works by nonentities—and this category tended to embrace both Bizet and Saint-Saëns—but the important thing was that their compositions actually got a hearing. An audience, hostile or otherwise, was a privilege which had often been denied to the musicians of an older generation. Of even greater value to the absolute beginner was to be the Société Nationale, an institution that did not come into being until 1871. Inspired by patriotic motives, it took as its motto the saying 'Ars Gallia' and as its object the advancement of native music and musicians. The society, which showed a great partiality towards chamber music, did sterling work in promoting concerts in the capital, and soon extended its activities to the provinces. At first the aim was to build up a body of French chamber music which would rival the German contribution, itself very imperfectly understood in France. In time the Société broadened its outlook to the extent of encouraging other and more popular forms of music, including orchestral music. The steady platform it provided for symphonic works became a good indication of its usefulness in this neglected sector. The driving forces behind the Société Nationale were Saint-Saëns (who was its first president), Gabriel Fauré, Ernest Guiraud, Romain Bussine, César Franck and Henri Duparc. The last-named composer, though he was led to resign through ill-health at quite an early stage, worked hard to publicize the committee's efforts, succeeding the unfortunate Alexis de Castillon as secretary and general factotum. Only about ten concerts a year were given under the society's auspices, but these quickly attained such prestige that they were almost sufficient to guarantee an interest in contemporary music on the part of the public, and to underwrite whatever works were forthcoming. Unhappily, there was a strong element of dissension in the attitudes adopted by the committee towards foreign music and its influence. The later history of the society was hence one of bitterness and acrimony. An important outbreak of squabbling occurred in the 1880s, when Saint-Saëns was ousted from his presidency by the anti-semitic d'Indy, and Franck elevated to the main office in his place. The establishment of a rival society—the lesser known Société Musicale Indépendente—by Fauré and others promised further opportunities for feuding, opportunities which were eagerly grasped by the various cults that sprang up at the time of the First World War. But by this time, the society's work had proved its value. It is worth remembering that its growth proceeded in step with, and largely by the aid of, the Franck group of composers.

Almost at the same moment in history as the founding of the Société Nationale, there evolved another concert-giving organization of equal interest to musicians. This was the Association Artistique des Concerts Colonne, founded in 1875. As an enterprise, it met with a subsidy from the publishing firm of Hartmann, so that its uses were doubly prized by the budding composer. Edouard Colonne had begun his career as a violinist in Pasdeloup's orchestra, but at great risk to his personal fortunes—for he was not a rich man—he launched out into concert promotion, partly in order to seek justice for Berlioz, whose ardent champion he became. His role as a conductor was something which he took deadly seriously, as he was also inclined to take his obligations towards improving public taste. The upshot was that he soon acquired an enviable reputation for his impassioned handling of romantic and modern music. It was largely due to his advocacy that composers as different from one another as Wagner, Saint-Saëns, Debussy and Ravel managed to win a following in France. One of Colonne's many innovations consisted of persuading the orchestra to accept a percentage of the receipts in lieu of a salary, thus providing the players with a strong motive for ensuring the success of any concert for which they had been engaged. Despite this precaution, the Concerts Colonne lost heavily during their early years, making up their deficit in the pride which accrued from such a courageous stand. The effect which they had upon the nation's musical taste was as valuable as it was incalculable. The success of one particular item which they popularized—bewilderingly entitled *Chevauchée des Walkyries*—heralded a revolution much greater than any Franck was destined to set in motion. It was the intrepid Colonne who directed the première of *Rédemption* in 1873—not very competently as it turned out—and he did a good deal to enhance the reputations of several of the master's pupils.

The last of the famous institutions to shape musical taste in France during the latter half of the nineteenth century was the Société des Nouveaux Concerts, under the direction of Charles Lamoureux. This body began work in 1881, by which time conditions looked like being more secure. Lamoureux was a wealthy professional—a rare and formidable combination—so that he was not put out by the idea of paying for extensive rehearsals. Moreover, he had no compunction about incurring the wrath of managements and public when the occasion seemed to warrant it. These factors undoubtedly assisted in easing the task he had set himself, which was nothing less than to win a sympathetic hearing for the most unpopular modern composers, among whom Wagner figured high on the list. His version of *Tristan*—first given in 1889—used to be held up as the acme of interpretive skill at the rostrum, especially by the older generation of Wagnerites. James Harding has given us a graphic portrait of the man, which also serves to underline the dictatorial influence he wielded upon French music-making during the last quarter of the century:

> He was a round, tubby little man with broad shoulders, bull neck, and a head shaped like a cannon ball. Late arrivals at his concerts were fixed with a terrifying glare as he stood, baton raised, and watched them from behind his enormous glasses while they crept down the aisle and scuttled into their seats like mice into holes.

With such a doughty protagonist at the helm, it is little wonder that the nation's musical life soon took a turn for the better, and that unpublished composers were again provided with the incentive to start writing.

Alongside the growth of concert-going went the decline of the salon, that sociable upholder of false values and enemy of progressivism. Having reached its pinnacle under Louis-Phillipe, the institution receded sharply during the parvenu age which followed. Unable any longer to recruit men and women of real breeding and cultivation, it gradually lost its value as an adjunct to culture and was barely successful in preserving its own existence. As the older aristocracy was replaced by an ambitious *haute bourgeoisie*, so the business of launching artistic satellites gave way to the scramble for office and the pursuit of commercial acclaim. Composers and performers who had trained themselves to follow in the footsteps of Chopin and Liszt were dismayed to discover that the new hostesses lacked the style shown by their predecessors and were interested only in furthering their husbands' careers. 'La France s'ennuie,' said the laconic Taine, hinting broadly at the nostalgia which many people still reserved for the old Bourbon monarchy. It was a complaint that struck a sympathetic echo in the minds of all who were continuing to aim at the sort of reputation which had sufficed for the romantics. Other grounds for disquiet arose out of the new attitudes which were being taken up towards the principle of patronage. Regarded as the keystone of the system during the years before 1848, this aristocratic privilege now stood in some danger of being revoked. Radicals had long come to revile its presence in the world of politics, and indications of its persistence in the arts were accordingly greeted with blunt hostility in certain quarters. D'Annunzio was to speak for nearly the whole of his tribe when he replied to Mme Aubernon's cultural entreaties by remarking: 'Read my books, madame, and let me eat my dinner!' The principle actually lingered for much longer than anyone could have predicted, as its deathbed chronicler—the merciless Marcel Proust—was to discover. But the fictional metamorphosis which transformed a Mme Verdurin into the Duchesse de Guermantes represented a social phenomenon only too rigorously attested during the closing decades of the nineteenth century.

On the whole, artists were quick to draw the moral from this lesson, which was that little profit could be derived from the time-honoured practice of selling their talents to the highest bidder. No longer content to remain a freak or a flunkey, the artist began to petition for a recognized place in society; and if this place could not, by the nature of things, be in the highest society, then he was quite willing to settle for something a little lower down. There were already signs that he was about to receive his due in some of the non-musical arts. The expansive Baron Haussmann—the natural successor to Mansart—was asked to build, not palaces, but a spacious array of boulevards designed to usher in a new era of city planning. When his colleague Charles Garnier was invited to construct a new opera-house right in the centre of the capital, there was no reason to doubt that the age of state patronage had begun. It is noteworthy that the term 'boulevardier'—which came into currency as a direct result of Haussmann's labours—referred to the kind of person whose promenades led him, almost by definition, to the café rather than the salon. Hence, by the time the impressionist revolution took hold, it had already become the practice for musicians, like painters, to meet and discuss their art in the bistros and absinthe dens of the city, while abandoning the rich to their generally stuffy and unimaginative pursuits. It is illustrative of this changing situation that an impecunious composer like Erik Satie, trying to make both ends meet, should have hired himself out as second pianist at the Chat Noir, the Montmartre café owned by the prosaic Rodolphe Salis; and that his richer fellow-artist, Ravel, should have chosen the role of 'apache' in preference to that of society darling, to which his talents and influence could easily have entitled him.

Reverting to the middle years of the century, it is of the greatest fascination to observe how César Franck began his career as an unsuccessful virtuoso; and how his entry into the sycophantic world of private patronage coincided so exactly with that world's decline and fall as to provide us with the perfect proof of our thesis. Still bemused by the triumphs of Liszt, Nicolas-Joseph Franck cosseted his son's talents in so snobbish and avaricious a fashion as to leave no doubt that his aim, even from the child's kindergarten days, was to stake all on a reputation to be won by playing at the chateaux and town-houses of the mighty. What defeated this aim was not so much the boy's gradual revulsion towards such a career as the censure he was forced to endure from critics, most of whom were quick to realize that it was they and not the diamond-studded dowagers who were to be the future arbiters of taste. It is symptomatic that more than one writer began by making fun of the pretentious Christian names with which Franck senior had ungraciously saddled his children. Blanchard, one of the deadliest commentators as far as the family was concerned, went further and actually stigmatized the luckless César as an extinct species:

A Roman Emperor and a sovereign pontiff joined together last Friday to give a concert at the rooms of the ancient chancellery of the Duke of Orléans in the Rue Valois.

It is hardly any wonder, after enduring such snubs, that the family lost heart and returned to their native Belgium. Perhaps we should see it as indicative of the slowness of this cultural revolution that, once they had arrived back in Liège, they set about planning another 'social' career by seeking out the favours of King Leopold. That this, too, was destined to reach a disappointing end must have been obvious to anyone who had followed the vagaries of the profession since the earlier years of the century. The fact that the Francks did not see their mistake until it was too late is only another pointer to Nicolas-Joseph's stupidity, and the stubborness with which he went on hammering at his original ambition.

In surveying Franck's development as an artist, it is easy to forget how difficult it was for any young man of talent to escape from the prevailing confusion of aim. This confusion was something that affected all the arts, but most of all the art of music. Even after the total destruction of Franck senior's hopes, it was a long time before it became apparent to his son what course he should pursue. A certain natural diffidence prevented him from plunging straight away into the more popular sectors of the musical life, so that what we witness during the composer's early maturity is a series of abortive attempts to establish himself, first of all in the chamber music field, then successively in oratorio and church music. It is significant that in none of these sectors did Franck find it possible to arrive at a living model to assist him in perfecting his technique. The Trios, which were his first major compositions, harked back to the Viennese masters: though they also contained several innovations for which Franck himself deserved the credit. It is easy to see how elements in these works reflected the changes which were taking place in the orchestra, and which may be glimpsed by comparing a score of Beethoven with one of Berlioz's complicated essays. To describe Franck's works as true examples of chamber music would accordingly be misleading. Much the same sort of thing happened when he transferred his ambitions to the larger vocal forms. Here his first experiments fell awkwardly between the rigid classicism of Méhul and the more expansive orientalism then on the point of becoming fashionable. In all of his pre-1870 works (except perhaps for the 'Six Pièces' for organ), we can recognize the uncertainties of gesture and inequalities of taste which go to characterize a culture bereft of tradition. It was the same kind of situation that was to confront a puzzled Elgar many years later in England. The main difference was that French attitudes were compromised by being more responsive to foreign stimulus, and were inherently less puritanical in tone.

Little more need be said about the state of music in Paris at the time of César Franck's arrival on the scene. It will have become evident that his retiring personality eluded the customary expectations, thwarted the ambitions of his family, and obstinately refused to coalesce into the pattern reserved for it by a venal and cynical public. Instead of conforming to the image of the conquering foreigner—the role Rossini and Meyerbeer had been alternately called upon to play—he was obliged to work his way up from the lower rungs of the social ladder, discovering his talents as he went along. His early showing as a prodigy proved that he possessed none of the dandy's mannerisms, while the unwordly habits he displayed confirmed that he would be better off in a less competitive sector of the musical life. Refused by the salons, he spent the next twenty-five years fighting down a persistent obscurity, and even after he had convinced people of his genius the satisfactions of fame still failed to come his way. Nothing he did up to the age of forty had the least bearing on his ultimate standing as a composer, unless we make an exception for the prolonged study of counterpoint which occupied him from his earliest youth onwards.

This study, and the grinding practice which he put in at the key-board, formed the whole extent of his universe until he was of an age when most men are content to reflect on their experience.

Nevertheless, the service which Franck was fated to perform on behalf of French music was among the most valuable ever rendered to that nation. By crowning his career with a set of brilliant chamber-works, he was able to propound an ideal that was quickly imitated by musicians as diverse as Debussy, d'Indy and Roussel. Not content with this achievement, he imposed a penance on future generations which it is still the practice for French composers to enact. To have placed a man of Franck's solemn cast in a city as simultaneously frivolous and degraded as Paris in the throes of the Empire might have suggested an act unparalleled perversity on the part of the Creator. Yet there was a certain justice in France's having inherited such a figure. For contained in his prescriptions were the remedies necessary to secure music's temporary abnegation, its purge after the banquet of romanticism; while mixed up with his solitary improvisations was a dose of the medicine needed to curb those graces, as dangerous as they were beguiling, to which the national character seemed fatally addicted.

The stance Franck assumed was unique by reason of its disinterestedness. It was through the stoicism which he exhibited, preferring to wait upon acclaim than to incur corruption by seeking it out, that he won the loyalty of those earnest young disciples who, having themselves become refugees from the more strident aspects of existence, were anxiously casting around for a prophet to guide them. Despising egotism, these men confined their search to those musicians in whom inner strength and probity were the signal virtues; and it was the presence of these qualities in César Franck which enabled him to fulfil their demands. Meantime, we should be less than just if we failed to make clear that the composer was not just another saintly ascetic. To his fellow-churchmen— and perhaps even to his family—his power of evoking the underside of the human spirit must have seemed no less pronounced than his grasp of its illuminations. His appeal therefore extended far beyond the devotional sphere, possibly reaching as far as the *musicien maudit*, that charioteer of the imagination in whom the final vestiges of the picturesque continued to struggle for expression. Franck is sometimes alleged to have been visited by angels, but it is probable that he was not unaware of the less beneficent orders and would have understood Theodore Dreiser's remark: 'I believe in the Furies . . . I have listened to the strange beating of their wings.'

II

The prodigy who failed
to conquer

So powerful is the animosity of nationalists everywhere that, remarkable though it may seem, the business of identifying César Franck's true country and allegiance has never been properly settled. His birthday—10 December 1822—remains fixed in the minds of musicians as a result of d'Indy superstitious reminder that this was the very day on which Beethoven completed his *Missa Solemnis*.[1] Unfortunately, much less unanimity has arisen from the consideration of where this happy event took place. Franck's pupil started something of a racial hare when he blandly asserted that his teacher had been born 'in a land that is peculiarly French, not only in sentiment and language, but also in its external aspect'. When we place this statement alongside the incontrovertible fact that César entered the world at Liège, an attractive provincial city in nearby Belgium, we get a clear inkling of the depths to which the controversy had sunk, even at the time of the earliest biographies.

Closer inspection of the problem reveals that d'Indy's proposition was not entirely the product of misplaced chauvinism. The position gains in clarity when we discover that Belgium was not granted its independence until 1830, up to which point the city of Liège, though officially described as being in the Walloon district of the Netherlands, had as good a claim to being called French as any overseas colony in which the French language was spoken. The state of affairs prior to independence was that the Flemish and Walloon districts each paid their separate allegiance, the former to the Dutch and the latter to the French nation. Eight

[1] Despite this clear indication, Professor Norman Demuth gives the date of the composer's birth as 22 December, which seems like a slip of the pen. The parish register at Liège is quite specific in adhering to the earlier date, giving the time as 7 a.m.

years after Franck was born, they were united under King Leopold and awarded the status of a country apart. Since the composer spanned both epochs, it is understandable that there should have been some confusion as to his real nationality. It is possible to think of him as having been originally French or Walloon, depending on the way the question is put. On the other hand, there can be no doubt that he became Belgian on the reading of the new proclamation. Taken thus far, the matter does not seem impossibly complicated. What makes it so is the fact that Franck's father—Nicolas-Joseph Franck—saw fit to re-apply for French nationality at the time of sending his son to the Paris Conservatoire. As if this were not enough, the composer himself is known to have taken a similar course as late as 1873, when accepting his appointment as Professor of Organ at that institution. Looking at the rest of the family, it is worth noting that Mme Franck, the composer's mother, was of German stock; while even his father's people came from the vicinity of Gemmenich, only a few miles west of the Aachen border. Such genealogical untidiness makes it hopeless to state with confidence which country should have the benefit of adding Franck's name to its musical heritage.

It is a relief to learn that the composer spent the whole of his childhood at 13 Rue St Pierre in Liège—a city which incidentally boasted a long list of musical celebrities. André Grétry, the composer of light operas, was originally a citizen, though he emigrated at a tender age to Paris, a course in which he was to be imitated by his younger fellow-townsman. Another inhabitant was the violinist Henri Vieuxtemps, a man only two years older than Franck. The subsequent appearance of the great virtuoso fiddler, Eugène Ysaÿe, only seemed to confirm the city's aptitude for producing players of this instrument. In earlier centuries, the fondness had been for choral singing. Dufay, Ockeghem and Josquin all lived and worked in the region of northern Burgundy, so that the land was renowned for the excellence of its traditions in this respect. Religious observance had always been strong there, and Franck's own forbears had occupied a respected place in ecclesiastical circles. This place was not, as may have been imagined, in the pulpit, but in the more humble sphere of stained-glass window making. The earliest known member of the family to have embarked on this craft was one Jerome Franck, a sixteenth-century artist who left his homeland to take up an appointment at the court of Henri III. The late Gothic style of religious painting was if anything a Flemish invention, owing much to that delicate blend of realism and spirituality which we find in Roger Van der Weyden, himself an admirer of the Van Eycks. No doubt Franck's ancestors practised this unselfconscious art with much the same devotion as the composer was to lavish on his music. It is interesting to learn that drawing was one of Franck's best subjects at school. That he was not obliged to follow the family vocation is evident from the fact of Nicolas-Joseph's earlier break with tradition. Having chosen a secular profession for himself, he was hardly in a position to insist that his son should do otherwise. In any case, his pecuniary urges were so compulsive that no spiritual considerations were permitted to influence his decision.

Because of the talent he displayed for music, César was marked down at a particularly early age for the profession of virtuoso. Despite this aim, the family did nothing at all to help nourish the finer aspects of the boy's sensibility. Quite to the contrary, his father seems to have imbued him with the conviction that the object of life was to make as much money as possible, and that to do this it was necessary to work unceasingly from dawn to dusk, shelving all matters which did not bear on the business in hand. The idea that a general education might have features to commend it was one that does not seem to have occurred to either parent. At least, there was no sign of a liberal outlook behind the régime to which they greedily subjected their offspring. Cortot's description of Nicolas-Joseph as a 'petit clerc' may have been accurate enough in its contemptuous implications, but scarcely takes account of the fact that, from the time his son reached the age of twelve, he did little work except that calculated to manoeuvre César into the position of being family provider. He had two children, both of them boys, the second being named after his father. Joseph was three years younger than César (not older, as Winton Dean suggests in his monograph on the composer), and at first seemed equally musical. The notion was quickly grasped of getting them to perform together as a duo, César at the piano and his brother on the violin. Their father resorted to every trick of propaganda to launch them on a lucrative career, which only his ineptness as an impresario prevented them from attaining. The story of the partnership is in many respects harrowing, bearing out the nineteenth century's reputation for exploiting child labour in the most evil manner. What remains unusual about it is that the manipulative element persisted well into César's twenties, and eventually came to incorporate creative as well as executant functions. The whole chronicle can be read as a lively documentary on the strains of the musical career, and is a most enlightening piece of social history.

That fame and fortune awaited all young men of personable appearance and moderate musical gifts was an illusion the romantic age did a great deal to foster. Disappointments must have been common even before Franck was drilled into investing his hopes. However, it almost seems as if Nicolas-Joseph had made up his

mind that his sons would succeed before setting out for the chris-
tening ceremony. In fact, the practice of naming infants after
classical kings and queens went back a lot further than this date.
Achieving its greatest popularity at the moment of renewed monarchical fervour in France, it mysteriously survived intact into the
age of republican dissent. It is odd to reflect that even that arch-
republican among composers, Georges Bizet, was originally
christened Alexandre-César-Leopold: a fact which the destruction
of his birth certificate during the Commune conveniently caused
him to forget. Franck, born some fifteen years before the composer
of *Carmen*, saw no reason to feel ashamed of his appellation,
though there must have been times when he bitterly regretted it.
Liszt, who knew better than anyone what was needed for success in
the world of the salons, lost no time in warning Nicolas-Joseph of
the harm he had done in so inaptly naming his children. In the same
letter, he expressed the opinion—shrewd enough as it turned out—
that young César seemed deficient in the social qualities required
by the career which had been proposed for him. Unfortunately,
Liszt's advice was ignored. Had it been accepted, and Franck diverted into a less tightly-knit sector of the musical life, it is possible
that his gifts would have been quicker to blossom. On the other
hand, he might never have developed the 'brilliant' qualities which
have given his music its wide appeal. Speculation of this sort does
not get us very far. It is more interesting to trace the steps in the
composer's early training, and examine what it was that led him to
make such a poor showing.

When he was only eight years of age, Franck was enrolled at the
Liège Conservatoire, an institution which acquired the prefix
'Royal' within a short time of his entering it. Here the boy was
given every opportunity to learn the rudiments of his profession,
and we have no reason to doubt the excellence of the instruction he
received. That he was a remarkable pupil is suggested by the fact
that he won his first prize after only a year's study. When he repeated his success, at the end of his third year, he was presented
with a full score of Meyerbeer's *Robert le Diable*. What he made of
this *tour-de-force* at his tender age can scarcely be imagined. We
do know, however, that he kept it with him for the remainder of
his life, a proud souvenir of his days as an infant prodigy. The
assessments of Franck's Belgian teachers are worth pondering, if
only for the light they shed on his subsequent career. Their praise
was by no means unrestricted—despite the boy's prize-winning
exploits—and it is significant that one teacher commented on his
over-ardent manner of expression. This was a defect for which his
future professor, Zimmermann, was also to rebuke him. Listeners
who find Franck's music cloying may be interested to note the

appearance of this trait, which was in all probability an innate aspect of his character. Another remark made by the child's examiners was that his intelligence did not seem equal to his musical gifts. This, too, has a slightly prophetic ring about it. For the most part, we get the impression of a fluent talent, far ahead of the ordinary in the mechanics of the art, but harbouring in its wake a number of disturbing qualifications. It is as well to be aware of what these qualifications were right from the beginning of our study.

That Franck was not a particularly astute man may have been gathered from preceding inquiries. Whether his lack of general intelligence was a handicap to him as a composer is a difficult question to answer. One quality which he signally lacked was the power of self-criticism, especially as it related to the planning and long term appraisal of his works. It was not that he had the stupidity of conceit, for no one could have been less vain about his abilities. It was simply that he did not possess that sharpness of acumen so often to be found in the literary or cosmopolitan musician. (Stravinsky is an excellent example of this.) Present-day listeners are sometimes inclined to think of Franck as 'an organ-loft composer', not without a modicum of reason. The fact is that he never managed to arrive at a universal musical language in the way that, say, Liszt and Berlioz did. Compared with them, he lacked culture and that sort of intellectual vision of his art which modern critics rate as indispensable. Despite d'Indy's vigorous arguments to the contrary, Franck was always in danger of being thought provincial; and it is on account of his failure to overcome this indictment that we hesitate to respond to him as fully as we might. The early testimonials he received—like the reviews of his first concerts—should not be dismissed as so much insensitive verbiage. They provide a valuable clue to some of the composer's cardinal weaknesses, and tell us, quite as clearly as any sociological analysis, why he met with such stiff opposition. Throughout his life Franck was subjected to moderate—and frequently immoderate—criticism, not just in his capacity as an executant, but in everything that he did. That some of this was motivated by spite is obvious. But it would be disingenuous to imply that a fair proportion did not reflect real deficiencies on his part.

The long struggle to win acclaim as a performer began while César was still a pupil at the Liège school of music. It was in 1834, while he was in his eleventh year, that his father took him on a tour of Belgium, the boy being made to play at Aix and Brussels as well as his home city. The presence of King Leopold at one of these concerts was probably what imbued Franck senior with the notion that he could enhance his son's prospects by attempting to pull strings at court. For the present, however, he was quite content to see the youngster acquit himself creditably, and share a platform with established artists. The pattern of concerts in those days was exceedingly haphazard. Programme planning had yet to be admitted as a subsidiary art, with the result that most musical evenings consisted of a puzzling hotch-potch of song and instrumental composition, the latter often consisting of fantasies and transcriptions based on the more popular operas. Any new work for solo instrument or chamber ensemble had to be squeezed ignominiously into the gaps between these fashionable numbers. Liszt alone was capable of giving solo piano recitals, and there are accounts of how even he was obliged to wave off unfortunate string players who had consented to make up the bill with him. The young Franck's role as a prospective prodigy was accordingly confined to padding out miscellaneous programmes in which others had been awarded highest rating.

On one of these evenings—an occasion he was to remember with pride for the rest of his days—he found himself billed alongside another rising star, two or three years older than himself. This turned out to be none other than the diva, Pauline Viardot, later to become one of the century's best known singers and hostess to a brilliant array of literary lions. She was the daughter of the tenor, Manuel Garcia, who had been the original Almaviva in Rossini's *The Barber of Seville*. Pauline, like Franck, was one of a set of musical siblings, her sister Maria having become famous as the immortal Malibran. Taken together, this blest pair of sirens, heartily stigmatized by later generations on account of their exhibitionism, were to steal an unfair proportion of the vocal honours accruing to the age.[1] Unlike many of our own *prima donnas*, they were both mezzo-sopranos; though, to judge from their repertoire, they must have been able to take some exceedingly high notes, Maria being as renowned for her 'Una voce poco fa' as for her powerful 'Abscheulicher!' Franck was to recall being introduced to this awe-inspiring lady and her husband, the violinist Charles de Bériot. Doubtless the couple had come to hear the inexperienced Pauline make her bid for fame. In a further year or two, memories were all that remained of the great *bel canto* exponent, for she died at the early age of twenty-eight, leaving her young sister to trudge

---

[1] Their standing with fashionable artists of the time may be gauged from the fact that Alfred de Musset wrote one of his poems in praise of Malibran, while Mme Viardot was described by Berlioz as 'one of the greatest artists in the past or present history of music'. Writing of Malibran's early death, Edgar Allan Poe said: 'She crowded ages into hours. She left the world at twenty-five [*sic*] having existed thousands of years.'

on to a ripe eighty-nine! One wonders whether Franck ever dreamed of including either of these singers in the plans for future vocal works which he may have had. Judging from the quality of his ill-fated *Le Valet de Ferme*—which he did not write until he was thirty—it would have taken more than their inspiration to have turned him into a figure of renown in the theatre. Probably he was content to think in terms of a few songs, a medium in which he experienced much less difficulty.

As it was, César's earliest compositions showed no hint of the prediction that he was more likely to be a creator than a performer. His father had been interested to see him turn out a couple of sets of *variations brilliantes* in the accepted fashion of the day, one of them on themes from the lauded *Gustav III*. When these were scored for small orchestra, it still did not seem a sufficiently alarming departure from the customary practice. In those days, the distinctions made between the various musical specialisms were hardly very acute, and it was easy to point to well-known executants who also dabbled in composition. Indeed, such a description might have seemed to fit both Liszt and Chopin, to say nothing of their various imitators. César's compositions for piano were accordingly quite acceptable to Nicolas-Joseph's ambitions. Since they helped to underline the boy's putative gifts as a virtuoso, they were eagerly included in the itinerant concerts which he was constantly being asked to give. Among the products of these early years were a 'Grand Rondo'; some variations on a theme from Hérold's *Pré-aux-Clercs*; a Concerto classed as op. 2; and two ambitious-sounding sonatas for the piano. There were also a number of other fantasias and trios, one of which was expanded to form the better-known Trio de Salon, now counted as no. 2 in the set of three Trios which Franck was to complete in 1841. Most of these works are tamely juvenile, and all remain unpublished. The manuscripts later fell into the possession of Franck's pupil, Pierre de Bréville, who generously presented them to the Bibliothèque Nationale in 1947. The only one of the childhood compositions which the composer did not disown was a 'Fantaisie', originally listed as op. 12, which he wrote at the age of thirteen and which he sometimes liked to play in his mature years.[1] Incidentally, this is not the work classed as op. 13, of which d'Indy complained of finding no trace; that particular piece continues to elude scrutiny and was quite probably never written at all.

[1] In the revised catalogue of the composer's works there is another 'Fantaisie' listed under the same opus number. This is a variant of the air 'Le point du jour' from de Dalayrac's *Gulistan*, which has nothing to do with the work in question. It was written much later, around 1844.

As may be surmised, it was the boy's father who took over the job of classifying his compositions, making sure that he added enough opus numbers to ensnare possible patrons. The gaps which appeared in the original, unrevised catalogue may be put down to this habit, and to the fact that César was given precious little time in which to demonstrate his fertility. The whole chain of numbers was re-started at op. 1 at the time of publishing the Trios, presumably in order to deter people from looking too closely at the juvenilia. It is noticeable that the titles of these youthful exercises tend to arouse expectations which the music does nothing to fulfil. One can imagine that they, too, were dreamed up by the resourceful Nicolas-Joseph. Symphonies written by boys in their 'teens are deservedly suspect (unless their name happens to be Mozart), and it should surprise no one to discover that the single work of this type attributed to the young Franck is rudimentary in the extreme. It is scored for all the instruments to be played continuously throughout! Considering what store the composer was later to put on his injunction 'Let a little air into your music!' this early effort must have come to seem an embarrassment of which he was eager not to be reminded. The paternal touch is once more evident in the trick César was encouraged to display of signing his scores 'César-Auguste Franck de Liège'. Ostensibly, this was in order to avoid confusion with another composer whose surname happened to be the same, one Edouard Franck of Berlin. It seems more likely, however, that it was intended as a grandiose gesture. Professor Demuth, in his book on the composer, draws attention to the fact that one early score reveals a defacement; a miscreant (could it have been Erik Satie, one wonders?) having inserted the word 'pompier' directly behind the signature. Despite all these attempts to gain attention, it is probable that Franck himself was far more craven than arrogant. His habits derived entirely from an exaggerated obedience to the parental will. That he eventually plucked up the courage to rebel must be everlastingly held up to his credit. Oddly enough, his servility did not extend to his academic superiors whose authority he delighted in flouting. Perhaps he regarded this as the sole means of retaliation left open to him.

The next glimpse we have of the *Wunderkind* is as an eager, though not very impressionable, pupil of Zimmermann. Sent to Paris to acquire the sort of technique that only a master could have been expected to impart, he found himself too young to be admitted to any of the recognized schools of music. He therefore had to pursue the alternative path of attaching himself to a private teacher. Thus in 1835 he came to be accepted by the man who had given lessons to the famous Marmontel, as well as a host of other well-known French pianists. What was to prove vastly more important was that he also presented himself for composition lessons to the Bohemian professor, Antonin Reicha, a cultivated immigrant whose liberal views were a mild source of annoyance to his colleagues at the Conservatoire to which he had coolly been appointed. This was a marvellous stroke of luck for Franck, one of the few that ever came his way, and the pity is that he did not enjoy it for long. Reicha had obtained his chair through the personal intervention of Louis XVIII, having previously distinguished himself as a member of the Electoral Orchestra at Bonn. It was there, of course, that he had matriculated in the company of Beethoven. Cherubini knew full well Reicha's reputation as a progressive thinker, and bitterly contested the appointment. For once his counsel proved useless. Franck was consequently very fortunate in being able to attach himself to that rarest of species, a rebel in authority.

The impact on his untutored mind of this good and kindly Czech, with his cultured interest in Kant and Aristotle, may be readily imagined. It is probable that the seeds of that gentle mysticism, later to express itself in works like *Rédemption* and *Les Béatitudes*, were sown during their short-lived relationship.[1] Moreover, since Reicha was an early advocate of polytonality (he was followed in this unlikely pursuit by the erudite Saint-Saëns, who typically gave a lecture on it to his colleagues at the Institut), it is at least arguable that Franck absorbed from him some of his taste for modulatory experiment. Sadly—for it is impossible not to feel that further contact with this enlightened humanist would have accelerated Franck's progress—Reicha was to die in 1836. In some ways, he had been dragged down by the stagnant ideals which had surrounded him in his adopted country. His own opera, *Natalie*, had been submitted to the Paris Opéra along with a hundred more superficial works, and he had nearly been driven out of his mind by the delays and prevarications it encountered before being pronounced a reject. Whether it was this disappointment that killed him, or a more conventional disease, there could be no doubt that he was a crushed man at the time of signing up his last pupil. It would have cheered him to learn that he provided Franck with the single ray of light he needed to see his way out of the drab tunnel which his family had dug for him.

Meantime, the lad had his duty to perform, and though he was able to enjoy an occasional holiday back in his native Belgium and at his uncle's house in Gemmenich (where he was described as a dreamy-looking youth, with long brown hair, dressed in a blue and

[1] One should not, of course, exaggerate this influence. As Maurice Emmanuel has pointed out in his study of the composer, Franck was a mere boy of thirteen or fourteen at the time of his association with Reicha.

white sailor's jacket), it was not long before his father had him battering at the gates of Paris once more like some future Achilles. This time the idea was that he should take the city by storm, capture the highest prizes on the basis of a single, triumphant recital. Nicolas-Joseph pulled off what he regarded as a valuable 'coup' in booking the enormous Gymnase Musical—a hall of vastly larger dimensions than any to which César was accustomed. Preparations for the great event soon reached the feverish stage, with carefully wangled testimonials being billed and publicity-seeking articles mysteriously appearing in the press. No one seems to have thought of tracing the latter back to the young man's parent. As usually happened when Nicolas-Joseph went to such pains, the concert itself proved a fiasco. Whether it was that the acoustics of the hall were too resonant, or simply that the right atmosphere was lacking, nothing seemed to create the desired effect. Rich in keyboard virtuosi, the city hardly bothered to notice the boy, except to say that he played well enough; and the battle had to be postponed to another day. Later on, when César renewed his bid by presenting dazzling fantasias of his own on *Lucia di Lammermoor* and *Anna Bolena*, he was smartly up-staged by Marmontel, who not unnaturally detected a threat to his prestige. In the general run, it was the avidly talked-about figure—a Weber or a Thalberg—who drew the crowds in Paris. An uncouth boy from Belgium, with his blundering father, attracted the attention of no one.

Reluctantly, the decision was then taken to enter the youngster at the Conservatoire, and see what the machinery could be made to produce. If he could not become an internationally fêted celebrity, at least he might put the time to good use while his father invented a fresh set of tactics. Hoping to qualify for naturalization, the entire Franck family moved to Paris in 1836. The circumstances surrounding this move are a little obscure, and the whole operation seems to have been planned with more haste than sense. Nicolas-Joseph, who had made a point of following Liszt's career in the minutest detail, abruptly seemed to have been made aware that the Hungarian master was once refused admission to the Paris Conservatoire. The grounds—rather speciously trumped up for the occasion by Cherubini—were said to have included the fact that he was a foreigner. Not wishing to be met with similar objections over César, his father went about everything in the most methodical way, taking out the necessary papers and putting in a tactful period of residence before pressing his application for admission. The plan was successful, and César was duly admitted on 4 October 1837. Ironically, he had to go through the same motions more than thirty years later, when his candidature as professor was under discussion. Meantime, it was enough that his father had taken these

precautions, and he embarked on a period of five years' study which
came to seem far more to his taste, despite some occasional chafing
under the yoke, than the dreary round of concert-giving to which
he had become accustomed.

Whilst at this most select of academies, Franck sought to enlarge and enrich his musical contacts. Though he continued with
Zimmermann for piano, he also found time to go to Leborne for
composition and Habeneck for violin. By and large, his teachers
were well disposed towards him, for he did not find theory in any
way a drudge. The Director himself soon noticed the boy's prowess.
taking it upon himself to inquire after him from time to time. The
goals which now raised themselves tended to be academic prizes;
and the Conservatoire awarded them in every department of skill
and knowledge. Still continuing to think of himself principally as an
executant, Franck began by addressing his efforts to the practical
tests. At the examination for piano in 1838, at which the judges were
Alkan and Adolphe Adam, he carried all before him with his
reading of the Hummel concerto, though he did not completely
satisfy his own teacher, Zimmermann. When it came to sight-
reading, he gave a still clearer indication of his superiority. Observing that the test-piece was well within his capabilities, he could not
resist the temptation to transpose it down a third as he was going
along. Expecting to hear a somewhat garbled account in E flat,
the judges were staggered to meet with a perfectly articulate performance in the key of C instead. At first, they were piqued with
the boy's impudence in tampering with the exercise he had been
set. The more they thought about it, however, the more they considered it would be unfair to deprive him of the honour which he
had so demonstrably won. As a compromise, it was decided to
award him a special 'Grand Prix d'Honneur', a course which succeeded in satisfying all parties, even the disgruntled Director who
had learnt about it at second-hand. This episode reveals with utmost clarity the astonishing nature of Franck's gifts at what might
be called the scholarly side of music. If the rest of the art had come
to him as easily, he would have been one of the greatest composers
who ever lived.

In 1840, Franck decided to transfer his attentions more to the
organ. François Benoist—for that was the name of the teacher to
whom he went for lessons—was easily the most respected player
in the country. He had won the Prix de Rome in 1815, afterwards
building up a huge reputation at the art of improvisation. It was due
to him that France managed to keep alive this practical art throughout the nineteenth century, his pupils forming a royal line no other
nation was able to match. The feats of men like Marcel Dupré
and André Marchal in the present century testify to the influence

of the tradition he helped inaugurate. In the course of time, Franck
was to succeed Benoist as Professor of Organ at the Conservatoire,
so that it is of some interest to inquire into his early showing at the
instrument. Surprisingly enough, he failed to repeat the success he
had achieved with the piano.[1] This, however, may have been due
to the obtuseness of the judges who, in relegating him to second
place, did not observe that he had taken the two themes proposed
for extemporization—one for sonata and the other for fugue—and
cleverly combined them. There is no question but that Franck
attained a prodigious skill at the organ: otherwise it is impossible
to account for the rapid promotion he won for himself in this
department. Nevertheless, it may be doubted whether he was ever
in the very top class of executants. Maurice Emmanuel, in his
biography of the composer, claims that he was much better as a
pianist, an opinion that would have brought a measure of consolation to the embittered Nicolas-Joseph had he lived to hear it
uttered. Franck's trouble as a performer—and this could be said
of his composing with equal justification—was that he improvised
when he should have been intent on perfection. The fault is scarcely
unique, and could be attributed to the kind of training meted out
to French students at this time. Making allowances for this tendency on his part, it is probably true to say that Franck had few
superiors as an organist up to the time the new instruments came
into circulation in the 1860s. After that time, he had much in the
way of technique to re-learn.

One more prize lay open to his talents while he remained a
student at the Conservatoire. This was the coveted Prix de Rome,
of which Gounod had been a holder. Girding his loins for the 1842
competition, which he might well have won on the form he had
shown to date, Franck found himself suddenly and inexplicably
removed from college by his impatient parent. Exasperated by the
delay in fulfilling his ambitions, Nicolas-Joseph had begun to fear
that César was heading for nothing more exalted than a career as a
music teacher: this was not at all what he had striven for. Having in
the meantime entered the younger brother, Joseph, at the same
institution, his father thought it would be quite enough for one of
the children to take up this more prosaic profession. In his estimate
of the talents of his two sons, he was perhaps not far wrong. As it
turned out, however, it was César who settled down to teaching,
and Joseph who persisted with the career of virtuoso. But a great
deal was to happen before this outcome was revealed. Coming at

[1] It may be of interest to note that Franck was unexpectedly slow to
win First Prize at counterpoint, another subject at which he was subsequently regarded as brilliant. He did, however, succeed with his third
attempt.

the end of four eminently successful years of study, his withdrawal must have been an acute shock to César; especially when he discovered himself back on the hated concert circuit within a few months of leaving. We have no record of how he reacted to the blow but it seems likely that he accepted it with his usual stoical reserve. Relations between the two brothers began to cool off a little from this time onwards, however, and one suspects that jealousies may have sprung up to separate them. When, in later years, Joseph tried to interest César in renewing their partnership, the response shown by the older boy was decidedly lukewarm. Despite its unsatisfactory dénouement, the period Franck spent at the Conservatoire was anything but wasted, since it enabled him to increase his theoretical and practical knowledge, as well as equipping him with valuable standards of comparison. As important as either of these things was the fact that he heard a great deal of unfamiliar music there, much of it at concerts organised by his teacher Habeneck.

The prospect which now spread itself before him was dismal and frustrating. Hurried back to Belgium in a rage of disappointment, he was quickly bullied and cajoled into taking part in a strenuous series of tours. Considered in bulk, these were no more effective in establishing him as a concert artist than had been the earlier cycle. It was accordingly not long before Nicolas-Joseph began to regret the high-handedness with which he had caused his family to quit the French capital. By 1844, he had made up his mind that there was nothing for it but to return and try again. Still thinking in terms of the concert world, he next gravitated to the role of ticket-agent, adding this to his already burdensome responsibilities as an impresario. Spending his first months in touting for patrons, he laid the foundations for another group of concerts in Paris. As he had been careful to ensure, these were somewhat better attended than the previous venture: with the result that the name of Franck eventually came to mean something to interested members of the public. Unfortunately, what it meant to the critics was a not altogether flattering reputation for persistence. Soon catching on to Nicolas-Joseph's little game, the more overworked reviewers could not resist the temptation to slip a spoke into his wheel. One of them came straight out and castigated the old man for exploiting his son's gifts, at the same time rebuking him for chattering to members of the audience while the boy was playing. On another occasion, César was unkindly compared to Vaucanson's mechanical puppet, one of the city's more popular attractions. Not all the criticism he received was proffered in this light-hearted spirit, and the pages of the *Revue Musicale* revealed numerous complaints about the standard of César's execution. This journal at first showed remarkable forbearance towards the boy, the critic Maurice Bourges having enough sense to realize the strain under which he was being made to perform. Unhappily, Bourges's successor on the paper was imbued with a more spiteful disposition. Blanchard, who was the new correspondent, lost no time in cutting the whole Franck family down to size. So vicious were his comments that even the un-snubbable Nicolas-Joseph was at last forced to take the hint.

Between the time of leaving the Conservatoire and being obliged to accept Blanchard's *coup de grâce*, César had experienced a fresh burst of creative activity. During the years 1840 and 1841, he had worked steadily on a series of Trios which marked a substantial advance over the trifling salon pieces of his boyhood. The most amazing thing about these new works was the form in which they were cast. As we have already had occasion to state, chamber music was in the doldrums in France throughout the whole of the first half of the century. Indeed, the art had not really flourished since the time of Couperin and Leclair. Franck's deliberate choice of the trio form must therefore be seen as an inspired effort at revival. Not content with having resurrected the form, it is very much to the composer's credit that he was able to add to it by introducing a startling modification. This was contained in the cyclical principle which he did so much to pioneer. In German chamber music, each movement of a composition tended to be complete in itself. Recapitulation was an accepted device, but normally operated only within the confines of a single allegro. Beethoven typically broke this rule in his Fifth Symphony and elsewhere, but his successors were more timid, exhibiting a degree of confusion as to what new amendments to the sonata form were possible. Brahms illustrates very clearly the dilemma into which these composers were plunged. Others, like Schumann and Mendelssohn, had not really tried to solve the problem, preferring to fall back on their powerful lyricism to see them through. Franck's respect for the classical forms was unusually marked, even at this early stage in his career, and it is not surprising that he wanted to take up from where Beethoven had left off. His ingenuity may be judged from the fact that, by intensively perusing the scores of his idol, he was able to conceive new possibilities in a cyclical handling of form. That is to say, he was able to grasp the advantage to the composer of permitting a recurrence of themes from movement to movement. In resorting to such a plan, it became easy to economize on material, while avoiding the temptation to make each work a string of un-related tunes.

It would be disingenuous to claim that Franck deserves all the credit for this idea. Many commentators have since pointed to Liszt as a musician whose early understanding of the cyclical principle was patently evident. There can be no doubt, for instance, that Liszt was using the device in superbly confident fashion at the time of writing his great Piano Sonata around 1852–3.[1] Not only did this work embody recurrent motifs, but ideas were contracted in such a way as to embrace within the sonata movement a rich variety of ancillary forms, including fugue, variation and free fantasia. What strikes us as most ingenious about this masterpiece is the manner in which certain small fragments of theme are subjected to continuous metamorphosis. Here is one indisputable use of the cyclical technique of composition. Wagner invented another when he created *The Ring*, with its multitude of references to character and place. By comparison, Franck's innovations were slow to develop. Even though he may still have been the first to give expression to the new philosophy, he can hardly be credited with having used it to create a masterwork. At least, nothing resembling this description flowed from his pen much before the 1870s, the Piano Quintet being perhaps the earliest of his works to qualify for the title. Yet it was something to have given birth to so fruitful a notion. Considering how out of touch with the major powers he was at the time of writing them, the three Trios constitute a remarkable feat of imagination. They are not great music, but few works in the repertory can claim to have been so prophetic in their implications. It is to them that musicologists must look if they wish to trace modern French chamber music to its source.

Looking at the characteristics they display in more detail, it is astonishing how many trademarks of the mature Franck stand out. For example, the first Trio is in the key of F sharp, his fondness for which was later mocked by Saint-Saëns. Rich keys held a perpetual fascination for the composer, and he made no attempt to resist their presence. B major became another of his addictions, as a glance at any of the big choral works will confirm. In regard to form, the first Trio possesses at least two unusual features: it has a scherzo which gives rise to a couple of contrasting sections instead of the customary one, and it employs several first movement themes in a later context. The precedents upon which Franck may have called when deciding on these departures are few. The Beethoven Quartets of the third period contain a number of analogous practices, and there is perhaps enough idiosyncrasy in a work like the Schubert E flat minor Quartet. It is probable that the composer

[1] It is generally conceded that the Weimar master derived some of his understanding of cyclical practice—especially as it applied to the piano—from Schubert's well-known 'Wanderer Fantasia'. Though scarcely a conscious contribution to the genre, this work could be described as the first cyclical piece of any substance to have been written.

knew all of these well enough to have made use of them. The combination for which he wrote—each of the Trios is for piano, violin and cello—was naturally very different from that employed in these models, setting its own problems of texture and balance. It was by no means an easy combination to write for, and if Franck

Ex. 1

César Franck: Trio in F sharp minor. Op. 1

occasionally resorted to a slick way out of his difficulties there are plenty of other eminent composers who would have done the same. Schumann found it necessary to make extensive use of doubling in his Piano Quintet—a splendid work, for all its unadventurousness. Franck also allows the piano to duplicate the cello's bass line in rather too many places. He is likewise guilty of giving the former instrument an excessive share of the attention. The hefty chords— more evident in the second Trio than the first—sometimes seem to anticipate the Brahms of op. 34; though they were doubtless suggested by the composer's own enormous stretch. He inherited his father's massive hands, and it amused him to think that every-one possessed similar advantages. It is not uncommon to come across chords of the twelfth in his keyboard music, setting the pianist a task that only one in a hundred can resolve without re-course to spreading.

The third Trio contains more in the way of clear part-writing than its two companions. It strikes the listener as a less unrelievedly harmonic work. In its original form, it had a long and impressive last movement (again, typically cyclical in character), and this so impressed Liszt that he advised abstracting it. His suggestion was that it should form an independent composition, a course his protégé was quite willing to follow. Hence, there came into being a fourth Trio, which is nothing more nor less than the last movement of the third, as it once stood. Having taken this step, Franck was obliged to write a new ending for the third of the series. Liszt's commendation of what is now the fourth Trio is not hard to under-stand, for it is a most original and inventive work to have sprung from a mere eighteen-year-old. The stepwise melodies are simple yet germinal in a style that reminds us of a composer who was later to be one of Franck's colleagues in the Société Nationale: the quiet and retiring Gabriel Fauré. Also like Fauré—and quite unlike the mature Franck—is the diatonic harmony which prevails for long periods throughout the work. Evidently, the composer's obsession with chromaticism had not yet made its appearance. An unorthodox touch in the recapitulation is the presenting of the second subject before the first; the sort of betrayal of expectation in which Beethoven was prone to indulge. Critics who continue to regard Franck as something of an academic hack may be surprised to learn that, hidden away in the bowels of this movement, lies a pair of consecutive fifths. One feels that Cherubini would have been sure to have spotted it. Typically romantic in sentiment, the Trios owe as much to Weber and Lesueur as they do to the Viennese masters, and part of their formal irregularity must be put down to the passionate rebelliousness which was so much a product of the age. In spite of his shyness, Franck had his own reasons for wishing to rebel, reasons which were all the more pressing for having been refused a proper outlet.

To give the family its due, all were eager to obtain maximum publicity for César's latest compositions. Nicolas-Joseph made every effort to get them read by the most advanced musicians of the day. Not only did he seek out Liszt's advice, but he hit upon the promising idea of issuing a de-luxe edition of the works, to be paid for by public subscription. Remembering the interest once shown by King Leopold, he considered that to obtain the royal imprimatur would be an excellent way in which to launch the scheme. After repeated imprecations, the King eventually gave his consent to the plan, though without displaying any sign of enthusiasm. No subsidies were offered—much to Nicolas-Joseph's disgust—and it was only by the most painful negotiations that a promise to perform the works under royal patronage was extorted. It is worth mentioning, however, that Franck was awarded a gold medal by order of the Belgian crown in November 1843. Whether or not this was intended to soften the blow is not clear. At all events, it did little to mollify Nicolas-Joseph's ruffled disposition. The Royal Family expressed only the most perfunctory interest in the arts at this time, and it was not until the First World War (during which Fauré dedicated his Second Violin Sonata to Queen Elizabeth) that a genuine sense of enthusiasm sprang up. It is symptomatic of the situation confronting the Franck family that nothing was done to honour the promise of a royal performance of the Trios. Despite this, the subscription edition was a great success. Asking for an advance price of twelve francs—as opposed to the expected retail price of forty-five—Nicolas-Joseph was able to secure a long list of distinguished names. Meyerbeer's headed the company, with Liszt as runner-up. Both Chopin and Halévy were also glad to contribute, and in all more than a dozen famous composers suffered to see themselves appended. The total number of subscribers, according to the publisher Schlesinger, was one hundred and seventy. Oddly enough, few Frenchmen ever took much interest in the works. In Germany, where they were issued in an ordinary edition by the firm of Schuberth, they aroused far more curiosity. It was a pity, as far as Franck's future was concerned, that Mendelssohn died just when he was on the point of sanctioning a performance of them. It was left to Liszt—always a dependable champion of the under-dog—to play them at Weimar in 1853, more than ten years after they had been written.[1] It seems unlikely that they will win fresh converts today. Their melancholy expressiveness—which Bourges compared to the feeling evoked by Ann Radcliffe's 'Gothic' novels —is too far removed from modern sensibilities.

Considering how inglorious had been his attempts to achieve wider fame, it hardly surprises us to learn that Franck's health showed signs of breaking down in the early part of 1844. Phlegmatic he may have been, but no one could have remained unaffected by the jeers and neglect with which he had to contend. Fickle comment was one thing; a steady and unremitting campaign of denigration quite another. ('And now for the three Francks,' scoffed one supercilious critic, 'Father, Son and Holy ———.') Equally enervating was the persistent round of teaching, much of it peripatetic, that he was forced to endure. Some creative artists do not hesitate to despise the task of instructing others less gifted than themselves. Franck was not one of these, and he willingly accepted a volume of work that only the most saintly would have been prepared to justify. Even he had his limits, however, and the tight-lipped Nicolas-Joseph's determination to fill every minute of his time-table meant that there was bound to come a time when he would begin to crack. While at the Conservatoire, he had managed to keep his part-time teaching within reasonable bounds, though he had always been compelled to open his studio in the Rue Montholon on Sunday afternoons. Now that he was condemned to make his living by teaching, his commitments increased to include visits to the city's boarding schools and a variety of religious institutions. For instance, he was a regular caller at the College Rollin, where the daughters of Auteuil were discreetly gathered. It was there that he met Offenbach, whose operettas he was to relish with a kind of secret joy. The Jesuit school of the Immaculate Conception in the Rue Vaugirard was another stopping place, housing at a somewhat later date his favourite Henri Duparc. At all these institutions, the fees which he earned were pitifully small. It is an indication of the

[1] Peter Cornelius was another admirer of the works, alongside Von Bülow. Ludwig Hermann is also known to have revived them at Dresden in 1861.

grimness of his existence that even these were instantly appropriated by his father.[1]

Perhaps we should see it as a proof of the robustness of Franck's constitution that he was visited by something less than a full scale nervous breakdown. Struggling to carry on as best he could, he delayed for a few more years the inevitable showdown which was threatening relations between him and his parent. The main fact to emerge from his trials was that the idea, to which Nicolas-Joseph had so tenaciously clung, of pursuing a family career was proving untenable. The last appearance of the brothers at a joint recital was on 1 June 1846, when a concert of pupils was organized. After this, each went his separate way, César never again appearing as a soloist, except in his capacity as organist or when he was required to launch a new composition. Joseph—whose poor showing may have done something to undermine the partnership—experienced none of his older brother's revulsion towards the virtuoso's existence, and we find him practising the same hopeful profession as late as 1860, still endeavouring to catch the eye of the unastonished Leopold. By that time, he had added the title of composer to his accomplishments, having prostratedly offered his patron a Requiem, a Piano Concerto and a number of minor works. Rather more imposing in his appearance than César, Joseph looked a good deal more distinguished than he was. With his neat pince-nez and well-kept whiskers, he could have passed for a classical scholar or the head of a respected law firm. As it turned out, he ended his flimsy career in the bankruptcy court, having inherited a good measure of his father's financial ineptness.

Meanwhile, César's indisposition had occurred at a point when he was half-way through a new composition, the most ambitious he had so far attempted. It is impossible to say whether anxieties over the writing of this work helped to accelerate his troubles, but it seems likely, in view of the composer's sudden switch from chamber music to oratorio, that he was in a perplexed state concerning the medium in which it would best pay to invest his talents. Could it have been Gounod, whom he met while that pious young man was battling with his vocation at the Mission Etrangères, who inspired him with the idea of an oratorio on the biblical subject of Ruth? Or did he, perhaps, react to Poussin's delicate painting of the meeting with Boaz? At all events, this was the theme that was turning over in his mind during the year 1843, while the abortive Belgian tours were dragging to an end. The public mood at that

[1] As evidence of César's lack of experience in handling money, it is worth relating that, when he was offered a bonus of sixty francs for appearing in a solo recital at Orléans some years later, he was too overcome to accept the fee.

time seemed about to favour religious subjects again, especially if they were dressed up in some exotic, oriental attire. The enthusiasm shown for Félicien David's curious symphonic ode, *Le Désert*, might well have had the effect of concentrating Franck's mind upon the idea which he had chosen. Frenchmen had long displayed an imaginative curiosity about the East, evident from the popularity of Montesquieu's *Lettres Persanes* and from the glut of 'chinoiserie' to be seen at Versailles. But the present vogue did not seem to be based so much on people's anthropological instincts as on their need for an idyllic fantasy by which to sustain their fading theological hopes. No doubt the drama inherent in the biblical stories was also being recognized by astute promoters, much as it was gratefully seized upon by their successors in the world of the cinema. The composer of *Le Désert*, though he could hardly have been accused of capitalizing on the trend, was quick to satisfy the public demand then springing up. There is no doubt that he possessed a remarkably fluent grasp of the idiom. Gustave Bertrand, writing in *Le Menestrel*, summarized his contribution by saying:

> David is a mirror that reflects the Orient admirably. He went there. What he saw impressed him strongly, and he renders it very well. What he does is ordinarily feeble. But give him a text about the Orient in which the words palm tree, minaret, camel, etc., appear, and he does some very nice things.

The first sentence of this review forms a good indication of the lack of sophistication which marked Parisian conceptions of the East. David, for all his charm, was nothing more than an illustrator, a Frenchified Rimsky-Korsakov without the Russian's orchestral showiness. It was to be a long time before the nation's composers began to write music having a genuine basis in Eastern scales and rhythms, music such as Roussel's *Padmâvatî* and de Bréville's *Stamboul*. Even Ravel, who was something of a connoisseur of Eastern culture, not infrequently relapsed into picture-postcard impressions; though since his aim was to create a pastiche he is less open to criticism than those who imagined that they were being authentic. Saint-Saëns, an inveterate globe-trotter throughout his eighty-six years, was so infatuated with the Orient that Debussy advised him to give up music and become an explorer. His approach to the music of other cultures typified that of the average educated Frenchman. It was an approach characterized by the search for local colour, and by a desire to embellish its findings with the romantic touches so indispensable to Western audiences. The results of his researches were embodied in nicely-turned diversions like the *Suite Algérienne*, which at best deserves to head a programme of popular seaside music. The movement had its parallel in literature through the sensuous evocations of Leconte de Lisle and Pierre Loti.[1]

David refrained from following up his success until 1862, when he returned to the new vein with his lesser-known *Lalla Roukh*. By that time, several rivals had appeared on the scene, with Bizet's *Pêcheurs de Perles* and Meyerbeer's *L'Africaine* looming on the horizon. Franck's *Ruth*, which was completed in September 1845, can accordingly be viewed as one of the earlier excursions into the genre. That it failed to win the same acclaim as David's work may be attributed partly to inexperience, but equally strongly, one suspects, to an absence of deliberate sensationalism in the music. His delay over finishing the work, while it can be accounted for in terms of the tense phase through which the composer was then passing, may just as easily have been due to other factors. The libretto, for example, had been very difficult to come by. Franck had not considered it possible to write his music directly from the Bible translations, so that he had been compelled to seek out a professional librettist who could arrange the words in a suitable sequence. This task was eventually accomplished by a second-rate poetaster by the name of Alexandre Guillemin, whose presentation of the story in fifteen parts must be held responsible for some of the work's shortcomings. Franck set his verses for chorus, soloists and full orchestra; making the whole thing a decidedly strenuous venture. As had been the case with his previous works, it was his father who took over the business of production. Ingenious as ever, Nicolas-Joseph considered it would be best to begin by giving a private performance to which various distinguished guests could be specially invited. Thus the première turned out to be a diversion prepared for certain select 'illuminati' who could be relied upon to spread the word concerning the young composer's gifts. Critics whose sharp tongues might have led them to take a less charitable view were carefully excluded. Among the audience which assembled was the aged Spontini, at seventy reckoned to be the grand old man of French music. In his train came Meyerbeer, Adolphe Adam, Halévy, Moscheles, Heller, Alkan and the faithful Liszt. What could these privileged beings do but murmur their fondest blessings?

When it came to an assessment, Liszt was the most fulsome in his praise, realizing that Franck would have much to overcome without being weighed down by the stigma of bad notices. His estimate of César's talent is contained in the following testimonial,

[1] The reader wishing to pursue the literary ramifications of French Orientalism is referred to James Baird's fascinating study *Ishmael* (Johns Hopkins Press, Baltimore, 1956.) This book brilliantly traces the entire movement from Loti to Verhaeren.

predictably wheedled out of him by Nicolas-Joseph with the object
of hastening a second performance:

> ... car parmi les jeunes gens qui suent sang et eau pour
> arriver a coucher quelques idées sur un méchant papier de
> musique, je n'en sache pas trois en France qui le vaillent.[1]*

This was indeed flattering, and it was hardly to be expected that
the other judges would be as kind. It is surprising to find that
Meyerbeer and Spontini, whose careers could be said to have
paraded the greatest compromise, were the most favourably inclined. Halévy may have been held back by a feeling that Franck's
music somewhat resembled his own; a comparison many writers
were later to make. The remainder blew neither hot nor cold. It
would have been interesting to have had Berlioz's opinion, but he
was the one unquestionable genius whose presence had not been
thought necessary. As the reactions were, by and large, on the positive side, Nicolas-Joseph rapidly addressed himself to the task of
securing a public première in some more auspicious locale. In the
end, the hall of the Conservatoire was chosen, and the date fixed
for 4 January 1846.

Both the composer and his family were deeply disappointed at
the response to this event. Critics found little to admire in the music,
the cruel Blanchard discovering excuses for a score of uncompli-
mentary epithets. Unfairly coupling Franck's name with that of
Rossini, it was not difficult for him to draw attention to certain
melodic deficiencies. By pitting *Ruth* against Méhul's *Joseph* in
terms of dignity and nobility, he was setting the work other standards which it could not have hoped to attain: for it was in their
mastery of these venerable emotions that the composers of the
First Empire had been prepared to rest all their claims. It would
have been far more to the point to have given readers some indication of the merits of Franck's score. Looked at through modern
eyes, it does seem as if the music of *Ruth* lacks colour and move-

---

[1] The opinion was expressed in a letter Liszt was asked to write to
the Comte de Montalivet, Ministre et Intendant de la Liste Civile. As
it happened, it had no effect as far as influencing the authorities went,
and *Ruth* never secured the second performance Nicolas-Joseph so
eagerly desired. At first, Franck's father went about assuring people that
a repeat would be given at the Italian Theatre. Since the Duke of
Montpensier had been present at the première, it was even rumoured
that further performances would take place at the court of Louis-
Phillipe!

* Among all the youngsters who expend blood and sweat to get their
ideas down on our recalcitrant manuscript paper, there are not three in
France who are his equal.

ment. But then the subject itself was scarcely dramatic, and was such as to preclude too much emphasis on these qualities. The work's instrumentation, on the contrary, is quite lively, and the duets between Ruth and Boaz tender enough to satisfy the most sensitive heart. More immediately appealing, perhaps, is the dis-

Ex. 2
César Franck: Ruth   Pt. III.   Duet for Ruth and Boaz.

creet 'Chant du Crépuscule', which was the subject of an encore during the 1871 performance. One of the most successful vocal sections of the work was the 'Choeur des Moissonneurs', an episode frequently abstracted for inclusion in miscellaneous programmes later in the century. By comparison, the 'Marche des Moabites' will be thought too banal to please present-day listeners, though it was greatly admired in its time. Léon Vallas has likened this number to the 'Marche des Pèlerins' from Berlioz's *Harold en Italie*. If this is justified, it is one of the few such similarities to be suggested by the score. A better indication of the general texture can be obtained from a glance at the milder choruses of Schubert. There is a common liking for elementary harmonies (hardly very prophetic of the mature Franck!), and a shared determination to avoid counterpoint. Moreover, these two composers display a similar artlessness which Schubert, at any rate, could afford not to look beyond. The weaknesses of *Ruth* have been clearly laid out by Jean Gallois in his recent and penetrating study of the composer:

> D'une façon générale cependant, la partition trahit une timidité, un manque d'aisance réels. Le plan est gauche, hésitant; l'harmonie souvant banale, les choeurs sans envolée —sauf le fameux Choeur des Moissonneurs—et l'absence de vision intérieure puissante ne contribuent naturellement pas à sauver une oeuvre donnant parfois dans les pires recettes que l'opéra d'alors exploitait sans vergogne.*

> * In terms of workmanship, the score exhibits timidity, a lack of real ease. The plan is awkward, hesitant; the harmony trite, the choral numbers without volition—except for the famous *Choeur des Moissonneurs*—and the want of mental vision naturally fails to save the work from occasionally relying on operatic formulae at that time shamelessly exploited.

The criticism he faced over this, his first large-scale composition, hurt Franck more deeply than any other disappointment of his life. The fact that the work appeared to sink without trace was something he could scarcely bring himself to understand. As things worked out, *Ruth* did secure a belated revival in 1871, when it was heard at the Cirque des Champs Elysées. D'Indy took that occasion to mount a full onslaught on the critics, including several who had assumed it to be a new composition, not having realized they had helped to shatter its chances many years previously. Perhaps it was not all unconscious hypocrisy on their part, however, since unknown to his pupil the composer had indeed made one or two alterations; nothing extensive, but enough to have removed the initial blemishes. At the same time, he transcribed the work for voice and piano, the form in which he allowed it to be published by Hartmann later in the season. Unfortunately, the original setback over *Ruth* did immense harm to Franck's ego, causing him to relapse into a stunned silence for more time than was wise. Equally deadened by the outcome, Nicolas-Joseph at last began to relax the pressure he had been bringing to bear on his son—at least from the creative angle. He had first of all tried to establish César as a lord of the salons using Liszt as the inevitable model. Then he turned his attention to producing a kind of all-round musical meteorite, after the fashion of Mozart or Beethoven.[1] Now both these policies had been shown to be futile. There seemed nothing left but to return to the treadmill of teaching, to coerce his prodigy into becoming a 'machine à leçons'. This was actually what came to pass, the old man inflicting his new sentence with all the ferocity of disappointment. Though he was too stupid to see it, it was this final twist of the screw that incited his son to rebel, causing him to cut free from that hated domination under which he had struggled since the days of his childhood.

[1] Some readers may be inclined to see a parallel between Nicolas-Joseph and Leopold Mozart. They were each very single-minded men who had no doubts as to the responsibility they had to discharge, but the difference is that Mozart's father was a first-rate musician who at least knew a great deal about the ways of the profession.

III

Marriage—revolutionary style

By one of those curious coincidences in which public and personal destinies seem to be marching hand in hand, the year 1848 signalled the emancipation of both César Franck and his adopted country. Duparc was later to attach much significance to the fact that he had been born in this year of revolutions, but it is surely of greater interest to observe that Franck actually came of age during it. It was not the year in which he attained the age of twenty-one, but it was that in which he married, assumed control of a household, witnessed the birth of his son Georges, whom he incidentally named 'barricades' on account of it, and generally settled down to a new life. In French law it was forbidden for a young man to marry without parental consent until he was twenty-five, so that earlier attempts to assert his independence would probably have been abortive. Bearing this in mind, it becomes even more fitting to suggest that the composer sprang to maturity at precisely that moment when, as one wit phrased it, 'France coughed and Europe sneezed'.

No one could have disputed the French nation's economic troubles under the indifferent administration of Louis-Phillipe. The 'bourgeois king', as he has since become known, was placid and mildly reformist by nature; but the restoration of royal privileges had soon resulted in him being faced with a resurgence of Bonapartism and anti-clericalism. Outbreaks of disobedience were not uncommon even in the earliest years of his reign, and the bad harvest in 1846 had reduced the population to a condition bordering on viciousness. Philosophers did not scruple to exploit old grievances, at the same time mesmerizing the people with blueprints of a promised utopia. Louis Blanc, whose statue gazes down so benevolently from the shade of the Luxembourg Gardens, hurried to make wider the circulation which attached to his *Mémoire sur l'Organiza-*

tion du Travail; while Proudhon, whose treatise had contained the infamous definition of property as theft, poured still more fiery rebukes on the head of the government. If these documents provided the workers with their charter, an altogether gentler summons to reform appeared in the form of Alexis de Tocqueville's *Democracy in America*, a work that had the effect of making many a Frenchman feel envious. Whether the cry was for a widening of the suffrage or a total dismantling of the régime, the impact on public decorum was similarly disturbing. As Louis's most recent biographer has put it:

> ... to an empty stomach in a Paris hovel either Proudhon's brand of misanthropic anarchism or the rosy visions of the utopians were equally attractive in the winter of 1846–7.[1]

Since the government comprised so high a proportion of farmers, it was a source of bafflement to the people that food supplies had been permitted to get into such a pass. To blame things on the professional classes was no better, since that too argued for a greater degree of radicalism.

Abroad, the record of the bourgeois monarchy stood in the sharpest possible contrast to that of Napoleon. Patriotic Frenchmen were accordingly prone to languish in a mood of cynicism or self-pity. One by one all of the major colonies had begun to disappear, making the country something of a laughing-stock in the club-rooms and political chambers of other nations. Holding onto Algeria as his single foreign possession ('Our expensive opera-box' was how one humourist was impelled to classify it), it was all the king could do to escape humiliation. As it was, the Foreign Office ran rings around his timid manoeuvres, and when he decided on an outright challenge to Britain over the question of the Spanish marriages, he was inconsiderately denounced at home for failing to keep the peace. Relying too heavily on the conservative Guizot—an historian turned Prime Minister—Louis could not understand that attempts were being made to light a bonfire under him. Always the political laboratory of Europe, France was anticipating the wish of the Continent as a whole in feeling that it was time to get rid of tyrants and incompetents, whether it was their habit to wear a crown or not. The age of the common man was being ushered in,

---

[1] The description is contained in T. E. B. Howarth's book *Citizen-King: the Life of Louis-Phillipe, King of the French* (Eyre & Spottiswoode, 1961). Interested readers may also refer to Stendhal's unfinished novel *Lucien Leuwen* for a fascinating satirical account of the events which led up to the King's reign. It was during his reign that one Minister launched the slogan ' "Enrichissez-vous!"—a call to villainy as unashamed as anything to have emerged from our "affluent society" '.

and the king's umbrella was hardly enough of a symbol by which to celebrate it. What also caused Louis to miscalculate was his ignorance of the extent to which his opponents had managed to embroider the legend of the little corporal. Having retrieved Napoleon's body from St Helena, the radicals clamoured to have it interred in a magnificent tomb at the Invalides. Even old soldiers could be heard declaiming Bonaparte's greatness in badly-rhyming quatrains throughout the streets of the capital. It was no wonder that poor Louis was compelled to hand over the legislature (and with it his crown) to that garrulous adventurer whose appeal rested so patently with his possession of the magic name.

While the insurgents plotted the downfall of the July monarchy, young César Franck was busy resisting the pestiferous influence of his father, whom he had at last been bold enough to confront. As usually happens in such cases, there were precipitating circumstances leading him to make his move. Enraged by his son's carelessness, Nicolas-Joseph one day taxed the young man with having pointlessly dedicated the song 'L'Ange et L'Enfant' to a certain Mlle Desmousseaux, one of the more insignificant of his pupils. When César attempted to remonstrate, his angry father tore the manuscript to shreds before his eyes. The effect of this action could hardly have been foreseen, for no one was yet aware that the lady in question had made the strongest of all impressions on the boy. Seething with a fury of which few would have thought him capable, young Franck declared his intention of marrying the girl as soon as it became practicable, leaving his family to fend for itself. The shock of this announcement left Nicolas-Joseph reeling, for the prospect of earning his own living was something this most parasitic of parents had rarely stopped to consider. Naturally he did everything in his power to forbid the marriage. First of all he threatened César in high-flown hysterical language, hoping that a show of authority would frighten the young man. When this failed, he changed to a whining approach, arguing that it was Franck's mother who would come off worst in the plan. Catherine Franck is a figure we have had no occasion to mention up to this point, and for good reason. Though six years older than her husband, she possessed no will of her own and meekly accepted the harsh conditions which reigned in her household. In this row over César's independence, she seems to have remained riveted to her role of non-participant. Perhaps it was on this account that César felt so few scruples about going through with what he had proposed. To use as a final argument, Nicolas-Joseph held up the case of Choiseul-Praslin, the notorious poisoner, whose murder of his wife had lately provided France with one of its juiciest scandals. Though he had escaped the guillotine by taking arsenic, this unsavoury

individual was still the subject of many a pointed homily in provincial homes, so that Franck senior's decision to brandish his name
was quite in keeping with the national mores. Whether he imagined his son would ever stoop to the same sort of deed is impossible
to say. If so, he might easily have saved his breath, for César was far
too gentle a soul ever to find himself at the mercy of his passions.
He was not, however, without the courage of his convictions, and
one day when the family was out walking he quietly packed his bags
and quit, leaving a note to say that he would pay off the debt of
eleven thousand francs his father was owing.

The young lady around whom this dispute raged was not
quite the 'femme fatale' the reader may have been led to expect.
She bore the name Desmousseaux only because it had been chosen
by her parents, both actors at the Comédie-Française, to use pro-
fessionally. Her birth certificate showed that she had been christened Félicité Saillot, and that her family had been in the theatre
for generations. Indeed, her grandfather (Mme Desmousseaux's
father) had been none other than the colourful tragedian, Baptiste,
several of whose roles were passed on to his son-in-law. Both
parents continued to act throughout the period when Franck was
courting their daughter, making the house a lively and excitable
one to visit. It must have struck César as a delightful port of call
after the glum abode he had been accustomed to. Taking an instant
fancy to the young music teacher, Mme Desmousseaux was probably responsible for throwing him into her daughter's arms; or
at any rate for giving his suit every encouragement. She regarded
him as an honest and upright person, and was even willing to
supplement his narrow education with her extensive knowledge of
the lighter arts. Not that she was a very erudite woman, but she had
a better grasp on reality than her unworldly son-in-law. She was
also no philistine when it came to the serious theatre. It was she,
for example, who persuaded César to attend the plays of Racine
and Corneille, much admired in Paris then as now, and it only
remains to admit that he could not sit through them without dozing
off. He much preferred the transitory productions at the Opéra-
Comique, having the same penchant as Elgar for their 'tinkling
little tunes'. Considering what a gloomy environment he had
sprung from, who can blame César for responding so readily to
the call of gaiety? If his contact with the Desmousseaux family did
nothing more for him, at least it enabled him to give up 'high seriousness' for a while and bask in the earthier humours of the people.

The house in the Rue Blanche where the Desmousseaux couple
lived, and where César had long been in the habit of calling,
became the young man's obvious place of refuge after his un-
ceremonious flight from home. Realizing that the engaged pair

would be unable to marry for some little time, Mme Desmousseaux was broadminded enough to offer them shelter under her roof. Despite being a 'theatrical'—almost a synonym for immoralist to certain people—she showed the most rigid concern for the moral welfare of her lodgers, always taking up her knitting basket at a point not too distant from them. Probably she had foreseen the part she would be expected to play in the domestic drama from the very beginning. Even before César had made known his intentions, she had conspired with him to hoodwink Nicolas-Joseph by letting him use her house to engage in composition. Her own training, musical as well as dramatic, had led her to recognize talent when she saw it, and she was no doubt won over by those other qualities of probity and dependability which Franck revealed, and which are so dear to the hearts of marriage-brokers everywhere. As for Félicité, she stood in no need of persuasion, her cousin Claire's diaries recounting, with a touch of feminine envy, how much she doted on her conscientious young instructor. Franck was undoubtedly a handsome figure of a man, not tall it is true, but offering a romantically pale complexion and candid, unflinching eyes. With his high collar and long side-burns, he must have corresponded to many a young girl's dream. That he could undertake to appear absent-minded, even at this early stage, is suggested by a daguerreotype in which he is revealed staring intricately into the distance, his waistcoat unbuttoned and askew. But it would be many years before he would develop those comical sartorial eccentricities that served to distinguish him from the more correct members of his congregation. For the present he adopted the manners of a dapper young blade, out to impress the lady of his choice and eager to benefit from the advantages of freedom.

The couple got married on 22 February 1848, at the church of Notre-Dame-de-Lorette; where, as it happened, the bridegroom was to obtain his first appointment as organist. During the previous December César had written to his father notifying him of the impending wedding. The presence of both families at the altar suggests that some measure of reconciliation had been reached. Félicité was not exactly a stranger to the rest of the Franck family, however, since she had appeared as a performer at one of the family's concerts; the very occasion, in fact, on which the two brothers had made their final showing. Joseph does not seem to have been present at the ceremony for all that. On the bride's side a full complement of actors and actresses from the Comédie-Française arrived to make up a party, and it seems likely that the event did not pass off without some jollification. Though he could not have been expected to know it, February was just about the worst month he could have chosen in order to celebrate his nuptials, for this was the month when the revolution first got under way. As the young musician made his way to the church, Paris erupted into a terrifying political turmoil, spreading pandemonium in the streets and driving everyone not involved in the fighting under cover. At nine o'clock, a procession of student demonstrators—alternately chanting the Marseillaise and the Girondin's chorus—tramped from the Panthéon to the Madeleine, causing government troops to throw a hasty cordon around the Chamber of Deputies. Shouts of 'A bas Guizot!' rang out, weapons were snatched from the shops of local gunsmiths, and a row of amateurish barricades was flung across the principal thoroughfares. At Notre-Dame-de-Lorette, a grill from the church was used to mount one of these obstacles, and the bridal pair, having been promised safe conduct, were helped over it and speeded on their way. Franck's introduction to matrimony could therefore be said to have taken place amid the stormiest of surroundings, in circumstances which, as Winton Dean has amusingly pointed out, would have been worthy of Berlioz.

In later years, Franck used to recall the hazards of his wedding day with wry humour. At the time, however, his feelings could well have been more complex. Like most Belgians, he had always been a moderate reformer, that country's struggle for independence having imbued most of its citizens with a sympathy for the radical cause. The establishment of the Second Republic must consequently have seemed a satisfactory outcome to the events which had almost succeeded in wrecking the composer's marriage. That this was indeed the case is suggested by a collection of patriotic pieces which Franck wrote during the interregnum. One of these —a setting of the poem 'Les Trois Exiles' by Bernard Delfosse— bore a colourful frontispiece containing pictures of the nation's military heroes. The three choleric gentlemen who gave the work its title were Napoleon I, the Duke of Reischtadt and the ubiquitous Louis. Some working men's songs are also listed among Franck's projects at this time, though no trace of them has been found. A hymn of glory, on the other hand, does exist and must be taken to comprise the composer's most considered tribute to the régime. He did not write any further *encomia* for the good reason that heavy bloodshed dampened his enthusiasm. Louis's seizure of the throne, following the famous 'coup d'état', was an adroit piece of opportunism, very much in the Bonaparte tradition, and Franck's reaction to it reminds us of that other and more publicized occasion when Beethoven ripped off the title-page of his 'Eroica' Symphony. It is not clear what Franck's politics were during his middle and later years, but it might be accurate to say that they hovered uneasily between desultoriness and cynicism. The June days had cured him of any belief in the extremes of action, while Louis's imperial

strutting was enough to have shattered his respect for the monarchical principle.[1] The essence of the matter is that he simply did
not aspire to be a political animal. His inward-turning imagination
made it inevitable that he would come to seek his convictions in the
shadow of the church rather than in the bright sunlight of the forum.

In this connection it is interesting to speculate on whether the
composer's friendship with Gounod, the seeds of which were sown
at this time, was inspired by their common uncertainties over
politics and religion. Having begun his training for holy orders in
1847, Gounod must have found himself in an embarrassing situation at the outbreak of the revolution, since the attack on the
priesthood was quite as vehement as anything directed against the
government. To have been seen wearing priest's robes during the
February days was to have courted grave personal risk. The
daughter of the famous singing teacher, Francis Delsarte, tells in
her letters of how her father was once compelled to intervene to
save an unfortunate Jesuit who was about to be tossed into the
Seine by an angry mob. Never insensitive to the perils that might
befall him, Gounod must surely have allowed this consideration to
weigh heavily with him in reaching his decision to renounce the
cloth. We know that he and Franck talked over the unhappy events
of that year, and it could well have been that some of each man's
philosophy rubbed off on the other, Franck acquiring a smattering
of theology and Gounod a whiff of radical politics. It is quite
certain that Gounod behaved generously in permitting César to
make free with his extensive library of books on religion. Indeed it
was at this juncture that the Belgian composer is said to have made
his deathless remark to the effect that he found Kant's *Critique*
'très amusant'—a word that does not, of course, carry quite the
light-hearted connotation of its English equivalent. Despite this
rare opportunity, and despite his long grounding in the Catholic
faith, Franck never really became a great reader. Books always
seemed a trifle boring to him, and they could not, by their nature,
exude the mystical atmosphere he so regularly sought to breathe.

Perhaps because of his lack of interest in theological matters,
critics have been led to doubt the sincerity of Franck's religious
beliefs. Was he at all times a devoted Catholic, or did he merely
respond to the musical side of the church? This is an awkward
question to have to answer. It would be absurd to propose that,
like Gabriel Fauré, he was really an unconscious agnostic. On the

[1] This makes it difficult to say whether Franck would have been
flattered or annoyed at the royal patronage accorded to his *Variations
Symphoniques* when it was mounted as a ballet at Covent Garden in the
late 1940s. The audience on that Gala Night incidentally included both
the King of England and the President of the French Republic.

contrary, all the evidence suggests that he sensed the presence of God beside him night and day. Pupils and friends—including the priest who administered the last sacrament—tend to agree on this point. Curious stories have nevertheless circulated about the composer's habits of worship, some acquaintances having claimed that he was prone to mutter his 'Ich heile dich' both in and out of service. Frequently one hears the accusation that Franck's religion was nothing more than the sublimation of powerful artistic and even erotic impulses. The evidence used to support such charges usually comes from the works, particularly *Psyché* and *Les Béatitudes*. These compositions are certainly unlike those of any other religious composer. They incline to the occult and are ripe with romantic feeling. D'Indy went to elaborate lengths to refute the notion that *Psyché* contains anything improper, spoiling his case a little by exaggerating the work's piety. To state, as he does, that it recalls 'the frescoes in the Arena of Padua or the Fioretti of St Francis of Assisi' seems to be stretching things too far, and incidentally falsifying the composer's purposes. For Franck can hardly be thought to have planned this as a liturgical composition: it was cast in the mould of a symphonic poem. As for the genuinely religious works—such as the Mass for Three Voices—one still cannot say that they are spurious. It must be remembered that in those times poetical concepts were allowed to exercise a far greater sway over religious sentiments than would be thought right today. After all, Liszt was the recipient of minor orders, and his church music made no effort to play down the romantic afflatus. Neither did that of Gounod, to witness the 'sugary' *Messe Solennelle de Ste Cécile* with its hints of theatrical pathos. We must surely defer to Martin Cooper when he writes of 'the extraordinary salon quality of even the best French music at this time'.

Franck's spiritual works—which we will not anticipate by discussing just yet—are rendered controversial by virtue of the excesses of the composer's temperament. Few would deny the weight of emotion which underlies them, and which carries them into a dimension beyond Gounod's sweetness and Liszt's unblushing sensuality. It relates somehow to the mystical conscience, and to that extent might be considered rather un-French. As Charles Bordes, an excellent witness in such matters, has pointed out: 'Franck was indeed a Christian artist, but more Evangelical than really Catholic'. And again, when discussing the composer's doctrinal position: 'The Christ who sang in him was rather the Jesus of the first centuries of the Christian Church than the Christ of Catholic doctrine'. All this confirms Franck's allegiance to the spirit of religion—especially if this is equated with the spirit of the Sermon on the Mount—but does little to allay the suspicions of those who detect in the composer, not a devout subscriber to church tenets, but a heretic and a visionary; a man who, paradoxically, had more in common with the milder English revivalists than with the dialectically-minded theologians of his own period. Works like *Psyché* and *les Béatitudes* have their true counterparts in the Prophetic Books of Blake, and in the sermons of some of the eighteenth-century divines. They lack the ritual element common to traditional Catholic music, and in any case appeal much more to Protestants. Certainly Franck's employers frequently thought them bizarre.

The strengthening of the composer's religious ties actually came about quite slowly and unspectacularly. As his work took him away from the salon and into the heart of the church, so his thoughts and feelings assumed a more pious character. The revolution had deprived him of a good number of pupils who, though no loss except in the purely financial sense, had caused him to move about the city a good deal, meeting new faces and discoursing on the day's events. Now that the appointment at Notre-Dame-de-Lorette became the mainstay of his existence, his experience grew more cloistered and there was far more time for meditation. This might have been an excellent time at which to settle down to a prolonged spell of composition. But that is precisely what did not happen. We shall probably never know why Franck virtually abandoned all idea of writing music for the greater part of the decade 1848–58. That he suffered acutely from discouragement is an obvious enough fact. Yet the creative urge, if strongly rooted, generally persists with semi-automatic vigour. It is more likely that Franck was still very much in the dark as to what his vocation really was. The ease with which he slid into the life of a hack music teacher gives the lie to any suggestion that he was constantly fired by the desire to get notes down on paper. Composers sometimes seem to be men of Promethean will, restlessly searching after self-expression in the way Beethoven did. At other times, they give the impression of being unceasing craftsmen, fated not to look up from the cluttered workbench that has become their life. Haydn was clearly one of these. Oddly enough, Franck conformed to neither species, being that *rara avis* the man of talent who does not know quite what is to become of himself, and who only dimly suspects that he might be different from other men. The line separating a Shakespeare from a village schoolmaster is often thinner than most of us care to admit. Franck's unconscious creative abstinence, and habit of sincere self-deprecation, show how easy it would have been for him never to have proceeded with his ambition.

For the next ten years, until he was selected for the better post at Sainte-Clotilde, Franck was content to remain an obscure vassal of the church. To the congregation trudging to Mass each day, their precentor was only 'poor old Franck'—an impoverished lay-figure in stove pipe hat and trousers that always seemed a little too short for him. He appeared to do nothing other than attend to the functions of his office, unless it was to irritate the clergy by indulging in one or two tiresomely prolonged anthems. When he forgot himself and failed to stop at the end of the offertory, church officials merely smiled generously and shook their heads. They preferred a certain amount of eccentricity to incompetence, and as long as their organist's fancies did not interrupt the service all was considered to have passed off fairly smoothly. Now and again an incumbent with livelier ideas would appear on the scene. The sympathetic de Rollot, at Franck's first church, was just such a man, taking an unexpectedly strenuous interest in the musical provisions. It was due to his energy that the Masses and motets of the great composers—Haydn, Mozart and Cherubini among them—were occasionally sung. It should be recalled that several members of the congregation at Notre-Dame-de-Lorette were professional singers employed at the Opéra. Their voices served to enrich the flow of sound to which César and his colleagues gave their close attention. After a few not unhappy years at this church, a more attractive appointment turned up. This came about through the intervention of the friendly Abbé Dancel, whose goodwill Franck had succeeded in gaining. This enlightened cleric—who had perhaps officiated at the composer's wedding—had been named curé of the church of Saint-Jean-François du Marais towards the end of 1851. Two years afterwards he asked to have Franck transferred to his parish as organist. The move could not have come at a better time, and the family quickly adapted itself to a new set of surroundings.

One of the benefits to emerge from the transfer was a change of instrument. ('Mon nouvel orgue?' Franck is said to have replied, when questioned about it, 'C'est un orchestre!') The builder of his Marais organ proved to have been none other than Aristide Cavaillé-Coll, inventor of the clarinet stop and modern manual coupling device, and one of the premier men in his field. It was Cavaillé-Coll's famous instrument at St Sulpice that later influenced our own Henry Willis in the construction of the Albert Hall organ. In the course of the years, Franck was to find himself accompanying this inventive genius on his tours of inspection throughout France.[1] Unhappily, Cavaillé-Coll died while still a

[1] In view of the damage done to the old Clicquot organs during the revolution, the Emperor appointed Cavaillé-Coll to inspect them and where necessary rebuild. Politically-speaking, this was an attempt to win back the favours of the Church.

young man, before giving full expression to his ideas. Even so, the innovations he fathered were sufficient to bring about a revolution in styles of playing and composing. As luck would have it, Franck's own training had been grounded in the older instruments, so that he was slow to adapt himself to these innovations. His pupils, however, enjoyed the full benefit of them. One of the more startling developments at about this time was the appearance of a new school of 'symphonic' organists, many of them of German origin. The years Franck spent at his second and third Parisian churches were accordingly taken up with a study of the technical and musical changes confronting his instrument. Hinting at the satisfactions which beckoned at Saint-Jean-Saint-François, the critic Emmanuel Buenzod comments:

> Installé à son banc, retranché derrière le triple clavier à pédales qui le défend du monde, il aura l'impression d'être l'interprète surnaturel d'un message grandiose, de déléguer la Parole sans avoir à l'expliquer, sans en faire un objet d'exégèse. Rien ne peut mieux lui convenir, rien ne peut s'accorder de façon plus intime avec son besoin de contemplation, du rêverie, dans l'ordre musical auquel sa vie est consacrée.*

The implications for his future as a composer were thus exceedingly far-reaching, even if they did not bear immediate exploitation. It is only by turning to a more detailed scrutiny of the state of organ-playing in France in the 1850s that we can hope to specify what these implications were.

Most musicians accept the view that the great age of French keyboard music was that over which the famous Couperin family presided. The members of this family had held appointments as organists more or less continuously from the middle of the seventeenth century to the beginning of the nineteenth, with the career of François (nicknamed 'Le Grand') running parallel to that of Bach in Germany. The style of playing and writing displayed in these times was determined, to a large extent, by the character of the instruments available. The so-called 'baroque' organ was not a powerful solo instrument, and often served merely to accompany singers in church services. In so far as the music of the seventeenth

---

* Attached to its console, tucked away behind the three manuals and pedals which are screened from the congregation, it will help convey, in spiritual fashion, an imposing message, passing on the Word without explanation, devoid of any proselytizing aim. Nothing could be better placed, nothing more compatible with its humble craftsmanship, its dreamy, meditative requirements, within the musical domain to which its life is dedicated.

and eighteenth centuries was primarily contrapuntal in texture, the period's keyboard instruments were made to serve the ideal of clarity rather than sonority. Moreover, since orchestras of that time tended to consist of simple string and wind bands, there was no temptation to burden the organ with a wide range of imitative devices. These would in any case have been beyond the skill of early inventors. With a few notable exceptions, the organist exploited the limited timbres put at his disposal in as simple and unaffected manner as possible. Additions to the catalogue of instruments, foreshadowed in particular by the Mannheim school, gradually helped to alter conceptions of the organ's role; so, too, did the discovery of virtuoso keyboard figuration for the piano. By the time the Romantic movement in music emerged to full expression, a substantial reassessment of the instrument's potentialities was accordingly at hand. It was somewhat to Franck's disadvantage—both as a player and a reformer—that this revaluation was a long time in coming, not really making itself felt until he moved to Sainte-Clotilde in 1858.

Knowledge of Couperin's works having become less scholarly, and ignorance of Bach allowed to gather momentum, it was inevitable that the organists Franck encountered as a young man should have seemed the inheritors of a debased musical coinage. Not only were they in the process of giving up the baroque repertoire, but they had also come to fall back on 'arrangements' rather than original compositions. It would be crediting Franck himself with too much insight to say that he was aware of this state of affairs and deplored it. His own programmes—at least up until the time he obtained his professorship at the Conservatoire—make dismaying reading, so easily do they seem to have been content with sentimental bits and pieces. During 1852–4, for example, the composer undertook a variety of recitals at Orléans, where he had been able to carve out a number of contacts for himself. Despite the interest which M. René Berthelot asked him to take in older music (this scholar was Director of the Conservatoire and author of a book on Orléans composers), Franck tamely reverted to the usual round of favourites when planning his concerts. One typical evening included a transcription of a Schubert song, the andante from Haydn's Symphony No. 36, a popular Chopin mazurka and a number of similar pieces. That this sort of 'pot-pourri' could not hope to be the means of restoring prestige to the instrument was a thought that never seems to have occurred to him. All the evidence points to the fact that Franck knew very few of Bach's organ works until he began to practise them a few years later at Sainte-Clotilde. According to Adrien de la Faye, in the *Gazette Musicale*, there were hardly any organists in France at that time who could be relied upon to play the fugues, toccatas and fantasias of the Leipzig master. Even the standard of execution was low compared with later in the century. This is confirmed by the fact that Franck's brother Joseph went on to win first prize for organ at the Paris Conservatoire in 1852, a distinction that would have been much more discriminatingly bestowed some thirty or forty years later.

The trouble with most of the older organists was that they failed to look beyond the teaching of men like Benoist. This venerable player was to continue in his post at the Conservatoire until 1872, by which time it was jokingly said that three republics and two empires had lived and died under him. While his methods had been reasonably up to date when Franck was a student, their usefulness to the rising generation was at best marginal. To some, his name was already synonymous with reaction, Saint-Saëns having had the gall to describe him as 'a mediocre player'. Others simply ignored his prescriptions, and attached themselves to one of the new German virtuosi. Foremost among these was Adolphe Hesse, a former pupil of Bach's biographer, Forkel, whose playing acted as a revelation to all who heard him. Hesse played accurately and without haste, obtaining his effects without a trace of exaggeration. The impression he conveyed with the pedals was altogether unprecedented.[1] One of those who took lessons with him was the Belgian, Lemmens, whom Franck listened to on more than one occasion. A teacher at the Brussels Conservatoire, this promising artist was actually a year younger than César, and his phenomenal legato must have aroused a definite sense of envy. Both Hesse and Lemmens were widely imitated by their juniors all over Europe. Their recitals communicated a feeling of excitement not dissimilar to that which Liszt and Paganini had been known to create. People went to hear them, not so much out of a liking for the music they played, as from a desire to witness their pyrotechnics. Hence, although the organ was never destined to appeal to a really wide musical public, a circle of devotees soon sprang up, and these surrounded the instrument with some of the fashionable airs formerly reserved for the piano. Indeed, as time progressed the situation attracted its Rubinsteins and Leschetitzkys, expert manipulators whose sole object was to stagger and ravish their audiences. The emancipation of the organ was therefore not without its dangers to musical integrity.

Alexandre Boëly, who ruled for many years over the organ at

[1] Reviewing one of his recitals in the *Gazette Musicale*, an anonymous critic wrote: 'Hesse plays better with his feet than most organists do with their hands.' This might have been construed as a knock at Franck and his kind, who still had not learned to master this aspect of their craft.

St Germain d'Auxerrois, was possibly the earliest of the breed which had taken France by storm. He died in the year Franck was appointed to Sainte-Clotilde, but his influence had already gone far towards entrenching the transcendental style of execution. The late Edward Dent once sarcastically credited him with having stolen a march on the *blasé* cinema organists of a later age. This is perhaps to encourage an unjust view of his talents. The fact that he played Bach with particular zest suggests that his example cannot have been wholly bad. However, it is to him as much as anyone that we owe the conception of the instrument as a pealing mechanical monstrosity. Later developments were the work of men like Charles Marie Widor, who occupied a post at St Sulpice from 1870 onwards, and whose knowledge came as such a bombshell to many Franck pupils at the Conservatoire. His grasp of the orchestra meant that he was interested in extending the instrument's range of stops, and it is to his practice that modern habits of registration are due. The ostentatious Lefébure-Wély first displayed his skill at the Madeleine, a church that was also to call on the services of both Fauré and Saint-Saëns. Though he invariably made a greater impression as a pianist, the latter was unquestionably fit to rank as one of the country's finest organists. His penchant for improvising mammoth fugues became so renowned that one prospective bride implored him not to play at her wedding in case he should frighten off all the guests. It is interesting to note, in passing, that Saint-Saëns played many of the piano works of Liszt in organ transcriptions. His account of *St Francois d'Assise predicant aux oiseaux* so amazed the composer that he was led to declare it the greatest feat he had ever heard. Saint-Saëns, like Widor, tended to maximize the instrument's power of simulating orchestral effects. It was he who claimed:

> . . . the organ is more than an instrument: it is an orchestra, a combination of Pan's pipes of every calibre, some of them tiny as children's playthings, others gigantic as the pillars of a temple.

As the century moved into its second half, the organ could indeed offer itself as a substitute for the orchestra in each and every one of its departments. Players found themselves possessed of a number of flute and clarinet stops: gamba stops capable of imitating the stringed instruments; a voix céleste rank; stops for the trumpet and the bassoon; and finally the much-abused vox humana, which emitted a slightly nasal sound. This last device was more commonly employed by French organists, reflecting their different approach to religious sentiment. Put at the disposal of the new virtuosi, all these advantages were apt to make people lose sight of the basic musical aims. It was partly due to the counter-influence of Franck and his school that French organ music was prevented from going the way of Central European piano music after the time of Liszt. The austerity which the circle displayed had the effect of turning musicians back from the abyss of exhibitionism and the worship of sheer bravura. Certainly, there can be no doubt that Franck's own playing—even after he had absorbed the lessons of his flashier contemporaries—was marked by an exceptional degree of restraint. Though addicted to improvisation, he never used the habit to astound his hearers; neither did he resort to the bizarre tricks of registration practised by his rivals. In his writing for the organ, he always allowed plenty of pauses to enable the less dexterous player to change manuals or pull out what, on many instruments, were very heavy stops. What is so remarkable is that, with all the self-effacement he preserved, he did not cause the organ to lose its new-found esteem and relapse into its former role of accompanying instrument. He played brilliantly without abandoning one whit of his concern for the musical ideas he was expressing, steering a middle course between virtuosity and unobtrusiveness. Remaining an *artisan d'église*, he was nevertheless a constant spur to the plodders who sought comfort amid the Church's ranks, and his powers of detachment served to make him a legend.

Although he used his years of silence to attend more closely to his church duties, Franck was able to leaven the tedium by writing at least two compositions of passing interest. Neither of these brought him fame or money, and neither can be said to occupy an honoured place among his finished works. The first helped to launch a genre in which a great deal of colourful music eventually came to be written; while the second led the composer into a painful 'cul-de-sac'. These works were the little known *Bergsymphonie* (which d'Indy mistook for an early draft of *Les Béatitudes*) and the ill-starred opera, *Le Valet de Ferme*. It will repay us to examine each, if only because each reflects, as the composer's maturer pieces do not, the growing pains he experienced while trying to decide on the right career. The state of mind in which they were conceived can only be vaguely surmised. D'Indy refers to another breakdown which evidently befell Franck in 1853, implying that a number of dissatisfactions began to crowd in upon him at that stage. The one specific cause he mentions is an overloaded teaching schedule. But this explanation scarcely makes much sense, for the burden Franck carried in this respect was lighter than that he had been used to facing earlier in his life. It is more probable that he was reacting, albeit quite unconsciously, to the thwarting of his creative ambitions; and perhaps to a temporary deterioration in his physical health. The fact that he was to spend a few weeks in Switzerland at this time suggests that his doctors may have been afraid he was contracting tuberculosis. Unfortunately, Franck was not given to declaring his troubles in outbursts of rage or anguish, so that his mentality is inferable only from his movements and from the general tenor of his work. In any case, it is worth recalling this illness when we come to assess the compositions of the late 1840s and early 1850s. The opera, in particular, would seem to have had some connection with his despair, since he was hardly acting according to his own wishes in writing it. As for the 'symphonie', that also brought him a run of bad luck, though of a somewhat different kind.

If importance can be ascribed to this last-named work, it is not so much on account of its musical substance—which is slight—as the manner in which it anticipates *Les Eolides* and the other tone-poems of the 1880s. It was typical of Franck's ill-fortune that the subject he chose for his first venture into the genre had also attracted the attention of Liszt. Whether this was just an unhappy coincidence, or whether we should concern ourselves with a question of stealing, is a matter that deserves to be cleared up. Julien Tiersot, writing in the *Revue Musicale* in 1922, proposed the view that as Franck had begun his version in 1845 or 1846 (whereas Liszt did not complete his until 1849), the Belgian should be credited with the prior claim; and hence the honour of having invented the symphonic poem. The snag with this argument is that Liszt, too, was a slow worker. Though Grove gives 1847 as the probable date of his inspiration, it is generally conceded that sketches for his work were in existence as early as 1833. The actual title—*Ce qu'on entend sur la montagne*—attaches to his composition as well as Franck's; but this tells us nothing, since both men worked from the same source, namely Victor Hugo's *Les Feuilles d'Automne*. The possibilities of plagiarism arise out of the fact that the two composers were acquainted, and may have known of each other's plans. Their earliest meeting seems to have been at the Grétry Festival in Liège during 1842, though it is just possible that they exchanged words on one of César's childhood tours a long time before. It is certain that they corresponded at intervals between the Liège meeting and the time of going to work on their respective enterprises. There seems no way of knowing, at this late date, whether the idea emanated from a single mind, and if so which of them it was. The irony is that, although Franck finished his work first, Liszt was the first to secure a performance. This he was able to do in 1852, not going on to publish for a further four years. The hearing of his composition obviously gave it the advantage as far as the public was concerned; especially since Franck was unsuccessful in finding the means of either publication or performance. The upshot of this unfairly balanced, and probably unconsciously pursued, rivalry was that Liszt was free to go forward and establish the symphonic poem as a novel medium, leaving Franck to languish in the wake of his success. When César returned to the attack in the 1870s, his rival had quit the scene in a flourish of self-abnegation.

A glance at Hugo's poem ought to be enough to convince listeners of the subject's wide romantic appeal. It is one of those pretentious effusions in which man's puny gifts are pointedly contrasted with the obstinacies of the cosmos. The poet imagines two voices. One springs from the sea and is carefree in its joyful declamation; the other emerges from the soil, pouring out its sadness in the accents of humanity:

> L'une venait des mers; chant de gloire! hymne heureux!
> C'était la voix des flots qui parlaient entre eux;
> L'autre, qui s'elevait de la terre ou nous sommes
> Etait triste: c'était le murmure des hommes.*

As with so many similar verses of the period, there is no attempt to resolve the metaphysical dilemma. It is sufficient that the poet can give vent to his anguish, and summarize his emotions in a grand and querulous gesture:

> Et pourquoi le Seigneur, qui seul lit a son livre,
> Mêle eternellement dans un fatal hymen
> Le chant de la nature au cri du genre humain.†

Franck's treatment of the theme is more pictorial than Liszt's. The future Abbé could not resist the temptation to intrude an *andante religioso* section near the end, effecting a reconciliation between the forces which the poem describes.[1] In so doing, he forfeited some of the quasi-impressionist quality which attaches to his rival's setting. Beginning with a slow and gentle woodwind theme in E major,

---

[1] That his fondness for religious perorations tended to serve Liszt very badly is suggested by the equally banal epilogue to the *Faust Symphony*. The drooling tenor solo he inserted at the end of this work was a disastrous miscalculation. The opposite of Franck, he was better at depicting devilry than spirituality.

* The one was coming from across the seas; song of glory! hymn of happiness! It was the voice of the waves speaking among their own kind; the other, which was reaching up from the ground where we are, was sad: it was the whisper of men.

† And why does the Lord, who alone pronounced in his book, eternally mingle in a doomed union nature's song with the cry of the human condition.

Franck's work almost looks forward to Debussy's *Nuages*. With its string harmonics, and block use of instrumental colour, it certainly marked an advance over the stylized scene-painting of David. Scored for full orchestra, *Ce qu'on entend sur la montagne* makes use of stereophonic effects in depicting 'le chant de la nature' and 'le cri humain'; and rises to an impressive fortissimo climax. The composer may have got the idea for the 'double' orchestra from Spohr's programme-symphony *Le Terrestre et le Divin dans la vie humaine*, a work that also expressed similar sentiments. It first appeared in 1841. From a retrospective point of view, it is interesting to note that Franck returned to this style of orchestration in his famous D minor Symphony. A final parallel seems to exist between the second subject of Franck's tone-poem and the main motif of Liszt's *Les Préludes*, a composition not written until 1854.

Tracing the course of a new art-form is liable to be an unrewarding business, and credit for having developed the symphonic poem depends as much as anything on the definition one cares to apply to it. If the term is construed to mean any short orchestral work in which certain fixed motifs evolve in accordance with a literary programme, then those magnificently solitary overtures, like Beethoven's *Coriolan* and *Egmont*, lay an obvious claim to precedence. Mendelssohn's *Hebrides* must be admitted as a further contender, since it appeared before anything by Franck or Liszt. On the other hand, none of these works was actually *called* a symphonic poem, and none comes within the orbit of high romanticism. Hector Berlioz, whose use of the *idée fixe* in works like the *Symphonie Fantastique* and *Harold en Italie* was undeniably prophetic, offers himself as yet another candidate for honours. Liszt was different from most of these men by virtue of his gift for transmuting literary impulses into musical coin of every denomination. So much more acutely than Franck, he was the possessor of an all-round aesthetic sensibility, capable of responding to the demands of architecture, painting and literature. Moreover, he found it possible to give the sharpest characterization to his sensations. It is curious that, despite his possession of such talents, Liszt rarely saddled himself with complicated programmes of the sort favoured by Berlioz and his successors among the French school. He shared the view, expressed by Beethoven in relation to the 'Pastoral' Symphony, that the composer's business was with the feelings aroused by natural objects, and not the objects themselves. His habit of prefacing his scores with evocative literary epigraphs shows how much more concerned he was with mood than vista. After the example set by Franck, there followed a long chain of these brief symphonic works, some of the most notable being Saint-Saëns's *Le Rouet d'Omphale* (1871), Duparc's *Lénore* (1874), Chausson's *Viviane* (1882), Debussy's *Prélude à l'après-midi d'un faune* (1894), and Dukas's *L'Apprenti Sorcier* (1897).

By comparison, the composer's *Le Valet de Ferme* seems almost a pure throwback. On the face of it, a comic opera might sound a most un-Franckian project, but the term implies something very different in France. It refers to any work in which spoken dialogue is allowed to appear, and is hence to be equated more with the German *Singspiel*. The theatrical leanings of the Desmousseaux family had made it inevitable that Franck would be persuaded to write such a work, the only cause for surprise being that he was allowed to choose so weak a subject. Perhaps his advisors were so intent on obtaining a quick success that they dared not look beyond the conventional formulae. It must be remembered that, whatever lonely trails were blazed after 1870, this was still 1850; and any composer living in France was under the strongest possible obligation to submit to facile operatic tastes. The whole system of education offered to prospective composers revolved around this aim. Among the compulsory courses at the Conservatoire, we find training in lyric declamation and in the defining and acting of roles. The Italian language, it need hardly be added, was a heavily subscribed subsidiary study. Several of the more distinguished teachers—men like Ambroise Thomas and Fromental Halévy— owed their positions entirely to their operatic triumphs. It is worth noting that to succeed the dour Cherubini—himself no stranger to the theatre—the Minister chose to appoint Daniel Auber, whose dry air of disenchantment extended to everything except the productions of the Opéra-Comique, where he could be found peacefully dozing on most evenings of the week. He performed this function, like all else that he did, with his hat on—a strange mannerism to have contracted.[1] Given a place of honour in the Director's box, this old cynic was later to remark:

> I never knew what it meant to snore until I took to sleeping in Veron's box; and, as it is, I do not snore now except under provocation. But there would be no possibility of sleeping by the side of Veron without snoring. You had to drown his, or else it would awaken you.

If Franck's attitude to his calling was somewhat less jaded, it still should not be assumed that his standards were incorruptible.

---

[1] There is a grisly story to the effect that when Gérard de Nerval's hatted body was found dangling from a lamp-post the police were persuaded of his suicide by Auber's comment: 'If I were going to kill myself, I should certainly take care not to remove my hat!'

He had, after all, gone through the same régime as most of the period's theatrical hacks, and it would be naïve to suppose that his training had left no mark on him. There exists a clumsy fragment of music, written while the composer was a student at the Conservatoire, which helps to bear out the assumption that he was not immune from being stage-struck. This is the sketch for an opera called *Stradella*, based on the life of the early Italian composer. Franck could never have expected to see this little 'pot-boiler' performed, as the libretto was already the property of another. Moreover, his musical score was not filled out. What it signifies, however, is that opera must always have had some lure for him; a proposition that gathers force from the fact that he returned to the form twice more after the failure of *Le Valet de Ferme*. All his attempts proved amateurish, and there is not much change to be had from the notion that he was a frustrated man of the theatre. To put no more complicated construction on the matter, it is probable that his tastes and aspirations reflected those of his age. We have already observed that he looked up to Meyerbeer in a way that marked him off from, let us say, Schumann, with whom he has otherwise been compared. In later life, his idols in the opera house went no higher than men like Massenet and Saint-Saëns. For some special reason (a personal or religious quarrel, perhaps?), he drew the line at Gounod. But there is nothing to suggest that he found French opera as a whole rather tawdry. The tepidness of his feelings towards Wagner may be contrasted with the keen awareness of this composer's genius displayed by pupils like Duparc and Chausson. Actually, one cannot help thinking that Franck steered clear of Wagner with deliberate intent. Both musicians were men of great passion, but Wagner's passion was more of an illicit quantity. Franck's was channelled uneasily into the respectable forms. When asked to give his opinion of the composer of *Tristan*, Franck is alleged to have said: 'What Wagner has done for human love, I have done for the divine.' One wonders, on the evidence of this assertion, whether his object was not to preserve uncontaminated the vehicle through which he was to express his deepest feelings.

However that may be, it seems as if he regarded the operatic form, not as a repository for his innermost thoughts, but as an artful set of conventions to be mastered; a legitimate and pre-eminently social genre in which it was his duty to register a triumph. It was probably with this philosophy that he approached the writing of *Le Valet de Ferme*, or *The Farmer's Man*. He was two years working at it, and the seriousness of his intentions may be gauged from the fact that he sought out the aid of two of the nation's leading librettists—Alphonse Royer and Gustav Vaez.

This pair had already provided the book for Donizetti's *Lucia* and Rossini's *Otello*, so that their collaboration was regarded as a good omen. Having also secured the approval of his mother-in-law, Franck had every reason to feel optimistic about the project he had set himself. Yet the plot of *Le Valet de Ferme* is so banal that one wonders how anyone could have given it a second glance. A rustic melodrama, cast in the most excruciating rhyming couplets, it exploits the theme of domestic infidelity in eighteenth century Ireland. Rugged and primitive country as it then was—rich in feuds and superstitions—Ireland might well have seemed the right locale by which to appeal to an audience of well-fed, comfortable Parisians. But the halting character of the story, with its cliché-ridden situations, put out of court any possibility of production. An indication of the dialogue may be had from the following homespun utterances:

C'est Dieu qui m'éclaire;
Betty, ton vieux père
Sera, je l'espère,
Sauvé du trépas!

Utilizing a minimum of scenic attraction, the opera could not even call on that interest in 'sentimental anthropology' which had been the instrument of Boieldieu's triumph in the Scottish scenes of *La Dame Blanche*; and which continued to fascinate in the paintings of Decamps and Longhi. Though Liszt once again attempted to intercede on his behalf, the management of the Théâtre Lyrique turned the opera down, and Franck had to put it in cold storage for a couple of years. This was in 1852, and his disappointment was cruelly renewed when, a little later on, Royer was lucky enough to get appointed Director of the Paris Opéra. The composer naturally took this promotion to signify that his work would go into immediate production. What he had not bargained for was the political nature of his friend's advancement. Given the post on the understanding that he would use it to bolster the régime, Royer rejected his own opera so as to make room for a run of new works by Meyerbeer. Thus the last of Franck's hopes was unceremoniously dashed. Many years afterwards, when he was asked to resubmit his manuscript for publication, the composer replied 'It is not worth printing.' Honesty accordingly took the place of rancour in his thinking.

Wearied by the collapse of his theatrical ambitions, Franck found himself greeting the nation's final monarchical fling with a mixture of contempt and indifference. Unable to summon up the smallest interest in politics, and repelled by the grotesque spectacles which filled the city's opera houses, the composer withdrew silently into the bosom of his family. Their solace and repose equipped him with the means of overcoming his disappointments, leaving the ensuing years in his career to be marked by nothing more sensational than an increase in feelings of security. He soon began making trips to Orléans, where he took on a teaching stint at the Conservatoire and gave occasional organ recitals. It was there that the Desmousseaux family had a cousin by the name of Féréol, a curious character who had graduated from being an opera singer to becoming chief of the local fire-brigade. This exuberant relative —who reminds us forcibly of someone in a Fernandel farce— opened the doors of a number of provincial musical establishments, enabling Franck to add handsomely to his annual income. It was also at Orléans that the composer renewed his acquaintance with Pauline Viardot, for whom he had meantime written his song, 'Souvenance', to words by Chateaubriand. Song-writing had been something of a hobby during the previous decade, 'Le Sylphe' and the well-known 'Robin Gray' having made their appearance around 1843. But it was not a hobby that took firm hold, and little else in the way of *mélodies* emerged until the writing of 'Le Mariage des Roses' and 'Roses et Papillons' in the early 1870s. The money Franck earned through his additional commitments helped to furnish the house in the Boulevard Montparnasse where he and Félicité were now residing. When M. Desmousseaux died of cholera in 1854, his widow came to live with the young couple, remaining as a jovial and businesslike companion until her own death three years later. Meanwhile, the members of Franck's original family receded into the limbo. The once hated Nicolas-Joseph did not relinquish his grip on life until 1871, a year in which death overtook so many Frenchmen that his passing slipped by unnoticed. By that time, his son had settled in the last of his churches, had become ensconced in the famous apartment at the Boulevard St Michel, and recovered his autonomy as man and artist.

IV

Rich strains from aloft

If the years of Franck's apprenticeship at the organ tended him
the emotional security he had lacked during his childhood and
adolescence, those which followed his installation at Sainte-
Clotilde were crowned with happiness and joy. The modest
basilican structure standing in its island of greenery off the Rue
las Cases could scarcely have been regarded as one of Paris's more
fashionable shrines, since it had only just taken its place alongside
the humble chapel of Sainte-Valère. Work on the new church was
still in progress when the composer reported for duty, with the
result that his occupation of the mammoth organ—alleged to be
Cavaillé-Coll's masterpiece to date—was delayed by a year. That
the post was worth waiting for is suggested by the rapturous comments the mighty instrument aroused. Moreover, the functions of
choirmaster and precentor were being thrown in. It was the
privacy of the loft that really attracted Franck, however, and we
may imagine him, much as he is represented in Rongier's famous
portrait, seated in wonder at the console that was to be his chief
abode for the next thirty-five years. The choral tasks he quickly
delegated to Théodore Dubois, a sound academic musician later to
become Director of the Conservatoire, where he was to meet with
resistance over the 'affaire Ravel'. What Franck desired for himself
was to be left to browse through the extensive repertory of keyboard music of which he had such limited knowledge, earnestly
hoping to complete that renovation of mind and spirit his promotion seemed to call for.

His new instrument was a three-manual affair, equipped with
forty-six stops (including a particularly excellent trumpet stop) and
fifteen pedals. Nothing the composer had played upon up to that
time came remotely within the same class. He was never to forget
the thrill he experienced on encountering this organ. His last

words were allegedly a fondly murmured attachment to it.[1] Its
swell and clarity were superb, the only problem being how to
manipulate the pedals. Here a deficiency resulted from the pianistic
bias his early training had imposed on him; and he attacked it with
the aid of a practice pedal-board supplied by the firm of Pleyel,
whose valiant service to Chopin had not gone unremembered.
Practice was a chore to which Franck had become thoroughly
accustomed, and it was no hardship to him to rise early and walk
the streets to the new church at which he was employed. He soon
found himself progressing with unexpected speed. Charles-Alexis
Chauvet, later to become organist of the Trinité, proved of the
greatest help in fostering his incomplete understanding of Bach, a
process that went on unhurriedly throughout the decades now
stretching ahead. Another colleague, Père Lambilloté, who had
been one of Franck's pupils at the Collège de Vaugirard, attempted
to enlist his interest in Gregorian music, but this art was presented
to him in such a narrowly-filtered and dogmatic fashion that his
response lit no new path. He persisted in his neglect of Palestrina
and the Italian school, even though the church authorities continued to ply him with requests for anthems and offertories. In
general, Franck did not find it easy to express himself through the
medium of church music, and it is worth remarking that he never
took to it as naturally as Bordes and Maurice Emmanuel. If it were
not too paradoxical, it might be said that his bent was towards
secular music with a religious bias. The distinction between these
two genres is best left undrawn, however, since there is more than
enough good music in existence which belongs to neither category.
At this stage in Franck's life—having regard to his failure in the
salon, concert-hall and opera-house—it must have seemed plausible
enough to contemplate a career as a church composer. Indeed, it
was about the only avenue he had left unexplored.

A fresh chapter in the composer's quest for recognition was
accordingly marked by the writing of a *Mass* for three voices and
a number of semi-ecclesiastical minor pieces. We have no option
but to regard this move as a resumption of ambition. There was
this difference nonetheless: that he no longer felt beset by fears for
his livelihood. This alone must have been consoling to one whose
anxieties over money had scarcely abated since the day he had left
school. Precisely what triggered off the new interest can only be
surmised. We know that the composer had a gratifying letter from
Von Bülow at about this time, telling him of the enthusiasm being
shown for his Trios in Germany. Yet he could scarcely have

[1] After Franck's death, when renovations were carried out, the
console came into the possession of his pupil, Charles Tournemire, who
in turn bequeathed it to Flor Peeters at Malines.

thought this a sufficient enhancement of his prospects. What is far more likely is that he was now beginning to be recognized as a minor figure in the professional life of the capital, and this recognition served to put him on good terms with a variety of influential people whose support he should otherwise have had to canvass. His Orléans tours had in the meantime won him some modest publicity, as did the consultant work he carried out in company with Cavaillé-Coll, Saint-Saëns and Widor. Moreover, he assisted in the inauguration of the St Sulpice instrument in 1862, and gave a recital when the re-built organ of St Etienne-du-Mont was put into commission the following year.[1] These happenings scarcely afforded Franck much opportunity for a personal triumph. They were not the kind of happenings his father would have rejoiced to witness. Yet they did confer something very valuable on the still struggling musician: an accredited position as advisor and exponent in what was clearly an expanding field.

If anything further were needed to galvanize his sluggish ambition, it was surely to be discovered in connection with his magnificent new organ. In the sphere of organ composition, technology has always been a spur to invention, and the desire to reveal to the public the full range of sounds now at his disposal must have figured prominently among Franck's motives for writing. At all events, it cannot have been accidental that, whereas his piano pieces are concentrated into two groups at the beginning and end of his career, it was the initial period at Sainte-Clotilde into which the impressive series of organ works was fitted. The earliest of these date from about 1860, when Franck embarked on a set of *Six Pièces*, each of which was dedicated to a different member of his circle as it then was. Chauvet, Alkan, Saint-Saëns, Cavaillé-Coll, Benoist and Lefébure-Wély were the names strewn across the title-pages, and these give a good indication of the range of Franck's acquaintances at this stage of his life. It will be observed that, as yet, his select band included no pupils of importance, and in reality consisted of men whose lives, like his own, were bounded by the keyboard. Saint-Saëns alone among this group suggests the possibility of other and wider horizons, but his altercations with Franck are sufficiently well known for us to suspect him of being the least sympathetic of the group. The pieces themselves are worthy of an honourable place in their composer's output, and are individual enough to merit separate comment. They became the first of Franck's compositions to win general acceptance with both players and the public.

[1] One of the notable features of this recital was evidently Franck's skilful handling of the 16-ft pedal, which seems to indicate that his assiduous application to M. Pleyel's device had achieved its object.

The initial number, listed as op. 16, is a *Fantaisie*—a title that might suggest a reversion to the virtuoso junketings of the composer's boyhood. Actually, nothing could be further removed from that period than this calm and controlled work in the unexpectedly 'white' key of C major. Unlike many of the organ compositions by that name by members of the Widor school, this fantasy avoids the slightest hint of rhetoric and is untypical of Franck in maintaining its elementary tonal scheme. The most remote of its sections, harmonically speaking, goes only as far as the subdominant. It is, however, a longish piece for inclusion in a set, having three sections, each in ternary form, with an interlude between the second and third. Professor Demuth accords it the highest praise in saying:

> There is little music as ineffably lovely as this *Fantaisie* . . . which suggests a dim religious light, evening with a few candles burning, lofty arches and a high ceiling.

Those who admire the gentle, unassertive qualities in Franck—and who can deny that they do most to reveal the quintessence of the man?—will also agree that such phrases seem to describe the music better than many a formal analysis. Indeed, there is a sense in which pieces like the *Fantaisie* resist erudite commentary. As with parts of *Ruth*, they appear to be the product of such unselfconscious craftsmanship that we feel it would be murder to dissect. Yet they are full of cunning as well as simplicity. Franck's canonic writing can be so natural that only a student, attempting to emulate him, is given cause to doubt its spontaneity. Counterpoint was an art over which he attained a rare mastery, and if he eventually came to practise it as if it were second nature, that still does not make it any the less remarkable an achievement. The second section of the *Fantaisie* provides us with a perfectly distilled example of his skill at invertible part-writing, taking the listener through a kaleidoscopic series of enharmonic changes before depositing him back in the home key of F minor. The easeful working of the first theme of the initial section into the final adagio once again proves how mindful Franck was of the degree to which the cyclical principle could be utilized to solve his difficulties over form. The worst that can be said about such music is that it exemplifies the limitations of mere competence, of substituting skill for inspiration. What is apt to be forgotten is that very few composers ever acquire the proficiency they mistakenly take for granted. When they do, a new quality of writing is often the unexpected result.

To follow, Franck inserted a *Grande Pièce Symphonique* which likewise turned out to be of sonata proportions. Having excised parts of the original *Fantaisie* on account of their diffuseness, the composer now strove to be more direct in his approach. It is interesting to observe a recurrence of the habit of combining themes in order to buttress his peroration, even though the effect is to come very near to bombast. One of Franck's constant shortcomings can be traced to his unsure command of mood. Where most musicians are firm in establishing the right atmosphere for a piece, Franck had a tendency to waver between two opposing poles. His music— and the first two of the 'Six Pieces' illustrate this very well—gives the impression of oscillating unconvincingly between the extremes of fragility and vulgarity, as if he were not quite certain how his audience would react. Where the *Fantaisie* strikes us as being timidly undemonstrative—his enemies would probably say pallid— the *Grande Pièce Symphonique* hurries us into a contrasting portentousness which almost suggests that the composer had suddenly detected his weakness and decided to cover it up in a massive display of confidence. Several critics have commented on the likeness

Ex. 3

César Franck: Grande Pièce Symphonique (for organ)

of its first theme to the opening of the D minor Symphony; and it is true that they both have a foreboding quality.[1] Such phraseology may be acceptable on the scale of the symphony, but is less so in a shortish keyboard work. The tonal scheme of the *Grande Pièce* also veers in the direction of pretentiousness—F sharp replacing C as the centre of gravity. Its sections resemble those of the Italian sonata, with a chordal second movement, a brisk section in triple time, and a concluding *fugato* passage. Texturally, there are interesting glimpses of the composer Franck was to become in the 1880s, though the figuration inevitably suggests the *Prélude, Choral et Fugue* as much as the last great organ *Chorals*. The crochet tune of the third section, with its truncated semiquaver accompaniment, is patently pianistic in the fashion adopted by so many of Franck's

[1] This is the theme the late Samuel Langford once described in the words—'The serpent lifts its head'. Perhaps it is just this element of sinuosity in Franck's music that a number of people find repellent.

pupils—witness the eighth variation in de la Presle's *Thème Varié* or the typical accompaniment to a French song of the *fin-de-siècle* period. The chief weakness of the piece is perhaps the inability of the final fugue to measure up to its own specifications.

Far more successful, if no less of a cousin to the ultimate piano works, is the *Prélude, Fugue et Variation* which forms number three in the series. This admirable piece has become a popular choice, partly because it is easy to play, but more especially, perhaps, on account of its availability in transcribed form for the piano, an exercise undertaken by Harold Bauer. Popular or not, it is one of the best of Franck's keyboard works, as most experts are willing to endorse. The principal tune of the *Prélude* is delicate and under-emphatic. It is supported by a rocking 9/8 rhythm and extends to form part of a ternary structure. Then follows a short link leading to the *Fugue*. This comes in three parts and is marked by its per-ference for stretti. The final *Variation* maintains the shape of the theme more or less intact, but alters the nature of the accompani-ment. Demuth condemns the piano version as 'completely un-suited'—a judgement we should be inclined to uphold were it not for the element of interchangeability which is present in most of Franck's instrumental thinking. Unwary critics might be led to suppose this triptych was conceived as a prototype of the three-movement essay for piano which the composer exploited so bril-liantly in his last decade. Actually, the model for those late and great compositions consisted of nothing Franck himself had con-tributed. It is to be found in Bach's *Forty-Eight*. Intent simply on writing a prelude and fugue, Franck found his form growing into a larger species as he worked at it. It is interesting that Bizet, at the time he joined Franck's organ class at the Conservatoire, expressed surprise and delight on hearing the *Prélude, Fugue et Variation*. 'Your piece is exquisite,' he told his embarrassed professor, 'I did not know you were a composer too.' This story incidentally illustra-tes very well the degree of obscurity which continued to attach to Franck as a creative artist, even after the dissolution of the Empire.

The *Pastorale* which comes next is arguably the most beguiling number of the six. Of its three sections, the second, with its mono-tonous pivotal movement, is the weakest. The clipped rhythm of the opening theme sounds fresh and taut, however, and cleverly avoids the obvious by tying the last note in each group of semi-quavers. The cyclical principle again intrudes in the manner in which the two themes of this first section combine to form the basis of the third. The ease with which Franck could slide into a fugal style of writing can be demonstrated in this piece, since it contains far more counterpoint than most others which bear the title. What saves the composer from the charge of academicism—he only narrowly escapes being convicted on this count at several points in the set, and once or twice goes up for a stiff sentence—is the unfailing charm of his cantabile melodies. The work *Lied* is often invoked by d'Indy to describe Franck's style—presumably in respect of its formal connotations. It is just as apt an expression to use when referring to the composer's gift of song. An ability to invent singing lines of melody is no common talent, and many great composers were without it. Franck's possession of this gift was not as complete as was the case with the German romantics, men like Schubert and Weber, but his melodies have a mysterious power of haunting the mind long after they have been heard. In stressing the composer's German ancestry, most critics are content to name Bach as Franck's obvious progenitor, without realizing the similarity he bears to the man who stands in a direct line between their respective paths—namely, Schumann. At any rate, it is the composer of songs like 'Mondnacht' and 'Der Nussbaum' who makes his presence felt when we listen to Franck's more ingratiating melodies, as in this gentle pastoral hymn.

The last two works—the *Prière* and *Final*—have in common a rough approximation to first movement form. The former is a diffuse construction, making over-use of a tame triplet accompanying figure, and at more than a dozen pages seeming to constitute an unduly demanding prayer. There are numerous weaknesses in this prolix essay. It is full of the most undistinguished recitative-like material and the layout is awkward in places. Franck's chromaticism, kept within reasonable bounds in most of the companion pieces, here becomes a shade oppressive. There is too much modulation and the tonal centre is often irritatingly ambiguous. Unfortunately, the *Final* is also something of a let-down, parading one of those jaunty tunes which seem pleasant enough on first hearing, but come to appear banal with repetition. This is the pedal solo which Franck inserted, no doubt to underline his current preoccupation with this aspect of the instrument's technique. Like Fauré, who may also have picked up the habit while improvising, Franck rather enjoyed straying into key-changes which, while natural enough to hand and ear, had the effect of producing some truly nightmarish notation. The plethora of double-sharps in this piece is an indication of how far he was inclined to go. Players can scarcely be blamed for neglecting music which starts by being so deliberately uninviting.

The final verdict on these six pieces, which were completed by 1862, must therefore be mixed. They do not comprise a consistently satisfying work, the first, third and fourth of the set standing out as more inspired than the remainder. Léon Vallas is guilty of exaggeration when he claims: '. . . they are solidly mortised and

mitred like the best works of Bach'. Nevertheless, their best
moments do invite such exalted comparisons, and even taking
account of their inconsistencies they emerge as vastly superior to
anything Franck had written up to that time. More important than
this, they went further towards establishing the composer's true
musical personality, pointing the way ahead with valuable assurance.

By comparison, the Mass for three voices, written around 1859–
60, takes its place as a more traditional work, meant to fit into the
framework of the liturgy. Without doubt the Sainte-Clotilde
appointment suggested a moral obligation to Franck—namely that
he ought to write something which would be of importance in the
eyes of the Church. This fairly ambitious choral work can be interpreted as an attempt at salving his conscience. That he was not too
happy with the way it progressed is inferable from the great many
revisions he saw fit to make. These became so protracted that the
date of publication of the work proved to be as late as 1872. Probably the composer wished to make sure that his rivals in other
church posts would not be given grounds for polite deprecation.
As it happened, the work Franck put in on this score had some real
value for him as a craftsman. It provided him with the first chance
he had encountered of polishing his vocal style since the writing of
Ruth. The solo voices he used were soprano, tenor and bass; and
the problem of linking their music to the choral sections presented
him with the usual difficulties of balance. Among the various sections of the Mass, the Kyrie, Sanctus and Gloria were the earliest
to be written, the Agnus Dei and Credo coming later. Finally, the
sentimental Panis Angelicus—one of Franck's best-known compositions and a piece nowadays played more often on its own—was
added to bring about the work's completion. Opinions of the whole
vary considerably. Some commentators have been inclined to view
it as the gateway to the composer's second manner—acting as a
forerunner to *Rédemption* and *Les Béatitudes*. Others, less charitably disposed, have remarked only on the distressing fashion in
which it adumbrates the notorious 'celestial choir' style of writing,
familiar to us from countless Hollywood films.

It would be fairer to Franck to admit, without prejudice, that
the Mass is a notably uneven work, as indeed are all of his choral
compositions. Probably its blemishes prevail since, among the many
parts, only the Agnus and Kyrie are exempt from faults. The former
is a most tender inspiration, the preliminary draft of which Franck
destroyed in one of his rare fits of self-criticism. The Kyrie, though
similarly uncomplicated, proved easier to write. On the evidence of
the score, it is the 'Credo' that must have cost the composer the
greatest effort. The choice of sonata-form for this episode shows

how hidebound by the rules of the Viennese school Franck could allow himself to become; even the academic d'Indy was embarrassed by its inaptness. D'Indy was also among those who looked askance at the Gloria—the one composition by his master about which he did not shrink from using the word 'vulgar'. Modern listeners are unlikely to dissent from these opinions, if only out of the feeling that religious works were not really Franck's strong suit. D'Indy's contempt was possibly aroused by the resemblance certain sections of this Mass bore to the choruses of Meyerbeer. Any debt to what he was tactless enough to call 'the Judaic period' in French music was always sufficient to bring out the worst in this racially-prejudiced scholar. Even allowing for this kind of accusation, however, the Gloria cannot easily be made an object of critical rescue. Of all Franck's compositions, it is the most glutted with clichés. Prominent among these is the habit of using the harp to render the ethereal emotions—a practice that has become all but unendurable with the passage of time. Professor Mellers not long ago took Rimsky-Korsakov to task for having been the arch-corrupter of musical expressiveness—the villain at whose door we should lay the blame for the soupy and uxorious music blared forth from the modern stage and screen. It should not be too difficult to shift some of this burden of guilt on to the broad shoulders of César Franck; and perhaps from there on to the equally sturdy frames of Wagner and Liszt. The heavenly fade-out and the tranquil broken-chord sequence cannot but seem in retrospect to have been Franckist inventions. To deny the charge would only be to bring down the wrath of the purists.

In this connection, it has to be admitted that Franck's middle-period music—and it should not be overlooked that the composer had now reached the age of forty—suffers from a patchiness it would be hard to match in the output of any other first-rate artist. The customary pattern of development, in which the artist begins uncertainly, goes on to exhibit a degree of mastery, and ends by adopting self-denial as his motto, can hardly be said to have existed in his case. On the contrary, he was threatened with all kinds of lapses right up to the last decade of his life, and the mood of his final compositions was not infrequently reckless. That he achieved greatness in this ultimate phase cannot be disputed. But it is odd to find it coming so late in his career. As Winton Dean has remarked: 'Had Franck died at fifty, or even a few years later, we should never have heard his name.' Comparing him with other well-known composers, he easily takes the palm for slow development. Why was it that he failed to achieve his consistency until reaching so advanced an age? Did he simply lack confidence, as Dean implies? Or was it that his training imposed some inhibition on him, forcing him to reject many of his best ideas? One could easily attribute the uneven quality he displays to a temporary confusion of the critical faculty—were it not for the stubborn fact that nothing Franck said or wrote can be taken to demonstrate his possession of such a faculty. Before settling for an explanation, it might repay us to inquire more closely into the conditions with which he had to contend in his early years. Chief among the handicaps he had to face was the persistence of a decadent romanticism as the prevailing musical philosophy. This legacy not only corrupted the talents of many minor composers, but what is more significant for Franck's case, wasted the time that gifted musicians would ordinarily have spent in finding their feet. Had there been no unprofitable trifling with the world of the salon, his career might well have taken a more straightforward course.

The church music which Franck wrote illustrates his mixed sense of commitment to perfection. For though his intention was too sincere to be impugned, it does begin to take on some of the character of an idle fancy once we acknowledge that it had no stronger backing than the sly clerical cajoling to which his appointment subjected him; and perhaps a rush of uninformed enthusiasm from within the family circle. What it signally fails to convey is the presence of a really developed ecclesiastical sensibility, such as might have acted as a springboard for the creative imagination. We are told that Mme Franck openly urged her husband to pursue the path of church musician, but could her own knowledge have been anything like sufficient to have appreciated the difficulties standing in his way? And, what is equally pertinent, were her motives entirely free from bourgeois scruples? It was one thing to stoke Franck's pettier ambitions as a church functionary—always assuming he had any—and quite another to launch him in the wake of the polyphonic masters of the past, trusting to luck that he would live up to their standards.

As we know from the reminiscences of his friends, Franck himself had no more than the sketchiest acquaintance with that great corpus of sacred music, stretching from Dufay to Couperin, that now springs to mind as one of the supreme treasures of the French school. Moreover, while opinions are nowadays unanimous as to the merits of this heritage, few scholars in Franck's day contested the view that ancient music was deservedly defunct. Even had Franck been one of these far-sighted prophets, it should be remembered that the tradition in question had run into the sands more than a hundred years before his time. To have revived it would have been manifestly impossible, while to have emulated it would merely have been to commit an anachronism. What was needed was a fresh appraisal of the role of music in church services, something that could only come about with the consent of the authorities and at the behest of the worshipful members of the public. Franck's modest knowledge and position scarcely equipped him to take account of such special factors. Neither could he easily invoke the aid of any living predecessor. The religious works of Berlioz—if one may use that term to describe such magnificent hybrids as the *Requiem*, the *Te Deum* and *L'Enfance du Christ*—had never achieved the impact their quality promised; partly owing to their creator's scanty respect for the order of the liturgy, but more especially, one suspects, on account of his professed revolutionary scepticism. The *Requiem* had in any case been commissioned by secular authority, and occupied no place in that febrile and cloistered world to which Franck had become attached.[1] The sad truth was that his friend Gounod was about the only French composer to whom Franck could look for guidance in attempting to develop a church style, and by that time it was apparent that the heart of this fickle genius was firmly set on storing up earthly prizes.

All might still have been well had Franck been able to call upon a profound understanding of the German choral tradition, such as one or two of his English contemporaries possessed. He was, after all, more than half-German, and his sympathies in the instru-mental sector went far towards betraying this bias. Unhappily, they were not accompanied by a corresponding zest for the sacred productions of that nation. At the root of this disinclination, exer-cising an unyielding influence, lay the composer's awareness of the religious differences between France and her next door neighbour. Franck was and remained a good Catholic. His whole background, to say nothing of his deepest feelings, was in conflict with the Protestant way of life. Hence, though his beloved Bach had founded what seemed like a distinctly imitable style, based on the grandeur of the baroque services, its adoption by a church lacking strict liturgical principles was an obvious embarrassment. Worse, the case of Mendelssohn provided composers with an object lesson to the effect that anyone wishing to follow the Leipzig tradition would have to retire from the Church and resume his fight from within the concert hall, if not from within the salon. Franck's plight as a Catholic was naturally somewhat different from Mendel-ssohn's, inviting a more accurate comparison with that of Elgar, whose struggle was still to come. The future composer of *Gerontius* was likewise to suffer the cruel handicap of not possessing a living tradition of which to avail himself; but the comparison cannot be

[1] Witness Sir Jack Westrup's comment: 'The tradition of pagan magnificence survived till the Empire and was suitably adapted to the needs of religion. Berlioz's "Messe des Morts" and "Te Deum" are the best known examples . . .' (*An Introduction to Musical History*, 1955.)

pushed too far. There are certain points of dissimilarity. For one thing, Elgar was to have the advantage of a public well conditioned to the acceptance of oratorio. Handel had been the national composer for as long as anyone in England could remember. (The extent of English enthusiasm for biblical choruses was a source of great astonishment to Saint-Saëns when he attended the Birmingham festival of 1879.) By a different token, the French—and Franck among them—cared for the composer of the *Messiah* not at all. His majesty and poise were treated as mere synonyms for dullness by the majority of Gallic minds, while his fondness for tonic-dominant harmonies was enough to have put him beyond the pale to the founder of chromaticism, even though their four-bar phrases might seem to have something in common. Forced up against the consequences of their prejudices, French musicians had to be content with a bastardised church medium—issuing from the union between theatre and conservatoire. It is a compromise which haunts them still.

As if these differences were not sufficient to dispel effort, other complications existed to prevent Franck from fulfilling the promise works like the Mass for three voices set out to suggest. The Romantic movement had intervened between the time of Mendelssohn and Franck's own day, with the result that attitudes to the faith had undergone a certain transformation. While we should be wrong to insinuate that Franck was influenced by the scepticism which quickly took possession of men like Brahms and Verdi, he could not avoid being affected by the tendency to emphasize the dramatic character of religious experience, its relation to the phenomenon of conversion. The fashion for enlarging on this phenomenon was a significant aspect of the movement.[1] This meant that, whereas the older composers had been content to let the message speak for itself, those who had been influenced by Romanticism felt compelled to register the impact. Franck's purpose in writing sacred cantatas was accordingly not so much to comfort the believer as to arouse the potential convert. The late Alfred Einstein made the very pertinent point that his works do not rest in faith; they effect a 'deliverance into faith'. One can appreciate that this subtle difference was not of a kind to commend itself to the church in all cases. Forms of observance are generally felt to be threatened by what the eighteenth century called 'enthusiasm'—as we can confirm today by reference to the American revivalist's willingness to

---

[1] It is clearly illustrated in the poetry of the age, as for example in the couplet of Emily Brontë's which runs:

> No, radiant angel, speak and say
> Why I did cast the world away . . .

dispense with ritual—so that most conservative churchmen of the middle decades of the nineteenth century had no option but to deplore the romantic dramatization of Christianity which was enacted in the literature and music of the time. Indeed, they were right to do so, since it was only to be a short while before French and German scholars were using the techniques of *Wissenschaft* to dispute the whole basis of theology, and to lend credence to the view that myth and not fact lay at the root of the religious outlook. It should not be imagined that Franck had any subversive part to play in this controversy, for he was much too ignorant of polemics to have assessed the social consequences of his actions. Yet in choosing to approach religious music in the manner he did, he could not have hoped to avoid criticism, nor could he have expected to find a ready-made vehicle close at hand, waiting to transmit his feelings.

The Mass, though intended for liturgical use, failed by reason of its over-expressiveness. A related fault can be traced throughout the composer's other sacred offering of this period—the unpublished *Tour de Babel*, which was written in 1865. Rather than make the building of the tower the chief focus of musical interest, as Stravinsky was to do when he decided to tackle the same theme in 1944, Franck made the mistake of casting the whole work in the form of a listless, proselytizing dialogue in which God and Humanity are brought face to face—a confrontation made more precarious by the adoption of Latin as the medium of communication. Considering what opportunities for aural experiment were being given away with this subject, it is surprising how lame and conventional Franck's treatment sounds. There is virtually no attempt at depicting the rowdiness of the tribe, neither is there any hint of the viciousness against which the parable warns. From the purely musical angle, the best feature displayed by the work is its contrapuntal assurance, a habit that marked a genuine advance over the unimaginatively four-square writing we observe in Franck's earlier vocal compositions. Considered as a practice exercise, the work had its value in helping to standardize certain technical procedures the composer was to employ on a more extended scale in his oratorio *Les Béatitudes*, where the voice of Christ is heard declaiming at the conclusion of each of its episodes. It is not clear why Franck failed to find a publisher for *La Tour de Babel*. The music itself is no worse than that which comprises the weaker passages of *Rédemption* and in some respects does its composer credit. It must be admitted, however, that nowhere does he succeed in doing justice to the subject.

A more congenial proposition pressed itself on Franck's attention in 1869. This was when he began the long haul that was to end

ten years later with the completion of *Les Béatitudes*. He had often
mused on the possibility of setting these undramatic biblical tenets,
drawn from the Sermon on the Mount, but held back in the absence of a suitable poetic version of them. Eventually, he persuaded
a Mme Colomb—the wife of a professor at one of the city's
lycées—to try her hand at providing him with the text he desired.
Though no Emily Dickinson, the lady complied by producing a full,
if somewhat insipid, collection of verses, possessing enough literary
merit to send the composer scuttling to his writing desk. Unlike
some of his poetry-conscious pupils—Duparc and Chausson for
example—Franck was hardly the man to be inhibited by a mediocre
text. He was too unheroic to have shared in the typical bad taste
of his age—symbolized by the passion for Hugo and Lamartine—
but this had not prevented him from developing his own unctuous
preferences. These consisted of such drably pious verses as English
readers might have found among the pages of their parish magazine.
Probably no one but Franck, among the circle he frequented, would
have failed to alert himself to the dangers of setting an eight-part
poem, all the parts of which aspired to create a similar mood of
benign exhortation. It did not seem to occur to him, either at the
time of commencing work or later, that most people would find the
subject intolerably monotonous. It was not that Franck himself
altogether lacked volatility—there are several anecdotes which
suggest that he would sometimes erupt in a memorable flood of rage
or passion. But being naturally inclined to the gentler conceptions
of Christian teaching, he did not think it odd to build his works
largely or entirely around these aspects. Thus while *Les Béatitudes*
beautifully expresses the humility that lies at the centre of the
gospel, it often seems to deny the listener access to the wider range
of experience upon which this quality must seek to base itself. It is
as if Franck could only invade these less salubrious areas of experience by recourse to the principle of *noli me tangere*. What is gained
through a detailed delineation of one emotion is accordingly lost
by reason of an absence of any accompanying sense of worldliness.
At least, this is the impression a modern, sophisticated hearer tends
to take away with him.

The simplicity of Franck's plan may be judged from the fact
that, aside from inserting a brief prologue, nothing is allowed to
corrupt the sequence of the text. Each beatitude follows a set form,
which soon becomes predictable. This makes for easy divisions
and it can scarcely have amazed anyone to discover that the practice of abstracting sections of the work was quickly approved.
Franck himself never heard the Second and Seventh Beatitudes,
since their inclusion at the première was considered impracticable.
Though later performances have aimed at a complete and unmuti-

lated presentation, it is still quite common to hear selections from
the work played as though they comprised the whole; and even
single beatitudes are sometimes removed from context and offered
as concert pieces in their own right. The upshot has been that
problems of nomenclature continue to cling to the work in such a
way as to render it almost unique in the repertory of choral music.
Scarcely varied enough to warrant the title of oratorio, it has more
the appearance of a gigantic cantata. Perhaps the best description of
it is that which reckons it a fresco-symphony, conceived in vocal
and instrumental terms; something like those vast biblical wall-
paintings of the Early Renaissance which permit of inspection either
piecemeal or as a whole, and whose sum is not necessarily greater
than their parts. D'Indy called it a 'musical epic' and thereby
invoked a different source of comparison. His instinct was to place
it in a special category, one which also included Beethoven's *Missa
Solemnis*, Schumann's *Faust*, Berlioz's *Damnation* and the music
dramas of Richard Wagner. H. C. Colles, on the other hand, has
stated that the only other work it can profitably be compared with is
Brahms's *Requiem*, written in 1866. Despite the similarity in date,
it is out of the question that there could have been any mutual influences. Franck and Brahms did not admire one another, and
César would probably have applauded his admirer Dukas's remark
that Brahms was 'all beer and beard'.

Examination of the eight parts of *Les Béatitudes* reveals that
each canto has a similar ground plan. To begin, there is an exposition of a particular set of evils which it becomes the duty of man to
expunge; then follows a celestial prophecy; and finally the Voice of
Christ pronounces the message. Thus a kind of ternary form is imposed through the subject matter. This does not prevent other and
more localized forms from appearing. There is a double use of the
chorus.[1] Franck worked very slowly and methodically at his task,
and had completed only the Prologue and the First Beatitude by the
outbreak of the Franco-Prussian War. Having become sensitive to
the likelihood of failure, he took the precaution of consulting his
friends and pupils at every step in the work's progress. His customary way of doing this was by inducing them to listen to him
playing over the finished episodes at his apartment. By a strange
quirk of irony, it was this room that became the venue of the first
performance on 20 February 1879.

Possibly on account of their earlier date—before the post-war
group of pupils could be at hand to advise—the Prologue and First
Beatitude came to be recognized as the weakest parts of Franck's
score. The function of the Prologue is made explicit enough, with

[1] This takes the form of a terrestial chorus, on the one plane, and a
celestial chorus on the other. The two are joined in unison in places.

its tenor recitative and anticipations of the Christ theme, but there
is precious little musical interest to salvage it from the charge of
desultoriness. The tentative character of the material, which is
coaxed along by means of tired sequences, engenders a certain

Ex. 4

César Franck: Prologue - "Les Béatitudes"

impatience in the listener, who might justifiably have been led to
expect a more awe-inspiring evocation of the mountainside, not to
mention some signs denoting the presence of the multitude. After
this tepid opening, the First Beatitude shocks by its trivial theatric-
ality. It reminds us once more of the composer's early encirclement
by the forces of popular reaction. Appropriately, Franck rises to
higher standards with his setting of the Second Beatitude—which
has as its text the benediction 'Blessed are the meek'. Resorting to
fugue—a form at which he could give most of his rivals a good head
start—he was here able to convey a real sense of nobility. The inter-
jectory theme in B flat—relapsing into an anacrusis at the commencement of each bar—has pronounced rhythmic ingenuity,
and its vigour is maintained throughout the beautifully managed
succession of entries which follows. It is balanced by a strongly
compassionate quintet.

By comparison, the Third Beatitude presents opportunities for
illustrative music. Held together by the text 'Blessed are they that
mourn', it offers a variety of scenes of lamentation. First of all, we
are shown the victims of personal tragedy: a cast-down orphan
unable to withstand the perils of loneliness, a widower left inconsolable by the death of his beloved, a sorrowing mother bereft of
her son. Then follows a section in which the mourners are of a
different and more world-forsaken stamp: a slave who laments the
loss of his freedom in company with all his kind, and a philosopher
whose search for truth has ended in failure. All are paraded in
music of sombre dignity, each section being punctuated by repeti-
tions of the textual theme. When the Voice of Christ enters, it is
with the ascending motif of the Prologue, but now shorn of its
syncopations and impelled to ring out in even crotchets, the full
choir reverting to a unison for the occasion. This forms a fitting
climax to the entire episode. Critics are agreed that this Third
Beatitude represents the first musical peak in the work; though many
would go on to claim that it is topped by the Fourth. Here Franck's
inspiration is difficult to fault. Centred upon the message 'Blessed

are they that hunger and thirst after righteousness', it poses two contrasting motifs—one signifying 'desire' and the other 'repose'—which are expanded to form a lengthy introduction. The tonality of this section hovers between major and minor. At the climax, a theme of supplication is heard in Franck's favourite key of B major, and the episode ends on a note of sublime confidence. This Beatitude is possibly the most characteristic of the eight. Its brooding chromaticism and falling melodic sixths and sevenths mark it out as very typical of the composer's style. It is the only episode d'Indy conceded to be unflawed.

The Fifth Beatitude concerns itself with condoning the world's violence. It begins with a description of the crimes of humanity, and attempts to be harrowing after the fashion of the many uncontrite imitators of Meyerbeer. It could easily have taken its place in one of those 'heretics-and-martyrs' scenes with which the operas of the Second Empire seem congenitally endowed. This is hardly to deny that it makes a striking enough effect in its legitimate con-context. Embedded in so unbelievably pious a work, its appearance must have been greeted with relief by many a torpid listener; and the weight of the choral writing is certainly better than in the corresponding section of the First Beatitude. The celestial chorus at the end nicely offsets the more rebellious one in the early part, and brings the whole episode more into line with the tone of the complete work. It also shows Franck's uncanny power of radiance, when expressing the emotions that lay closest to his heart. 'Blessed are the pure in heart' becomes the appropriate theme of the Sixth Beatitude—which contrasts hypocritical sects like the Pharisees with those whose sincerity is adamant. Its most impressive moment comes when both are summoned before the Angel of Death at the last judgement. Franck for once makes a splendidly dramatic effect by modulating into the key of F sharp as a means of suggesting the recession of the heavenly portals. In the succeeding section, depicting the flight of angels, lies one of the finest melodies in the entire work. The climax is reached by an exhibition of decorative counterpoint for the soloists, a feat which provoked d'Indy to compare Franck's notation to the ornate floral garlands painted by Lippo Lippi and Fra Angelico.

After such sustained attempts to render the ineffable, it was essential for the remaining Beatitudes to feature more tangible emotions. The Seventh accordingly introduces the character of Satan, whose *esprit du mal* lacks any hint of Miltonic grandeur.[1]

---

[1] It certainly could not be said of Franck, as Dr L. A. Cormican has said of Milton, that '. . . his obvious emphasis falls on the vigour and resoluteness of Satan'.

Ex. 5

César Franck: Sixth Beatitude

His motif—beginning with a rising fourth and tracing the notes of the minor common chord—strikes us as suspiciously Wagnerian, and if we are not careful transports us from Hell to Valhalla in the space of a few bars. Set against the C minor reserved for the Prince of Darkness, Christ's recitative is sunk in the unassertive key of B flat. These tonal juxtapositions are extremely important to any consideration of the work as a whole. They rest on Franck's avowed principle of 'tonal architecture'. As with *The Ring* there is a mystical cycle of key relationships to be discerned in the work's successive episodes, a fact that makes nonsense of any cut version. In general, it could be said that Franck uses tonality according to what a psychologist would recognize as the principle of *synaesthesia*—or attribution of colour to sound. His heavily notated tonalities, such as D flat or F sharp, are meant to produce the effect of a sudden, rich splash of primary colour of the kind we experience when confronted by a flamboyant Veronese painting. Simpler keys, like F major or B flat, seem on the contrary to aim at a monochromatic vision such as we might get from looking at the work of an older master. Several times in the course of this composition the key of D major is singled out to express the Divine Mission, most notably at the end of the Sixth and Eighth Beatitudes. Occasionally, Franck seems to depart from this practice by utilizing the extreme flat keys to symbolize mourning. The far-reaching sharp keys, on the other hand, are always employed to suggest what d'Indy describes as 'the light of paradise'. Doubtless it was Beethoven who, more than Wagner, influenced Franck to think of identifying certain keys with particular sensations. Tonal architecture is not a principle that has commended itself to French composers of a later generation

than Franck. Instrumental coloration has proved a far more enticing rule, as we can confirm by a glance at the scores of Ravel or
Poulenc. It is significant that Honegger—another member of
'Les Six'—spoke out strongly against tonal architecture shortly
before his death in 1956, saying that he likened it to painting in
which the artist selected his palette beforehand.[1] To that extent, it
does seem opposed to the principle of inspiration. For Franck,
however, with his organist's feeling for long-range modulation, it
obviously had its advantages.

The character of the Eighth Beatitude once again takes shape
from the dialogue between Christ and Satan. Cast down at the
end of the previous episode, the latter is vastly more impressive on
his re-appearance. Stepping out of the cardboard frame in which he
had been encased, he strikes a menacing note for the first time.
Christ's role is limited to simple expressions of denial. This situation should have offered Franck unequivocal scope for a dramatic
representation of evil, yet the opportunity is fumbled. The devilish
threats which emerge are cast in music that is much too suave to
arouse a genuine sense of horror, while the choral invocations, with
the exception of the celebrated 'O Eternal Justice', do little to
exonerate the composer from the charge of flatulence. We have to
wait for the Virgin's delicate Mater Dolorosa, expressing the self-
sacrifice that lies at the heart of love, before encountering a fresh
spurt of inspiration. At this point in the narrative, Satan is forced
to acknowledge the hopelessness of his cause, and retires to the
outer regions. To end, the pure Voice of Christ is heard, proclaiming humanity regenerate, while the choirs, terrestial and celestial,
are massed in a triumphal succession of hosannas. The abrupt
modulations of this Eighth Beatitude go further towards defining
the essential Franck than any other passages in the work. Their
originality may be deduced from the embarrassments they caused
the singers when the score was at last brought to light. Adverse
critics have nevertheless complained that Franck's obsession with
modulation is nothing more than a careful ruse, designed to divert
attention from the work's melodic paucity. Yet the composer surely
deserves some credit for having led his contemporaries away from
the stodgy round of keys favoured by imitators of the classical
tradition. It is not too much to claim that, because of Franck's
willingness to pioneer in this matter, the way was left open for
truly *avant-garde* composers like Satie and Debussy.

[1] It is interesting to recall that more than one painter has none the
less detected in Franck a legitimate model for his own activities. Thus
Gauguin wrote: 'Cézanne, pour citer un ancien, semble être un élève de
César Franck.' His remark gives us a further insight into the period's
astonishing artistic fusion.

Despite the experimental character of the harmony, and a few supremely successful moments of drama, the effect of this composition in performance is curiously unsatisfying. Critics are inclined to turn, in the end, to more conventional works, such as the Requiems of Fauré and Brahms, in preference to Franck's *magnum opus*. It would take a rescue operation of the greatest ingenuity to restore *Les Béatitudes* to the high pedestal it occupied in its composer's imagination. That Franck never ceased to set enormous store by the work is quite evident from his reported conversations. We may guess, therefore, how painful must have been the spectacle presented by the first performance, when the audience straggled out one by one, leaving only the faithful Lalo and Joncières to stay to the end. Buoyed up by his own enthusiasm, Franck had sent out invitations to a wide range of celebrities, including the Minister of Fine Arts, and the Directors of both the Opéra and the Conservatoire, only to have them returned with polite regrets a few days later. When the evening of the performance came round, he found himself with only twenty singers to act as the chorus, and was reduced to substituting a piano for the score's full orchestra. Somewhat characteristically, he was even prevented from taking a personal role, a sprained wrist having put him out of action a mere twenty-four hours beforehand. D'Indy has recorded how unnerved he was at having the piano score thrust into his hands at such short notice. By all accounts, the performance was so bad as to have rendered any judgement of music premature. Franck disguised his disappointment by a brilliant display of tact. 'Of one thing I am certain,' he is reported to have said to his wife at the end of the evening, 'it is a very fine work.' This excess of charity towards those responsible for desecrating his efforts seems to have been a firmly entrenched habit with the composer. He is remembered for the bland satisfaction he exhibited after Colonne had botched the première of *Rédemption* in 1873; and again when the Third and Eighth Beatitudes were mishandled by Lamoureux's orchestra during the 1887 festival. It could not have been that he was all that modest about his achievements; merely perhaps that he had been deprived of recognition for so long that even the most blundering restitution had come to seem acceptable.

The first uncut performance of *Les Béatitudes* had to wait until after Franck's death. It took place on 19 March 1893, at one of the Concerts Colonne. Reviews of this event are quite likely to have been coloured by the guilt critics felt at having helped to send the composer to his grave unsung. Jullien was obliged to restrain certain remorseful commentators whose efforts to redress the balance had clearly gone too far. He drew attention to one article in the *Débats* which described *Les Béatitudes* as:

... the most powerful work produced for at least thirty years ... on a level with Bach's B minor Mass and Wagner's *Parsifal*.

As Franck's posthumous reputation gathered strength, many identical testimonials were hastily trumped up. M. Georges Servières, for example, spoke of:

... this grand musical work, where the severity of the oratorio form is tempered by the tenderest inspiration; where Christian mysticism expresses itself with a wonderful suavity, without the melodic grace ever degenerating into mawkishness or insipidity; where is revealed a sincere compassion for the humble, the suffering and the afflicted; where the depth of feeling is only equalled by the most consummate contrapuntal science, the purity of style, the elegance and boldness of the harmony; where the employment of scholastic forms and polyphonic complexity blend in a stream of exquisite melodies.

This style of encomium quickly spread to England where, as may be imagined, the attractions of a large-scale choral work on a biblical theme were not permitted to pass unnoticed. The late Sir Henry Wood gave a performance of it at the Sheffield Festival of 1908, though it had previously been performed, either in part or as a whole, at Cardiff, Hereford and Glasgow. By this time, the British public was ready to be enlightened about the composer's merits, and reviews of his compositions had begun to appear in several of the leading journals. The wide circulation which attached to Arthur Hervey's book, *French Music in the Nineteenth Century*, must also have had its effect. This author did much to stimulate the vogue for Franck, which reached a chauvinistic peak at the time of the Allied struggle against Germany, when the reaction to Wagner became less worshipful. His summing-up of *Les Béatitudes* carries all the marks of lavishness first detectable in his French predecessors:

The profound humanity, the depth of feeling, the transcendental beauty of the music, all combine to render *Les Béatitudes* one of the greatest masterpieces of the art.

Even so, there had remained musicians in both countries whose attitudes were not so charitable. Camille Bellaigue proved obdurate in his dislike of Franck, finding the work in question lacking in melody and variety of expression, strained in harmony and opaque in orchestration. Ravel was another detractor, though not Debussy.

The former remained unrepentant to the extent of writing to his friend Jean Marnold: 'I know what to expect from those neo-Christian adepts, but I don't care!' In 1906 his protests did not meet with much approval, and he had to wait for the 1920s to break down the soggy climate of adulation that had sprung up. When the reaction set in, it was not so much bitter as derisive. André de Ternant's hoax in *The Choir*—in which he portrayed an imaginary Franck living it up in the London taverns—was typical of the debunking spirit soon to follow.[1] Meantime, English critics were also slow to give up their admiration. Constant Lambert roused the opposition in his *Music Ho!*, but W. J. Turner and others continued to present a strong case for the defence. At the present time, opinions of Franck's churchly works have tended to lower his stock rather than raise it. The more cynical critics are inclined to stigmatize him as an *eminence grise* whose influence has been emasculating. To this extent, it is tempting to compare his effect on French music to that of Catholic writers, such as Claudel and Mauriac, on French literature. Franck's straightforward goodness—as represented in his religious works—has come to seem merely sanctimonious to a generation which prefers its saints tainted with the flavour of sin. Among the composer's main offences is the shallow treatment he accords to evil, an error for which existentialists will find it hard to forgive him. As Martin Cooper has wittily suggested:

> ... there is no strong contrast between evil and good, merely a beautiful, if rather insipid, atmosphere of religious tenderness broken here and there by descents, not into Hell, but into the duller purlieus of the Opera.

Until there is a return to the fashion which exalts pure faith, this is the verdict with which we are most likely to be left.

Meantime, it is necessary to pick up the train of events comprising the composer's daily existence. Long before that fateful day in 1879, when *Les Béatitudes* fell so excruciatingly upon the ear, there had been happenings of paramount importance for Franck's later career as a teacher. He had begun, in the middle of the 1860s, to gather about him a tiny, but highly talented, band of more advanced pupils. These men expressed an admiration that was soon to transcend all contractual obligations. Included among his circle of wider acquaintances, there appeared a number of established artists whose gifts had already stood them firmly on their own feet. It was to them that the composer came to look for moral support

---

[1] The locale in which de Ternant cast his victim was particularly misleading, since Franck was never known to have set foot in England.

and encouragement. Assurance was likewise becoming the keynote of his domestic life, the deaths of two children in infancy having by now become a memory.[1] His surviving sons, Georges and Germain, were growing up at an alarming rate; they would soon be of marriageable age themselves. Meanwhile, he and Félicité had settled down to a long period of contentment, with no hint of the rifts destined to cloud their later years. She delighted in copying out his scores, and in advising him on the tactful handling of his charges. While Franck continued to write in the vein of *Les Béatitudes* and *Rédemption* her disposition sweetened visibly. Her habit of prolonged nagging—ostensibly caused by the composer's decision to switch to the writing of chamber music—was something that did not develop for another decade. Finally, and most crucially of all, came the calamitous war with Prussia, followed immediately by the horrors of the Commune. These tragic events temporarily overshadowed everything else in Franck's life, as well as in the lives of his pupils and family. Since he chose to remain in the capital during the upheavals they caused, it is not surprising that he was forced to break his routine to the extent of helping to relieve the famine, and learning to write, not religious epics, but patriotic odes, akin to those wrung from him by the 1848 catastrophe. Indeed the year 1871 may be regarded—in the light of its similarity to the earlier revolutionary date—as a second turning point in Franck's career. Though he was not to know it then, it marked the end of his most intense period of hibernation, and signalled the beginning of what was eventually to be a new and talked-about career as a teacher at the Conservatoire and official at the Société Nationale. It is to the earliest of these changes that we must now give our attention.

The widening of Franck's social contacts came about gradually and undramatically. We have already stated that his organ playing tended to attract a large crowd of casual visitors to Sainte-Clotilde. By the middle of the 1860s, it became apparent to the authorities that they had a very remarkable person in their employ. One fine day in April 1866 no less a figure than Franz Liszt—now penitently clad in a black cassock, though still out to impress the villagers with his knee-breeches and buckled shoes—turned up at the church to hear his old protégé perform. Brushing aside Franck's modest protestations, he demanded a preview of the organist's compo-

[1] These were Marie-Joseph (1849–50) and Paul (1856–9). Georges, who was the eldest, lived on until 1910, pursuing a reasonably distinguished career in academic circles and rigorously defending his father's memory. The remaining son, Germain, was born in 1853 and died in 1912. He became an Inspector with the French Railways, working in the department of bridges and footpaths.

sitions; and was rewarded with the *Six Pièces* and the works of other musicians. Deeply moved by what he had heard, the ageing maestro was seen leaving the church muttering the name of J. S. Bach in comparison. At their reunion, Liszt had remarked—'How could I ever forget the composer of those Trios?' The reply which came back—'I fancy I have done better things since'—proves that Franck's self-effacement had its limits, and that he was not above a friendly dig at the complacency of his well-wishers.[1] It is also interesting to have evidence, directly in Liszt's own words, of the great impression made by the early chamber music. Much could be learnt from a comparative study of the styles of Franck and Liszt, not all of which would point to the superiority of the Hungarian composer. Liszt's pilgrimage to Sainte-Clotilde must be regarded as an entirely unbidden proclamation of debt from one of the major names in European music. And as such it was undoubtedly viewed by all who were appraised of it. Whether or not Franck's colleagues were taken aback by the veneration accorded to their local precentor, their attitudes were henceforth considerably more respectful. It had become evident that the new organist of Sainte-Clotilde was a figure to be reckoned with.

Several years later, as if by grateful reparation, it was Franck's own turn to pay tribute to a neglected organist-composer. This was none other than Anton Bruckner, whom he chanced to hear at Notre-Dame in May, 1869. The shy and gauche Austrian musician from the Abbey of St Florian, near Linz, bore a striking resemblance to Franck in background, character and musical inclinations. They had both been handicapped by a provincial upbringing, yet had managed to win a host of prizes. Their paths, moreover, had led in the common direction of the church, and what was more the Catholic Church. Add to this the fact that each man could be described as a great organist who perversely cherished the vocation of composer, and the likeness seems near enough to complete. Yet they had their differences. Unlikely as it may sound, Franck was probably the more worldly of the pair. It would be ludicrous to imagine that Liszt, with his cosmopolitan airs, could have found anything to admire in the Austrian composer's rustic simplicity. And try as we may, we can never credit Franck with the tactlessness of which Bruckner was guilty on innumerable occasions—as for example when he pressed a coin into the great Hans Richter's unsuspecting palm, after that conductor had directed the première

[1] On another occasion, Franck is said to have told a tactless pupil who waxed eloquent about Wagner in his presence—'I have no need of being reminded what he did'. There is no doubt that certain of these innocent-sounding rebukes were meant to point up the shameful neglect from which the composer suffered.

of his Fourth Symphony.[1] The differences emerge equally clearly
from a consideration of their respective musical canons. Bruckner,
being unwaveringly devout in his habits, regarded each and every
work he wrote as an offering to his God. Franck, on the other hand,
had been an active, if not very willing, supporter of Mammon; at
least to the extent of having courted a reputation in both the
theatre and salon. It is a pity that no one thought of recording the
conversation these two spiritual giants had at Notre-Dame on that
touching visit. Perhaps they actually said very little to each other,
since neither man could be said to have been strikingly articulate
and it is most unlikely that they were familiar with one another's
compositions or language. All we know is that Franck was thrilled
by what he heard.

At the time of this meeting, Bruckner had written only the first
of his nine symphonies and had just moved from Linz to Vienna.
These two cities played much the same part in his development as
Liège and Paris had done in Franck's. That is to say, they symbolized the limits within which his ambition had been obliged to concentrate. Assured of his organist's post at St Florian, Bruckner,
like Franck, had not been able to resist the temptation to sound the
pulse of the big city; though in his case the object of his quest was
nothing more reproachful than a chair at the university. Both composers found their excursion into the metropolis more than they
bargained for, and both came near to despairing over the tedium
of having to pursue futile, underpaid appointments. Sir Neville
Cardus has penetratingly conveyed their differences in stating:

> The two composers lived and worked at the same time, but
> they really had little in common except devotion to the organ
> and religion. Bruckner was very much the peasant by nature;
> Franck can never be thought of as a peasant. He was not naïve
> and unworldly in Bruckner's way. The chromatic melody of
> Franck lapses often into sentimentality or the sensuous. In
> Bruckner there is no weak or lush chromaticism, no senti-
> mentality, certainly little or no sensuousness. Architecturally,
> Franck may be related to the Gothic, Bruckner to the
> Baroque . . .[2]

[1] The story goes that when the Emperor Franz Josef once asked
Bruckner whether there was anything he could do for him, the harassed
composer begged him to do something about Hanslick, the Viennese
music critic whose animosity he had aroused.

[2] Essays on both composers are contained in Sir Neville's book, *A
Composer's Eleven* (Jonathan Cape, 1958). For a fuller account of
Bruckner's concert tours in France and England, the reader is recom-
mended to consult E. Doernberg: *The Life and Symphonies of Anton
Bruckner* (Barrie & Rockliff, 1960).

Bruckner's journey to France seems to have been made at the suggestion of his future enemy Hanslick; who at that time had no special cause to feel relieved at his absence. The tour included a recital at Nancy, where he played on the new organ at Sainte-Epvre. The organ-building firms, like Merklin-Schutze and Cavaillé-Coll, took immense satisfaction in his performances, since they had the effect, like Franck's own, of helping to sell instruments. The French press was also extremely enthusiastic, unlike the English papers were to be a few years later during the composer's London debut. Among the audience at his Notre-Dame recital were Saint-Saëns, Gounod and Auber; and all these astute judges were quick to echo Franck's praise.

A third acquaintance with whom Franck was to strike up a lasting friendship dating from this time was the ebullient Chabrier. Historians will continue to remain puzzled at the attractions which brought these two men together. For if Bruckner had his resemblances to Franck, none could have been more of his opposite than this roisterous Southerner, who combined an unlikely career as a clerk in the Ministry of the Interior with a fanatical passion for Wagner and Spanish señoras. One can imagine that Franck's theatrical mother-in-law would have found much to delight her in Chabrier's scabrous behaviour, so well adapted was it to providing entertainment for his less prudish friends. To Franck, on the other hand, his antics must have seemed vaguely embarrassing. Demuth relates with what delight the portly little extrovert sought to bring a flush of colour to the cheeks of his more pious companion, regaling him with racy accounts of his meetings with the toreros and hip-swinging beauties of Andalusia. Knowing Franck's highly circumspect tastes, it surprises us to learn how benignly he tolerated these good-natured provocations. Perhaps he looked upon their author, much like the ephemeral operettas he sometimes sneaked off to see, as a necessary projection of the lighter and more repressed side to his nature; a harmless personification of the fantasies his sterner self proscribed. At all events, so perfect were their respective impersonations of the spirit and the flesh that, were it not for a common want of height, their appearance together must inevitably have suggested Don Quixote and Sancho Panza. They were unlike in many other respects too: Chabrier always striving to be in the midst of every artistic coterie (he was an avid collector who became the first owner of Manet's celebrated 'Bar aux Folies-Bergère' as well as a number of Monets, Renoirs and Sisleys), while Franck seemed to retreat further and further into his encapsulated world of crotchets and quavers. Equally divergent were their literary inclinations, Franck accepting whatever text was thrust at him, while Chabrier was busy being initiated into the cult of Verlaine. Even their personal habits were incompatible, one proving an inveterate traveller, telling lies to his superior at the Ministry so that he could slide off to Germany, while the other remained an incorrigible stay-at-home to the end of his days. Most astonishing of all is the fact that their music stood at the widest possible extremes—the 'Marche Joyeuse' and 'España' as against the Panis Angelicus and the Trios. Yet somehow, despite all their oppositions of purpose and temperament, these two men found it possible to love and respect one another with that fervour which seems reserved for those who are both French and middle-aged.

But this is to anticipate. At the time of their first meeting Chabrier was no more than a promising amateur to whom Franck must have appeared, if not quite in the guise of 'Father Franck', at least as more of a mentor than a friend. Their gradual intimacy was something that emerged out of the shoulder-to-shoulder campaign they undertook on behalf of the Société Nationale; and that benevolent institution was not formed until the way had been cleared for a more worthy expression of national pride. During the early days of his clerkship—which he was unable to relinquish until 1880—Chabrier's boon companions were the voluble idlers who met at Nina's salon, in particular the Parnassian poets Leconte de Lisle and Théodore de Banville.[1] These men taught that art was a religion whose practice depended on a scrupulous use of form, combined with an ability to handle the subtlest shades of colour. The latter principle strikes us as having helped to determine Chabrier's own approach to his medium, since there have been few composers more deft in applying tonal contrasts. Though he is best known today for his operas and orchestral show-pieces, this typical native of Auvergne began his musical career at the piano—an instrument he soon became notorious for abusing. Detaille's famous caricature—in which he is portrayed thundering away at the keyboard, swaddled in a shapeless overcoat and surrounded by a litter of empty bottles—illustrates both the character and the style of life this engaging bohemian delighted in displaying. Cortot has recorded that after one visit the composer paid to Ambert, all the pianos in the district had to be sent away for repair, eye-witnesses having testified that broken strings and fragments of ivory were to be seen hurtling from his vicinity like mortar fire. He did not travel to Spain—the country evoked in so many of his compositions—until 1882, so that at this time his sentiments were unexceptionably French. His presence at Franck's side is worth mentioning, if only to point up his superiority as a builder of

[1] De Lisle was a source of inspiration to many French musicians—providing Fauré with the lyrics for *Nell* and *Les Roses d'Ispahan* and Franck himself with the text of *Les Eolides*.

literary rapprochements. It was this failure to look beyond the boundaries of his art that was to mark off Franck from the other progressive musicians of the Republic, those whose talents were to unite under the banner of Impressionism.

The pupils who joined him during the years immediately preceding the war were the first to be recognized as belonging to 'la bande à Franck'. What brought them together as much as anything was their feeling that the composer of *Les Béatitudes* was exploring a world apart. The late William McNaught once remarked that French music could be likened to a light and elegant fabric; but that Franck's school stood to one side like 'a solid and heavily built annexe'. It may have been just this desire to escape the taint of finery—exchanging graceful lines for the security of bricks and mortar—that inspired the original nucleus of students. The forceful advocacy of Henri Duparc, however, was what prompted their decision. To him also goes the distinction of having been the first of the few. To state that the coming together of the remainder was in some measure accidental would be to cast doubt on our principal thesis. Yet there was an element of chance in the fortuitousness by which Franck hit upon Duparc as the self-appointed recruiting officer for his troop. The Collège de Vaugirard was, after all, only one of his many ports of call as a teacher, and there was no reason to think that young Duparc had ever contemplated a career in music. Once his interest had been enlisted, however, things began to move. The image of Duparc which often percolates down to us from surveys of the period is that of a withdrawn and neurotic aesthete.[1] This altogether fails to make clear the incomparable role he pursued as a catalyst of talent—not merely during his later championship of the Wagnerian cause, but at the time of the Franck circle's inception. It is well known that he ministered to the growing pains of the Société Nationale, but few critics seem to realize what a crucial function he performed on behalf of French music even before the founding of that admirable institution. Right from the start of his pupillage, he showed a rare understanding of his teacher's gifts, making it his duty to acquaint others with the quality of instruction he was receiving.[2] When he persuaded Alexis

[1] I have attempted to correct this image in the chapter—entitled 'Henri Duparc: An Aesthetic Tragedy'—contained in my book *The Gallic Muse* (Dent, 1967). Interested readers should also consult Dr Northcote's admirable book on the composer.

[2] It is worth stressing his work as a propagandist for Franck as a corrective to the widely-held assumption that it was d'Indy alone who did all the canvassing. The point is that, whereas d'Indy did miracles for Franck's posthumous reputation, Duparc performed his part while the composer was still alive and unknown.

de Castillon to drop his lessons with the superficial Victor Massé, and d'Indy to renounce his fashionable interest in the city's operatic cliques, he went far towards setting these musicians a more ascetic ideal—one that was bound, in the end, to lead to Franck. That he was unwilling to leave even this to chance is proved by the fact that it was Duparc himself who introduced both musicians to their future master. Meanwhile, Arthur Coquard—who stood midway between Castillon and d'Indy in age, and shared some of the latter's infatuation with opera—took advantage of his position as a fellow-pupil at Vaugirard to find his own way into the composer's graces. His period of advocacy was to come later, when he fulfilled a valuable role in attracting students to Franck's organ class at the Conservatoire. Albert Cahen, yet another Parisian, brought up the rear. What distinguished these pupils from the earlier batch Franck had taught was their overriding quality of seriousness. In making no secret of their intention to become composers, they showed themselves capable of looking beyond the executant aim. Moreover, they were eager to submit to the most rigorous criticism, having no illusions about the corrupt state of musical taste. Essentially reflective in their outlook, they sought escape from the shallow values of the metropolis, being anxious to repair to a place of artistic sanctuary where they could nurture their gifts in peace and silence. Too individual to have made headway under a conventional teacher—though not clever enough to dispense with all instruction—their search was for a man who could coerce without stooping to humiliate. In Franck they discovered the object of their quest.

The expansion of this straggle of followers into a tightly-knit community did not come about at once. Their affiliations took place at different times and in different circumstances. Castillon, who was among the earliest to have attached himself, was present in 1868, while d'Indy did not officially join with the others until 1872, the year in which he enrolled in Franck's class at the Conservatoire. One of the intriguing features displayed by the group as a whole was its exalted social caste. Entitled to describe himself as a Vicomte, d'Indy could trace his ancestry back to Henri IV. This did not succeed in raising him above the level of his fellow-pupils, since Castillon laid claim to the same rank, and was possibly from an even richer family. They were both aristocrats of unimpeachable standing in the community. Though none of the remaining pupils offered such an impressive pedigree, there were several who had no need to work for a living. Chausson, to take the obvious case, was an extremely wealthy man, to whom music figured as something of an avocation. It was a matter of continual annoyance to him that critics paid all their attention to professionals. The rest of the group were used to a mundane existence, but they did not lack connections. They were not, as Debussy was revealed to be, products of an artisan environment.[1]

The other characteristic Franck's earliest pupils had in common was a decided military fervour and allegiance. Duparc was quick to enlist in the 18th Battalion of the Mobile Guard as soon as hostilities threatened, leaving Coquard and d'Indy to take up their positions with other units. All three played a part in the defence of Paris. Meantime, Castillon, who had previously held a commission in the Imperial Cavalry, was recalled to his regiment elsewhere. Even the comically inglorious figure of Saint-Saëns was to be seen staggering through the Faubourg St Honoré in a shapeless private's regalia. This eagerness to leap into uniform may be attributed in part to the exceptionally combative outlook Frenchmen were encouraged to display during the time of Louis Napoléon, when no effort was spared to revive the concept of heroism which had been expressed earlier at Jena and Wagram. Even making full allowance for this tendency, however, the forcefulness of Franck's gathering cannot help imposing itself, for it stands in blunt contrast to the master's own timidity.

The war was crucial to the lives of all who elected to remain in Paris in the face of the Prussian invasion. Although the Emperor's adventuresome foreign policy had contributed to the state of tension which existed between the two nations, it was actually Bismarck's falsification of King William's telegram (on the business of the Hohenzollern candidacy and the Spanish Crown) that provoked them into slaughter. It was a flimsy excuse to go to war on, but it sufficed to satisfy the German dream of a renewed European hegemony. At the outset, few Frenchmen took the fighting seriously. 'There seems to be a great deal of prologue to the Taming of this German Shrew', was how one literate Parisian was inclined to put it. But the facts were more pessimistic. They revealed an absent Emperor—laid low by an attack of gall stones—and a badly divided populace. Having foolishly proclaimed the Empress as regent, Louis was surprised at the depth of resentment the country directed at her. A silly and superstitious woman—nicknamed 'L'Espagnole' by sceptical republicans—she had aroused public wrath on more than one occasion by her unwise attempts to influence imperial decisions. Now that she was in control, a spirited liberal opposition sprang up which had the effect of placing the country's unity in jeopardy. The cries of 'À Berlin' which had emanated from every corner cafe during the opening phase of the campaign rapidly gave way to a more realistic

[1] Among other Franck pupils, Pierre de Bréville, Paul de Wailly and Louis de Serres all belonged to the upper reaches of the bourgeoisie.

appraisal of the situation. One of the few French officers to sense the danger the nation was in was General d'Hautpoul. His summing-up of his Prussian opposite number had a fatalistic ring to it: 'Moltke has the gift of the great billiard-player. He knows beforehand the exact results of a shock between two bodies at a certain angle'. Beginning with a crushing defeat at Wissembourg (wrongly reported in the French press as a victory), and an even more humiliating one at Metz to follow, the Empire could do little to withstand the pressure. It conceded at Sedan on 2 September, 1870.

Within a fortnight of the capitulation, Prussian troops were besieging the gates of Paris, and there began four gruelling months of cruelty and starvation. Every able-bodied man offered to help in easing the terrible hardships to be witnessed on all sides. Franck's sons had already pledged themselves to their country, and it says much for the composer's own loyalty that he did not allow his advancing years to keep him from volunteering. As it turned out, his role was confined to seeing that the food and fuel supplies were kept running—an arduous enough undertaking in circumstances of looting and malnutrition. Duparc, writing in the *Revue Musicale* in 1922, recalled with emotion the sight of Franck stumbling from street to street with buckets full of coal to warm the aged. His own family was reduced to serving hot chocolate in place of meals. It was during this year of tragedy that Franck composed his ode 'Paris, queen of all cities'. Actually, it was never completely written out, possibly because a performance at that time would have seemed particularly inopportune. The loss of his pupils permitted the composer ample time in which to continue other musical projects which he had begun, the most important of all being *Les Béatitudes*.[1] Castillon has recorded how he listened to parts of the work at the apartment in the Boulevard St Michel during the early days of the siege. The experience compelled him to remark:

> People have said that Fra Angelico painted with his inner soul, and the same might be said of Franck. He has the soul of a seraph.

This power of spiritual isolation in moments of crisis was always to serve the composer well. It may be that the quiet meditation in which he was forced to indulge at this period was what led directly to the formation of his third and most serene manner. Those

[1] There was also another patriotic ode—based on Hugo's *Les Chatiments*—which Duparc encouraged the composer to write during the Commune. It was not published until 1917.

friends and pupils who were stationed in the capital did not lose time in visiting him whenever the opportunity presented itself, which was more often than might be supposed. The joy attaching to these evenings was unforgettable, and the ties formed in happier days were not broken. Thus when the fighting at last came to an end, it was possible to visualize the moment when the circle would re-unite, its members more determined than ever to assert the ideals they had come together to serve.

Unfortunately, the armistice brought with it only the promise of further conflict. This appeared in the shape of the Commune, whose object was to secure acceptance for the revolutionary ideas France had seen fit to betray—once in 1793 and again in 1848. This time the party began with more advantages. The folly of the monarchy needed no demonstrating, and the ineptitude of the right-wing stood revealed for all to see. Most reasonable men were accordingly inclined to uphold the progressive cause. The withdrawal of the Government to Versailles became the signal for a surge of confidence in the republican camp. If only the provinces had been behind the insurgents at this stage, France would quickly have fallen into their hands. But the reverse proved to be the case. Though impotent to restrain the rebels, Thiers could afford to play a waiting game, building up his troops till the moment came for a return coup. By ridding himself of the extremists and issuing a number of false promises to the waverers (many of whom were shamelessly massacred once order had been restored), the cunning old fox was able to get round his difficulties and put the Assembly back on its feet. During these unsettling manoeuvres, most of the ex-National Guardsmen in Paris were subjected to the threats of the Communards. Fauré fled to Rambouillet, while Saint-Saëns beat a hasty retreat across the channel to England, where Gounod was waiting to receive him. Franck, whose republican sentiments had worn a trifle thin with the years, decided to stay where he was —though not without considerable apprehension. That he too feared some kind of reprisal is suggested by the tentative plan he worked out to remove himself to Belgium. This scheme might have materialized if Franck had been appointed to the Directorship of the Liège Conservatoire, a post for which he applied unsuccessfully at this time. Fortunately for French music, nothing else intervened to uproot him from what he had by now come to regard as his native soil.

What the war—both at home and abroad—succeeded in doing for Franck and his pupils cannot be measured in terms of posts occupied or loyalties strengthened. Its impact was so drastic and purifying as to transform the entire fabric of French culture, proposing a new set of goals for both society and the artist. One thing that stood out was that the Empire's decadence would not be allowed to corrupt the taste of yet another generation. National pride—sorely inflamed by revelations of incompetence—at last turned to ways of amending the country's archaic institutional structure. Bored with the perennial round of valour and gaiety, the people quickly assumed a more serious aspect, wishing to restore to their proper place the useful and self-improving pursuits which their former Emperor had seen fit to spurn. The time was in fact ripe for a thorough re-appraisal of the role of the arts in a well-regulated community. Already a vigorous group of literary critics, historians and philosophers were at hand to point out the changes needed. Taine, Renan and Zola were among these torch-bearers of the new society. Scolded or made to languish in obscurity by the pre-war public, they were now elevated to positions of power and influence; positions they were not slow to use to the maximum of their very persuasive talents. Most of the darlings of the romantic age had in any case died off either during or shortly after the struggle, so that the way was left open for a fresh series of prophets. Victor Hugo, it is true, managed to soldier on until 1885, but his premature semblance to a national monument was sufficiently indicated by the army of top-hatted bureaucrats who followed his remains to their resting-place in the Pantheon. For the more progressive individual, the Third Republic offered un-limited scope for social and cultural experiment, greater frankness and realism, and an end to mirthless frivolity.

It would be pointless to pretend that the high-minded visions of the Franck circle were of signal importance in spurring on these changes. Rather they were lucky to reap the consequences of the new climate of enlightenment. As a non-representational art, music lagged behind in its capacity to reflect these and other transforma-tions, and the first thrusts of progress were observed in literature and painting. Franck accordingly had to wait another full decade —longer if we think of him primarily as a composer—before his work was appreciated. Even so, the years immediately following the war were among the most essential in laying the foundation for his acclaim. They saw him move from his secluded position in the wings of French cultural life nearer and nearer to the centre of the stage. They carried him from his modest outpost at Sainte-Clotilde to the headquarters of musical planning and consultation. The next steps in his career—signified by the founding of the Société Nationale; the acquisition of a further batch of talented pupils; and the appointment to a professorship at the Conservatoire —belong to a later stage of the story we have to tell. Meantime, it is necessary to take leave of Franck himself and turn to the con-tribution made by his principal disciples. For it is surely incumbent upon us to assess how far the achievements of the circle rested on their shoulders as opposed to those of the founder. In examining the work and personalities of d'Indy, Castillon, Coquard, Cahen, Duparc and Chausson—to say nothing of the less prominent figures—we may hope to reveal something of the rich variety of talent to which the circle gave birth. Only afterwards shall we be justified in returning to describe Franck's last phase. For if it is true that the composer of *Les Béatitudes* had a marked and lasting influence on his pupils, so these same young men contributed to create the man who was to sign his name to the Symphony in D minor, the String Quartet and the Violin Sonata.

Before embarking on this survey, there may be some advantage in pausing to consider the prospect which spread itself beneath their gaze. We have already commented on the change of public conscience brought about by the establishing of the Third Republic. At the same time as we begin our analysis of the musical achievements of the new age, it might be as well to remind ourselves of what an extraordinary flowering of aesthetic ideas was about to take place. Historians of culture have been inclined to label it a silver age: and measured against the standards of the High Renaissance this is perhaps the highest accolade we can confer upon it. Yet the period from 1870 to the outbreak of the First World War must be seen as one during which the level of attainment was fixed at an astonishingly stable point, not simply in one particular art but in all of the arts. It was the period, above all, which gave rise to the modern movement, the tendrils of which are still reaching out into our present civilization. Richard Anthony Leonard has indicated the magnificent tide of imagination that swept through the visual and literary cultures once the gates of freedom had been flung open:

> There is no mystery about the after-effect of the Franco-Prussian War of 1870. Following that humiliating defeat the entire French nation underwent a catharsis. Revolt against the existing order was nowhere more strongly motivated than in the arts. In literature, the lead passed to the realists, headed by Zola, Maupassant and Daudet. Zola's theme was a gigantic scouring of the degenerate society whose diseased roots trailing back to the Second Empire, had ruined France. From his naturalism grew a new literature all over Europe and America. In painting, there arose the most famous art movement in modern times—impressionism. It was founded by Manet, Pisarro, Monet, Renoir, Sisley, Guillaumin and Cézanne; and it indirectly sired Degas, Toulouse-Lautrec, Van Gogh, Gauguin and Seurat. The movement began with

Manet's struggles against the reactionary salon painters, as early as 1859: but the First Impressionist Exhibition which crystallized the idea dated from 1874. In the next twenty-five years these men and their followers produced an art which is one of the permanent assets of French culture.[1]

The musical counterpart to these brilliant uprisings did not get under way with anything like the same speed, not gathering its full force until the *fin-de-siècle* and beyond. It began with the writing of Debussy's *Prélude à l'après-midi d'un faune* in 1894, and reached a pinnacle of success with the Diaghilev ballet's production of Ravel's *Daphnis et Chloé* in 1912. Between these years French music displayed something of that confidence and élan which had been evident at the earlier stage in the representational arts. They were the years of *Pelléas et Mélisande* and *Ariane et Barbe-bleue* at the opera; of the *Histoires Naturelles* and *Fêtes Galantes* in the sphere of song; of pianistic triumphs such as *Gaspard de la Nuit* and the *Images*; and finally of the early chamber music of Magnard and Roussel. The interest which attaches to the music of Franck's pupils lies chiefly in the degree to which it anticipates these revolutionary developments. Yet it would be shameful if our curiosity were to proceed no further. For composers like Castillon, d'Indy, Duparc and Chausson demand—and fully deserve—the most individual critical treatment. To regard them simply as precursors—even though that is what, in certain respects, they were—would be to acquiesce in the tamest of musical judgements. In fact each of these men had something intensely personal to say, something no other musician has been able to voice on their behalf. As well as being pioneers, busily engaged in forging a sense of national pride, they were unique and subjective artists. And in many cases, it was the artist who managed to triumph over the innovator, the *homme de goût* over the propagandist. It is to a consideration of the achievements of these neglected figures that we must now turn.

[1] The description is contained in Mr Leonard's general historical survey—*The Stream of Music* (Hutchinson, 1945). But for a further account of the arts in France during the Third Republic the reader may consult Roger Shattuck's *The Banquet Years* (Faber, 1955), which deals with representatives of drama, poetry, music and painting between 1885 and 1914.

PART TWO

V

Aristocrats and soldiers

An artist's life always furnishes us with material for speculation of a kind that no biographer can resist. If the subject died young, the temptation intrudes itself to legislate on what he might have achieved had his promise not been cut short by events. If, on the other hand, we have to deal with someone of longer span, it becomes irresistible to point to the various turnings taken by his life and enquire what would have happened if he had pursued a different path from that recorded in his obituary. Either way, the game of cataloguing the contingencies can be vastly entertaining; though the chances are that it will end in sterility. In any case, it cannot possibly concern the critic, who is in the position that he must accept what the gods have offered him. As Browning makes his Bishop Blougram say:

> . . . But, friend,
> We speak of what is; not of what might be,
> And how 'twere better if 'twere otherwise.
> I am the man you see here plain enough:
> Grant I'm a beast, why, beasts must lead beasts' lives!

Confronted with the same counsel, we cannot do more than relate the few facts history allows us about those of Franck's pupils whose careers were tragically brief; while our interest in the remainder must reside more in what they did than in what they were capable of doing.

What prompts these cheerless reflections is the thought of how capriciously Franck's tiny band responded to the hazards of early death and premature senility. Among the army of figures, large and small, who came into contact with him, few had the good fortune to lead full and productive lives. Looking at the circle as a whole, it is possible to point to a variety of destinies. Some, and

one thinks at once of Chausson and Lekeu, were struck down at
what seemed the very hour of their maturity; there were others,
like Duparc and Benôit, who, despite surviving to an advanced
age, took a wrong turning somewhere early on, and ended by
becoming the anguished spectators of their own impotence; and
still others again who, like d'Indy and Guy Ropartz, managed to
make the widest possible use of their gifts, fulfilling their destinies
as both men and artists. Without, for the moment, venturing to
speculate on whether Franck's own personality was the principal
factor in fashioning the lives of his pupils, it is at any rate possible
to claim that some of the vagaries attendant upon those lives could
not have been predicted, and may be attributed either to the war,
some unfortunate mishap, or simply susceptibility to illness. There
is, for example, nothing sinister to be read into the fact that both
Chausson and Franck himself became the victims of traffic
accidents. This being the case, we should not treat the success or
failure of any individual musician as if it were the product of
mysterious currents operating within or upon the circle. Things
might well have turned out differently for many members had not
France been in the grip of a military crisis at the time of the circle's
foundation. Similarly, we must be careful not to give too much
weight to psychological explanations. 'Anatomy is destiny' is an
interesting proposition to consider, but very often chance takes an
equally strenuous hand in the shaping of lives.

The oldest musician to become associated with Franck in the
years leading up to the war was Marie de Saint-Victor Alexis,
Vicomte de Castillon, who was born in 1838 and had attained the
age of thirty at the time of his admission to the circle. He was thus
ten years Duparc's senior, and a strict contemporary of Bizet,
whose added loss at a comparatively early age helped to make this
a specially ill-fated generation as far as French music was concerned. Whereas the composer of *L'Arlésienne* was an extremely
precocious artist, however, there are signs that Castillon did not
mature until it was too late. Almost all his principal works were
written during the last five years of his life. These fell between
1868—the year in which he was officially introduced to Franck—
and 1873, of which he only survived to see the first few months.
When we take into account the fact that he did not get properly
started under Franck's guidance until well into 1870, and add to
this the knowledge that ill-health prevented him from doing more
than glance wistfully at those projects begun after the autumn of
1872, then his productive period appears even more cruelly fore-
shortened. Léon Vallas, no doubt bearing these facts in mind, goes
as far as to deny him the right to be regarded as a Franck pupil,
stating that he was a follower only. Perhaps what M. Vallas was

intending to convey here was the suggestion—in itself indisputable
—that Castillon never lived to occupy an official relationship to
Franck, such as d'Indy and most of the other pupils came to enjoy
by virtue of their attendance at the master's organ classes. The
evidence is certainly quite clear on this point, in that Castillon's
health had become so precarious by the middle of 1872 that he was
forced to quit the capital and take up residence at Pau, where the
climate offered better prospects of improvement. He could therefore never have been present during Franck's first session as
Professor at the Conservatoire. However, it seems a trifle pedantic
to insist that Castillon was nothing more than an admirer when it
is obvious that a good deal of informal tuition was meted out to
him at the musical *soirées* held at Franck's apartment in the wartime period. While on leave from his regiment, the young man
took every opportunity of visiting his new tutor, and their evenings
together were passed in the detailed examination and playing of
works one or other had written. There is certainly a wealth of
internal evidence derivable from Castillon's scores which goes to
show how powerfully indebted he was to the Belgian composer.

The Castillon family had their estates near Chartres, and young
Alexis gained his earliest introduction to music by being allowed
to listen and perform at the grand organ of the cathedral. He was
an unusually bright child; though, aside from having a father who
cultivated his voice after the fashion of the dandy, he had no
musical forbears upon whom to fall back. The prevailing outlook
of the household was unremittingly aristocratic—which meant that
sport, agriculture and militarism were the approved topics of conversation. It is not surprising that the boy was singled out for a
career as a soldier and dispatched to the military academy at St
Cyr in 1856. We know little of the hardships he must have endured
at this disciplined institution—the French equivalent of Sandhurst
—but it is evident that he soon sickened of the life. Giving up his
commission to devote himself entirely to music, he made the
initial mistake of attaching himself to Victor Massé, a hack composer whose chief claim to fame consisted of a trite operetta entitled *Les Noces de Jeannette*. This had won him a certain jejune
repute among the excitable patrons of the Opéra-Comique, where
his presence continued to provoke the rivalry of Ambroise Thomas
and Aimé Maillart. That he did make some effort to move with the
times was proved by his later opera *Paul et Virginie*, which
attempted to occupy the ground so well charted by Bizet in *La
Jolie Fille de Perth* and *Carmen*. At the time of his accepting
Castillon as a pupil, however, Massé's artistic credo was lamentably
superficial. Bitterly disappointed by his teacher's disdainful lack of
interest in the *Lied* and chamber music forms, Alexis was on the

point of turning his back on his chosen vocation when he had the good luck to run into Duparc. The meeting convinced him that he would do best to give up Massé and take his chances as an informal pupil of Franck. This meant renouncing his studentship at the Conservatoire and pursuing the harder path of private study. As he had just inherited a fortune from his father, the course presented no financial obstacles. The rub came when it was discovered, a few months later, that his country would have a renewed use for his services. It was then that he had to set about resuming his military commitments.

One of the first acts Castillon undertook on allying himself with Franck was the destruction of all those works he had written under the influence of Massé. Whether the world has been deprived of a masterpiece as a result of this ritual purgation is a matter of speculation.[1] The chances are that nothing of value was permitted to perish. A symphony written in 1865 was one of the principal casualties, but considering how prone young composers generally are to embrace the most ambitious forms, it hardly seems as if the work was anything more than an immature expression of over-confidence. Fauré, it will be recalled, consigned a similar orchestral epic to the flames. To judge from Castillon's later—and it must be conceded very accomplished—essays in sonata form, he could not have possessed the power of development necessary to write successfully on the symphonic scale at this early date. He was, indeed, unable to finish a Second Symphony, of which the parts remain. Looking through the catalogue of his extant works, we are inclined to fix 1868 as about the earliest date at which music of high quality could have begun to appear. This, for instance, is the date of the first of the composer's *Six Poésies de Armand Silvestre* a song-cycle that went far to establish him as more than a mere bearer of promise. But he was an exceptionally prolific artist for one who had suffered so late a start, and it remains conceivable that his judgement on his own work was too severe.

At least there is no doubt that the chamber-works upon which he embarked in 1870—and which came to include a Piano Quintet, Piano Quartet, String Quartet, Trio and Violin Sonata—represent an amazingly rich and pioneering contribution to a genre of which the French have not been among the hardiest exponents. The quality displayed by these works makes it tempting to echo the verdict expressed in Cobbett's *Cyclopedic Survey of Chamber Music* that: 'In the whole history of music we find no composer

---

[1] A comparison here suggests itself with Henri Duparc and Paul Dukas, two further members of the Franck circle who were addicted to destroying what they wrote. Such firmness reflects the lofty critical temper adopted by the group as a whole.

who has written so many really fine works during so brief a career.'

No less fascinating to the historian is the question of why Castillon allowed himself to become interested in such an ascetic form at a time when all ambition pointed towards other sectors. It is true that France could boast trios for harpsichord and strings by Rameau and Couperin (as well as some exquisite violin sonatas by Jean-Marie Leclair) but these works were scarcely in the forefront of the repertory. The French had in fact forsaken chamber music for the better part of a century, letting it be understood that they regarded this medium as the prerogative of their German colleagues. Apart from Franck himself, there were only a handful of musicians who were making it their business to reverse the trend. One of these was Edouard Lalo, who played the viola in the Armingaud Quartet, and who had graced the repertory with three attractive trios, owing much in style to Weber and Schumann. Another was the ubiquitous Saint-Saëns, whose Piano Quintet dated from 1865 and must therefore have helped to inspire the quintets of both Castillon and Franck. Possibly a more accessible model could be found among the many chamber-works of the little known Anglo-French composer, Georges Onslow.[1] And we should not forget that Félicien David—whose Oriental fantasies were so much admired by the undiscriminating—redeemed himself by writing in this genre. Hardly any of these men had done much to make the genre popular, however, and Castillon accordingly deserves credit for initiative in the matter. If for nothing else, he should go down as one of music's typical archaeologists, notable for having retrieved an exciting mode of composition from its place of obscurity.

That Castillon's chamber music should have exuded a faintly Teutonic flavour ought not to be thought surprising in the circumstances. He was always a keen student of the past, and in this case the past meant the Austro-Germanic tradition. Among the various composers who influenced him, Schumann was dearest to his heart. A refusal to employ virtuoso figuration is common to both composers, while the same rather solid blocks of chords appear in their respective piano works. A comparison of Schumann's op. 44 with the Quintet of Castillon yields further similarities, the most conspicuous being a tendency to repeat material in place of development. It is also possible that Castillon

---

[1] Onslow's name had appeared on the list of subscribers to Franck's early Trios. His position as an obscure specialist in chamber music invites comparison with that of Alkan *vis-à-vis* the piano. Incredible though it may seem, Onslow wrote no less than thirty Piano Quintets, and was for many years an influential figure in French musical life. He succeeded Cherubini at the Institut and died in 1852.

derived certain of his cyclical habits from Schumann rather than Franck. The coda to Schumann's last movement, for example, begins with a fugal subject which turns out to be an augmentation of the work's opening theme. In Castillon's Quintet, there is a comparable abstraction of material from the Adagio. Two themes are carried over from this movement to the Finale, where they combine with new figures to bring about the peroration. Some differences are nevertheless clearly observable. The techniques utilized for the two scherzo movements are in marked contrast. Schumann's creation is brisk and fiery, Castillon's all lightness and grace. The model for this section of the French composer's work was in all probability one of Saint-Saëns's mercurial compositions. An interesting personal characteristic of Castillon's is his preference for intruding ecclesiastical modes into his chamber-works. The figure consisting of four semibreves in the A flat minor movement of the Quintet offers a case in point. This is perhaps a Franckist touch, such as would not have occurred to a non-Catholic. It underlines the religious nature of the ethos in which the composer moved.

A Schumann-like lyricism aspires to be the dominant influence in the Piano Quartet, op. 7, which Castillon did not embark upon until the end of 1871. This is another fine work, well worthy of inclusion in the repertory. However, the largo introduction and exploiting of a motto theme tend in the last resort to place this composition more in the Beethoven tradition than any other. As with d'Indy, Beethoven was a powerful formative example in Castillon's eyes, and his romantic texture was always carefully woven into classical designs. The late Quartets of the Bonn master were actually slow to get a hearing in France, having to wait for inclusion in the programmes of the Maurin Quartet for the year 1852. But from that date on, they gained plenty of adherents— especially among the *avant-garde*—and both Franck and Castillon were of their number. In spite of his adulation of Beethoven, it is evident that Castillon was capable of tonal misadventures of a kind quite absent from the work of his idol. His fault was most commonly to draw back from the consequences of his own logic. Having established a particularly audacious pattern of modulation, he had a habit of failing to follow it through, tamely reverting to the original key at a critical moment. This is something his German predecessors would have had the courage to avoid; and it is not a fault Franck could be accused of having contracted. In such unfulfilled promises, we detect a hint of the haste with which Castillon was forced to work. His genius was invariably at the mercy of a somewhat sketchy training—though the many felicitous touches of scoring and sheer breadth of melodic invention are often sufficient to redeem his works from their inevitable shortcomings. The Piano Quartet is a typical instance. In this impressive work, the superbly broad melodies—of which the first subject of the opening movement is a good specimen—are alone a guarantee of merit. It is worth noting that the composer's modal preference also makes its appearance in this composition, in the form of a 'quasi-marcia' section belonging to the larghetto. Whether Castillon would ever have gone on to display the assurance in the handling of modal sequences which is a feature of the work of Gabriel Fauré remains a matter for speculation. What is quite unlike Fauré is his penchant for brilliant codas—witness the bravura ending of this Quartet and the Violin Sonata. These imitate the reckless panache of Liszt, and perhaps helped to confirm in Franck himself a fondness for the dazzling conclusion, such as we get in the *Prélude, Choral et Fugue* and in his own Violin Sonata, not written until 1886. It is important to bear in mind instances of this kind, where the pupil appears to have taught the master.

Mention of the respective violin sonatas of these composers serves to remind us that Castillon's work was written some fourteen years before Franck's and six years before that of Fauré. Considering how often the sonatas of these musicians are announced as having helped to resuscitate the form, it might be thought that Castillon has had much less than his due in the matter. It is all the more unjust when we acknowledge that his work is pitched on the same level of inspiration as theirs. If it does not quite attain the monumental sublimity of the Franck sonata, nor the shining effulgence of the Fauré, it can at any rate stand its ground with either in the sphere of formal innovation. The linking of its first movement to the scherzo by means of a bridge passage must be looked upon as a particularly happy stroke of invention. It relates the work to the ancient sonata principle and shows how a baroque form can be utilized in a modern composition with complete success. The fugal development of the first movement again invites comparison with the famous fugue-like intrusions of Beethoven, to say nothing of the canonical episode in the finale of the Franck sonata. Other original interpolations include the Gregorian melody which helps to sustain the work's song-like andante. But the attention of most listeners will be most effectively captured by the striking rhythm employed for the Finale. It is as subtle and compulsive as anything in Roussel and points to another aspect of technique in which this enormously gifted pupil might easily have gone on to eclipse his master.

Much of the success of the foregoing chamber-works results from Castillon's masterly handling of the piano, an instrument several members of the Franck school did well to cultivate. Writing of what he terms 'the great tradition' of keyboard music initiated by Franck and his disciples, Professor Demuth singles out Castillon and de Bréville as among the most important exponents. The Piano Concerto of the former composer and the Piano Sonata of the latter are held up to represent all that was best in that tradition. Certainly the quantity of music Castillon left for the piano suggests that it was the presence of this instrument among the strings that appealed to him quite as much as the possibilities of ensemble. His assorted piano pieces often revert to archaic forms; yet in so doing they had the paradoxical effect of looking forward as well as back. This was because the succeeding age developed a strong preference for the old dance forms, and for the type of figuration invented by the clavecinistes. The titles *Le Tombeau de Couperin* and *Hommage à Rameau*, which were to attach to suites by Ravel and Debussy, are a clear indication of this fashion. So is the preoccupation, very evident in the case of Saint-Saëns, with preparing authentic editions of baroque music. It seems symptomatic of this revival that several of Castillon's pieces were given the suffix, 'dans le style ancien'. Among the pieces thus described is a fugue and a set of five contrasting dances. There are also two suites in which recollections of pre-classical idioms occur. What is interesting to us —at this late date—is that not merely Castillon, but other Franck pupils too, figured among the pioneers of this movement. Chausson's *Quelques Danses*, though not written until 1896, still manage to pre-date Debussy's *Pour le Piano*; while the *Suite en sol* by Samazeuilh was composed sixteen years before Ravel paid his famous tribute to Couperin. That this is a genre which continues to attract French musicians may be attested by taking works as far apart as the *Petite Suite* of George Auric (1928)—which revives the villanelle, sarabande and voltes—and the more recent *Suite de Danses* by Jean-Jacques Grunenwald (1959), who teaches the organ at the Schola Cantorum.[1] But the cult of antiquity was not something the Franckists helped to perpetuate, if only because they lived before the concept of 'time-travelling' became viable. It is to Stravinsky and Poulenc that we must attribute this bizarre maladaptation of the research instinct. Castillon's pieces in the ancient style spring from an interest in form and not mannerism.

The tentativeness of these experiments is thrown into relief by the habit—characteristic of Saint-Saëns and Castillon—of composing in both the romantic and pre-classical styles. These two styles would ordinarily be construed as antithetical. Yet they exist,

---

[1] One might also cite the *Sarabande et Menuet* (op.24) of d'Indy; the sprightly *Suite Française* of Daniel-Lesur (formerly a Director of the Schola); and, most impressive of all, Roussel's four-movement Suite in F sharp minor, op.14.

cheek by jowl, in the works of a number of French composers of
the period, which in this sense deserves to be classified as transitional. To consider the case of Castillon, it surprises us to find such
'modern' works as the *Cinq Pièces* taking their place alongside conventional salon products like the *Six Valses Humoristiques*. It is as
if the dividing line separating these tastes only became visible in
retrospect. Nor are they the sole alternatives to be suggested. For
there are hints of the impressionist outlook in certain other pieces
the composer wrote; witness the twenty-four *Pensées Fugitives*
which anticipate the method, if not the harmonic astringency, of
Prokoviev. The truth is that in writing for the keyboard, Castillon
betrays a variety of not always reconcilable influences. His themes
have a decidedly linear quality reminiscent of Saint-Saëns; a composer whose influence was clearly just as potent as that of Franck.
On the other hand, it could not be said that Castillon was as pianistic in his figuration as this admission might lead us to suppose. The
reception awarded to his Piano Concerto, when Saint-Saëns performed it in 1872 at a Pasdeloup concert, was so lukewarm that the
pianist was actually compelled to slam down the lid of his instrument and march off the platform, warning the audience that he
would not continue until they acquired a little more respect
('Camille was magnificent!' was the heckled composer's reaction to
the event). This surely indicates how far removed from the customary virtuoso pattern the work set out to be. Probably the main
reason why so few of Castillon's piano pieces are ever played today
is that they have never been able to break down this prejudice on
the part of performers and audience. Their style is considered too
unadorned to maintain interest. Also, Castillon's conception of the
Piano Concerto was to regard the solo part as virtually *obligato*.
Once again, the parallel with Franck's *Les Djinns* is instructive.

It is arguable that the most significant contribution Castillon
made to French music occurred in none of these forms, but in the
vocal works which he wrote. For although he possessed a remarkable
flair for ensemble, it is to the solitary song-cycle with which he
began his career that modern critics are inclined to look when seeking to assess his importance. The tradition of song in French-
speaking countries stretches back many centuries. But it is imperative to distinguish between the popular air—of which there were
several manifestations ranging from the medieval chanson to the
courtly bergerette of the seventeenth century—and the kind of
melody attempted by Castillon and his colleagues. Early French
song, despite its efforts at literary rapprochement, had given rise
to nothing which could be compared to the German lied. It is true
that as time went on Berlioz, Meyerbeer and Liszt all interested
themselves in just such a challenge. But the results they achieved

were scarcely worthy of their intentions. Still later, Gounod and Bizet produced romances of memorable quality, but these were only a more stylish counterpart to the English drawing-room ballad. The trouble lay in the fact that each of these composers relied too much on adapting traditions that had formerly existed in the theatre; or else shamelessly plundered the work of rival nations.

What France needed was an altogether new vocal form which would be equal to exploiting the rich vein of Parnassian and symbolist poetry which was about to open at the feet of its musicians. It is idle to suppose that such a form could have been invented much before the poets themselves had put their house in order. Hence it required a period of patient waiting for ideas to generate. Hugo's romanticism remained a powerful force up until the war of 1870, and the conventional settings of his verse by Lalo, Franck and Fauré did little more than corroborate the view that this literary cult offered no scope for musical embellishment. The poetry it produced was too corpulent to lend itself to variation. By comparison, the German romantics had at least professed genuine sentiments, and they had not allowed their verses to be defiled by rhetoric or affectation. Moreover, their outlook found a ready counterpart in the uncomplicated stream of melody poured forth by men of the stamp of Schubert and Brahms. The situation in France was, on the contrary, that poets and musicians professed to have little in common, and even appeared hopelessly disaffected.[1] The breakthrough, when it came, consisted of the efforts of composers like Castillon, Duparc and Fauré, who chose to apply their supersensitive powers to a novel and elegant collection of texts.

Among the songs left by these musicians, those by Castillon are easily the least appreciated. One may account for this neglect by reference to the question of bulk. His mere six settings constitute an absurdly meagre offering. Yet it should be remembered that Duparc himself bequeathed only sixteen. Moreover, at the time of Castillon's death in 1873, Fauré had written nothing to words by Verlaine, neither had Duparc got much beyond his first encounter with Baudelaire, while Chausson had not even appeared on the scene. This makes it tenable to suggest that had he been spared Castillon would have added a body of song equal in quantity, if not in quality, to that provided by the great masters of the French *mélodie*. We cannot prophesy which poets would have appealed most to his fancy, nor is it possible to guess whether he would have

[1] The French Romantic poets were a particularly unmusical crew. Hugo preferred painting, while Gautier went to the Opera only to please his daughters, usually finding an excuse to disappear after the first Act. Baudelaire proved an exception, but he was Wagnerian in his sympathies.

been side-tracked by his obsessive interest in chamber music. It is, however, possible to make some tentative assessment of the contribution he did leave us.

The six songs, contrary to expectations, were written at fairly widely-spaced intervals, and only two of them were dated by the composer. 'Le Semeur' carries a note with it, in the composer's handwriting, giving the date of its composition as 28 June 1869; while the succeeding song, 'Sonnet Mélancolique', has a similar subscription dated 27 June 1871. It may be estimated that the whole cycle took about four years to complete, the first song almost certainly going back to 1868 and the sixth falling into the last year of his life, perhaps his very last act of creation. It seems, from the original titling of the work, that the composer intended to set only two poems, and was impelled to contribute the remainder as an afterthought. Despite the fact that they do not hang together as an indivisible cycle—in the manner of, say, Fauré's Verlaine cycles—these songs do have a common subject-matter in that they all depict aspects of the French countryside.

The writer who provided Castillon with his source of inspiration does not deserve to rank very highly in the symbolist hierarchy. He was an essentially minor figure, perpetually on the threshold of greatness but never able to attain it. Born in 1837, Armand Silvestre was almost exactly the same age as his collaborator, and the two men were officers in the army during the war. This common ordeal is doubtless what served to unite their otherwise not specially compatible temperaments. It is true, however, that in the humble portrayals of springtime in the fields, the grape-harvest, the grain-sower and the woodsman, Castillon might well have discovered a nostalgic reflection of the scenes of his boyhood around the landscape of Chartres. Unlike his brother officer, Silvestre survived the conflict of war and went on to take a post at the Ministry of Finance. He died in 1901, after a moderately successful career in which he eventually became an Inspecteur des Beaux-Arts. His verses were admired by Fauré, who was indebted to him for the texts of 'Aurore' and 'Le Secret', and by Duparc, whose lugubrious song 'Testament' is a tribute to the poet's hold over him.

As in the composer's instrumental works, the German influence is at once detectable in Castillon's settings of Silvestre; which incidentally pre-date Duparc's single song by a clear decade, as they also anticipate the settings of Fauré. The chief influence tends once again to be Schumann, and this is apparent in the habit of appending a piano postlude to one or two of the songs—most notably in 'Vendange' and 'Renouveau'. Both Lalo and Castillon, being among the earliest to experiment with the *mélodie*, suffered from an absence of native models; with the result that they leaned heavily on the *Lieder* tradition. This meant that, like several of their German exemplars, they betrayed an improper understanding of prosody. Castillon's first song, 'Le Bûcher', accordingly reveals a number of metrical clashes in which the musical accent tends to fall on the definite article rather than the appropriate syllable of the noun; while in other songs there is so much doubling of the vocal line by the piano that the possibilities for subtle rhythmical inflection are simply not present. Unfortunately, neither Massé nor Franck were capable of giving the composer the advice he needed in such matters. Franck's own approach to song-writing was befuddled by an equally gauche misconception of the musician's obligation to the poet. He did set—more by convention than any expression of personal taste—a wide selection of verses by well-known masters, including Hugo, Musset and Sully-Prudhomme; but his handling of the words shows him guilty of the same misdemeanours as his pupil, with the stress falling on prepositions and mute endings, anywhere in fact but on the parts of the line demanded by the poem's metre. Scansion was not an exercise that preceded the setting of words to music at this stage in the growth of the art, and France had still to introduce the reforms that were called for if literary and musical impulses were to meet in intensity. Without the example set by Hugo Wolf in Germany and Claude Debussy in his own country, Castillon was unable to rise above these crucial limitations.

Ex. 6

Alexis de Castillon: Le Semeur

Even so, the feeling expressed in the Silvestre songs comes so near to capturing the poet's mood that, defective though they may be in technical accomplishment, they mark a real advance in musical sensibility. No French composer had previously addressed himself, in quite the same vivid fashion, to the business of achieving complete emotional identification with the subject. Frits Noske, in his authoritative study 'La Mélodie Française de

Berlioz à Duparc', puts his finger on the exact impression made by Castillon's vocal works:

> Comme artiste, Castillon était assurément très doué. En dépit du manque de perfection, ses mélodies présentent des marques de genié.*

Others, like Paul Landormy, have expressed the point differently by claiming that even though the composer's forms tended to be poorly realized, his artistic conceptions had a way of breaking through to the listener. In possessing this power of direct speech—transcending whatever limitations were inherent in the medium—Castillon revealed himself as a true follower of Franck. For alongside the clumsiness which most of the band were fated to display went a certain strength of inspiration, a determination to confront the unsurmountable, which in the end enabled them to triumph over the purely formal obstacles that stood in their path. None of the group—not even the luckless Duparc—had more to contend with than Castillon. It is accordingly only right and proper that history should judge him charitably.

The vicissitudes this young man had to face as a cavalry officer went far towards duplicating the struggles he had undergone as a composer. Saddled with the most arduous missions, he was constantly being forced to camp out in bad weather, and in a variety of appalling conditions. A snowstorm in which he and his troop were engulfed became the occasion of his contracting tuberculosis, a disease that quickly strengthened its grip on him once the food shortage became acute. When he was released from the army, he seemed only a shadow of his former self. Advised to spend the winter of 1872 in Pau, it was while he was returning to the capital that he caught pneumonia. The effect of this misfortune, in his generally precarious state of health, was all too foreseeable. By March 1873 he was dead, and the hopes he had aroused on behalf of French music irretrievably blasted. Anxious to pay their respects to the dead man's family, a delegation of musicians assembled at the Castillon ancestral home a few days before the funeral. To their surprise and consternation, they discovered that the composer's mother knew little of her son's ambitions. 'Je ne connais pas des personnes musicales' was her chilling comment on his circle of acquaintances. Invitations were none the less sent out to the leading figures in the profession, and the earliest and most passionately lamented of the circle's victims was decently laid to rest. Aside from the chamber-works which he had hastened to com-

---

* As an artist, Castillon was surely very talented. Despite their lack of perfection, his melodies carry the marks of genius.

plete, the only major projects left open at the time of the composer's death turned out to be a Symphony—which would have been No. 2 in his canon—and part of a Mass for solo voices, chorus and orchestra. This last work was a paraphrase of Psalm LXXXIV, and represents a genre to which Roussel was also to give his attention. No more songs were discovered, beyond those which have been described, and nothing else of importance emerged for the piano. Thus ended one of the saddest chapters in the history of nineteenth-century music in France.

Although it is imperative that interest should not be diverted away from Castillon's musical achievements, we should be unjust if we failed to give an account of the work he did as an administrator. Much has been made of the Franck circle's indifference to other arts than music. Yet it is surprising how many of the group found the time to engage in society activities and to carry on the trade of journalist.[1] Castillon threw what little energies he had left on his demobilization into the formation and running of a society to be devoted to the propagation of French music. This was to be known as the Société Nationale de Musique—founded in February 1871 by Romaine Bussine, a singing teacher at the Conservatoire, together with Saint-Saëns, who became Vice-President, and Castillon, whose services were invoked as Secretary. Other musicians who took an active interest in this venture were Fauré, Duparc, Lalo, Massenet, Ernest Guiraud, Théodore Dubois and Franck himself. They adopted the motto 'Ars Gallica' —hardly a very tactful rallying cry at that precise moment in French history —and quickly set about the task of framing a constitution. It became the practice to assemble on Monday evenings for committee meetings, and these were held in close conjunction with Pasdeloup's Thursday orchestral rehearsals. The idea was that members of the society would be encouraged to lay down a realistic policy for introducing new works as a result of their observation of the concert machinery in action. The forces at work within the Nationale were fairly evenly divided between those who wanted to advance French music as such (Saint-Saëns was the champion of this group), and those who had become influenced by Wagner. The latter group—whose enthusiasm had been sparked off by the concert performance of some of Wagner's works which had been held at the Théâtre des Italiens in 1860—later came to include d'Indy, and reached a peak of persuasion in the 1880s. At the time of the society's inception, the nationalist faction expressed itself more power-

[1] Among those who undertook some journalistic commitments may be counted Coquard, de Bréville, Benôit, Paul de Wailly and Dukas. Several of these wrote for such influential periodicals as the *Mercure de France*, *La Revue Hebdomadaire*, etc.

fully. This is confirmed by a reading of the statutes, which included the following explicit statement of intent:

> The aim of the society is to aid the production and populariza-
> tion of all serious musical works, whether published or
> unpublished, of French composers; to encourage and bring
> to light, so far as it is in its power, all musical endeavour, what-
> form it may take, on condition that there is evidence of high
> artistic aspiration on the part of the author . . . It is in
> brotherly love, with complete forgetfulness of self and with
> the firm intention of aiding one another as much as they can,
> that the members of the society will co-operate, each in his
> own sphere of activity, in the study and performance of works
> they shall be called upon to select and to interpret.[1]

Not only does this statement reveal the strength of that progressivism which was already emergent in the minds of the more dedicated musicians of the age, but it patently betrays the idealism,
ethical as well as artistic, which was beginning to emanate from
their midst. It is obvious that Castillon, Duparc and other admirers
of Franck played an important part in shaping such sentiments.

The next oldest member of the circle did not exhibit Castillon's
promise, nor did he ever manage to become a major composer. Despite his limitations, or perhaps because of them, he succeeded in
attaching himself to Franck with a very special grace. He was
Albert Cahen, and he was born in Paris in 1846. Though it is sometimes assumed that he was Belgian, and hence able to use his
nationality to ingratiate himself with his teacher, he was actually a
Frenchman who lived most of his life in the capital. It was only
later that his profession took him to Brussels and Antwerp, where
he counted on a more benevolent public to elevate him to a position of repute.[2] Financially, the Cahens were exceedingly well off
and scarcely needed his support. Though not of the older aristocracy, the composer's brother was Count Louis Cahen d'Anvers, a
rich and self-indulgent socialite. Albert himself married a high
born Polish *emigrée* named Lulia Warchawska, an aunt of the
dancer Ida Rubinstein. At the beginning of his career, he devoted
his energies to the piano, obtaining lessons from Mme Szarvady

---

[1] As secretary of the Society, Castillon was entrusted with the task
of framing this very declaration, and it is obvious that it reflected his
own feelings as well as those of his fellow-members.

[2] An alternative course for composers who found it difficult to get
their stage-works mounted in Paris was to apply to the Théâtre de la
Monnaie at Brussels. A second escape route presented itself at Monte
Carlo.

and subsequently from Franck. He entrusted himself to the latter at about the same time as his friends Coquard and Duparc; that is to say, well before the outbreak of the war. His musical inclinations soon veered away from the keyboard, the earliest things he wrote showing that he was content to follow his master at a respectful distance. A biblical drama on the life of John the Baptist suggests a decidedly Franckist preference for the ponderous and the sanctimonious. It was performed in 1874, the year in which the revisions to *Rédemption* were carried out, and the sponsor was the Société Nationale. His second major work—a mythological 'poème' entitled *Endymion*—followed at the Concerts Darbé a year or two later. Neither of these long-winded compositions achieved much success, suffering a fate similar to that which had engulfed Franck's pious offerings. Whether it was on account of this discouraging start, or perhaps the disdain which d'Indy and his friends showered on the cantata form, Cahen lost no time in pitching his ambitions in the world of the theatre, where he was known to a wide circle of friends. It was upon this heavily commercialized world that he was to depend for the remainder of what became a mediocre and protracted career.

His stage début was made with a one-act opera entitled *Le Bois* which, owing to the monopoly in force at the Opéra, had to take its chances at the Opéra-Comique. It was not at all uncommon at this time for composers with serious intentions to find themselves relegated to the same institution as the successors of Offenbach. Works so much the opposite of 'comic' as Massenet's *Manon*, Charpentier's *Louise* and Debussy's *Pelléas et Mélisande* were all to end up receiving their premières from the stage of this smaller theatre in the Rue Favart. It is hardly surprising that the audience which, only five years previously, had pronounced with disfavour on *Carmen* should have discovered little to titillate in Cahen's opera. The success of the year turned out to be Delibes's *Jean de Nivelle*, and even this was quickly eclipsed by the same composer's *Lakmé* in 1883. Realizing that it was useless to aim at overcoming these obstacles, Cahen took the only sensible course open to him when he decided to withdraw his next work. A fairy-tale on the theme of *La Belle au Bois Dormant*, this opened in Geneva in 1886. Like many another outsider, it failed to survive the return journey. The composer's best-known opera, *Le Venitien*, obtained its première a little nearer home, though still not in the capital itself. It was put on in Rouen, to which city Franck travelled in April 1890—only six months before his death—so that he could be present for the launching. It is an indication of the older man's critical complacency that he was led to describe Cahen's opera as 'having provided me with one of the best moments of my musical life'.

His pupil was to reciprocate this loyalty by making a special trip from Antwerp to attend Franck's funeral; a courtesy many more famous musicians would have been glad to deny him. Following his master's death, Cahen tended to drop out of the circle, his lax Jewish friends having gone some way towards making him *non persona grata* with the anti-semitic d'Indy.[1] He went on, however, to compose a ballet, *Fleur de Neige*, and yet another opera, *La Femme de Claude*, which briefly reinstated him at the Opéra-Comique in 1896. Neither of these works brought him the acclaim he desired, and he died a disappointed man at Cap d'Ail, some seven years later.

His companion Arthur Coquard, though he too failed to win real renown as a composer, met with a slightly less withering fate. A more versatile figure, he found it possible to practise several professions, and he was prudent in not setting too much store by his musical hopes. Originally from Burgundy, his family had settled in Paris before he was born, and he was sent to the seminary of Auxerre for his early education. Like Duparc, to whom he remained harnessed by academic and professional ties, he proceeded to the Collège de Vaugirard, which was where he first encountered Franck. They met in 1865 for a course of harmony lessons, which Coquard discontinued after only one year, not resuming his musical studies until after the war. Meantime, he pursued a diligent path in the law, obtaining his doctorate of jurisprudence in 1870. Afterwards, he was appointed secretary to Martel in the Senate, enjoying a typically industrious career on the fringe of politics. During the war itself he served with distinction in the National Guard, and it was while on leave from his duties that he began helping Franck to organise the musical evenings which did so much to lay the foundation for the circle's later activities. Coquard was very interested in keyboard music. He renewed his contacts with Franck on the establishment of peace, becoming one of the keenest members of the composer's organ class at the Conservatoire. It was in this last capacity that he was to prove invaluable to his master; for it was his willingness to campaign on Franck's behalf that caused so many Conservatoire students to become periodic *auditeurs* within this class when their official commitments resided elsewhere. Franck's habit of teaching composition in place of the instrument over which he had been asked to preside led a number of curious spirits to wish to sample his wares. Some of these

[1] One should not nevertheless think that d'Indy ostracized all his Jewish acquaintances—his behaviour towards men like Dukas and Octave Maus was invariably 'très correct'. But later in life he certainly became obsessed on this question, joining Maurras's 'Action Française' and other racial groups.

came merely in order to poke fun, or ferret out slanderous allegations. But a nucleus 'remained to pray'—much to the annoyance of the authorities—and it was Coquard who always sought to guarantee their presence.

His own ambitions as a composer were slow in appearing. He was thirty before writing 'Le Chant des Epées', a ballad for baritone and orchestra which might well have been prompted by a desire to emulate Duparc. Such a gory theme would have been outside the range of his friend's sympathies, however, and it is only the work's form that invites the comparison. Such promise as this held out was not to be rapidly fulfilled, for it was followed by a period of five years during which music seemed to have vanished from the young man's thoughts. Renewal of interest came about in 1881, when he decided to put away his law books in favour of the lyric stage. Coquard had a formidable knowledge of classical literature, and was very responsive to the spirit of contemporary writing. His tastes actually ran the gamut from Corneille and Racine to the 'cloak-and-dagger' romances of his own day. To do him justice, he strove to keep these tastes in watertight compartments, writing sober incidental music for the serious theatre and reserving his more flamboyant urges for the opera-house. The dramatic scores which he wrote included music for productions of *Hero et Léandre* (a theme later to interest his fellow-pupil, Augusta Holmès); *Andromaque; Cassandre*; and *Christophe Colomb*. He also produced choruses for Racine's *Esther*, de Bornier's *Agamemnon* and Longhaye's *Helvetia*. All these works are distinguished by fluency, skill and definite theatrical flair. His possession of these qualities—like his wide reading—tended to put him at the opposite remove from most of Franck's organ scholars. During the last decades of the century, Coquard went on to write a succession of militant operas embodying the adventurous features we associate today with Alexandre Dumas and his followers. *L'Epée du Roi* (1884) was a two-act melodrama which had its première at Angers, while *Le Mari d'un Jour* (1886) followed at the Opéra-Comique. One of his most ambitious undertakings was a completion of Lalo's fragment, *La Jacquerie*—a revolutionary tale of blood-and-thunder which made its appearance at Monte Carlo in 1895. To find a truly prophetic expression of Coquard's talents, however, we must turn to his opera, *La Troupe Jolicoeur* (1902). This was inspired by the composer's growing belief in naturalism as a mode of dramatic presentation. Fired by the success of Bruneau's *Le Rêve* and *Messidor*—the two attempts at Zolaesque realism to have been imported into the French theatre—he wanted above all to liberate a new popular urge. As he himself phrased it in an interview with a journalist, his aim was 'fouiller l'âme populaire'. Written, though not performed, before Charpentier's *Louise*, his *Troupe Jolicoeur* embodied all the up-to-date aspirations of the literary clique. Based on a novel by Henri Cain, it recounts the life of a band of circus folk, looking forward in its subject-matter to Sauguet's *Les Forains*. The scenes are extremely bright and colourful, without any of the period's customary factitiousness. The death of Loustic is done with touching refinement, while the 14 July celebrations are rendered with a vividness almost worthy of *Petruschka*. As René Dumesnil has said, the whole opera represents 'un charivari pittoresque et toujours musical'.

But the full extent of Coquard's versatility can only be gauged by examining his work as a critic. He wrote chiefly for *Le Monde*, a leading journal in which his slender memoir of Franck was republished in 1904. First conceived as an obituary, this tribute displays all the hallmarks of respect due on such an occasion. It does not attempt an examination of the music, but relies instead on a series of anecdotes revealing the now familiar traits of gentleness and benignity. Not surprisingly, in view of the author's commitment to the stage, a good deal of the space is taken up in describing Franck's reactions to various popular successes of the day. These are useful in confirming the assumption that the composer was exceedingly generous in his praise of his contemporaries. The account of his response to Saint-Saëns's *Samson et Dalila* is worth quoting as an indication of his charitableness, and of the tone in which the master and his disciple conversed:

> . . . Naturally, I told him all about the first night of the season, and how *Samson et Dalila* had obtained a great success, and I spoke *en passant* of my admiration for M. Saint-Saëns's masterpiece. I can see him still, turning his worn and suffering face towards me, saying eagerly and almost joyfully in that deep and vibrant tone so familiar to all his friends: 'Very fine! very fine!'

Much of Coquard's monograph conveys just this limp spirit of adulation, reminding us that his devotion was no less uncritical than d'Indy's. These two senior members of the circle had many other things in common.[1] Their military interests helped to establish one bond, while the fact that they were chosen by Franck to carry out some of the chores involved in revising or transcribing his music quickly set up another. Coquard was given the job of orchestrating the fourth act of Franck's opera *Hulda*; and he shared with d'Indy, Chausson, de Bréville and Rousseau the task of preparing *Ghisèle* for its posthumous première in April 1896. The

[1] Their letters have been preserved and may be examined in the collection, edited by Norbert Dufourcq, entitled *Coquard, César Franck & D'Indy* (Editions du Coudrier, 1952).

later career of this gifted disciple brought him further honours. He received the Prix Bordin from the Académie des Beaux-Arts for his book, *De la Musique en France depuis Rameau*, and also spent a number of years as a lecturer at the National Institute for the Blind. His death in 1910 robbed the circle, if not of a major composer, at least of a distinguished public figure.

Of the group which built itself around Franck just after the war of 1870, the most vigorous and prepossessing was surely Vincent d'Indy. Whatever we may think of his unsubtle attempts to canonize his master, his ignorant and aggressive dislike of intruders, and his ruthless pursuit of authority at the Schola, he must be seen as a musician of towering stature when set alongside the majority of his rivals. A descendant of the Vivarais, he came from the Faugs district of upper Ardèche, a region to which he attached a great deal of importance, musically and historically. Its picturesque landscape formed the background of his holidays both as a child and an adult. Unfortunately, he never had the benefit of his mother's care. Instead, he had a grim—almost tyrannical—upbringing, chiefly at the hands of his paternal grandmother, the Comtesse Rézia, a lady whose name had appeared on the list of subscribers to César Franck's early Trios. This musical connection did not occur entirely by accident, since Wilfrid d'Indy (the elder son of the Countess, and uncle of the composer) had already pursued a private career as a musician, and had become known to Franck through his interest in both chamber music and comic opera. As a matter of fact, Franck had given him a brief series of lessons at Liège during 1842. His nephew Vincent was not born until 1851, however, and his decision to make use of the same teacher was the result of little more than a coincidence. That the d'Indy family had a pronounced musical streak is nevertheless worth remembering. It reminds us that, despite a number of superficial resemblances, it was never possessed of the same indigenous philistinism as could be found among the Castillons. Wilfrid d'Indy was not its only musical scion, his brother Antonin being equally industrious in pursuit of the art. This second uncle of Vincent's also strove to retain his amateur status, even though he had studied the piano with Zimmerman and been intimately acquainted with Berlioz. Tempting as it may be, therefore, to write off the d'Indys as a race of complacent landowners, the facts do not quite fit such an explanation. Despite the atmosphere of harshness which undoubtedly existed in the household, sweetness and light were continually threatening to break in.

The Paris home of this formidable family lay in the Rue du Bac. and it was here that the young Vincent was subjected to the strict régime which did so much to turn him into one of music's most notorious martinets. As a child, he was not at all put out by the inflexible time-table his grandmother successfully imposed upon him from dawn until dusk.[1] Though he showed early indications of a zest for music, he was just as tireless in the pursuit of his other hobbies. The greatest of these was a passion for soldiering. At first this merely took the form of fighting toy battles, but later on it developed into an almost unhealthy predilection for French military history, a subject upon which he became something of a spare-time authority. At no time in his adult life was it easy to restrain him from re-staging the Battle of Waterloo wherever and whenever the occasion prompted it. In this tiresome habit he was probably no different from thousands of other Frenchmen. What really distinguished d'Indy from the rest of his compatriots was the rigour with which he followed up his interests (he made two visits to the battlefield in 1865 and 1897, making use of the second occasion to give his son—a lieutenant in the Dragoons—a typical dressing-down on the subject). As with everything else he took up, including his profession of music, this uncompromising thoroughness and refusal to admit opposition became the rule by which to proceed. It is scarcely surprising that others found him an obstinate man. Dispassionate concern and a willingness to understand both sides of a dispute were simply not qualities he cherished. Yet the astonishing thing about d'Indy is that the more one examines his philosophy of life the more apparent it becomes that he was a victim of contrariness. Such an assertion would have been contested by most of the composer's contemporaries, almost all of whom regarded him as a single-minded fanatic. Judging him in retrospect, however, it is remarkable how many of his strong opinions contained a hint of their opposite.

Basil Deane, writing about the composer's influence on Roussel, has summed up d'Indy's peculiar inconsistencies so searchingly that no other words serve as well to illustrate the point. He states:

> Vincent d'Indy is one of the most fascinating and paradoxical figures in the history of French music. A devout Catholic, acutely conscious of his divinely-inspired mission as a teacher, he was a man of strong prejudices and had a medieval propensity for developing elaborate theories from unsound premises, twisting or ignoring inconvenient facts which might present themselves. As a musician he was capable of extraordinary insight and amazing obtuseness; he regarded the Renaissance and Reformation as unmitigated evils, yet he was one of the first to recognise the greatness of Monteverdi

[1] It was said that even after the old lady had become blind, she took to wearing a repeater watch in order to maintain the rigid schedule she had mapped out for her grandson.

and he was a lifelong propagandist for Bach and Beethoven. A fervent nationalist with a genuine and practical enthusiasm for his native traditions and culture, he nevertheless believed that the future of French music lay along the paths explored by Wagner. In his teaching he continually emphasised the importance of inspiration, yet he evolved a system of composition which virtually excluded it, and he was suspicious of any signs of individuality in his pupils. Although disliked by many, he was universally respected, and he extended his considerable charm and courtesy to all, including those whose music, ideas or religion he most violently attacked.

It is hard to say how far these contradictions were the result of d'Indy's upbringing, which seemed to have the effect of both encouraging and restraining his gifts. His fearlessness certainly owed something to the training he had undergone, since it is well known that the Countess forced him to submit to needlessly cruel ordeals in order to test his manliness. She compelled him to stand in front of an open window during thunderstorms so that he would overcome his sense of fright. In the same way, she insisted on his assuming an erect posture at the keyboard, and rapped him fiercely on the knuckles every time he relapsed into a more slovenly pose. Such disciplinary measures undoubtedly played their part in shaping the young man's character.

Oddly enough, there seems to have been no attempt to stifle d'Indy's early enthusiasm for the arts, and he was not discouraged from placing himself under the tutorship of top-flight musicians. Family connections were invoked to enable him to learn the piano with Marmontel, whose virtuoso talents had been sufficient to dissuade the public from paying attention to the young Franck many years previously, and his assistant Louis Diémer. Though he was to become a very creditable performer at the piano, the instrument was not big enough to contain his ambitions. At this point, it looked as if he might try his hand at half a dozen instruments. None succeeded in claiming him, however, and he soon found more to interest him in the harmony lessons he had from Albert Lavignac. This distinguished teacher offered d'Indy many things he would not have obtained from anyone else. To begin with, Lavignac was quite an advanced theorist by the standards of the day. It was his progressive outlook which provided Debussy with the stimulus he needed to look beyond conventional practices. A keen student of Eastern music, he adopted a very wide-ranging attitude to the problems of tonality, while his rigorous system of sight-reading became of revolutionary importance at the Paris Conservatoire where he taught. More significant than any of these things was the fact that it was Lavignac who established himself as the major French authority on Wagner. His book *Voyage Artistique à Bayreuth* was not written until 1897, but to judge from its impressive array of charts and catalogues of *leit-motifs* it must have occupied him for a very long time previously. That he was already an active partisan of the German composer at the moment of his meeting with the adolescent d'Indy cannot be doubted. His enthusiasm, together with the new ideas he picked up, laid the basis for those sympathies so many were to dislike in his pupil.

The decision to become a professional musician seems to have given d'Indy hardly any trouble. With all his wealth awaiting him (his parents had died and he was shortly to inherit their share of the family estates), he was not embarrassed by doubts about securing a livelihood. Neither did he feel, as Chausson was so poignantly to do, that it was still incumbent on him to prove that he possessed genius. Rather, it was d'Indy's good fortune to pursue a run-of-the-mill musical career without enduring any of the frustrations this would normally have involved. When we observe him becoming occasional horn-player and drummer at the Théâtre Italien, and timpanist with the Colonne orchestra, we cannot help thinking that these experiences served to give him a good taste of the pedestrian aspects of the musician's existence without committing him to any of its hardships. D'Indy's introduction to the profession resulted in one or two setbacks all the same. Although he had privately decided, by the age of eighteen, that he wanted to become a composer, his earliest efforts at writing music unhappily coincided with the onset of war. Granted such a dutiful temperament, it was not possible for the young man to act according to his resolve. His first choice was to volunteer his services on behalf of his country. Appearing one day in the uniform of a National Guardsman, he earned the surprise and approval of his enfeebled grandmother, who was well used to seeing her menfolk take this course, but had not anticipated that things would occur quite so precipitately. From then onwards, d'Indy was permitted only the most intermittent contacts with the profession he had hoped to enter. He was stationed in Paris throughout the duration of the conflict, but the cessation of musical activities made it impossible to think of having any of his works performed. His interests—as much through social as artistic pressure—were directed towards dramatic music, though it is to his credit that he refused to make use of his many influential contacts to further a career in this sector. Instead, he accepted the need for a disciplined study of the classics, and began his creative apprenticeship with a number of sonatas, songs and smaller pieces, all of which were destroyed once he had established himself as a Franck pupil. The only large work to have been started during the

war was his *Symphonie Italienne*—a programmatic representation of
two civilizations, that of Ancient Rome, symbolized by the Coli-
seum, and Christian Rome, as expressed by the noble architecture
of St Peter's. This immature work was later performed by Pasdeloup, with whom d'Indy always maintained a close relationship, at
one of his Sunday symphony concerts.

Though Duparc's friendship secured him an introduction to
Franck whilst the war was still in progress, we have it on d'Indy's
own testimony that he did not dare to divulge his musical ambitions
at this stage. It was only after Franck's appointment to the Conservatoire that the young officer plucked up the courage to ask for
lessons. His first step—necessarily rather cautious—was to show
the older man a movement from a Quartet which he had been
writing. It is an interesting gloss on Franck's response that he did
not waste time on his customary equivocal praise. D'Indy himself
relates what happened with painful objectivity:

After I had played him a movement of my Quartet (which I
fondly imagined to be of such a nature as to win his approba-
tion), he was silent for a moment; then, turning to me with a
melancholy air, he spoke the words I have never been able to
forget, since they had a decisive action upon my life: 'There
are some good things in it; it shows spirit and a certain instinct
for dialogue between the parts; the ideas would not be bad—
but—that is not enough; the work is not finished—in fact, you
really know nothing whatever.' Seeing that I was dreadfully
mortified by this opinion, for which I was not at all prepared,
he went on to explain his reasons, and wound up by saying:
'Come to see me, if you want us to work together. I could teach
you composition.'
    When I got home—the interview took place very late in the
evening—I lay awake at night, rebelling against the severity
of this sentence, but agitated in the depths of my heart, and
I said to myself that Franck was an old-fashioned musician
who knew nothing of a young and progressive art. Nevertheless, the next day, having calmed down, I took up my unfortunate Quartet and went over, one by one, the observations
which the master had made, emphasising his words the
while, according to his custom, by innumerable arabesques
scrawled in pencil over the manuscript, and I was obliged to
own to myself that he was perfectly right—I knew nothing. I
went to him, almost in fear and trembling, to ask if he would
be good enough to take me as a pupil, and he admitted me
to the organ class at the Conservatoire, of which he had just
been appointed professor.

This incident shows that, when necessary, Franck was capable of considerable firmness and directness in dealing with his prospective pupils. It also shows that it was not the quality of 'progressiveness' that attracted these young men. If anything, they tended to regard Franck's outlook as a trifle *vieux jeu*. Clearly, it was Wagner who represented the Music of the Future, and hardly any French musicians had the imagination to sense how prophetic Franck's contribution, particularly in the sphere of harmony, was to become. They revered him, in the beginning, for his integrity, his patient sense of abnegation, rather than for any revolutionary zeal.

In time, of course, d'Indy came to appreciate the striking nature of many of his teacher's innovations. It is important not to be misled by this, however, since it was chiefly as the successor to Beethoven, and heir to the classical tradition, that Franck was fated to appear to him. Classicism remained d'Indy's supreme ideal, even after he had absorbed the lessons of his contemporaries, and it is only one more proof of the man's essential contrariness the he could see no dichotomy between this ideal and the Teutonic-Romantic principles to which he also professed attachment. In the field of instrumentation, he gave an enthusiastic welcome to the discoveries of Berlioz, whilst the few days he spent at Weimar in 1873 had the effect of turning him into a part-time disciple of both Liszt and Brahms. When he put in an appearance at the opening cycle of *The Ring* at the newly-built theatre of Bayreuth in 1876, the admiration he had long extended to Wagner was given added strength and tenacity.[1] Equipped with this very mixed background, d'Indy cannot be accused of having developed through a narrow obsession with Franckist ideas. On the contrary, he had the most wide-ranging sympathies of any of the pupils. That he was bigoted in some matters is indisputable. But he never suffered, like so many others, from too great an exclusiveness in his musical relationships. Although he can be convicted of having made a false monument out of his teacher, he was saved from the worst perils of illiberalism by the great breadth of his scholarly pretensions. These certainly proved far in advance of most other musicians of his day. He was thoroughly alive to the possibilities of a science of musicology, and even in the present age of research there can be precious few pedagogues with anything like the same inclusive attitude to music as he possessed. This catholicity of taste served him in particularly good stead during the years when Franck no longer stood at his side.

[1] This was not d'Indy's earliest introduction to the later music-dramas, since he had made a trip to Munich in the company of Duparc in 1869. It was there that the two men heard 'Das Rheingold' and 'Tristan und Isolde'.

One of the inhibiting consequences of Franck's role as a teacher was that his pupils too quickly imitated his feelings of modesty and resignation. Realising that their master had waited whole decades without securing recognition, they drew the erroneous conclusion that it would be improper for them to submit too many works of their own. As Chausson was later to put it in a letter he wrote to d'Indy: 'When I think of our teacher Franck, I am truly amazed if anyone dares to complain.' This willingness to languish in a self-inflicted exile was characteristic of even the most gifted members of the circle, including the artistically-constipated Duparc. D'Indy proved untypical in going on to write a massive and varied body of music, though he too underwent a brief period when it looked as if he would not become prolific. This phase lasted from about 1872 to 1876 or a little later. Between these dates he attempted several works but was unable to finish anything of importance. Such lethargy in one who scarcely had it in him to be inactive was unusual. It suggests that, out of deference to his teacher's feelings, he deliberately refrained from making a display of his ambitions. It also remains true that d'Indy, like many of his fellow aristocrats, affected a perpetual disdain for publicity.[1] He considered it bad form to want to press one's own claims in company, and the fact that Franck himself was from a lower social class urged the necessity of a little 'noblesse oblige'. Reticence of this kind went far towards depriving the group, not only of its essential creative vigour, but also of the element of glamour which it might otherwise have exhibited. Comparing them with their counterparts among, say, the Debussy circle, the Franckists cannot help making a somewhat colourless showing. Even when severely criticised, they had the good manners to remain silent, and for all their elaborate journalistic connections, they were slow to take advantage of what interest the public took in their works.

As a composer, d'Indy did not restrict himself to a single genre. He wrote fluently on all fronts, though his early work shows a preference for the standard Franckist forms—especially the ballad for voice and orchestra, and the piece with an informal literary pro-gramme. Like Franck himself, he was attracted to the poetry of Hugo, with the result that he was led to set his 'Chanson des Adventuriers de la Mer' for baritone, choir and piano in 1870, following it two years later with the songs 'Attente' and 'Clair de

---

[1] It is perhaps on this account that he never engaged in the writing of manifestoes—a task for which he might have seemed eminently fitted. Though he wrote profusely to the newspapers, most of his polemics centred upon academic matters. It is typical of him that he looked to an *official* organisation like the Société Nationale to do all his propaganda for him.

Lune', the last-named being scored for soprano and orchestra. The 'art-song' was never to be developed by d'Indy, however, and he even omitted to give tuition in this branch of music when he became Director of the Schola. Whether he recognized, after these early trials, that he lacked the gift for melody demanded by the form, or whether there was an element of philistinism in his decision, we shall never be quite sure. In either case, he deserves to be rebuked for neglecting this one sector in which the Franck school made an undoubted breakthrough.[1] Long-range musical thinking was far more of a strong suit of d'Indy's, and the tone-poem or programme symphony represented him at his most natural. The *Wallenstein* overtures which he began in 1873 accordingly seem very expressive of his interests. The first of these to be written was the one we now know as No. 2, entitled *Max et Thécla*. In its initial form it was

Ex. 7
Vincent d' Indy: Wallenstein (Max)

(Thécla)

called *Overture Piccolomini*, and it was performed by Pasdeloup at one of the Concerts Populaires in 1875. It was this work that won the composer his first hint of recognition, though that did not prevent him from making the alterations of title and substance to which we have referred. He also went on to add a prologue, *Le Camp*, and an epilogue, *Le Mort de Wallenstein*, the entire trilogy not being completed until 1881. The subject of this extended portrait does much to lay bare d'Indy's religious sentiments. Wallenstein was the great Jesuit-trained general of the Emperor Ferdinand, the ruler whose bitter scourging of the seventeenth-century Protestants had helped to maintain Hapsburg supremacy and prolong the Thirty Years War. D'Indy's militant Catholicism and love of authority were doubtless what impelled him to choose such a theme. Indeed the work could be said to illustrate his position *vis-à-vis* his religious faith as decisively as *Les Béatitudes* illustrates the very different position of Franck.

[1] About a dozen other songs—including three to verses by Duparc's favourite Robert de Bonnières—do little to mitigate this judgement. It was Bordes and de Bréville who did most to keep this art alive at the Schola, though Roussel also became a notable exponent later on.

Many of the succeeding works which d'Indy wrote betray his unswerving penchant for the stage. This was something for which the Wagnerian influence should not be held solely responsible. At first, he had been willing to write a comic opera—the now forgotten *Attendez-moi sous l'Orme*—but the triteness of this composition made him hesitate before casting his next work in an explicitly dramatic form. Known as *Le Chant de la Cloche*, it was a setting of a text by Schiller (who had incidentally been the author of the Wallenstein story) for soloists, double choir and orchestra. Although planned as a 'légende dramatique' for the concert hall—the form in which it received its first performance—it later proved easily adaptable to stage presentation, as was shown by the success it won at the Théâtre de la Monnaie in 1912. The plot recounts the behaviour of Wilhelm, a megalomanic bell-maker, whose efforts to cast a magic spell over his products arouses the fierce suspicion of his colleagues. Desirous of immortality, he bends his will towards producing a mammoth construction which will have the effect of outringing every other bell in the city. His wish is granted only after his death, since on the day of his funeral the procession is interrupted by a tremendous pealing and tolling—signifying that Wilhelm's creation had set off a reaction in each surrounding belfry. As may be imagined, the subject lent itself well to musical treatment. D'Indy's handling of the percussion department—and the massiveness of his scoring—proved how audacious a composer he was even at the age of thirty. In terms of orchestration, the work looks back to Berlioz and forward to Honegger. Its deliberately aural conceptions also make it among the forerunners of the impressionist works of the early twentieth century. Its major weakness can be found in the too frequent resemblance it bears to 'Die Meistersinger'. The chorus of guildsmen and general atmosphere of intrigue are not its only points of similarity. As Martin Cooper has acutely detected, it contains:

> . . . a Beckmesser with the glorious name of Dietrich Leerschwulst, a misunderstood and noble artist, Wilhelm, instead of Wagner's Walther, and a perfect counterpart to Eva in Lenore.

Certainly, the final impression left by both this cantata and the Wallenstein trilogy is that they are the work of a progressive henchman of Liszt and his unsettling son-in-law.

An unexpected honour which came d'Indy's way as a result of *Le Chant de la Cloche* was the prize he received from the City of Paris in 1885. This had the effect of helping to make his name as a composer. At that point in his career, d'Indy found himself in the somewhat embarrassing position of being more famous than his

teacher. His experience as choirmaster to Colonne had assured him
of a small following, and now that he had caught the public ear with
one or two substantial works of his own his prospects had come to
seem lively indeed. His aim was never to gain a quick success,
however, and he spent many of the ensuing years working hard on
an opera, or 'action musicale' as it was eventually termed. This
project had been on the stocks since 1881, and altogether it was
to take the composer fourteen years to finish. The inspiration
behind it was still Wagner, but this time *Parsifal* rather than *Meistersinger*. The title d'Indy gave to this work was *Fervaal*—a name
chosen to replace the Scandinavian Axel of Exsaias Tegner's drama,
upon which the opera was being based. That it was intended as a
strong bid for major status may be gathered from an inspection of
the forces for which it was written. Utilizing a modern sized
orchestra, the parts called for quadruple woodwind and brass,
coupled with a variety of outsize bass instruments, including bass
and double bass clarinet and bass tuba. Also specified were eight
saxhorns and a 'cornet à bouquin' or mountain horn.[1] Such an
array proves how industrious the composer had been in studying
Berlioz's famous treatise on instrumentation, and how eager he
still was to shift some of the lavish Bayreuth sonorities to the
French theatre.

Ex. 8

Vincent d' Indy: Prélude - Fervaal

Très lent et calme

Fervaal had a reasonably smooth passage at Brussels on 12
March 1897, having to wait a further year before being mounted

[1] A further innovation in the percussion department consisted of a
set of kettle-drums which enabled the composer to obtain all twelve
notes of the chromatic scale.

at the Comique. It did not succeed in gaining admittance to the
Opéra itself until 1913—a reflection on the attitudes of those in
authority to what was unquestionably an important attempt to
resurrect the form. Some of the dislike the work aroused stemmed
from its subject-matter, and this proved difficult to accept even in
Belgium. One critic declared that it would have been better
entitled *Le Crépuscule des Druides*, while others objected to the
clumsy and mechanical fashion in which the various symbolic and
mythological elements had been put together. That there was
much truth in these objections cannot be denied. Fervaal himself
was patently designed to stand for Humanity, Guilhen for Love
and Arfgaard for Error. The manner in which the story evolved
served merely to bind these abstractions. Foster-child of the old
druid Arfgaard, the hero is brought up to fulfil an ancient prophecy
that he will one day rule over the kingdom of Cravann. Intent on
confronting his destiny, Fervaal finds himself diverted by the
charms of Guilhen, who becomes his enemy in battle. After being
defeated, he listens to the advice of the goddess Kaito, who tells
him that if only he will submit to sacrifice a new child will be born
to bear out the prophecy in his place. At the moment of yielding
to the knife, Fervaal hears Guilhen's cries and rushes to comfort
her, at the same time killing the meddling Arfgaard. In the third
act, the hero is seen carrying the body of his beloved, who has died
of neglect, up into the cloud-capped mountains of his homeland.
Even stated so baldly, the action has obvious resemblances to the
typical Wagnerian music-drama. The similarities to *The Ring* are
sufficiently observable—especially if one compares Fervaal's role
with that of Siegfried, and Arfgaard's with that of Mime. The
work's likenesses to *Parsifal* are still more striking. Fervaal, for
example, is made to take an oath of chastity, and is lured into a
Zaubergarten of the kind that has become all too familiar from the
sets of Appia and Tietjen. The Guilhen-Kundry parallel is just as
pronounced as that between Fervaal and Parsifal. In the end, we
are forced to acknowledge the second-handness of much of d'Indy's
dramatic concept.

Musically speaking, the debts owed by *Fervaal* are no less
explicit, even if they do not all relate to Wagner. The habit of
associating certain tonalities with story-elements is something that
can just as properly be attributed to Franck—especially in the
fashion used in d'Indy's opera. As in *Les Béatitudes*, the richer keys
are singled out to express the varieties of human and divine love,
whilst themes of grief and unrest are presented, either as enharmonic inversions of these, or as simplified modulations. What
is indubitably redolent of Wagner is the fixing of definite *leit-
motifs*, some of which signify the old Druidic kingdom and others

the new world which Fervaal is bringing into being. D'Indy made poetic play with these motives in his Cours de Composition Musicale, in which the existence of allegorical counterparts is freely acknowledged. The comparison which the composer allows himself is with *Pelléas et Mélisande*, however, and not any of Wagner's dramas. Since Debussy's opera followed rather than preceded d'Indy's, this is perhaps being too disingenuous. Both composers must have learnt much from their German predecessor. Yet when all is said, there is a great deal in both works that remains French in feeling and tone. We know that d'Indy was deeply impressed by Wagner's remark (apparently conveyed to him by Duparc) that it was time French composers learnt to exploit the legends of their own country. It was to be some years before they were able to follow this advice, and *Fervaal* cannot truthfully be accorded a place in the experiment.[1] Its Northern origins are too well known. What the opera does do is more subtle. It attempts, through its extensive use of folk-like melodies, to impose a Gallic flavour upon the Scandinavian material it employs.[2] It will be worth our while to elaborate briefly on this suggestion.

By the time he was well advanced on the writing of *Fervaal*, d'Indy had settled on the practice of spending his summers back at Faugs, where he had built a villa in which to do his composing. The pattern of his life—which was to remain virtually unchanged —then became established, and it consisted of a teaching and organising stint in the capital, followed by a creative period in the Ardèche. Like Mahler, he found it necessary to become a 'vacation composer', otherwise he would have had to forfeit the many executive interests he had developed. This practice not only bore fruit in terms of the quantity of work d'Indy produced, but it also led him to further the regional studies in which he had always shown curiosity. It was while he put up at Faugs that he continued the long series of explorations of folksong for which he was to become well known. The songs he noted down were mainly mountain airs associated with his native region. Hugues Imbert, writing of the influences which he considered helped to mould d'Indy's style, has commented on the three most outstanding. These, he claims, were Nature, Berlioz, and Wagner. The second and third of these influences we have already dealt with. They are apparent in the composer's use of instruments and of the stage,

[1] Lalo's opera *Le Roi d'Ys* (1888) is usually thought to be the earliest work to have been directly inspired by French folklore. It was instigated by an interest in Breton legends, while at the same time remaining faithful to Wagnerian conceptions.

[2] This flavour is, of course, much enhanced by having the action transferred from its Northern locale to d'Indy's native Cévennes region.

respectively. The power of Nature is conversely most evident in d'Indy's style of melodic construction, in which there is an overt reliance upon simple folk tunes. For the most part, these tend to be diatonic, step-wise melodies of no great complexity or distinction. They are frequently in triple-time, and avoid any suggestion of the jaggedness we associate with the Central European idiom. A good example is the opening theme of the *Symphonie Cévenole*.

Ex. 9

Vincent d' Indy: Symphonie Cévenole

Cor Anglais

The regular use of such tunes is what serves to make d'Indy's music—despite all its indebtedness to the classical tradition—fundamentally and unmistakably national in character.

Nothing the composer wrote demonstrates his acceptance of the French influence better than this *Symphonie sur un Chant Montagnard Français*, completed in 1886. An important essay in the concertante style, it must rank as one of d'Indy's finest compositions. The work is in three movements, and is thus too long to have been given the title of Ballade, after the fashion of Fauré's otherwise similar work. To all intents and purposes, it could have been called a Piano Concerto. The main point of difference lies in the fact that the soloist is treated, not as the dominating power, but as a mere *primus inter pares*. We have already noted how original Castillon had been in introducing something of this kind, aiming at the chamber music balance only on a larger scale.[1] Since d'Indy's work was to make use of Vivarais folk-material, it could hardly have striven for the same purity of expression. But between the writing of Castillon's concerto and d'Indy's, there had been two significant additions to the genre made by Franck himself. These were *Les Djinns* (1884) and the *Variations Symphoniques* (1885). The first-named was a symphonic poem in which the piano was awarded 'obligato' status, whilst the latter proved to be a set of linked variations employing the dialogue principle. There can be little doubt that d'Indy modelled his writing on the experience contained in all three previous ventures. The *Symphonie Cévenole* (the alternative title is much easier to use) shows the influence of Franck's brilliant piano figuration, without reflecting his habit of lapsing into virtuosity. Compared with the Castillon concerto, its

[1] Actually, the first French composer to have used the piano as a *symphonic* instrument seems to have been Saint-Saëns, whose Third Symphony (1886) contains parts for no less than three keyboard players.

style seems more buoyant and continuously varied. What is certainly to d'Indy's credit is the manner in which he appears to have pruned his orchestral imagination. For instead of the thick, heavily-massed scoring of the Wagnerian works, what we have is a light and airy semi-chamber style. There are even certain passages in which the melody is allowed to remain unaccompanied. One suspects that the mountain air may have had refreshing effects on the composer's intellectual processes as well as his general outlook.

The other works of the early years confirm the difficulty d'Indy experienced in striking a balance between the 'choral' manner he had inherited and the natural graces arising out of folk-song. In this sense, Berlioz, whose *Damnation of Faust* had greatly impressed him in 1877, proved to be both a good and a bad influence. The magical interplay of strings and woodwind that we find in the more lightly-scored works of this master (especially in parts of *Romeo and Juliet*) was thus of some importance in teaching d'Indy to orchestrate with economy; while the musical hyperbole employed in works like the *Requiem* and *Lélio* left a contrary and too often detrimental legacy. The pity is that d'Indy's lack of melodic facility caused him to lean rather heavily on the *chanson populaire* as a way out of his creative dilemmas. It is not surprising that repetitiveness presented itself as a hazard in nearly all the works he wrote at about this time.[1] The curbing of his tendency to grandiosity may therefore have given rise to other faults, peculiar to the new medium to which he turned his attention. Aside from the *Symphonie*, few of the composer's regional works form satisfying wholes. The upshot is that d'Indy—far more than Franck—has a way of boring his listeners. This he does either through deliberate pretension, or by naïve reliance on local colour. Only very rarely does he succeed in ravishing the senses. The novelist E. M. Forster once remarked enviously: 'I can't soar; I can only indicate. That's where the musicians have the pull, for music has wings.' But the trouble with so much of d'Indy's music is that it signally forfeits this ability. Invented in a spirit of prosaic determination, it constantly refuses to embrace those qualities which could have done so much to vindicate it. The struggle between technique and inspiration—always an unequal struggle as far as this composer was concerned—shows itself in the allegory, *Saugefleurie* and the ballade-symphonie, *La Forêt Enchantée*, based on Uhland's poem 'Harald'. Both works contain subtleties of orchestration, but neither quite overcomes its inevitable *longueurs*.

[1] Typically pertinent is William Mann's remark apropos the *Symphonie Cévenole*: 'It is a pity the shepherd only knows one tune.' (The Gramophone, August, 1962).

Far better able to stand on its own feet is the suite of orchestral variations entitled *Istar* (1896). Orientalism was not of such compelling appeal to d'Indy as it was to de Bréville, but this Arabian Nights fantasy (which was actually drawn from one of Idzubar's Assyrian epics) proved an interesting challenge. It describes the ordeals of the goddess Istar, who has to pass through seven gates in order to reach her lover, at each of which she is required to shed some article of apparel. In the end, she stands revealed in all her nakedness. Such a theme would have seemed well suited to Richard Strauss or Bartók, but scarcely fitted what we know of d'Indy's more austere inclinations. What probably attracted him to the subject was the ingenious fashion in which it could be adapted to serve the variation technique, each of the goddess's ordeals suggesting a possible transformation of the original musical idea. D'Indy actually carried this notion to an added pitch of cleverness by not presenting the main theme until *after* all the variations had been heard. In this way, its eventual appearance duplicated that of Istar herself, both having managed to divest themselves of every encumbrance. Though the work is singularly unexpressive of sensuality, it remains in quite another sense highly indicative of its composer's skills. This is the sense in which it permits him to demonstrate—in a way that is readily understandable by all—the skeletal processes at work in the act of composition. A close analysis of *Istar* shows that each variation takes a particular aspect of the creative function and deals with it in isolation. Thus Variation I simply lays down the harmonic substratum which the theme sets out to specify, whilst Variation VII passionately pursues its melodic implications. The instrumentation is also sufficiently explicit to act as a 'young person's guide' to this department of the musician's thinking. Considered as a whole, *Istar* is one of those fortunate works which succeed in meeting the demands of art without sacrificing their power to instruct. Its place in French music lies somewhere between Franck's *Variations Symphoniques* and Roussel's *Evocations*.

In terms of day-to-day activities, d'Indy did not wait too long before moving up into the policy-making echelons of life in the capital. The years from 1872 to 1890 saw him busily laying the foundation for his later apostolic role. When the death of Castillon created a gap in the administrative machinery, he did not waste much time in filling it. From 1876 he assumed the joint title of Secretary of the Société Nationale along with his colleague Henri Duparc. As may be surmised, it was d'Indy who took on the lion's share of the activity, devoting hour after hour to the business of tidying up the procedural mess into which the Society's affairs had fallen. Up to this time, none of the members had thought it worthwhile to keep an accurate transcript of their meetings, so that the records of the Society were in a richly chaotic state. D'Indy immediately set about rectifying things, jotting down the minutes in his own punctilious hand. He also took on the job of rearranging the files into some semblance of order. In thus ensuring that he became indispensable, the composer established the pattern that was to lead him to his unique position of authority in the years ahead. He showed cool judgement in not rushing his bid for power until opinion had come round to his point of view. Realizing the unifying qualities which resided in Franck's person, he took the alternative course of manoeuvring his teacher into a succession of key roles, taking all the steps necessary to see that he eventually became president. Meantime he devoted the bulk of his efforts to attacking what he took to be the reactionary faction on the committee. Among the proponents of this faction's views, Saint-Saëns presented himself as easily the most formidable figure, and for a number of years he became the chief obstacle to d'Indy's policies.[1] Having worked his way up the ladder of success with considerable precariousness, this practically-minded ex-prodigy harboured an acute fear of German musical invasions. He thought the acceptance of Wagner would mean stiffer competition than most working French musicians could afford to face. Moreover, he had been mortified by the Bayreuth master's contemptuous attacks on France at the time of the Franco-Prussian War. D'Indy's position as a rich acolyte caused him to discount such fears as unrealistic.

The quarrels at the Nationale came to a head around 1886, when Saint-Saëns's grumbling behaviour (he was always jealous of Franck's esteem, and deplored the atmosphere of heavy piety which surrounded him) exposed him to the charge of rudeness. During November of that year, d'Indy succeeded in getting a resolution passed which lifted the ban on foreign music at the Society's concerts. Predictably enough, this had the effect of ensuring Saint-Saëns's prompt resignation, and Franck was hustled into the principal office in his place. From then onwards, it became simple for d'Indy to get his own way about almost everything. Chabrier and Duparc, who had acted as fellow conspirators in the whole venture, were quite content to further the Wagnerian cause, as long as it did not interfere with winning acclaim for the Franck circle's members. The seeds were thus sown for that bipartite domination of French musical life which became apparent

[1] The enmity between these two musicians was to culminate many years later in the publication of Saint-Saëns's scathing critique *Les Idées de M. Vincent d'Indy*—the book in which he made his strongest assault on the Franckist-Wagnerian hegemony from which he had suffered all his life.

in the last decade of the nineteenth century. It is unfortunate that Franck himself died just at the point when his star had reached its ascendancy, but the result of this was that d'Indy's inheritance of power was considerably facilitated. To do him justice, it is only fair to add that he would probably have been willing to share much of this power with those remaining Franck disciples who had assisted him in his task, had they not found reasons of their own for relinquishing all claims. Duparc's nervous breakdown and abrupt termination as a composer—which took place at about the same time as the administrative changes referred to above—was one signal instance of the withdrawal of rivalry. Similarly, the accident to Chausson in 1899 removed the last possibility of usurpation by a younger member of the set. As for the others, they were none of them possessed of sufficient musical talent to divert any of the homage which d'Indy now began to receive as his due. His greater energy alone suggested him as the most logical person to propagate the circle's work, whilst the habit of system-building to which he was prone singled him out as the obvious codifier of Franck's haphazard teachings.

To share the trials of his personal life, d'Indy chose to marry his cousin, Isabelle de Pampelonne. The match had been opposed by Rézia, so that the couple had to wait until after her death in 1872 to proceed with their plans. She seems to have made him a more docile wife than most, willingly accepting the fact that music came first in his aspirations. Legend has it that when his friend Charles Langrand, who was called upon to play the organ at the wedding, put the question: 'Did I play my part satisfactorily?' the maestro replied: 'Perfectly, but why did you modulate to the sub-dominant at the end of the first section?' Although he must have seemed a curious figure to his bride's friends and acquaintances, d'Indy never felt it necessary to apologize for his profession. His musical activities were planned in exactly the cold-blooded fashion of a military commander deploying his forces. Each operation presupposed an objective to be gained, a victory to be won. The same business-like attitudes were observable in his dealings with the rank and file of orchestral musicians. Not sensing the element of eccentricity in his behaviour, these ordinary folk often took offence at what they imagined was an arrogantly paternal stance on his part. Once, when the composer was rehearsing an orchestra in place of its regular conductor, he discovered a note on his desk which read: 'Death to the aristocrats! Next time we'll finish off you and your kind.' It is inconceivable that he could have been intimidated by threats of this kind, and it probably never occurred to him to assume a more tactful form of address. What saved him from being ostracized was the unexpected power of charm which he was suddenly capable of switching on. This was not something slimy or insincere. It sprang quite naturally from his complex character. Indeed, once his musical recriminations had secured an outlet, it was unusual for him to bear a grudge. The letters which he wrote to his friend Auguste Sérieyx show a real concern for the health and welfare of those around him, and it is obvious that nothing was too much trouble if they had need of his services. The selfless manner in which he laboured to complete certain scores of Chausson and Lekeu underlines the essential kindliness of the man, and serves to make clear the altruism which dominated his thinking. It will be agreed that d'Indy's eminence was in a good measure due to the many-sidedness of his work, and the mysterious gift he possessed of being able to contain a host of contradictions.

In taking our leave of this pertinacious champion of French music—we shall be returning to consider his later career in Chapter XI—it is hardly necessary to summarize what he achieved. His work as founder and administrator of the Schola Cantorum was to prove the most important single contribution of any Franck pupil, and one of the supreme educational ventures of the age. Even at this early point in his career, however, the convergent effect he had can scarcely be exaggerated. Genius or not, he was the one member of the group—apart from Franck himself—to whom potential recruits could look for guidance. This was because he alone possessed the technical knowledge of a *grand maître*. Freed from the self-doubts and fears of the more conventional artist, he could and did devote the bulk of his time to overhauling the machinery of music as he found it; and in so doing he provided the art with a succession of growth points for the age to come. Taking advantage of the services he made available, sophisticated composers of a younger generation—men like Paul Dukas and Albéric Magnard—found it possible to express their ideas without embarrassment, while the less robust members of Franck's loyal band discovered in him a new saviour to whom they would be able, once the fateful day came around, to transfer what was left of their allegiance.

VI

The imperfect Wagnerite

If Wagner went a long way towards mesmerizing so determined an individualist as d'Indy, it may be imagined how much more potent was his effect on the less resolute musicians of the age. Duparc, Chausson, Chabrier, Lekeu—all these were to discover in the music-drama an influence at least as nourishing as anything they acquired through Franck. Everyone knows the story of Wagner's earliest sojourn in Paris during 1839, when he failed to dislodge Meyerbeer from his throne at the Opéra. What is not so clearly recalled is the prurient air of expectation that was made to surround the composer's later assaults on the capital, each of which served to whet the appetites of that small band of progressives whose lot it had been merely to stand and wait. When the famous production of *Tannhäuser* also misfired in 1861, Wagner was compelled to undertake a second retreat, after which he foolishly sought revenge in a tasteless lampoon mocking the agonies of the occupation. It was not to be wondered that, by the time he came to make his final attack on the city, feelings had mounted to fever pitch. The sensible course for those who could afford it was therefore to invest in a prior trip to Munich, where the operas could be heard without prejudice, and avoid having to take part in a sordid squabble.[1]

Those who were wise enough to have decided on this course found that they had been spared a very long wait. For despite the

[1] After 1876 it naturally became much more fashionable to go direct to Bayreuth, and in the course of time this shrine was visited by a whole host of French musicians, including Saint-Saëns (1876), Chausson (1882), Dukas (1886) and Debussy (1888). The climax to these pilgrimages was reached during the 1889 season, when Lekeu and Chabrier gave way to their respective outbursts. The list of French visitors to Bayreuth may be found in Lavignac (*op. cit.*).

propaganda begun by Pasdeloup in 1873, and the concert devoted
entirely to Wagner's works given by Lamoureux some twelve years
later, the next attempt at staging a complete opera did not take
place until *Lohengrin* was admitted to the Eden Theatre in 1887.
This was conducted in French, and it was to be a further four years
before the German version was sanctified by being presented at
the Opéra itself. Turning to the later music-dramas, it is remarkable to recollect that it was not until 1914—almost a quarter of a
century after Franck's death—that Parisians had their first chance
of hearing the original text of *Tristan* sung in the theatre; whilst
Debussy himself did not live long enough to attend the first complete performance of *The Ring* in 1921. Knowing these facts, it
becomes a little difficult to credit the enormous influence Wagner
is acknowledged to have exercised over the composers of the Third
Republic. What has to be understood is that, precisely because his
music had the flavour of forbidden fruit, it aroused an exaggerated
sense of yearning in the minds of sensitive Frenchmen. Those who
made the expedition to Germany returned with spell-binding tales
which involved the man as much as his music. To the less adventurous spirits who had remained at home, on the other hand,
the feeling of frustration gained in importance for every year it was
allowed to fester. Surmounting it all was the hysterical behaviour
of the anti-Wagnerites, those backward-looking academics and
supporters of cultural nationalism whose policies only had the
effect of stirring up curiosity where none had previously existed.
In such an aggravated atmosphere, it was ironical that the only
pieces of Wagner to find their way into the concert-life of the
capital were the more sensational transcriptions like 'The Ride of
the Valkyries' and the 'Overture to Tannhäuser'.

The unique power of fascination possessed by the German composer did not reside in his music alone, however, and it would be
wrong to underestimate the insidious attraction of his philosophy.[1]
Poets who had already been won over to the Baudelairean theory
of correspondences could be excused for seeing in the Wagnerian
Gesamtkunstwerk a larger vehicle for the expression of their ideas.
The notion of a synthesis of the arts appealed strongly to French
Platonists, as well as to those ex-Romantics whose reading had
been confined more to writers like Poe and Hoffmann. Added to
these, there were a number of dilettantes, such as Catulle Mendès
and Judith Gautier, to whom the name Wagner was synonymous
with exciting developments in aesthetic theory and practice.

[1] Indeed, it could be said that Wagnerism (as opposed to what Mr
Elliott Zuckermann has aptly called 'Tristanism') was not primarily a
musical movement in France. It became a branch of the Symbolist
philosophy.

Mendès was a symbolist poet whose place in music became assured by his writing the libretti for Chabrier's *Gwendoline* (possibly the most Wagnerian of all French operas) and Debussy's unfinished *Rodrigues et Chimène*. He and Gautier's daughter were married in 1867, after which they paid several visits to Wagner at his home at Triebschen. The object of their quest was to reformulate the great man's philosophy in terms calculated to appeal to the hypothetical French genius whose presence they were bent on invoking. Prophesying the creation of a national music-drama to rival that begun in Germany, Mendès wrote:

> Whoever creates such a work will be a great man and he will earn our love. For, even though he borrows his forms from Germany, he will modify them, and in his inspiration he will remain a Frenchman.

Unhappily his dreams received an unexpected jolt in the publication of *Eine Kapitulation*, and by the amorous attachment which suddenly sprang up between Wagner and his wife, Judith. After these happenings, Mendés's enthusiasm simmered down, though the campaign he had waged reverberated through the literary circles in which he moved with resounding effect.[1]

During the years that followed a motley collection of Wagnerian novels, treatises and guide-books began to appear in France, and in 1885 the writer Edouard Dujardin founded the notorious *Revue Wagnérienne*, a periodical whose contributors came to include Verlaine, Huysmans and Houston Stewart Chamberlain. These were the salad days of the French Wagnerian movement, which did not reach its peak until the last decade of the century. To be accused of being a Wagnerite soon became a mark of fashion among the intelligentsia of all classes, as painters like Fantin-Latour and Odilon Redon were quick to realize. These artists not only sketched devotees in the act of worship, but actually issued lithographs depicting scenes from the operas, much as Beardsley was to do in England. Like all fashionable expressions of *kitsch*, the cult of Wagner was bound to end by receding in popularity. One significant factor in accounting for its decline was the attack mounted by Nietzsche in 1888, five years after the death of the composer. This drew much of its sting from the fact that the author had once been counted among Wagner's staunchest sup-

---

[1] The poet eventually had his revenge on Wagner for these infidelities by writing a novel—*Le Roi Vierge* (1881)—in which the composer and his patron, King Ludwig II of Bavaria, are cruelly parodied. He continued, however, to admire the operas, and to expound a second-hand version of Wagner's theories.

porters. Having come to feel that rhetoric and egoism were bringing an element of speciousness to the music-drama, Nietzsche did
not waste time in announcing his reversion to the traditional Gallic
ideals of wit and gaiety. These ideals he considered best expressed
in a work like Bizet's 'Carmen'. Such a conclusion is nowadays apt
to seem too glib, but it embraced a point of view that many patriots
were glad enough to uphold. The pomposity and solemnity of
much that Wagner wrote must be regarded as cutting clean against
the grain of French sensibilities. It was therefore inevitable that
the more indigenous traits would one day seek to reassert themselves. By 1906, when Debussy wrote his *Children's Corner Suite*,
it had become feasible to poke fun at the dying Tristan—even
though many who did so were forced to choke back a tear on visiting the theatre itself.[1]

The attitude taken up by Franck and his pupils did not differ
in essentials from that displayed by the average composer. The
expression given to this attitude, however, was frequently shrill
and erratic. Franck himself always managed to avoid the extremes
of prostration and revulsion. There is no evidence that he was ever
swept off his feet by Wagner's music, and we know that he was not
impelled to make the journey to Bayreuth. His knowledge of the
music-dramas was accordingly gained chiefly from a study of the
scores. What sort of an impression they made on him is hard to
estimate with accuracy. Being rather insensitive to literary and
ideological values, he tended to regard the works purely in the
light of their musical innovations. It is probable that all he discovered in the *Tristan* story was a celebration of the fleshly love he
is so renowned for repressing. From a narrowly musical standpoint,
however, he may have found more to admire. The score's unyielding chromaticism must have made a decided appeal to him,
even though he never went on record as saying so. Possibly his
enthusiasm for this aspect of Wagner's work was tempered by
feelings of rivalry. A close comparison of the styles of the two
composers would nevertheless reveal definite disparities. Franck's
chromatic leanings were always aimed at making modulation
easier. That is to say, he never wished to remain in one key for
long enough to establish a fixed sense of tonality. Wagner, on the
other hand, was inclined to prefer static (or at best slow-changing)
harmony, using chromatic movement to give a sense of inflection.
It is true that in *Tristan* the inflections become so marked as to
threaten the listener's awareness of the basic key, but this would

[1] A much more hilarious parody of Wagner was contained in the
Souvenirs de Bayreuth which Fauré and his friend Messager used to play
as a piano duet. This quadrille consisted of comical re-arrangements of
the principal *leit-motifs*.

not have happened so easily if Wagner had speeded up the rate of harmonic change. It is the *length* rather than the inflection of the harmonic period which is so destructive of tonality in this work. Whether Franck noted any kinship between himself and Wagner is accordingly rather dubious. It is quite possible that he remained baffled as to what Wagner was trying to do with the musical language he had inherited, not understanding that to a dramatic composer the abstract or theoretical values of music are of secondary interest. To Wagner—as to Alban Berg many years later—expression seemed more important than grammar. As a more academically-minded musician, Franck could not have been expected to agree with this. His attitude can be summed up by stating that he treasured his copy of *Tristan*, without ever removing the word 'Poison' which he had once seen fit to scrawl on the title-page.

It is a pity that the toxic properties of this score were not so readily appreciated by the composer's pupils. Among the many Franckists who had the misfortune to get lost 'dans la forêt Wagnerienne', none had a more difficult time than Henri Duparc. As a visitor to Munich in 1869, he was virtually the first of the band to be seduced by the new sounds. That it was Duparc's talent for instigation which led to the spread of interest among other French musicians is suggested by his having taken, first of all d'Indy, and then Chabrier, along with him on his travels. Each of these composers wrote music that seems more unashamedly Wagnerian than anything by Duparc, but this may have been because they were operatic in their ambitions and he was not. A deeply fastidious man in all he did, he felt himself better equipped to explore the miniature world of the song, though even this was to pose insoluble problems for him in the end. Unlike his fellow-Wagnerians, Duparc harboured terrible misgivings about his ability. Scarcely anything he wrote came easily to him, and that which did gave rise to copious revision. Of all Franck's children, he strikes us as having been the least sure of himself, the most addicted to fits of depression. He thus stands in sharp contrast to Wagner himself, who never for a moment had cause to question his genius. The pathological character of Duparc's inhibition is apparent to the simplest layman, and his story could almost be taken for a sermon on the evils of self-abasement. That he also gave the impression of being among the most gifted musicians of his generation only makes it harder to write.

Three years older than his colleague d'Indy, Duparc was born during the 'Year of Revolutions'—a fact which may have helped to foster his lifelong interest in politics. He was not a precocious child, either in his approach to music or general subjects. The

piano lessons which he received from Franck were not particularly
fruitful, if they were intended to train his abilities as a performer.
By the time he was nineteen, however, and had decided on a career
as a lawyer, he found himself able to compose short instrumental
pieces of a moderately high degree of accomplishment. Among
these a Cello Sonata (1867) and a set of Schumannesque *Album-
leaves* for piano (1868) seemed the most promising. Being a friend
of Castillon and Fauré, he was naturally interested in the songs
they were writing, and was especially intrigued by the new direction in which this art-form appeared to be moving. Having the
example of the latter's epoch-making *Lydia* to guide him, he
quickly seized the initiative by writing five songs of his own to
poems by Sully-Prudhomme, Lahor and others. Each of these
melodies survives, though it was feared for a long time that all but
two had been destroyed.[1] They confirm that the composer never
lacked skill in the handling of his craft, and comparing them with
Castillon's handful of songs there is no denying their superior
fluency and sophistication. 'Soupir'—which offers itself as the best
of them—shows a marked flair for counter-melody, and a Wolf-
like mastery of pianistic idiom. The words concern a death-laden
love of the kind Wagner expressed in *Tristan*. Equally Wagnerian
is the chromatic intensification of the music. The fact that one of
the remaining four songs is called 'Chanson Triste' (the first to be
written according to the composer) seems a verification of that
obsession with sadness and desolation which it is tempting to
ascribe to Duparc. Fauré's influence is detectable in the richly-
flowing accompaniments attaching to many of the songs. We can
point to an instance of this in the rediscovered 'Sérénade', though
the greater flourishes employed in this song hint as broadly at
Franck's more substantive pianism. Taken as a group, the 1868
songs stand as an impressive achievement on the part of so youthful
a composer. If their salon style and generally strophic forms deprive
them of pioneer importance, their finished quality was not something other musicians found it easy to match. They proved invaluable in helping to entrench the new medium.

It was with the three songs he wrote between 1869 and 1871 that
Duparc really pressed his claims as an original force. Taking an
immense amount of care over each of these compositions, he aimed
at equipping them with an amplitude and sumptuousness unknown
to French music. In a song like 'L'Invitation au Voyage', he
succeeded beyond his wildest hopes. This superb realization of

[1] The lost 'Le Galop' turned up in 1945 and was published by
Messrs Durand in due course. The remaining two—'Sérénade' and
'Romance de Mignon'—continue unpublished, but the manuscripts of
both songs may be seen at the Bibliothèque Nationale.

Ex. 10
Henri Duparc: Sérénade

Baudelaire's famous poem not only aspires to be Duparc's finest legacy, but in the opinion of many remains the brightest jewel in the entire crown of modern song. Duparc possessed an uncannily acute literary sense, and much of the song's haunting quality is directly traceable to the romantic 'spleen' of his collaborator. It is a tribute to the composer, however, that his music ascends to the same level of inspiration. Baudelaire's purpose in the poem was to conjure up a dream-like vision of the land of Holland, to which he and his actress friend, Marie Daubron, had high hopes of escaping. The flat, clean countryside—with its rolling tulip fields and picturesque canals—is made to seem the natural counterpart to his mistress's beauty:

> Les soleils mouillés
> De ces ciels brouillés
> Pour mon esprit ont les charmes
> Si mystérieux
> De tes traîtres yeux,
> Brillant à travers leurs larmes.
>
> Là, tout n'est qu'ordre et beauté,
> Luxe, calme et volupté.

Duparc sets these serene lines to slow, sweet music underlying which a broken-chord accompaniment shimmers discreetly. The unworldly effect of the poem is accentuated by the soft tolling of a tonic-dominant pedal which persists for close on fifty bars in the

Ex. 11

Henri Duparc: accompaniment to L' Invitation au Voyage

bass register of the keyboard. As Gerald Moore has astutely observed, this opening section really requires a three-pedal piano to do it full justice. The composer himself may have thought differently since he later produced an orchestral version which some critics have found preferable. There are certainly times when the song cries out for the grandeur of a full complement of instruments. The high tessitura in which the voice is placed, on the other hand, calls for delicate support at the key points—especially in the pianissimo refrain.

Markedly contrasting in tone is 'La Vague et la Cloche', one of the dramatic companions to the Baudelaire song which Duparc completed about a year later. This time the verses were drawn from the lesser-known François Coppée, christened 'le poète des humbles' and caricatured in the Goncourt journals as 'a green-eyed old sea-salt'. They describe in a particularly horrifying manner an alcoholic nightmare in which the poet imagines himself to be alternately cast adrift in a sinking boat and swung aloft by some monstrous bell, whose clanging and swaying terrify him to no understandable purpose. The symbolism of the first part of the poem is not unlike that to which Baudelaire resorted in his 'Don Juan aux Enfers' and must be considered part of the satanic heritage French writers had recently acquired from Edgar Allan Poe. Duparc's setting is full of rhythmical menace and abandon. It is unquestionably the most tempestuous song he ever attempted. The piano is once again subjected to quasi-orchestral treatment, the hammering bass motifs producing a dangerously percussive sound that almost threatens the voice with extinction.[1] A pro-

[1] In this instance, Duparc reversed the practice he had followed with 'L'Invitation au Voyage' by writing an orchestral version first and then proceeding to a piano transcription. The whole question of the right medium for Duparc's songs is one that has aroused heated controversy.

grammatic element creeps in when successions of open fifths are
employed to imitate the crashing of the bell. It was typical of
Duparc not to shrink from using the most extravagant effects if he
felt they were justified by the words of the poem. He was not
normally attracted to such bizarre themes as appear in Coppée's
verses, but it was entirely characteristic of him to treat each poem
as a separate problem. If it called for unusual resources, he would
never think of going back on the obligation. The letters he wrote
to Chausson show this tenacity he adopted towards his texts with
unmistakable clarity. When asked to comment on his friend's
'Poème de l'amour et de la mer', he spoke out fearlessly in defence
of his position:

> En somme—et ceci est peut-être plus clair—j'ai eu
> plus d'une fois l'impression que les paroles avaient
> été adaptées a la musique, et qu'il n'y avait pas entre
> les deux cohésion absolue . . .*

'Au pays où se fait la guerre'—the last of the three wartime
songs—is a sweetheart's lament. It expresses sentiments more
readily associated with the romance, a form in which French
composers had intermittently excelled ever since the days of
Rousseau and Monsigny. After 1815, however, there evolved a
tendency to modify this form in a number of different directions,
one of which was in imitation of the operatic *scène*. Duparc's song
belongs to this latter genre in that it endeavours to follow the *récit*
and *chanson* principle so much in favour with certain sections of
the public. Structurally, the song is an old French rondeau, but
the impression it creates is that of an extended dramatic mono-
logue. In some respects, it is one of the composer's best songs. It is
certainly of great interest to those of his admirers who regret that
he never managed to fulfil his dream of writing an opera. For what
it shows is that Duparc was amply gifted with the propensity for
dénouement, and understood well the techniques of expression
which the theatre composer must master. Not all exponents of the
mélodie were equipped with this power. Fauré, for example, was
notably lacking in it. Like the other songs in this group, 'Au pays
où se fait la guerre' strives to include specific references to the
events of the poem. A martial figure in thirds which occurs in the
middle register of the piano (recalling Wolf's famous 'Ihr Jungen
Leute' and the many military intrusions in the songs of Mahler) is
one indication of this. It is in the setting of the last stanza that

---

* To sum up—and this perhaps puts it more clearly—I have tried
harder for once to give the impression that the words were geared to the
music, and that absolutely no dual context existed between them.

Duparc gives most play to his operatic talents, the intense recitative and stridently Wagnerian climax going far towards banishing all thoughts of the drawing-room. Though the words of this song are by Gautier, and the theme one of recurring topicality, it is not as frequently heard as many of its companions. Perhaps it is too much at variance with the surface mood celebrated in the better-known French songs, and too demanding in its characterization. A key to its interpretation has been provided by Lotte Lehmann.[1]

Although Duparc never succeeded in rising above his limitations as a song-composer, there were times in his life when he urgently sought expression in the larger media. His meeting with Liszt at Weimar was what probably inspired him to try his hand at the symphonic poem, though the chances are that he was familiar enough with Franck's abortive attempts at introducing this form. As it happened, Saint-Saëns had taken over the role of pioneer as far as French audiences were concerned, his *Le Rouet d'Omphale* and *Phaëton* having been performed in 1872 and 1873 respectively. It was he who undertook the job of transcribing Duparc's only excursion into the field in 1875. Since listeners were still a little disconcerted by the novelty of the form, Saint-Saëns had originally planned his own contribution for two pianos, and it was through this less ambitious medium that he advised Duparc to seek acclaim. The latter was an intrepid orchestrator, however, and he had no cause to fear that his full-scale version would be regarded as clumsy. The work—which was based on Bürgher's ballad 'Lénore' —had its première under the auspices of the Société on 15 May 1875, and was successful in securing other performances by Pasdeloup in 1876 and 1877, and by Colonne at the Trocadéro in 1878. What is interesting to us today is to speculate on whether Duparc had been long at work on this project before he consented to have it performed. We know from the habits he displayed in relation to his songs that he frequently used to tinker with a composition for anything up to a few years before expressing himself satisfied with it. There is some evidence that something of this kind may have happened with *Lénore*. The visit to Liszt had occurred in 1869, and it was while he was a guest at Weimar that he was taken to hear the gypsy violinist Paticarius, whose startling improvisations were a source of common admiration. According to Duparc himself, he offered the Hungarian the principal theme of *Lénore* as a basis for improvisation. If this is true, it suggests that the ideas for the composition, if not the form, were already decided upon five years before its completion. In that case, it was Duparc's misfortune that he was slow in working out the details

[1] The analysis is contained in her book *More than Singing*, published by Messrs Boosey & Hawkes Inc., 1945.

of his task. Had he been a little quicker, he would have deprived
Saint-Saëns of the honour (which he eventually came to covet) of
having been the first French composer to win success with the
new form.

Audience reaction to *Lénore* was extremely mixed to begin with.
On the first night, some listeners went as far as to hiss loudly. On
the other hand, progressive musicians who attended the concert—
a few like de Bréville having forced their way in without a ticket
—were immediately impressed by the work's modernity. The
handling of the orchestra seemed more than usually assured, and
hardly anyone realized that the composer had put in several
anxious days revising parts of the score just prior to the performance. Despite the tributes of his colleagues, Duparc continued to
make small alterations to the work during the years ahead, when
amendments to his existing oeuvre came to constitute his only
remaining outlet. Franck was so taken with the piece that he was
led to make an arrangement for piano duet. The content of *Lénore*
is perhaps more derivative than its instrumentation. Looked at in
the light of the models Duparc had before him, the work betrays
unmistakable signs of Liszt's influence in the impetuous 'allegro'
section; whilst its opening theme on the cellos pivots around a low
G in a manner strictly redolent of Franck. The ideas have struck
certain critics as too clogged, with the whole composition being
blocked off in discrete sections. Yet others have acclaimed it as one
of the best examples to have emerged from the period. Julien
Tiersot, writing in 1924, awarded it high praise in saying:

> Le Poème Symphonique *Lénore*, exactement contemporain
> des créations analogues de M. Saint-Saëns, reste comme un
> des meilleurs modèles du genre.

It has since been revived at the Strasbourg Festival, and its place
as a formative experiment widely recognized.

The only song the composer wrote in the year of completing
Lénore was the neglected 'Elégie'—a setting of Thomas Moore's
lament on the death of Robert Emmet. He did not return to his
favourite mode of expression until 1878, when he began by penning
a triumphantly lyrical tribute to Wagner. The vicious feelings
aroused by *Eine Kapitulation* had by this time clashed with the
more reverent emotions of those bent on admitting the composer
to Paris, so that just about every musician in the capital was being
rudely solicited for his allegiance. Though Duparc had never lost
his head over Wagner (his enthusiasm remained a little more
circumspect than that of Chausson, if a trifle less so than that of
Franck), he was still sufficient of a devotee to feel that positive
steps were needed to rebut the libels circulating about his music.

As his own contribution to the debate, he composed 'Extase'—a tremulous invocation to death which duplicates the message of the Liebestod from *Tristan und Isolde*. Actually, a better source of comparison (especially for those anxious to compensate for differences in scale between these two works) is the song 'Schmerzen' from the five Wesendonk *Lieder* which Wagner wrote prior to embarking on his opera. The highly-charged character of these brief melodies makes it probable that they were conceived as studies for *Tristan*, so that they could be said to adumbrate the traits found in the mature work. The similarity they bear to the more expansive songs of Duparc is quite striking, and one tends to think of 'Extase' as forming a belated sequel to them. Employing a lengthy introduction and postlude, Duparc's setting permits the voice to unfold gradually and then allows it to die away with a subtle effect of perceptible silence. Despite its Wagnerisms, the song has merits which seem very characteristic of the composer. The facile internal polyphony and gently sonorous pedal-points should be counted among these. As always with Duparc, the tessitura is expertly laid out so as to encompass but not over-stretch the voice. The mistake many commentators make in relation to this song is to think of it merely as a pastiche. In fact it is an exquisite addition to the literature for which it was intended.

Still more marvellous songs were jotted down at intervals between 1879 and 1884. Duparc rarely wrote more than one a year, and their quality is at least partly attributable to the uniquely gestatory approach he adopted. 'Le Manoir de Rosamonde' (1879) is a lacerating complaint issued by one of those lovesick wanderers of the kind Schubert immortalized in his two great Müller cycles. The verses—taken from Robert de Bonnières's 'Contes de Fées'— are enlivened by far more daring conceits than anything to be found in Muller, and utilize an almost Jacobean violence of imagery suggestive of Webster or Middleton. The song itself derives its agitated quality from the reiterated octave figure which begins the accompaniment, and the rising scale passage in the bass. These devices give what Dr Sydney Northcote has termed 'an expressive kind of breathlessness to the dramatic content' which turns out to be singularly appropriate. There is considerable variety of mood, and the whole composition is rich in tonal contrasts. The simile in which love is compared to a dog's bite and the lover's pain to a trail of shed blood is set to savage, declamatory music; while the poet's dying image of 'the blue manor of Rosamonde' (which he has been unable to find) is accompanied by a quiet, whispering repetition of the opening motif, now shorn of all its urgency and passion and made to do duty as a terse coda on the keyboard. The intelligent blending of declamation with epigram in this song makes

it one of Duparc's most admired creations, and a great favourite
with singers good enough to do it justice. Less characteristic is the
short 'Sérénade Florentine' which the composer wrote in the
ensuing year, and which might almost seem a product of the young
Fauré. The melody of this song has a tinkling charm which links
it more closely to the general run of the period's vocalizations. Also
reminiscent of Fauré is the melancholy 'Lamento' of 1883. This
setting is remarkable only for its peroration (starting with the
words 'Ah! jamais plus'), embodying yet another instance of
Duparc's melodramatic tactics.

Easily the most symphonic of all the composer's sixteen melodies
is the tender 'Phidylé', written to words by Fauré's poet, Leconte
de Lisle, in 1882. Dedicated to the circle's newest inhabitant—the
self-effacing Ernest Chausson—the song shows what a highly-
developed sense of climax Duparc possessed, and how unerringly
he was able to gauge the span of a musical phrase. The accompaniment begins with an innocent chordal progression, devoid of the
slightest rhythmical inflection. Stage by stage, however, it gathers
momentum until it breaks out into a paean of sound so encircling
as to justify—and indeed demand—orchestral expression. Vocally,
each limb of the melody reaches just far enough to prolong the
tension, while the song's tonal centre, prosaically driven home in
the opening bar, is enharmonically transformed the moment the
voice enters, with magical effect. Henceforth, the tonality exhibits
a pull towards the aurally ambiguous mediant, another factor
which adds to the suspense. The poem on which the song is based
was considerably shortened by Duparc when he came to make his
setting, its ten stanzas being reduced to four. This is not a practice
other musicians would do well to imitate, but in this case the resulting verses make sense in the order in which Duparc presents them.
They describe a peaceful lovers' tryst beneath the hot Mediter-
ranean sun, the landscape scattered with red flowers and out-
stretched cornfields. Overhead, humming flights of bees circulate,
and tired birds skim downwards in search of the briar tree's shade.
The splendid sensuality of these images is rapturously caught in
Duparc's music, which looks forward in immediacy to Debussy's
L'Après-midi d'un faune and the more sumptuous works of Ravel.
It is a pity that the song continues to be sung by women singers
(nothing irritated the composer more than this flagrant falsification
of his intentions), and is too often heard in the inadequate piano
version. Given its proper form, it lays claim to being one of the
finest of all vocal effusions, certainly among the French school. By
comparison, the scene set in the next of the composer's songs—the
expressively anguished 'Testament'—is bleak and wintry. Deriving
from Armand Silvestre, it portrays the remorseful lover in self-

pitying mood. Duparc had become attracted to sketching as a hobby by the time he wrote this melody (his meeting with the painter Harpignies at La Bourboule did something to spark off this interest), with the result that there exists a sensitive water-colour transposing the theme into visual terms. As a piece of music, 'Testament' displays a fondness for the augmented triad and other Franckist devices.

The last of the wine was quick to flow, and in the space of a further year the compact body of song created by this immensely talented man was complete. 'La Vie Antérieure', perhaps because it was taken from Baudelaire, inspired the composer to heights not far short of those he had reached in 'L'Invitation au Voyage' and 'Phidylé'. Like them, the song is a product of that ineffable nostalgia which seems to have affected a whole generation of French romantics. It again recounts the events of a dream, but this time a comforting Oriental soliloquy, undistraught by fear or longing. Recollecting the conditions of a past life, the poet summons up a vision of some vast palace under the sea, in which perfumed slaves are imagined cooling his brow. While he condescends to their attentions, the play of sun on water creates flickering shapes which stimulate his fancy. Careworn though he is made to appear, the secret of his sadness is never revealed. The familiar Duparc trade-marks are present once more in the dominant pivot and pedal bass of the opening measures. Unlike the strophic 'Lamento', this setting tends to be through-composed, the third and last section giving rise to an extended recitative. The impassioned climax which occurs at the words 'mes yeux' calls for a cadenza-like flourish from the accompanist, while the wide compass the song exhibits would put a strain on all but the professional singer. Harmonically, it shares with 'Phidylé' a preference for audacious modulations, passing dissonances and subtle 'internal' resolutions. Far from suggesting any decline in its composer's powers, it pro-claims itself as the work of a man in full maturity. The long legato phrases are handled with consummate assurance, and the tiny syncopations by which they are offset leave no doubt as to the element of mastery. Duparc himself retained a special affection for this song. Along with 'Le Manoir de Rosamonde', it struck him as exemplifying those qualities he had in common with the best of his race.

After this beautiful outpouring, the rest was silence. Unable to carry on writing, the composer suffered a mysterious nervous breakdown, the effects of which he supposed would be temporary. His friend de Bréville had sensed this overtaking him, however, and suspected, quite correctly, that the outcome would be more disastrous. Revealing itself in failing sight, feelings of self-disgust, and a curious inability to put the finishing touches to anything he wrote, the disorder remains as puzzling to us today as it did to the unfortunate victim. Part of the trouble lay in Duparc's agonizing sense of creative inadequacy, his determination to disparage everything that did not come up to the very highest standards. When caught in one of his artistic dilemmas, he would frequently display symptoms of acute hysteria. As time progressed, and he began to understand that he would never compose again, other and more alarming signs of deterioration were revealed. Paralysis implanted itself in parts of his limbs, and he was occasionally wracked by neuralgia. That he could sometimes recover well enough to go about the ordinary duties of life is proved by the spasmodic public forays which he undertook.[1] Leaving Paris to live in Switzerland, he conceived the idea of a cure at one of that nation's spas, but no treatment he received was of any avail. He settled first of all at the Villa Amélie in La Tour de Peilz, near Lake Leman. From there he moved on to Tarbes—so as to be close to his son Charles—and eventually established himself at Mont-de-Marsan in 1919. It was there that he died, aged eighty-five, in 1933. During all this time, he was never once able to repossess his lost gifts, neither was he able to free himself from the torments posed by revision to existing compositions. He kept most of the bitterness he felt away from his wife, and declined to disclose the possible origins of his neurosis to his many friends. The stoicism he was compelled to adopt inevitably drew him in the direction of religion, with the result that his last years were shrouded in mysticism. Like Scriabin, he ended by invoking a harmony of the spheres, built up out of an assortment of theosophical teachings. These he managed to equate with his Catholicism to the extent of indulging in regular prayers and embarking on an ultimate pilgrimage, not to his beloved Bayreuth, but to Lourdes in the company of his friends Francis Jammes and Paul Claudel.

The few works for larger forces which Duparc attempted in the years following his eclipse as a song-writer met with such stern censorship that they never emerged into the light of day. His masochistic urges led him to burn two parts of a triptych for orchestra (the third part survives under the title 'Aux Etoiles'), while projects involving music to Molière's *Amphitryon* and the Italian drama *Francesca da Rimini* were either not started or else rapidly abandoned once they were under way. By far the most formidable task the composer set himself in his middle years was

---

[1] Chiefly during the period when he was mayor of Marnes-la-Coquette. It was part of the paradox of Duparc that he could experience such anguish while presenting the outward appearance of a Theodore Roosevelt.

the completion of an opera—his one and only commitment to the form—on Pushkin's story *Roussalka*. He had always been an admirer of Russian literature, having a great zest for Tolstoy in particular. The search for a suitable libretto therefore occupied him a little longer than would have been the case with a less cultivated man. Possibly he spent some time probing various Scandinavian sources, for he was also very much enamoured of Ibsen and his colleagues. When, in the end, he decided on Pushkin's tale, he still had no idea of the complexities which awaited him in adapting his music to the demands of the theatre. The first Act was actually written down in the 1880s, and Duparc is known to have made sketches for the remainder. In all he had probably set about two-thirds of the poem when he was caught up in a cycle of despair. This was in June 1900, and though it was summertime he had a roaring fire lit so that he could experience the satisfaction of plunging his manuscript dramatically into the flames. Shocked by what he had done, the composer spent the next three months re-writing the entire score from memory, only to work himself up into another fit of destructiveness in which the whole process was to be repeated. The indecisive character of his behaviour was as typical as the impulsiveness which underlay his acts. Few artists can ever have experienced such a purgatorial blightening of their talents.

While he was shut up in this self-contained rage, other musicians took the trouble to plead Duparc's cause. In 1912 a veritable Duparc festival took place at Montreux and Lausanne. Jeanne Raunay sang a number of the composer's songs, and *Lénore* secured another performance under Ehrenberg's direction. This was during October, and three months later there followed a concert at which Mme Lula Mysz-Gmeiner (a Vienna Court Opera singer whose style was not quite idiomatic enough to suit Duparc) sang 'L'Invitation' and 'Phidylé' to a mixed but on the whole appreciative audience. At about the same time, the young Ernest Ansermet wrote several laudatory articles which were printed in the tablets put out by the Schola Cantorum. The critics Tiersot and Servières were also keen to join in the revaluation, and had little hesitation in placing Duparc among the masters of French song. The composer himself was not thrown off balance by this unexpected recognition, for he had reached the stage when attitudes to his work left him cold. He had evolved an ideal of order and beauty that went beyond earthly realization. That this vision was not sufficient to bring him the happiness he desired is indicated by the complaining tone of many of the letters he wrote from Tarbes and Mont-de-Marsan. It is true that by this time his sons had been conscripted to serve in the First World War, so that some of his anxiety probably stemmed from worry as to their whereabouts. Nevertheless, the outlook to which he clung took on an increasingly sombre colouring as this correspondence drew to its close, making it open to question whether he was ever able to derive spiritual comfort from the faith he had so pitifully embraced. As his companion Claudel has written in another context: 'Quand l'homme essaie d'imaginer le Paradis sur terre, ca fait tout de suite un Enfer très convenable.'* With his eyes no longer of any use to him, Duparc's ultimate satisfactions came from the music he heard in his mind's ear. Who can say what compensations it afforded him?

Speculation relating to the composer's mental collapse has yielded curiously conflicting results. Psycho-analysts have traced his difficulties to childhood frustration. Others with a less clinical bias have preferred to argue that he was a victim of hyper-aestheticism. Professor Wilfrid Mellers has proposed a third interpretation in stating that Duparc's life should be construed as 'a parable of the terrors of moral isolation'. That there is some truth in each of these views seems incontestable. Nevertheless, it would be interesting to be given more information of an organic nature. The composer's grand-daughter—the Comtesse Marie Thérèse d'Armagnac—has claimed, for instance, that her grandfather's poor sight was due entirely to a cataract which could easily have been removed. It was caused, she suggests, by an excess of tobacco fumes. Duparc himself took steps to consult an ophthalmologist at Lausanne, and returned with the diagnosis of glaucoma, leading to progressive optic atrophy. Either of these conditions could be made to account for his having gone blind. The paralysis—creative as well as physical it should be remembered—is not so readily explained away. Here we must defer to the idea of some psychological impediment. 'Je veux être ému' was the cry the composer uttered on being admitted to the ranks of Franck's followers, and this vow may have imposed its own constraint on his system. But we cannot presume that Duparc was necessarily and only a casualty of Franckist idealism. Like most remarkable men, he had himself to thank for most of what happened to him.

* 'When man tries to conceive a Paradise on earth, it immediately turns into a very respectable form of Hell.'

VII

A time of lilacs and roses

The composer of *Lénore* could scarcely be said to have left any
pupils, unless we make an exception for the faithful Jean Cras. But
the advice he so assiduously urged upon younger members of the
circle meant that many found themselves exposed to his theories.
Among these none stood to gain or lose more than Ernest Chausson,
whose natural reluctance as a composer made him the perfect
target of Duparc's vacillations. It is tempting to attribute much of
the diffidence shown by this artist to the criticism he faced from
his older contemporary. The forty-page letter Duparc wrote him
on *Le Roi Arthus* stands as an ominous reminder of the lengths to
which this criticism went. Fortunately, Chausson did not allow
himself to be overcome by it, extracting what he needed to complete his scores without falling prey to the disease of impotence.
Perseverance is as necessary to the artist as self-understanding, and
it would have been to the advantage of each of these Franck pupils
if they had been quicker to grasp the point.

Although Chausson was more effective than Duparc in maintaining his creative equilibrium, it should not be assumed that he
was ever a master of his fate. His struggles over the B flat Symphony,
while less permanently crippling than any which marked his
friend's decline, were severe enough to have proposed a real
handicap which it became the composer's penance to overcome.
Luckily, he possessed some of the industry of another of his
advisers, the gentle and prolific Gabriel Fauré, so that he did not
capitulate in the manner certain critics would have us believe. That
he was badly divided in his loyalties—revealing the familiar double
allegiance to Franck and Wagner—almost goes without saying.
But he was fortunate in preserving a touch of that aristocratic
pudeur with which so many French musicians have been endowed;
and he accordingly learnt how to hold his head up in a crisis. Not

only that, but he was young enough to have been aware of new aesthetic currents that did not arise until after the old guard of pupils had matured. In this sense, he helped to foreshadow Debussy, whose close friend and mentor he became towards the end of his short life. These factors, along with the comfortable privileges of a moneyed background, helped to equip Chausson with just enough self-confidence to surmount the obstacles which might otherwise have brought him crashing to the ground.

Born in 1855, he came from a family that was rising in the social and financial scale. His father, Prosper Chausson, had been appointed one of Haussmann's building contractors, and had already played a considerable part in creating the new Paris. Two previous children of the marriage had been lost, so that when Ernest was growing up his parents spared no effort to protect him from harm. Their over-solicitous attitude may have been decisive in sapping the child's initiative, since it is clear that he found difficulty, even from his earliest days, in giving firm expression to his convictions. Rather than send him to school like other children, his father decided to engage a tutor—the cultured Brethous-Lafargue—whose task it became to watch over the boy in all he did. In certain respects, this plan proved successful. It was his tutor who first kindled Chausson's interest in the arts, and these were never allowed to make their appeal in a narrow or merely technical fashion. Drawing and literature, as well as music, were among the subjects he was encouraged to study. Nevertheless, the impact of his companion's personality could scarcely help being too adult, with the result that Chausson was denied much of the rough-and-tumble which ensues from mixing with youthful spirits. As he grew up, he began to appreciate that his outlook was compounded of far more reflective qualities than he was accustomed to find in others. That he also recognized the strain of pessimism which he had inherited is suggested by the following admission: 'I was sad without quite knowing why, but firmly convinced that I had the best reason in the world for it.' By the time he came to indulge in such flights of self-analysis, his character had gone a long way towards being formed, and all he could do was learn to live with it.

More out of respect for his father's wishes than from any inner prompting, Chausson took it into his head to enroll as a law student at the University of Paris, receiving his degree in 1877. Though he was faced with what many other young men would have regarded as an enviable future, he worried incessantly about his career, not finding as much to interest him in the law as he did in music, painting and literature. One of the persons from whom he sought advice was his godmother, Mme de Rayssac, whose husband had been a poet, and who had herself studied art as a young woman. After becoming widowed, she had gone to live in a convent, renouncing most of her worldly interests. It was there that Chausson fell into the habit of visiting her during his vacations from the university. They also corresponded in an intimate and confidential fashion. In their relationship, the young student looked for the key to his predicament, and for a measure of the comfort he needed. She was careful, however, not to lend too much encouragement to his dreams of becoming an artist. Nearly everyone to whom Chausson went for guidance greeted him with this excessive caution, perhaps because there was little sign that his own resolve was sufficiently firm. Discouragement was always something that weighed heavily on his shoulders, and he was in all probability one of those young people who have to be pushed into a course of action. In the end, what caused him to make up his mind was a visit he paid to the opera at Munich, where he succumbed immediately to the spell of Wagner. This was in 1879—exactly ten years after d'Indy and Duparc had made their pilgrimage—when he had reached an age at which further postponement seemed inadvisable. Within a few days of making his visit, Chausson was writing to Mme Rayssac that he must act at once if he is ever to achieve his goal. A month after his return he registered at the Conservatoire in the classes of Franck and Massenet, and abandoned all thoughts of the profession in which he had qualified. 'Franck is an admirable musician,' he wrote after his first meeting, 'though somewhat mystical.' With this shrewd judgement he began the association which was to carry him speedily into the heart of his vocation.

It was in the first year of attending the Conservatoire that the composer wrote his earliest published songs, those forming the initial portion of his op. 2. They include the well-known 'Nanny' (Leconte de Lisle), 'Le Charme' (Armand Silvestre), 'Les Papillons' and 'La Dernière Feuille' (Théophile Gautier). Considered as specimens of the *mélodie*, they are fluent and accomplished, melodious in style, and generally light in texture. 'Les Papillons', for example, floats airily above a springing accompaniment, which is cleverly divided between the hands. It has all the charm we associate with Grieg's or Schumann's similarly-titled pieces. In the same way, 'La Dernière Feuille'—which caption might be used to epitomize the wistful feelings the composer expresses in this set—is as simple a statement as one could hope to find in the best Bizet or Gounod. At no time in his career was Chausson to plumb the extremes of emotion generated by the most intense Wagnerism. Acute passion and despair were qualities that passed him by in music—though perhaps not in real life. Certainly these early songs—written before the urge towards complexity took possession of the composer—offer no hint of the torments which we must assume Wagner's music inspired in him. As his biographers, Barricelli and Weinstein, have pointed out: 'Their lyrical directness is such that, if we did not have evidence to the contrary, we might be tempted to ascribe to Chausson the facility of musical inventiveness of a Schubert.' What serves most clearly to reveal the individual sensibility at work in these compositions is the slight sense of emotional fatigue which now and then becomes evident. In a song like 'Le Colibri', which forms the last of the op. 2 collection, there is also an element of indulgence towards the properties of pure sound (cf. the eight bars of spread chords which interrupt the melody at its climax) which cannot be found among the less sensuous masters of the *Lied*.[1] The theme of this last poem also betrays the direction in which the composer's sympathies were tending. In its comparison of the poet's soul with the life and death of a hummingbird, it symbolizes that elegaic attitude to art of which he was to partake all too ruinously in the years ahead. Also belonging to the period 1879–80 are the *Cinq Fantaisies pour piano* (of which the plates were destroyed, but a few copies remain at the Memorial Library of Music, Stanford University), and a Sonata in F minor. Franck was duly impressed with the sonata, though Massenet professed to discover in it an unconscious plagiarism of Meyerbeer. A Sonatina for four hands completes the music of this preliminary stage in Chausson's career.

During 1880, the composer was unable to resist making a return journey to Munich—this time to hear *Tristan und Isolde*. As may be imagined, the work had a profound effect on him, beginning with its theoretical implications. Sensing that Wagner had recovered in this opera some of that respect for dramatic values which had been absent since the time of Gluck, he was quick to seize on the possibilities which the new medium presented. This did not prevent him from criticizing Wagner's touching-up of *Iphigénie en Aulide*, the revival of which he also managed to attend. Like d'Indy—and for that matter most of the French composers we have chosen to investigate—Chausson maintained a drily puritanical attitude to the texts of the old masters, and he did not think of baroque opera as a mere horse-drawn version of what was happening at Bayreuth. It is more than likely that the difficulties Chausson had in freeing himself from the domination of Wagner stemmed, not so much from any fearful infatuation which he contracted at his first performance of *Tristan*, but from his ill-

[1] A direct French comparison is possible with this song, since the poem has also been set by Charles Koechlin. It is difficult to say which version is the finer.

advisedness in choosing so similar a subject for his own opera. *Le Roi Arthus* was still six years off at this time, however, and the composer's commitment to the stage was far from being established. His loyalty to Franck (and also to Fauré, whom he admired very much indeed, and whose influence on his songs should not be discounted) probably weighed more heavily with him at this stage in his ambitions, as may be confirmed by a glance at the compositions he was writing. A Trio in G minor for piano, violin, and cello dates from 1881, and this work coincided with Chausson's decision to break with Massenet and attach himself exclusively to Franck. It is not a particularly impressive work, only the animated final movement exhibiting any real confidence. Its reliance on the cyclical return of a previous theme marks it out as characteristic, while the pure tone of the andante provides a clear indication of the mood in which it was written. Needless to say, Franck found much to praise in it, and it was performed through the Society's offices in April 1882.

It was doubtless on account of Franck's encouragement that Chausson embarked on his first orchestral composition—a symphonic poem based on the Merlin legend—shortly afterwards.[1] This was certainly a step forward in the composer's progress. Not only was it an excellent subject to have chosen, but the grace and brilliance of the instrumentation help to single it out as worth maintaining in the repertory. The part of the legend treated by Chausson concerns Merlin's ensnarement in the trap laid for him by his mistress, Viviane. Having been seduced into parting with one of his spells, the magician is surprised at being its victim, suffering himself to be put to sleep in the middle of a hawthorn bush. The music divides this story into four distinct episodes— the first is a love scene, followed by King Arthur's search for the missing magician; then comes Merlin's attempt to end the reverie and his ultimate capitulation to the spell. Points to notice in the score include a series of off-stage trumpet calls (after the manner of *Leonora* No. 3), some beautifully soothing horn music during the love episode, and the very daring cadenzas for harp which are meant to depict the entanglement. The work has more of a Wagnerian flavour than the composer's previous essays, if only on account of the obvious temptations implicit in writing in a 'forest murmurs' style. Nevertheless, it was a first-rate achievement for one who was technically still a student, and pointed the way to the opera which centres upon different aspects of the same myth. *Viviane*—together with its counterpart *Lénore*—proved that

[1] He had in the meantime attempted some incidental music for Alfred de Musset's comedy *Les Caprices de Marianne* (1880–2), but this was never published and only the Entracte performed.

Franck's pupils were capable of producing competent work in a genre in which their teacher himself had been slow to win distinction. Chausson's poem was played for the first time on 31 March 1883, and was revived by Lamoureux on 29 January 1888. Between these dates the composer undertook a small amount of revision of the work—a practice that was all but standard with the less independent pupils—and this may have been responsible for the greater applause it eventually obtained.

Viviane was dedicated to a young lady by the name of Jeanne Escudier, and in the same year as it received its première she and the composer got married. They had been introduced by the sculptor Alfred Lenoir (the artist who was commissioned to execute the Franck monument which now stands in the grounds of Sainte-Clotilde). Since Jeanne was a pianist, they were able to share many of their interests, and there is no question but that the marriage was exceedingly happy. Together they must have formed a particularly handsome couple, he with his flowing features and high-domed forehead and she with her piercing blue eyes. Everyone liked them, even such a notorious womanizer as Albeniz paying tribute to the union. They were to have five children in all, and were rarely content to be away from one another for more than a few days at a time. Chausson always loved solitude to engage in his work, hating the bustle and gossip of the city. Like Sibelius, he had to get away to the calmness of the countryside before his inspiration began to flow, and he was rich enough to enjoy a succession of retreats at which to carry out his wishes. In his journeys to these luxurious country seats he was almost invariably accompanied by his wife. It was rather hard luck on the pair that only a year after they had been married Chausson received his calling-up papers for the army. He was not obliged to remain conscripted for very long, however, and was able to return home later in the year. Military life he found abhorrent, not so much because he disbelieved in it as because it brought about an interruption in his creative thinking. Whatever reasons he gave for his attitude, it is hard to imagine that Chausson would ever have made a successful soldier. D'Indy and Duparc each had a pronounced patriotic streak, deducible from their somewhat retaliatory bearing. By comparison, the composer of *Viviane* was all gentleness and compassion. If he had been forced to witness the horrors of war, it is highly probable that, like Ravel, he would have been sickened by them. Even in the bosom of his family he continued to experience a constant premonitoriness about death that was not simply an Elizabethan affectation, but reflected his conviction that human life was too short to achieve all he desired. Whether or not he survived to express the best of himself was a vital and brooding speculation in which he indulged. By today's standards, he would certainly have been regarded as morbid, though this ignores the genuine sense of happiness he often felt and displayed. His pessimism derived as much as anything from his acute perception of the grandeur of art, and his awareness of how much it had to depend on an ungenerous fate. Stephen Spender, in his line 'I think continually of those who were truly great', came closest to capturing the disposition upon which Chausson's life was founded. In retrospect, it may be conceded that his outlook was in a large measure justified.

Once he had returned to civilian life, the composer set to work ; on the incidental music for a two-act lyric drama entitled *Hélène*, and also on a lament for the death of Hercules. These projects anticipate the pre-occupation with the stage which was to characterize the next phase of his career. It was in *Hélène* that he first began to realize the recalcitrance of Wagner's image. Though not an opera, it induced him to express operatic sentiments, and it shocked him to discover that they were derivative. His correspondence with Paul Poujaud reveals the consternation he felt on finding that he could not evolve a personal style. Dogged by a persistent lack of facility, he saw only too vividly the role of mediocrity which beckoned, and the prospect was more than he could bear. As he put it in one of the letters from Villiers-sur-Mer:

> Besides the great men, there are thousands of little ants which grind away, sweating conscientiously, without receiving any appreciation; what they do is of little consequence; it does not change anything and yet they cannot do otherwise. Why the deuce am I one of those beasts?

Obviously, it was the comparison with Wagner which was helping to elicit this inferiority complex. Hard as he tried, he could not wipe out the feeling that it was his destiny to remain a mere bit-player in the drama he was witnessing. Ever since writing *Viviane* he had allowed himself to aspire idly to the larger forms again, and it was not long before his sights became firmly focussed on the theatre. The high prestige which opera continued to enjoy in France (rather similar in many ways to the lure it exercised for German composers after the reign of Richard Strauss) made it unlikely that a man with Chausson's exalted mission could be kept away. It was not that he wanted to follow the example of the Second Empire plutocrats, but simply that there was still no other way of being taken seriously as far as the general public went. It should be remembered that even so introverted a figure as Debussy, writing almost a full decade later, felt no hesitation in committing the largest share his time and effort to the stage. As with his successor, 'the red spectre of Wagner' continued to haunt Chausson throughout the remainder of his career, sometimes merely hovering in the background but at other times painfully and terrifyingly visible. What began as an enthusiasm gradually evolved into an inhibition and ended by becoming a phobia. During this intense inner struggle, the example set by Franck was rendered temporarily remote.

As Chausson himself had predicted, 'Hélène' died a slow death on account of its languishments. Based on de Lisle's pagan verses, it was never the right vehicle for his talents, any more than the opera which followed it. *Arthus*—begun in 1886 but not finished for a further nine years—became the cross which he bore throughout the next decade. In the meantime, there were additional songs, some incidental work to plays by Shakespeare and Aristophanes, and a courageous if tentative return to chamber music. Among these varied offerings, the songs have best withstood the test of time—perhaps because the gift they required did not need elaborate nurturing. At all events, the short cycles the composer continued to write for the remainder of his career are an excellent guide to the way his abilities evolved. Some of the melodies they contain are over-complicated, judged by the standards of a Fauré or Debussy, but they all bear the stamp of Chausson's refined personality, and many are assured of a permanent place in the repertory. The poets chosen overlap with those of other musicians. Gautier and Lahor he continued to share with Duparc, and Verlaine with a whole host of composers. His special tastes are disclosed by a preference for Camille Mauclair, Jean Richepin and Maurice Bouchor—the last-named being a friend whose claims he found it difficult to resist. Above all, the composer will probably be remembered for his idiomatic settings of Maeterlinck, the poet whose dream-world was to be of such signal inspiration to both Satie and Debussy. With this distinguished company from which to choose, it is not surprising that Chausson was able to carve an important niche for himself in the annals of French song. Altogether, he wrote close on fifty melodies, a few of them for voice and orchestra, but the majority requiring only piano accompaniment. Nearly all form part of a cycle of not more than three or four numbers. It is not a vast collection—quite small by the standards of the *Lieder* composers—but it is sufficiently large to presuppose a measure of development. It will repay us to select a bouquet of his songs for closer scrutiny.

We may begin by looking at some of the Bouchor settings. This elegant poet was actually the first to stimulate Chausson's fancy, two of his poems having been transposed into music as early as

1878, before the op. 2 cycle was envisaged. After by-passing the verses of his friend for a number of years, he picked up his trail again with 'Nocturne', 'Amour d'Antan', 'Nos Souvenirs' and 'Printemps Triste'. None of these strikes us as of the highest aesthetic importance—despite the ingenuity of some of their accompaniments—and we have to move on to the famous 'Poème de l'Amour et de la Mer' (1893) before discovering a worthy expression of the partnership. The three songs in this orchestral cycle were written at widely-spaced intervals, and it is only the last which has become memorable. Originally described as 'La Mort de l'Amour', it has since won acclaim under the title 'Le Temps des Lilas'. As such it has become Chausson's most popular *mélodie*, and one nowadays sung on its own. When it was first performed, alongside its companions, it attracted no attention, either from the critics or the public. In Paris, the reviewer of *Figaro* found it 'crushingly monotonous'—a charge that was repeated *ad nauseam* in connection with music by the Franck school. Possibly the excuse for its employment can be traced to Bouchor's heavily-scented verses. The 1880s gave rise to what might almost be called a cult of erotic lassitude in literature and music.[1] It was a period of sighs and regrets for the romantic age which was passing. Poets and musicians took advantage of this situation to indulge their neurasthenic fantasies, and to persuade the public that their function was to celebrate the act of reminiscence. It can be no accident that some of the commonest symbols to be adopted were those which emphasized the motive of change and decay—poppies with fallen petals, trees with their black branches shorn of leaves, old love letters yellowing with age. Such are the depressing images which recur in the work of Chausson's poets, and they help to condense a philosophy of which he approved. 'The time of lilacs and roses has passed' runs the refrain of Bouchor's poem. It expresses a sentiment which can be found in each of the principal song-writers from Fauré to Poulenc, but most characteristically of all in the composer of 'Nanny'.

'Le Temps des Lilas' does not make use of an unusual time-signature, like 'Le Colibri', but its oblique rhythmical hesitations single it out as one of the subtlest of Chausson's songs. The

---

[1] Verlaine himself may be said to have started this cult when he penned the lines:

> C'est l'extase langoureuse,
> C'est la fatigue amoureuse.

The poem from which they are taken was set, significantly enough, by both Debussy and Fauré, the former in 1888 and the latter in 1890.

accents are not over-stressed, and the artlessness of the modulation serves to contrast favourably with the more intemperate Franckist procedures. The rather limited musical material of the complete 'Poème'—which incidentally falls back on the cyclical principle in place of development—does not seem too thinly spread in the single song, so that we do not tire of the sombre D minor theme in the way that the critic of *Figaro* presumably did. Chausson's plunge into a foreign key on the words 'le vent a changé' is adroitly managed, as are the tonal fluctuations contained in the middle-section (bars 38–55). On the return of the melody, there is a breath-taking change of register and an exquisite tilting of the major/minor axis. The song demonstrates the composer's admired *souplesse* as well as any in his output. The only other Bouchor settings worth examining are translations from Shakespeare. These are late works, written between 1890 and 1897, consisting of one song each from *Twelfth Night*, *Measure for Measure*, *Hamlet* and *Much Ado About Nothing*. Predictably enough, they are all laments of one kind or another. The clown's song from *Twelfth Night* is passionate and declamatory judged by Chausson's normal standards. It is the most operatic of all his songs. Equally agitated is the lover's dream—ending in futility—from the second of the four plays. In the 'Chanson d'Ophélie' on the other hand, the composer found a ready-made situation of the utmost privacy and poignancy. The last song differs from the rest in being a 'Chant Funèbre' for women's voices. Its classicism makes it less typical than its companions, and it really needs placing in a category of its own. The same might be said of the vocal numbers from Chausson's incidental music to *The Tempest*, a project undertaken with Bouchor's translation again in mind. These include two charming Ariel songs, one arch and frivolous and the other gently introspective. The entire score of this venture is worth preserving. It presents Shakespeare in innocently Gallic disguise, but the music can scarcely be thought any the worse for that, and the rambling piper's tunes and quaint duet for Juno and Ceres are a decided tribute to the composer's skill. Considered as a whole, the collaboration with Bouchor must be regarded as only moderately rewarding. His verses, while tender and nostalgic, lacked the innate propulsion required to bring out the best in Chausson. Certainly they did not possess the qualities he later came to find so receptive in Maeterlinck and Verlaine.

Granted the composer's literary prescience, it is inconceivable that he could have developed much further without encountering the poetry of these great masters of the symbolist movement. There is a strong possibility that in time he would have concluded a definite alliance with one or other of them. As things stand, the high prestige enjoyed by both Fauré and Debussy as interpreters of Verlaine has militated against the acceptance of Chausson in a comparable role. It is true that he did not set enough of Verlaine's poems to give us any indication of the depth of his sympathies— we have to be content with his three settings as against Fauré's seventeen and Debussy's eighteen—but those we do have suggest that an affinity was in the process of being reached. 'Apaisement' belongs with the Quatre Mélodies which the composer wrote between 1885 and 1887, and constitutes the only Verlaine song to be admitted to this group, while 'La Chanson bien douce' and 'Le Chévalier Malheur' join to form a short cycle dating from 1898. The second of the three—taken from the poet's contrite 'Sagesse' —goes furthest towards epitomizing the close rapport which was clearly brewing between these two subtle artists. It is a lovely setting, resigned yet pure in mood, capturing to perfection the spirit of forbearance emanating from every line of the poem. The way in which the drooping curve of the melody is offset by strivings in the accompaniment gives an example of the eager fashion in which the composer laboured to strike the right balance. There is buoyancy as well as sadness in the best of Verlaine's verses, and this is precisely the quality Chausson needed to develop in order to counteract his defects. Whether he would have been successful in embodying this lesson in the work of his middle-age is a matter upon which it is useless to speculate. Like all amateurs (and poor Chausson never ceased to suffer from this indictment) the composer was impelled to demonstrate the complexity of his musical knowledge, and the later phases of his career provide dismaying instances of inspiration being swamped by technical abstraction. Pre-occupation with what Debussy called 'les dessous' (the inner parts) came near to bringing about Chausson's downfall, not only in the mature songs but in practically all of the compositions which he wrote after 1890.[1] Making allowance for this shortcoming, the five *Serres Chaudes* which he based on Maeterlinck's poems occupy an ambiguous position in the history of French song. They are too slack and corporeal to be ranked as masterpieces, yet they undoubtedly distil a measure of the poet's essence. And since he is not a writer who is well represented in the tradition, this in itself must amount to a recommendation of sorts. That Debussy found these songs admirable—using the surgent phrase 'little dramas of impassioned metaphysics' by which to describe them—ought to be clinching testimony, in view of his authoritative relationship to the poet.

[1] Among the composer's vocal works, the *Trois Lieder* based on poems by Camille Mauclair do most to absolve him from this charge. Written in 1896, they revert to a simpler and cleaner style.

During most of the 1880s, Chausson and his wife were installed for several months of each year at a grand town house in the Boulevard de Courcelles. It was here that they put into practice their habit of entertaining the most famous writers, painters and musicians of the age. Mingling together as guests at these sybaritic gatherings were Manet, Degas and Rodin among the painters; Gide, Colette and her husband 'Willy' to represent literature; and a whole galaxy of musicians ranging through Franck, Chabrier, Fauré, Duparc and Satie. Intended as a substitute venue, in place of the established institutions at which so many were still failing to be acclaimed, Chausson's home was first and foremost an un-official 'salon des refusés' to which artists were encouraged to bring their works.[1] Mallarmé read his poems there, paintings by Renoir and Gauguin could be seen hanging from the walls, and the company was enlivened by brilliant recitals from performers like Cortot and Ysaÿe. One of the few descriptions of these evenings to survive records how d'Indy once played parts of *Fervaal* to a distinguished (and possibly somewhat bored) assembly, and Debussy was unwillingly coaxed into running through his new opera, *Pelléas*. During the days between, life was hard for this young impressionist composer, and Chausson's rich connections were invoked to help find him work. This usually consisted of playing transcriptions from Wagner at various house-parties in the vicinity. Knowing Debussy's independent temperament, we can imagine how he must have hated this job. Nevertheless, he had cause to be grateful, since it was also Chausson who paid for his de-luxe editions of the *Cinq Poèmes de Baudelaire* and *La Damoiselle Elue*—works which might otherwise have had to wait a long time before seeing publication. Businessmen took advantage of Chausson in a variety of ways. Never anxious to make money out of the publication of his own compositions, he was once asked by Hamelle to pay a subsidy of five hundred francs on his setting of Gautier's 'La Caravane'. This was too much even for his generous nature, and he stormed out of the publisher's office in disgust. Despite the success of his role as host to fashionable Paris, Chausson never completely got over his shyness in dealing with people. As Camille Mauclair has penetratingly observed: 'His gaiety was often a form of deference which he adopted towards others.'

The decorator of Chausson's house on the Boulevard de Courcelles had been his brother-in-law, Henri Lerolle, and it was

[1] The original use of this expression was to describe the salon instituted by Napoleon III in 1863 to accommodate work which had been rejected by the official bodies. Manet exhibited his 'Déjeuner sur l'herbe' at this gathering, and Cézanne, Pissarro and Fantin-Latour were among others who participated.

he who first broached the idea of the composer writing a symphony. As we know, the form was not highly regarded by Frenchmen, but Lalo, Saint-Saëns and Franck had all made recent exertions on its behalf. It was not as if Chausson needed to be persuaded of their good intentions, and the only thing which seemed to be holding him back was his sense of awe at the prospect. Nevertheless, he came round to a decision quickly enough, once the seriousness of the project had been recognized, and in 1889 he left Paris for the quiet of his villa near Cibourre in the South of France, where he counted on getting down to a long spell of work at it. Even he could have had little notion of how long these labours were to be protracted. At first all went smoothly, but by the time he began making sketches for the andante it became apparent that a crisis was looming. Pouring his strongest feelings into the slow movement had meant that an abrupt change of mood was threatening to destroy the finale. Moreover, there was the question of where the scherzo best fitted into the scheme. The long phrases for which, like Duparc, he possessed a decided gift did not invariably fit together in the way he had expected. The result was a period of hellish concentration which came close to breaking his spirit. The letters to Lerolle show that if he had not drawn back from the intellectual maelstrom which beckoned to him at this stage he would in all probability have gone mad. Luckily for him, his family sense of poise came to the rescue. Turning aside from his task, the composer immersed himself in the score of *The Magic Flute*, the calm and sanity of which did much to restore his scattered wits. Analysing the reasons for his failure in a letter to Poujaud, Chausson was inclined to put most of the blame on his song training. He wrote:

> In my lucid moments, I try to recognize my malady. And I have found it, all of a sudden. It comes from my songs. Ah! I detest them now, and I hope never to write any again. All of them bad, except Hebe perhaps and fifteen measures of Nanny.

It is clear that the spectre who was momentarily troubling him had changed from Wagner to being Duparc. At any rate, he was tempting posterity once more by picturing himself as a thwarted miniaturist. In the very same letter, he asks Poujaud to warn his friend de Bréville against becoming a song-writer, expatiating on the terrors of what he describes as 'un abime ouvert'. Critics may question whether Chausson was right to give way to this unashamed piece of self-flagellation. It was not so much his song training that was leading him astray as his lack of experience in handling the larger forms.

Despite all obstacles, the symphony was finished during the last months of 1890, and it only remained to arrange for its first performance. The work is as fully extended in form as one would expect from so conscientious a craftsman, being one of the few French symphonies to measure up to the protean demands implied by the medium. Like Franck's single contribution, it begins with a slow introduction, broadly stated by the clarinet in its lower register. The theme is little more than a simple, scalewise construction which serves to establish the spacious mood out of which the movement grows. Listeners would do well to mark this tune, since it recurs in the finale with greater climactic effect. After several pages of finely-worked string passages, the first section reaches an impassioned close, and a new subject enters on horn and bassoon. Utilizing a quicker tempo, its deep contours seem

Ex. 12

Ernest Chausson: 1st Movement - Symphony in B flat

Horn and Bassoon

about to suggest a Wagnerian call to arms, though the allusion is dissipated by a counterstatement on the oboe.[1] Following in the wake of this theme is a series of brisk and staccato figures given out by the upper woodwind. These in turn lead to a plaintive sliver of a tune that is extremely characteristic of Chausson himself. In the remote key of F sharp (the tonality of the whole movement resides firmly in B flat), it is again played by the clarinet, with the assistance of violas and cellos. A final limb is added to the exposition in the form of a high-pitched episode for violins. Nearly all the foregoing subjects are mingled together in the development section, which is distinguished by the variety of its modulations. On the first return of the allegro vivo theme, there is a slight change in the instrumentation, while the remaining material is subjected to a good deal of compression. A presto coda ends the movement in brilliant style. By comparison, the andante aspires to be a solemn lament, deeply shot through with the changing colours

[1] Whether it was this or another theme that led Paul Henry Lang to describe the symphony as 'filled with the brassy glory of Tannhäuser' is hard to say with confidence. In any case, it is a singularly inapt piece of characterization. (cf. 'Music in Western Civilisation'. Norton. N.Y. 1941, p. 928.)

of the composer's melancholy. A ray of light appears in the middle-section with the melody for cor anglais, an instrument borrowed from the Franck symphony. This tune is expressively varied in the bars which follow. The climax reverts to the most intense anguish, only the last chord being allowed to settle in the major key. It is obvious that Chausson threw the whole of himself into this impressive movement, which looks forward in profundity of conception to many a similar movement in the works of Roussel. Having decided to eliminate the scherzo, the composer proceeded straight from this lament into the finale, the weakest portion of the score. The faults here stem from too conscious an imitation of Franck's last movement, and too great a reliance on the cyclical method. The opening subject is tamely anchored to the same cluster of notes and fails to surmount its strained chromatic quality. It has none of the free play so much in evidence in other parts of the symphony. An excessive use of scales and repeated notes towards the conclusion does even less to reassure the listener. A culminating Franckist touch can be found in the chorale which is inserted mid-way through this disappointing movement. Unfortunately, it does not succeed in drawing attention away from the composer's flagging inspiration. The B flat Symphony had its première on 18 April 1891, with Chausson himself conducting. It aroused a favourable response in the audience, which included a powerful contingent of supporters, but drew only the usual tepid dismissal from the critics. To many who were present, the gloom created by Franck's death cast its own pall over the proceedings.

Benumbed by the efforts he had put into writing this work, Chausson did not feel inclined to remain in the capital to witness the aftermath. Instead, he decided to go on a trip to Italy and recuperate. He had visited the country on a previous occasion, but this time its charms were the means he needed to regain his composure. In Florence he met Cosima and Siegfried Wagner, finding the latter shockingly reactionary in his views. As a genteel member of the upper-classes, he was also taken aback by the manners of the tourists. Complaining of 'old Englishwomen who threaten the holiest virgins of Botticelli with their long teeth', he did not feel happy in his new surroundings, and he was not long in making up his mind to return to Paris. Soon after his arrival, he completed more music to words by his friend Bouchor, this time for a drama entitled *La Légende de Sainte-Cécile*, a work that had the most unfortunate première in January 1892. Bellaigue—the critic who was destined to throw cold water on the posthumous performance of *Les Béatitudes*—did a neat hatchet job on this production, accusing Chausson's music of being 'ugly, shrill, thin and grating'. Other critics referred to it as 'puerile' and 'more cruel than the tortures

of Gaymas'. It is of interest to uncover the objections these contemporaries had to the composer's art. They did not find his
music—as we are often inclined to do today—too elegaic and
lowering. On the contrary, it was its modernism that struck the
wrong note. Just as Debussy was at first considered barbaric
(though he strikes most present-day listeners as exceptionally
refined), so Chausson was thought to be harmonically obscure and
audacious. It is true that the word 'restrained' was frequently used
in a derogatory sense about his work, but this hardly chimes with
the current opinion that it suffers from too many 'swooning'
phrases. A standard criticism of his music was expressed in the
comment of one unfavourable observer who likened it to 'stew
without meat'. Even after the second—and unquestionably more
successful—presentation of his symphony by Nikisch and the
Berlin Philharmonic, the press still thought fit to attack him as 'the
Mallarmé of music'. This might have been interpreted as a com-
pliment had it sprung from really informed sources. Unfortunately,
all it reflected was the enormous public ignorance surrounding
matters of aesthetic theory. The delicate presentiments contained
in the work of men like Chausson and Mallarmé simply failed to
penetrate the average hidebound sensibility. People were taught to
appreciate only what was concrete and unequivocal. It is symptomatic that audiences revelled in works like Rimsky-Korsakov's
Antar, while being utterly blind to experiments in a less blatant
vein carried out by members of the Franck school. As long as such
philistinism persisted, there was no real chance that Chausson's
music would be taken seriously.

To state that these attacks were a discouragement to the composer would only be to give rise to a further platitude. The situation in which he found himself was actually a good deal more
complex. For although he continued to suffer occasional fits of
depression right up to the end of his life, Chausson had by this
time managed to acquire a measure of control over his emotions.[1]
His preoccupation with death began to be less marked with the
passing of the years, and he relinquished the habit of reading
pessimistic messages into the novels of Balzac and Stendhal.
Aware of the contradiction existing between his disenchantment
and the comfortable circumstances of his private life, the composer
gradually renounced the idea that he was in some way a victim of
affliction. As he had the frankness to admit in one of his confessional
letters to Raymond Bonheur:

[1] One of the signs by which his stability became recognized was the
increasingly active role he was called upon to play in the affairs of the
Société Nationale. He followed d'Indy and Duparc as Secretary from
about 1894 onwards.

Good Heavens, I know very well that I am what people call
fortunate, almost frightfully so. And doubtless I would be too
much so without this wretched, uneasy and violent brain of
mine.

This shows that the real source of Chausson's melancholy can be
summed up in one word—imagination. He had the sort of imagination we associate with figures like Shelley and Coleridge. Like
them, he pondered on the problems of human frailty and the
limits of human aspiration. But as time progressed, he also
accepted the need for mental discipline. Thus he learned to bear
criticism of his work without affront, and retreated somewhat from
the practice of opposing his standards to those of the masses. The
upshot was that his poise was never faced with total disintegration
—except perhaps in private and at times of acute crisis—and he
escaped the taint of permanent neurosis. While discussing the art
with his friends, he would often deplore the contemporary taste for
'programme music' and the more unthinking forms of Italian
opera, but the existence of such things became a fact which he
ended by tolerating.[1] It is all the more tragic, perhaps, that he did
not survive to make good use of this new-found equanimity.

Setting out in search of his next retreat, Chausson discovered
what he was looking for in the magnificent country residence at
Luzancy, which his biographers have aptly described as 'a
nineteenth-century Ferney'. Once again, it was his rich in-laws
who had been responsible for renting this mansion, and all the
composer had to do was transport his family there, along with a
few carefully selected possessions. Since he had by this time
strengthened his comradeship with Debussy, it seemed quite
natural to invite the young man to share their company. Both
composers were busy at work on their respective operas, and the
enthusiasm which they were on the point of developing for Russian
music gave them an added reason for wanting to be together.
Without either feeling the need to make great demands on the
other, they began what was to be one of the most idyllic episodes
in Chausson's life. Activities consisted of aimless boat-rides,
heated discussions on the music of *Boris Godounov*, and indolent
afternoons spent at the billiard table. Debussy thrilled everyone
with his subtle piano playing, while on fine days they all went out-
doors to indulge in an orgy of photography. This exciting invention—which Corot and his followers at Barbizon had already come

---

[1] Programme music created what psychologists used to call an
'approach-avoidance conflict' in many of the Franck school—they professed to despise it, while at the same time were busy writing it. D'Indy
is the supreme instance of this paradox.

to regret—has left us a touching pictorial narrative of the occasion. On one print, we easily recognize the two composers waiting to cast off on the banks of the Marne, their swarthy features partly hidden by gay straw-hats, worn à la Maupassant. On another, the entire family is grouped around the piano, Mme Chausson resplendently dressed in a white evening gown, while the composer of *L'après-midi d'un faune* weaves his spell. Looking at such pictures from across three-quarters of a century, it is surprising how undated they appear. One could almost mistake them for stills from a Max Ophuls film. All was not lived in idleness, however and when the time came for the two men to separate it was found that each had learnt a great deal from the other. In the correspondence which they kept up for more than a year afterwards, Chausson recalls benefiting from his friend's warning not to overload his scores with too much part-writing; while Debussy comments on the advice he has obtained regarding his *Proses Lyriques* and certain sections of *Pelléas*. A note of acrimony creeps into their letters now and again, especially when Chausson makes it plain that he cannot enthuse over the younger man's String Quartet. We know little of the circumstances which eventually drove a breach between them. Mme Etiennette Lerolle-Chausson (the composer's daughter) has implied that they quarrelled over money, and that there was an element of 'double-dealing' in Debussy's behaviour. This would not be out of character, judging by what we know of his actions in other financial contexts. In any case, it does not alter the fact that for a short period they enjoyed the most happy and fruitful relationship, and it is significant that Debussy was among the mourners at Chausson's funeral, five years after their alleged estrangement.

Another colleague who was to have a marked influence on Chausson's career was the Belgian violinist, Eugène Ysaÿe. This boisterous extrovert was in amicable mood when in the company of the Franck school of composers, and he had a genuine desire to present the public with their works. He and Chausson had met frequently at Paris concerts, and over the dinner-table at the Boulevard de Courcelles. When in Brussels, the composer would stay with the Ysaÿes at their home in the Avenue Brugmann. Several valuable developments accrued from their friendship, not least the performance of Chausson's Concerto in D for piano and chamber ensemble, which was given under Ysaÿe's auspices at Brussels's famous Twenty Club in 1892.[1] More important than this even was a suggestion—persistently hammered home by the

[1] This astonishing work for piano, violin and string quartet must be unique in the chamber repertory. It aspires to be a kind of miniature concerto grosso.

Belgian player—that the composer should write something for violin and orchestra. This came at a time when Chausson was hard at work on *Arthus*, so that for a long period he did nothing about it. Eventually, however, his conscience began to prick him a little, and he wrote to his friend telling him that, if he could not spare the time to compose a full concerto, at least he would soon let him have a work of smaller dimensions. As it happened, Ysaÿe himself had written a *Poème Elégiaque* which was notable for having broken away from the rakish tradition of Bériot and Vieuxtemps. This unpretentious piece was probably what inspired Chausson to create his famous *Poème*, op. 25. Ysaÿe was resting at Yvoir, after an exhausting American tour, when he received the manuscript of the work, and he was so thrilled with it that he could hardly wait to announce its first performance. It was then the autumn of 1896, and before either the composer or the performer could do anything to prevent it, one of Franck's other pupils—the energetic Guy Ropartz—stepped in and requested the rights to the première. Ropartz was at that time Director of the Nancy Conservatoire, so that he represented a powerful voice from the provinces. Chausson could not refuse the honour, and the *Poème* was first heard in that city on 27 December. Meantime, Ysaÿe had not been able to resist giving a private performance of the work before a gathering of artists in Spain during the previous October. Legend has it that the violinist played from the music on that occasion, and did not actually memorise the composition until he was on the train from Brussels to Nancy. Afterwards, he took it with him to Germany, where Albeniz, who was to become another of the composer's staunchest allies, was instrumental in getting Breitkopf and Härtel to publish it. Unknown to Chausson, the Spanish pianist paid out of his own pocket for this to be done. It was a fine gesture which had the effect of bolstering the composer's shaky confidence.

The 'Poème' is a splendid example of what Chausson could do when he had the sense to invest in the right medium. Though fully scored for soloist and orchestra, the work lasts less than twenty minutes. It thus cleverly avoids the longueurs of a multi-movement essay in the same vein. The mood is passive and improvisatory, recalling the Delius Violin Concerto to English listeners. The harmonic language of these two works is also somewhat similar. Chausson's harmony was always very advanced for his day, making free use of chromatic sevenths and ninths. His whole idiom came close to the impressionists in this respect. If nowadays we tend to find this idiom a trifle cloying, it is only because it was over-employed by later composers like Bax, who used it to create the illusion of a Celtic twilight. One of the reasons why the *Poème* seems so much more successful than the composer's other works is that the violin's ascending and descending cantilena gave him special opportunities for exhibiting his lyrical gift. This gift emerges to far greater effect than in the Symphony. The beautifully proportionate 'lento e misterioso' theme which appears at the beginning of the work is among the composer's best melodies. Its

Ex. 13

Ernest Chausson: Poème for Violin and Orchestra

Lento e misterioso

intervals are as pleasing to the eye as the arches of a classical building. Every composer is said to have his favourite interval, Elgar being notable for his falling seventh and Fauré for his modal tritone. Chausson more often than not exploited the concordant interval of a third. This makes his music excessively euphonious and lacking in angularity. To modern ears, the *Poème* can accordingly sound over-sweet.[1] But the form of the composition is so flexible (not presenting the composer with his usual constructional difficulties), and the cut of the melodies so distinguished, that most listeners are prepared to ignore occasional lapses of taste. Above all, there is no striving after effect in this profoundly sincere work, surely the composer's finest effort. What Chausson would have made of Anthony Tudor's ballet *Lilac Garden*—which presents it in choreographic apparel—is not hard to imagine.

During the Christmas preceding the playing of his *Poème*, the composer had reluctantly put the finishing touches to his opera *Arthus*, though as yet he had been unable to find a theatre willing to perform it. Considered in the light of its Wagnerian affinities, the work was bound to propose certain difficulties of acceptance. It was not only France which rejected it, however, but also Spain, Belgium and Germany. For a while it seemed probable that the Director of the Prague Opera would make a bid, but he was prevented from doing so by a publisher's agreement. In the outcome, production had to wait until 1903, four years after the composer's death, and then it fell to the Théâtre de la Monnaie to do the honours. The work thus ran true to form, casting a jinx on its creator which reached out even beyond the grave. As is well known, the Arthurian legend has taken a multitude of forms and is

[1] Another possible reason for the work's voluptuousness is that it is said to have been inspired by a reading of one of Turgenev's tender nouvelles. Jean Gallois, in his recent biography of the composer, offers a fascinating account of its genesis, seen from this angle.

to be encountered in more than one country. The aspects chosen by Chausson concern Lancelot's guilty love for Guinevere, and Mordred's betrayal of the pair to King Arthur. The situation is therefore very similar to that of *Tristan*—where the lovers are threatened by Melot and King Mark. The fact that in both operas the hero and heroine are made to die, while the King survives to pronounce on the tragedy, would seem to render the parallel conclusive. It is important to realize, however, that narrative coincidence does not imply sameness of emotional accent. To that extent, it is worth reminding ourselves of the very different standpoints which Wagner and Chausson adopt towards their material. The composer of *Tristan* allows the emphasis to fall on passion, whereas in *Arthus* it is duty which receives the greater uplift. There is nothing resembling a *Liebestod* in Chausson's opera, for the reason that he was unable to conceive of love in quite such self-annihilating terms. The revolution Wagner brought about lay in his cavilling at traditional morality. In Chausson's philosophy, on the contrary, moral obligation assumed a place of highest urgency. Looking at the relationships of his characters, it is unquestionably Arthur who bears the heaviest burden, with Lancelot's passion curbed by his sense of the King's destiny. As the composer himself expressed it in a letter written during one of his creative crises:

> You will not be surprised if I tell you that I do not at all share your opinion about 'relaxed morality'. I understand only effort, constant effort in all things, and always directed towards the same goal. What do you see that is not an effort!

These sentiments made it impossible for Chausson to have written his opera as a thinly-disguised apology for eroticism. When Arthur surveys the scene at the end of Act III, it is not as the typical chorus-like figure we may have been led to expect, but as the chief protagonist of the drama, ready to embrace the claims which have been made upon him.[1] Moreover, there is never any doubt that Guinevere is motivated by selfishness.

Viewed in purely musical terms, *Arthus* has an equally strong case for being granted independence. Wagner's orchestra in *Tristan* is highlighted by the excessively solo character of the playing, which sometimes threatens to turn the work into a gigantic divertimento for instruments. We do not find this method imitated in Chausson's opera. There the writing is more conventionally orchestral, though not to the point of being prejudicial. Scoring is smooth and tightly-knit, aimed at producing a firm support for

---

[1] Cf. Jean Gallois, who writes: 'C'est Arthus, qui, donnant d'ailleurs son nom à l'opéra, forme l'élément moteur, le centre de l'action.'

the voices. Where the action calls for a prelude or interlude, this is tactfully intruded without making unseemly demands on the audience. Since Chausson wrote his own libretto for the work, he was able to bring about a particularly close link between music and text. He avoided the recitative and aria pattern, choosing to maintain the continuity of vocal and orchestral sound. So far this merely duplicates Wagnerian practice. The difference comes in the composer's astute grasp of French prosody, which enabled him to adapt his sequences to the barely perceptible accents of the characters. It is simply untrue to say, as Donald Grout does in his *Short History of Opera*, that 'neither libretto nor music offers any passages of real distinction'. The dialogue between Arthur and Merlin (Act II Sc. I) beginning 'Ta parole est sombre' provides a fine example of Chausson's power to heighten the drama by the use of expressive language; while almost any episode from Act III can be shown to possess musical merit of the subtlest kind. Taken as a whole, it is this last section which compels admiration. Act I is overburdened with a pallid and derivative love duet, as well as a bardic chorus that harks back suspiciously to the days of Grand Opera. Things improve towards the end of Act II, and from that point on the work's quality is never in serious doubt. Lancelot's death-scene has no difficulty in provoking a positive response, while the moving farewell which Arthur bids must rank among the best finales in modern French opera. These sequences alone suffice to justify a revival. If criticism is urged, it should be to call attention to limitations of sensibility rather than outmoded Wagnerisms. In this connection, it ought to be admitted that Chausson fails to make the theme of betrayal really convincing. Like Franck, he was much better at depicting loyalty than evil, with the result that Arthur's music seems more persuasive than that of Mordred. Similarly, the remorse which Lancelot exhibits in Act III Sc. I rings out more truthfully than his earlier turpitude. Indeed, the entire opera could be viewed—contrary to all intention—as a parable of honesty and high-mindedness. Perhaps that critic was near the mark who identified the Knights of the Round Table with the various members of the Franck circle, and King Arthur himself with the Pater Seraphicus. But such a caricature does not invalidate Chausson's claims to have written some first-rate music for the theatre, and to have given a new 'point d'appui' to the Wagnerian ideal. No other composer, with the exception of Debussy, came nearer towards accommodating this ideal to the conditions of French cultural life.[1]

[1] Comparisons may be sought with Reyer's *Sigurd* (1883), Chabrier's *Gwendoline* (1886) and d'Indy's *Fervaal* (1897)—all of which may be thought demonstrably inferior to Chausson's opera.

Deeply disappointed by his inability to discover a venue for
Arthus, Chausson spent his last few years regretting that he had
ever ventured into such dangerous waters. 'Leave it all to Bruneau
and Wagner' was his usual rejoinder when asked whether he saw
any point in continuing as an operatic composer. The entire paraphernalia of stage production was something he found frightening
and more than a little sickening. It could hardly have been much of
a surprise to his friends when the composer announced his further
secession from the metropolitan world that had treated him so
shabbily. The district to which he now retired was Veyrier, near
the Lake of Annecy. It was there that he composed his Piano
Quartet in A, generally conceded to be the best of his chamber-
works. The whole operation took him a mere five weeks, being
marked by a complete absence of struggle. Whether this showed that
Chausson had at last reached a stage of fluency, or whether it was
simply one of those lucky flukes which all artists have reason to
hope for, no one can tell. What is certain is that it proved the best
received of any of the composer's works. When Auguste Pierret
performed it on 2 April 1898, the audience responded in the most
heart-warming fashion. It is not difficult to see why this should have
been so, for the Quartet is full of marvellous things, instantly
attractive to the discriminating listener. The plangent viola theme
in D flat which begins the slow movement was a truly magnificent
inspiration which Chausson managed to carry through with fault-
less logic. Similarly fetching is the naïve folk-like melody in 3/4

Ex. 14

Ernest Chausson: 2nd Movement - Piano Quartet in A.

time which speeds the third movement on its way. As we should
expect from any Franck pupil, there are hints of thematic reminiscence, most patently in the reappearance of the viola tune in the
fourth movement. Augmentation of the note values has the effect
of broadening the melody's gait on the second time around. Critics
of Chausson's chamber music have drawn attention to the composer's habit of padding out his textures, and the Piano Quartet
cannot be exempted from this failing. Recourse to tremolo filling
is more than once apparent, the pity being that it occurs most often
when the music seems to be crying out for a genuinely expressive
climax. Neither Castillon nor Duparc entirely overcame a comparable weakness, so that one is inclined to attribute it to inadequacies in Franck's teaching. Even allowing for the fullest lapses,

however, the A major Quartet must be regarded as a splendid addition to the repertory. It deserves a place alongside the two superb works for this combination written by Fauré.

Surging with enthusiasm at the prospect now springing up before him, and brandishing the score of an unpublished symphonic poem called *Soir de Fête*, Chausson could scarcely help feeling on top of the world again. At last it seemed as if his career were about to enter its most majestic phase. But as so often happens, fate had already decided otherwise. During the summer of 1899, when the streets of Paris had become too hot for comfort, the composer took himself off once more to Limay, near Nantes, where he expected to work at a second Quartet and incidentally enjoy a few days' cycling in the open-air. He had been settled in this pleasant environment only a short while when disaster struck. Out for a spin one afternoon, he lost control of his machine and smashed into a wall, suffering a severe fracture of the skull. No one appears to have witnessed the accident, but there seems no doubt that the composer was killed instantly. When the information was relayed to his family, they were so stunned they could hardly take it in. By the day of the funeral, however, all Paris had been informed, and people from every district of the capital flocked to the graveside to pay their respects. Debussy, Fauré, Duparc, Magnard and Dukas were among the musicians present, while Rodin, Degas and Carrière represented the artists. Chausson's friend Pierre Louÿs wrote a moving tribute on behalf of those who were less well acquainted with the composer, and the faithful Ysaÿe gave a tremulous rendering of the *Poème* before an audience in London. Everywhere there were expressions of surprise and regret that so promising an artist had not lived to complete his work. Only a few months previously, the composer had received news that *Viviane* was being heard in Moscow. At the same time, Jeanne Raunay was busy preparing a new song—the haunting *Chanson perpétuelle*—for performance at Le Havre. On the larger front, the conductor Felix Mottl had pledged himself to introduce *Arthus* at Karlsruhe, a promise that was leading the composer to toy with the idea of another opera based on one of Calderon's plays. Now all his plans had suffered a shattering blow, as final as it was unexpected. It only remained for the survivors to take stock of the damage, and set about the task of closing the circle's ranks.

Asked to give an appraisal of Chausson's status, few present-day listeners would hesitate to express their opinion. What is so remarkable is the regularity with which such opinions seem based on mere whim or fancy. Like many other Franck pupils, the composer seems destined to depend for his standing on unimportant fluctuations of taste and temperament. Those who look to music to equip them with 'sensations sweet, felt in the blood and felt along the heart' cannot help finding much consolation in his art. As de Bréville acutely suggested, it is an art that constantly strives to say the word 'cher'. On the other hand, we must not underestimate the influence of those crusading spirits to whom all manifestations of tenderness, whether in music or any other art, are anathema. Perhaps the truth is that Chausson was not a sufficiently inclusive figure to have contained within his vision that variety of feeling needed to appeal on a succession of fronts. Precisely because his mood was so individual and consistent, he forfeited the power of being liked by everybody, though this has resulted in him being liked all the more by his adherents. Viewing him alongside other members of the Franck circle, he cannot help striking us as more talented than d'Indy, less constricted than Duparc. It might be conceded that his best work does not suffer by being brought into relation with that of Franck himself. Indeed, a comparison of their respective symphonies might lead us to the conclusion that the pupil sometimes triumphed over the master. Wherever we have pledged our loyalties, it will scarcely be denied that Chausson was the most lovable of Franck's followers, and a man whose life was lived in the service of the highest and most refined ideals.

VIII

Professor without portfolio

The last twenty years in the career of César Franck wrought no
dramatic changes in the composer's *modus vivendi*. Those intimations of fame which had so faithfully pursued him throughout the
middle stages of his journey were never destined to take on fuller
possession; so that he remained to the end unmolested by public
adulation. He rose early, ate a frugal breakfast, and embarked on
his usual day's teaching, proving that neither the ravages of age nor
the pangs of discontent were sufficient to undermine his carefully
prepared routine. Gifted with an excellent physique, and a larger
than average share of nervous resilience, there was no reason to
suppose he would not become an octogenarian. A portrait taken of
the composer at Tournai in April 1890 shows him to have been
almost totally unaffected by the passage of time. As Winton Dean
has remarked when assessing the discrepancies in his features, 'the
only marked change . . . over forty years was a gradual whitening
of the hirsute portions.' Nor was this Franck's sole feat of resistance,
for the passionate character of his late music hints strongly at a
similar preservation of his emotional reflexes. Such an all-round
power to withstand decline serves to make this terminal phase by
far the most significant in the composer's progress.

It was a phase that began, somewhat unexpectedly, with the
retirement of Franck's old organ professor, Benoist. His tenure at
the Conservatoire had persisted for so long that ambitious young
teachers might have been forgiven for assuming it would go on for
ever. Once he was safely shunted out of the way, however, there
was no dearth of speculation about whom to appoint as his successor. On grounds of skill and experience, the obvious candidate
appeared to be Saint-Saëns, but his busy life as a composer was
already making strenuous demands upon him, to say nothing
of the astonishing range of scholarly hobbies to which he was

addicted.[1] It was at this point that Franck's former choirmaster and friend at Sainte-Clotilde, the conservative Théodore Dubois, saw his chance to put in a word. Since working with Franck as choirmaster, Dubois had gone on to carve out a more worldly career in academic circles, and his opinions already carried a good deal of weight at the Conservatoire. Allegedly, it was he who approached the Director, Ambroise Thomas, with a view to pressing Franck's claims for the vacant post. 'There is at the moment only one man who is fit for this post,' Dubois is said to have told him, 'and that is César Franck.' Thomas, very much to his surprise, agreed with the assessment, and promptly went ahead to issue his formal invitation. Others have implied that it was really Saint-Saëns who, having willingly forfeited his own candidature, took the trouble to go around canvassing on behalf of Franck. Either way, the appointment seems to have been slightly mysterious, and d'Indy, writing thirty years later, still could not understand how it had all been managed. Whether there was a conspiracy or not, Franck was clearly the right man for the job, any doubts being due solely to malice or envy. He was naturally very pleased to have been offered it, not merely because it was well paid, but on account of the honour it would bring him. Not that it was one of the key chairs within the institution. The three professorships of composition—occupied by such mediocrities as Victor Massé, Henri Reber and François Bazin—counted for far more in the way of public esteem, and their holders were inclined to lord it over Franck in a thoroughly galling fashion. It is directly symptomatic of the low rating ascribed to the composer that he was never able to aspire to one of these senior positions, even though his interests were slanted more in the direction of composition than anything else. Attempts to elevate Franck from inside met with the usual resistance, and when the vacancies came up they were filled by men of the calibre of Guiraud and Delibes. Despite the limits placed upon his prospects, no one could have been more content with his new post than the composer of 'Ruth'. His father had taught him never to look a gift horse in the mouth, and the advantages promised were certainly numerous enough to give cause for rejoicing.

In terms of pupils, everyone was impressed by the flock which now found an official nesting-place under the composer's wing. Many of these, of course, lacked a special feeling of attachment to their teacher. They were simply young men and women who had been drafted to learn the organ as part of the school's curriculum.

[1] As James Harding has lately shown, Saint-Saëns was a genuine polymath with interests in archaeology, astronomy, botany, philosophy and even the antique theatre. (See *Saint-Saëns and his Circle*, Chapman & Hall, 1965).

Probably Debussy was the most celebrated of the 'captive' pupils Franck acquired in this way, and he was no exception in finding his lessons something of a bore.[1] Others, however, came entirely of their own will, bringing with them a welcome touch of enthusiasm. Bizet, though he stayed too short a time to be counted a disciple, may be considered one of these. Since Franck was not really a name in musical circles at the time of his appointment, the bulk of students were content to suffer rather than enjoy his presence, and given half a chance they would slip off to listen in at the lectures of someone more famous. One of the composer's initial mistakes was to time-table his classes at the same hours as Massenet's. As a result he was frequently compelled to knock on his colleague's door and enquire whether there were any strays within. This habit caused Franck to emerge as a kind of unconscious music-hall comic in the minds of dozens of observers. As time wore on, however, the humour of the situation gave way to grumbles. The fact that he continued to hang on to the loyalties of a small core of students made certain insecure professors very angry; and when a few of Franck's charges looked like carrying off prizes at the annual examinations their anger erupted into open hostility. No better reception awaited the composer among the more high and mighty of his colleagues, several of whom did not scruple to manipulate the juries in such a way as to deprive him of his successes. D'Indy's winning a *primus accessit* during the second year of his studies with Franck showed that now and again their manoeuvres were outwitted by sheer force of ability. It was hardly to be expected that Franck's reputation as a teacher would spread like wildfire. He was too modest and self-effacing for that. It took him nearly the whole twenty years to achieve the standing he desired, and there remained plenty of crabbed spirits who refused to credit him with any skill at all. At the end of that time, however, he could truthfully be said to have made his mark on the institution of his choice—whether as an influence for good or evil was hotly debated.

One of the minor irregularities the composer was obliged to put right before taking up his duties lay in the sphere of nationality. Technically, Franck was still Belgian at this time, despite Nicolas-Joseph's elaborate bureaucratic precautions, so that he was now required to go through the motions of taking out French citizenship. This course presented him with no crisis of conscience, and the papers were duly authorized in time for him to proceed. What his position would have been like had he refused to take this step is hard to assess. Apart from the effect on his appointment,

---

[1] One of the things Debussy found objectionable in Franck's teaching was his constant urge to modulate. His later description of his teacher was as a 'modulating machine'.

there is the question of whether he would have been claimed in time as a Belgian nationalist composer, as happened, for example, with Lekeu. In the interval since his death, many commentators have speculated on how oddly Franck fits in to the French cultural tradition. Some have branded him as a German intruder who helped to implant dangerously foreign habits. Others, less open to prejudice, have still felt inclined to question the sources of his inspiration. Jean-Aubry, for instance, raised an important issue in asking: 'Is it really French, this mysticism, this readiness to take everything seriously?' Without wishing to impute too many national characteristics to music, it is perhaps the case that Franck's 'supplicative' style owes much to Belgian practice, and would have been seized upon by the 'separatists' of that nation had not the composer acted to deprive them of their catch. The fact is that Franck was never very interested in being thought a nationalist, either in regard to politics or music. He possessed absolutely none of that patriotic ardour we attribute to men like Dvořák and Verdi. Moreover, the dominance of German culture was hardly something that resulted from the work of a few accidental expatriates. It was deeply rooted in the attitudes of all who were intelligent enough to have recognized the genius of Bach and Handel, Beethoven and Brahms. It is significant that d'Indy, Duparc and Castillon—each of whom was unequivocally French—were as subject to this domination as Franck, and not simply because they reflected his sympathies. All the same, it is worth remembering that Franck was not native born, and that his descent involved conflicting ethnic strains.

The creative leap forward inspired by the peace did not assist the composer to develop a fresh style, neither did it impel him to select new forms. His setting of Edouard Blau's *Rédemption* (1871–3) displayed much the same assortment of virtues and vices as had gone into the composition of *Ruth*—though it turned out to be a far more polished exercise.[1] It was in order to work on this project that Franck laid aside *Les Béatitudes*. The text was not unfashionable, Massenet having toyed with the idea of using it, while Gounod did not disdain to claim it later on. It traces, somewhat unctuously, the rise of humanity from mindless paganism to Christian redemption. There are a number of different versions of the score, the earliest having been written in 1871, the second in hasty preparation for a performance in April 1873, and a final revision made at

[1] The cantata *Rebecca* proves that even as late as 1880–1 Franck was not above reverting to the style he had epitomized in *Ruth*. Of the five sections comprising this uninspired work, only the lusty camel-drivers' chorus stood out. This won repeated hearings as a concert-piece in its own right.

the behest of d'Indy and Duparc which appeared the year after. In its definitive form the work is spread over three sections, the first and third of which are choral invocations, the second being a symphonic interlude. It contains parts for mezzo-soprano, mixed choir and orchestra. Like *Les Béatitudes*, the cycle of keys through which it progresses follows a definite scheme. Part I portrays the dawn of life on earth, representing man as a creature who is merely responsive to pleasure and pain. This is one of the least successful sections of the work, partly owing to the static nature of the writing, but also to the absence of any impression of savagery. After a turgid fifty bars of introduction, the opening chorus is conventional in its blocked-off phrasing and repetitive accompaniment. The tunes are mawkish and the aria and recitative for the archangel depressingly flat. The whole section ends with a chorus proclaiming the birth of Christ. Probably the best parts of this preludial music are the adroit canonic episodes, though even these pall by virtue of constant reappearance. To state, as d'Indy does, that it gives rise to 'all the vilest passions of the heathen world' is laughable. The function of the symphonic interlude which follows seems to have been to indicate time passing. During this section, which was incidentally omitted from the first performance, the intention of the composer was to portray a reversion to pre-religious modes of thought, a kind of lapse into the Dark Ages. Franck's orchestral tool-kit hardly shows much change here or elsewhere in the work. The glutinous use of the harp is again prominent, and there is a preponderance of low-pitched string sequences. The pedal notes for double-bass are actually so low as to produce a soft 'buzz' which goes far towards spoiling the texture. After the interlude, Part II presents us with the archangel once more, this time singing the praises of prayer, penitence and brotherly love as means to redemption. The music, however, is anything but awesome. For the most part, it moves at an incredibly jocose pace, and it is only in the final declamation that some semblance of dignity returns.

Criticism of 'Rédemption' has sought to underline many of the shortcomings to which we have pointed. Speaking of the ineffective portrait of degeneracy, Norman Demuth has rightly contested: 'If humanity was no more evil than this, then there was not very much wrong with it.' Other commentators have drawn attention to the lack of exuberant rhythms, and the substitution of 'melopoeia' for melody. It is true that Franck's music never dances, least of all in this sober work. What is perhaps more reprehensible is the continued failure to dramatize sufficiently. Adolphe Jullien, writing in *Français* complained most pertinently of this fault when he argued:

'To attack a superhuman poem of this kind something more is needed than the pure and polished talent which created *Ruth*—something like the thundering genius of Beethoven or the extravagant imagination of Berlioz.'

To heap all the blame on Franck and refer to the poem as 'superhuman' will nevertheless seem unjust to the more literate observer, since the text itself was hardly of this stature. Banalities can easily be found in the parts covered by the symphonic interlude, while the ingenuous sub-titles which appeared in the first version nowadays seem unbearably coy. On the credit side, there are occasional felicities of scoring which would not have been nearly so apparent in the younger Franck. The effective use of horns and trombones comes into this category, as does the employment of the full ensemble for the climax in Part II. Less commendable is the composer's habit of writing in fourths for the woodwind—something that produced a notably shrill and ungrateful sound in places—and his careful avoidance of brass solos. Suspicious critics may be inclined to raise the question of Wagner's influence on this work. At the time of writing, however, Franck had heard only *Lohengrin* and *Tannhäuser*, and to judge from the tepid remarks he made to Duparc in 1873 on the subject of *Die Walküre*, nothing in this later masterpiece could have induced him to undertake the revisions. Berlioz, Meyerbeer and Gounod in all probability continued to be the chief models. It is interesting to note that other contemporary composers were not much impressed by Franck's latest *magnum opus*. Amy Fay, in her charming book of musical recollections based on study in Germany, records that Liszt showed next to no interest when d'Indy passed him a copy of *Rédemption* shortly after its first production. Brahms, as was his custom, proved even ruder by refusing to read through the score.

The acuteness of the public was once again brought into question when Franck's cantata—which d'Indy incidentally insisted upon describing as an oratorio—was given its première. This took place at the Odéon Theatre during Holy Week, with Colonne directing. At an early stage in the rehearsals, it became apparent that poor copying of the parts was going to lead to difficulty. An unprecedented number of mistakes had somehow crept into the score. In the two days leading up to the second rehearsal, d'Indy, Benoît and Duparc were accordingly entrusted with the unenviable job of re-copying all the erroneous and illegible portions. This they were able to do by staying up all night—fortified by Duparc's brandy— cutting and pasting away with furious energy. When the performance came around, it was obvious how unprepared the orchestra was to cope with the extreme sharp keys. The publisher Hartmann was partly to blame for this débâcle, having failed to send on the parts at a suitably early date. As if these upsets were not enough, the soloist, Mme de Caters, took it into her head to object to a lack of cantilena for the voice, with the result that her singing assumed a pompous and aggrieved tone. All might still have passed unnoticed had Colonne made himself responsible for covering up. Unfortunately, he too appeared less than fully familiar with the music. It has even been implied that he was unsympathetic to Franck, and took a perverse delight in seeming incompetent. This interpretation is probably unjust, though it must be emphasized that, despite their generally willing spirit, neither Colonne nor Lamoureux could have been described as devoted Franckists. For one thing, they considered him an unhelpful orchestrator, suspecting that he transferred all his ideas *en bloc* from the organ loft. For another, they reserved a good deal of their sympathy for the composer's pupils, many of whom were better at striking the modern note demanded of them.

Because the symphonic interlude had been left out, *Rédemption* created an impression of incompleteness, and all but about fifty of the audience trooped out before the end had been reached.[1] Franck was naturally wounded by this affront, but as usual he elected to keep his own counsel. The modifications made later were unquestionably provoked by the composer's pupils. D'Indy relates how for a long time Franck refused to be talked into making any changes. Surprisingly for him, he even forbade his disciple ever to mention the subject again. Within a year, however, other approaches had been made, and it became clear that grounds for revision existed. Included among the amendments were the transformation of the archangel's F sharp aria into the less intractable key of E; the re-modelling of large sections of the interlude; and the ruling out of the sub-titles. Like so many other of his works, *Rédemption* had to wait until after Franck's death before securing its first worthy interpretation. This came about in December 1896, when the Concerts Colonne went some way towards rectifying their initial blunder. The novelist Octave Mirbeau allowed himself to become one of the acknowledged partisans on that happy occasion, echoing Franck's own belief that the work was superior to Gounod's more popular setting of the text.[2] Sound though this judgement turned out to be, it was hardly enough to

[1] The reason for this serious omission was that Massenet, some of whose works were also being performed in the programme, demanded an excessive share of the rehearsal time.

[2] Mirbeau is best remembered today for his daring exposure of class and sexual habits in the novel *Journal d'une femme de chambre* (1901) which both Jean Renoir and Luis Bunuel have since turned into a successful film. In addition to his espousal of Franck, he was renowned for his astute championship of Cézanne and Maeterlinck.

warrant a complete re-instatement, and *Rédemption* must be viewed alongside *Les Béatitudes* as a much flawed contribution to a less than clearly defined genre.

A couple of years later, Franck hit upon—or perhaps it would be truer to say rediscovered—a promising alternative medium. This was the faithful symphonic poem, to which he now returned in three triumphantly imaginative essays. *Les Eolides*—being the first of the three—appeared almost out of the blue in 1876. No one could have been prepared for it, since the work was both inspired and composed at the far-off home of Auguste Sanches in the Azille district of Languedoc. Franck had often planned to visit his friend in this region, and when he set out in September 1875 he had no thought of making his vacation an excuse for musical composition. Finding the journey rather long, however, he was obliged to stop over at Valence for a few days. While he was there he encountered the *mistral*—that much-discussed poetical and geographical phenomenon. Its sight and sound caused the composer to recall some verses by Leconte de Lisle which celebrate the arrival of the Aeolids, fleeting inhabitants of a classical fairyland. The poem begins with the lines:

> Brises flottantes des cieux . . . qui de baisers capricieux caressant les monts et les plaines.*

The mingling of memory and sensation implied in these events went on to inspire Franck to the writing of music—not for full orchestra, but for the more delectable combination of horns, woodwind, cornet, trumpet, harp, percussion and divided strings. The resulting texture proved as light and airy as that employed by Mendelssohn in his well-known scherzo movements, and as resolutely unlike Franck as anything that could be imagined. Whether for that reason or another, the work has been acclaimed as one of the composer's best. That it allowed him greater freedom than usual will scarcely be contested. The episodes are extremely loosely strung together, despite the canonical tricks in which they abound, and the first theme is languid enough to please the most devout Wagnerian. By this time—and certainly by the time of the Symphony in D minor—the influence of *Tristan* and *The Ring* had begun to be discernible. The second and third themes are firmer and broader, and Franck could not resist blending all three in his richly stratified counterpoint to form the conclusion. What remains so endearing in this work is the care the composer seems to have taken to avoid chromatic meanderings. Furthermore, there is no ugly polarization around a predictable cluster of notes.

*Floating breezes of the skies . . . implanting kisses with fickle tenderness on the mountains and plains.

Right throughout, the melodic lines appear much less regimented than is customary, and the interplay of strings and woodwind (especially clarinets) is skilful enough to have provided d'Indy with a precedent for his *Symphonie Cévenole*. More than that, *Les Eolides* is perhaps the only work by Franck to have anticipated the method of the impressionists. It was first performed in Paris during November 1876, there being a revival at the Salle Erard the following year.

By comparison, the second of the composer's late tone-poems is a more conventional work, at least as far as its subject-matter is concerned. *Le Chasseur Maudit* (1882) unfolds a Lisztian tale of adventure about a Count who defies the Sabbath to go hunting. The ballad on which it was based was written, like Duparc's *Lénore*, by the morbidly-inclined Burgher. Franck's treatment is refreshingly brassy and full-blooded, if a trifle thick in scoring, with strenuous attention given to depicting the horde of devils which end by pursuing the unfortunate huntsman into eternity. As a theme, it strikes a vaguely unserious note, more reminiscent of Walt Disney than German Romanticism. But this may be because the temper of our present age is jocular rather than theological. If Franck intended the work as a serious demonstration of the Church's teachings, he did not reckon with a public that has become conditioned to all manner of Sunday indulgences. Even so, some of the work's details are vividly picturesque. For instance, galloping music used to suggest the Count's ride is piquantly contrasted with the holy strains emanating from the village churches which he thunders past. Indeed, all of the specific aural references—including the tolling of the bell and the chanting of the choir—emerge with as much clarity and succinctness as one would expect from a work by Richard Strauss. This reversion to a narrative-pictorial mode of composition also meant that Franck had less need of his stock cyclical techniques, and their absence renders this symphonic poem almost unique in the composer's output. *Le Chasseur Maudit* reveals a side to Franck's nature which he was probably loath to develop too systematically. For one thing, many of his pupils—especially Chausson and d'Indy—outwardly disapproved of what they took to be an exhibitionist strain in their teacher, believing that respectability resided in the classical forms. Rival musicians also tended to regard his excursions into the realm of the bizarre as naïve and embarrassing.[1] For another, Franck's own pious sensi-

---

[1] This, for example, was the view to which Saint-Saëns gave currency when he remarked: 'Berlioz was more artist than musician; Franck was more musician than artist. He was no poet, and a sense of the picturesque is entirely lacking in his music.' Such a judgement is not unjust, though it has to be set against its author's well-known weakness for spite. As a matter of fact, Saint-Saëns's own sense of colour was distinctly artificial.

bility generally put a brake on his secular and dramatic instincts, sometimes to the great detriment of his creative development. We must be grateful that he was not deterred from returning to the purer forms of music—especially if this includes chamber music—but he would probably also have gained by cultivating his taste for the ridiculous. At least it would have helped to make him a somewhat less priggish figure in the eyes of his descendants.

Horror rather than ridicule emerges as the dominant emotion in *Les Djinns* (1883–4), which was the last of the three orchestral works to appear. Also concerned with evil spirits, it makes a stronger bid for seriousness than its predecessor, if only on account of the conflict between faith and diabolism which it successfully exhibits. The 'djinns' of the title are actually winged devils who arise, shrieking horribly, from their sepulchral resting place amid the catacombs. The work was based on an Oriental fable by Victor Hugo in which the author strives to impart something like a Christian emphasis to the message.[1] Instead of being infidels in revolt against Islam, the evil denizens are seen as an embodiment of man's cruel and vicious propensities. Their power of temptation is pitted against the serene wisdom of the converted, and in the end victory emerges on the side of faith. In choosing to use the piano to symbolize the good elements and the orchestra the bad, Franck unconsciously reversed the practice which Liszt had followed in his *Malédiction*. Whether he was actually influenced by this work is not known. It is quite likely that the famous 'Danse Macabre' of Saint-Saëns, which had made its appearance in 1875, helped to put the idea into his head. The employment of the piano, however, must be attributed to a suggestion from Mme de Serres who, under her maiden name of Caroline Montigny-Rémaury, was on the lookout for a short concertante work to use in filling her concert programmes. This lady-pianist also happened to be Ambroise Thomas's sister-in-law, so that Franck was hardly in a position to ignore her request. In the event, the work was written, like *Les Eolides*, while the composer was on vacation. This time he was staying at Quincy, Seine-et-Marne, with his children and grandchildren, spending part of the holiday flying kites for the benefit of the family. Charles Bordes joined him there during the days he was at work on *Les Djinns*. This was in September 1884, though Alfred Cortot has intimated that the composition had been started in the previous year, only the orchestration being left unfinished. Whether or not

---

[1] Hugo's poem is sometimes cryptically described as a 'lozenge', a term that accurately conveys the shape of the lines, which are short to begin with, and then lengthen towards the middle, finally reverting to the shorter unit again to end.

this was the case, it was certainly not performed before January 1885, when rehearsals were set in motion for the presentation by Louis Diémer and Colonne's orchestra at the Châtelet Theatre. Notices of this concert, which took place on the 15 March, were not entirely unfavourable to Franck. Mersac, writing in *Le Menestrel*, referred to the work's 'originality of thought and admirable polish of style'—going on to add that it was a pity Franck's name appeared so rarely on concert posters. But it should be remembered that by this time the composer had entered upon the penultimate stage of his career.

Possible forerunners of *Les Djinns* have already been discussed, but it is important to underline the work's key affiliations. The existence of Castillon's concerto was probably the most significant factor in the situation. Another was Berlioz's *Harold en Italie*—a work in which the viola is treated as the concertante instrument. Each of these antecedents was known to Franck, and there seems little doubt that he allowed himself to profit from their example. It is equally interesting to speculate on the effect *Les Djinns* may have had upon subsequent compositions for piano and orchestra. Aside from d'Indy's one essay, those which come soonest to mind in this connection are Strauss's *Burleske* and Fauré's late *Fantaisie*. Unlike these formally emancipated works, however, Franck's symphonic poem retains the classical divisions of exposition, development and recapitulation. Essentially, it makes do with two themes, one aggressive and the other pleading. Their opposition in itself pays lip-service to the notion of sonata form, but detailed analysis of the work as a whole reveals other and more strict expressions of allegiance. The orchestra is made to begin with a wild, scherzo-like episode, at times sinister but more often martial, and this leads to the principal idea, which is presented in the form of a dialogue. The second subject is at first allotted to the piano alone, but a swirling accompaniment is soon invoked to bring it to its climax. A change of rhythm, from duple to triple time, announces the development, and from this point on the soloist engages in a number of increasingly expressive, almost ecstatic, interludes. One of the instructions to the player characteristically reads: 'In the mood of a prayer, but with a certain uneasy agitation'. This is exactly the realm most suited to Franck's genius, and it does not take him long to get into his stride. The soaring lyrical flights appear to generate their volition from some far-off mystical source, while the piano's submissive chords are inexorably removed from the sphere of declamation. When the re-capitulation appears, it is with sober exactness, even the second subject going into the tonic. After a coda which briefly exalts virtuosity, a series of plain statements from the keyboard, carefully transformed into the

major key, proclaims a victory for hope and piety. Critics have
not been uniformly kind to *Les Djinns*—perhaps on account of
Franck's rigid habits of schematization—but the work stands in no
need of apology. If it has any marked faults, they are too great a
reliance on string tremolo writing and perhaps one or two stretchily
ungrateful passages for the soloist.

Surprising though it may seem, in the light of his previous
failures, Franck spent much of his time between 1881 and 1886
busy at work on a new opera. It is doubtful whether he would ever
have got started on this if it had not been for the repeated impor-
tunities of his family. Félicité, taking her cue from various theatrical friends, had always harboured a secret desire that he should
become a composer for the stage. Part of this desire reflected her
strong pecuniary urges. She had tolerated her husband's religious
music chiefly because it posed the possibility of richer stipends from
the church. As soon as it became obvious that such rewards were
not forthcoming, she began to consider other ways in which the
family income might be augmented. No doubt it is easy to criticize
her for the avarice she displayed, and it ought to be said in her
favour that she had already endured a painfully long period of
penury. Yet one cannot help feeling that she was wrong to show so
much contempt for Franck's more unworldly interests, such as his
interest in chamber music. If she had not constantly goaded him
into attempting projects which were quite outside the ordinary scope
of his abilities, it is probable that he would have reached creative
maturity as an artist much sooner than he did. As it was, she acted
as one voice and the composer's conscience as another. Later in
their lives, she discovered a powerful ally in her son, Georges,
whose work as a teacher at the Lycée Lakanal (and as a lecturer at
the university) brought him into touch with a persuasive group of
literary intellectuals. Georges was a 'progressive' who belonged to
that tiresome breed which cannot rest content until it has probed
and remodelled the lives of all those with whom it has come into
contact. The attitude which he took up towards his father proved
a mixture of care and condescension. Perhaps because his own subject was anthropology, he took a lively interest in the myths and
legends of other lands, feeling that it would be easy for him to select
material for an opera. The urge to stage-manage his father's career
was thereafter to express itself in a variety of ways (it is tempting to
detect a hint of Nicolas-Joseph in Georges, though without much
trace of authoritarianism). His best-laid plan was to mount a somewhat transmogrified version of a play about the eleventh-century
Aslaks by the Norwegian dramatist, Bjornson. The idea may have
had something to commend it in the first place, but unfortunately
it degenerated in the hands of the librettist, Grandmougin, into a

typically nonsensical melodrama of the kind for which France had become all too notorious. It is rather odd, considering George's professedly *avant-garde* outlook on morals and politics, that he was inveigled into championing the operatic ideals of the 1840s. Yet that is precisely what happened. Seeing that money and fame had accrued to the more spectacular opera composers, he was perhaps unconsciously led to pervert his up-to-date urges; or, more likely, Félicité prevailed on him to gamble all for the sake of the family fortunes. In any case, there was no difficulty in persuading Franck himself to participate in the scheme. To any reasonably worldly individual, it would have seemed idiotic to try to break into the theatre for the first time at the age of sixty-three. Franck, however, was a very gullible man, and he allowed himself to be carried away by dreams of triumph.

Hulda was written at a furious pace, despite its eight hundred pages of score. In the outcome, it spread itself over four long acts and included everything from a ballet to a set of Norwegian popular tunes. The plot describes the trials of a young woman of the house of Hustawick, whose kinsmen have been killed or taken captive by the marauding Aslaks. During the first act, she is dragged off by an Aslak chief, the combative Gudleik, against whom she has made a vow of vengeance. Held prisoner in the castle of the victors, Hulda finds a way out of her dilemma by instigating a fight between Gudleik and his brother Gunther in which the former is mortally wounded. At the same time, another of the visiting chieftains, Eiolf, has taken a fancy to her, despite his being officially betrothed to an Aslak girl named Swannhilde. This brings us to the end of Act II. What follows is a kind of extended interlude in which the Aslak king and queen commiserate bitterly on their misfortunes, and Hulda meditates on what the future holds for her. The ballet (which turns out to be an allegorical affair concerning winter and spring) comes at the beginning of the fourth act, into which a further load of bloodshed is mechanically disgorged. It is now Swannhilde's turn to win back Eiolf, while Hulda jealously conspires with the Aslak people to bring about his death. At the moment of Eiolf's assassination, Hulda finds herself pursued by her fellow-conspirators, and ends by throwing herself into the sea in a grand gesture of renunciation. To modern sensibilities, all these absurd heroics have a flavour of Meyerbeer about them, the main difference being that Franck was unable to comply with a musical parallel. In every act, the music fails to rise to the occasion, there being no rise or swell of sound to generate dramatic emotion. Between the staggeringly large number of killings, both the action and the musical pulse come near to stopping altogether. Act III, for instance, drags interminably, with Hulda occupying far too much of the stage. On the other hand, the ballet is entertaining enough, and the 'Marche Royale', *à la Tannhäuser*, a splendid point of wakefulness.

Not surprisingly, *Hulda* was refused by the Director of the Paris Opéra, who nevertheless liked the ballet well enough to propose that Franck should recast the work in this form. As it transpired, nothing was done with the opera until after the composer's death, when Georges and Samuel Rousseau made some changes with a view to getting it performed at Monte Carlo. It is interesting to note that one of the reasons why Franck's son chose Rousseau as his collaborator was to avoid having to consult d'Indy, who had maintained a frostily disapproving attitude over the whole project. Indeed, it was not only *Hulda* of which he disapproved, but the entire paraphernalia of progressivism which Georges was bringing to bear on his father. D'Indy prided himself on being a Royalist of the old school, a diehard Catholic to whom all manifestations of social change were anathema. He suspected Georges, rightly or wrongly, of parading his advanced views as a cloak by which to disguise his commercialism. Looked at from the opposite angle, this young university lecturer could not resist flinging Voltaire in the face of his adversary, arguing that what was best in French thought had always been on the side of enlightenment. They never actually came to blows over their respective philosophies, probably because each had too much respect for Franck to wish to hurt his feelings. Nevertheless, their falling-out, coupled with Félicité's increasing coolness, had the effect of introducing a measure of sadness into the composer's last years. When the family at last got *Hulda* on to the boards in 1894, it was patently as a survivor from another operatic period. A few critics were kind about it, most notably the faithful Tiersot, who praised the diversity of its numbers (it had included a prisoners' chorus, a sword-song, one or two expressive preludes for orchestra, and the usual sprinkling of love-duets), and excused its lack of drama by describing it as a 'lyrical' work. Otherwise, not much interest was aroused. It had a second lease of life at the Theatre Royal, the Hague, in March 1895, but thereafter quickly dropped out of the repertory. That Franck never succeeded in learning his lesson on the subject of opera is proved by his returning to write *Ghisèle* between 1888 and 1890. Here the *mise-en-scène* is transferred to the Merovingian court of Neustria, with equally tendentious results. The libretto, by Augustin-Thierry, reveals a definite advance over *Hulda*, and the church scenes look as if they would come over well. Inspiration, however, is conspicuously absent. *Ghisèle* also obtained a posthumous performance in Monaco during April 1896. Despite its completion, it has never won any adherents and the fact remains that Franck was ill-advised ever to have strayed into the glamorous but razor-edged world of the theatre.

The years during which the composer toiled away at *Hulda* were also those in which his disciples were driven to show their keenest sympathy and regard. In tracing the evolution of the circle from its earliest days up to the time of its absorption into the Schola, we can identify three distinct stages. At the beginning, between 1865 and 1870, came a phase when loyalties were too embryonic to give rise to self-consciousness. Following this there arose that tense and soulful period best associated with *Rédemption* and *Les Béatitudes*; when the burden of morality which Franck imposed upon his friends was at its weightiest. At this point, the circle's reputation for gloominess was earned. Finally, by the middle of the next decade, a new spirit of energy and assertiveness sprang up, engendered in the main by the successful palace revolution at the Société Nationale and the rising esteem surrounding the person of its president. It was alongside this last phase that cries for recognition became more angry and overt. D'Indy was by that time furious at the authorities for having neglected to honour his teacher. It happened that in 1880 the composer's *alma mater* had awarded him a laurel wreath to commemorate his many examination successes, while shortly afterwards he was fortunate enough to be elected an Officier de l'Académie. But neither of these tributes seemed a proper reward for one who had devoted a lifetime's skill and effort to developing French music. Something more substantial was accordingly demanded on his behalf.

During the years which followed, concerts were held of the composer's works, letters were addressed to influential public figures, and interviews sought with ministers of state—all with the object of drawing attention to Franck's case. Characteristically, none of these manoeuvres proved of the slightest avail. It was then that Albert Cahen hit upon a sly but profitable idea. He learned that the President was at that moment having his portrait painted by Bonnat.[1] Luckily, this artist was also known to frequent the lavish salons given by Lulia Cahen and her scandalous sister Marie.[2] A

---

[1] Léon Bonnat was the Republic's most fashionable portrait painter. It was maliciously said of him that he changed his decorations according to the houses he visited. As a teacher, he is remembered for having instructed the young Toulouse-Lautrec.

[2] Scandalous on account of her *liaison amoureuse* with the priapic novelist and short-story writer, Guy de Maupassant. Albert Cahen himself became a close friend of the author of *Bel-Ami*, and was reputedly the last person to see him alive in the asylum at Passy. (cf. the comments of Maupassant's latest biographer Paul Ignotus in his book *The Paradox of Maupassant*, University of London Press 1966, page 244 *et seq.*)

plan was therefore hatched whereby Bonnat was briefed to tip off
the President of Franck's patient candidacy. Much to everyone's
surprise, the trick worked and an insertion was made in the forthcoming honours list. In August 1885, at the Conservatoire's annual
prize-giving, Franck was duly invested with the cross of a Chevalier
of the Legion of Honour. It was not the highest insignia attaching
to the order, and cynics were quick to point out that it had been
habitually bestowed on teachers of Franck's particular rank. All
the same, the gesture had been made. In some respects, it was unfortunate that the citation referred only to the composer's work as a
professor of the organ, saying nothing of the influence he had
exerted on music in general. The choleric d'Indy once more rose up
in wrath at this oblique insult, but his rallying of the group's
militant feelings embarrassed neither the honourers nor the hon-
ourand. 'My friends, you expect too much. I am quite satisfied,'
was Franck's modest comment. And in personal terms he had good
reason to rest content. The four hundred cards and letters of greeting which he received probably warmed his heart far more than
any decoration could have done, and if this were not enough the
news also came that Rongier's portrait of him would be hung at one
of the Salons later in the year. It helped to immortalize the composer in the role he loved best.

Throughout the period of renewed orchestral and operatic
experiment, Franck had been in some danger of forgetting that he
was first and foremost a keyboard musician. Having begun his
career with works for the piano, and crowned it with the impressive
Six Pièces for organ, it was a cause for dismay among certain
friends that he had not gone on to exploit this aptitude more
systematically. In fact the composer had written nothing for the
piano between 1846 and 1884 (*Les Plaintes d'une Poupée* hardly
constitutes an exception) and nothing specifically for the organ
between 1863 and 1878. His return to the latter instrument was
occasioned by the *Trois Pièces* he was obliged to produce in honour
of Guilmant's recital at the Trocadéro. They were the first of
Franck's pieces for 'grand organ'—that is to say, they may be
classed among those works written in a symphonic style and intended for performance in the concert-hall. As such, they hardly
gave rise to the composer's deepest feelings. The *Fantaisie* which
begins the set is the least interesting. Its themes are fetching and
lucid, but their development is too arbitrary. Moreover, the mood is
strangely supplicative, with weak reliance on pianistic habits that
should have been discarded. The succeeding *Cantabile* is better,
though here again one notes a preference for holding down certain
treble notes while moving the accompanying chords in a chromatic
sequence, a practice vaguely reminiscent of Chopin. By far the most

popular is the last of the three, the confident *Pièce Héroique*. This has two main themes, one rhythmic and the other melodic, and they give way to a meditative chorale at the climax. It is perhaps all to the good that Franck did not spend too much time pursuing the ideals contained in these pieces, for they are not as free from display as one might wish. The student would be best encouraged to treat them as transitional works, useful in having helped to keep the composer's hand in, but scarcely to be placed among his greatest offerings.

Much less apology is needed on behalf of the compositions for piano which made their appearance some six years later. The period from 1884 to 1887 must be regarded as one of intense pianistic activity. It had the effect of establishing Franck among the supreme masters of the instrument, rivalled only by Fauré in France and Brahms in Germany. His *Prélude, Choral et Fugue* (1884) has been acclaimed one of the major test-pieces for players of the nineteenth-century repertoire; while the brilliant *Variations Symphoniques* (1885) remains the composition by which Franck is best known to the thousands attending 'pops' concerts in Britain and the United States. By comparison, the lesser-known *Prélude, Aria et Final* (1886–7) seems the property of a select circle of critics and devotees. What decided the composer to return to his first love is still an open question. As a rule, his choice of a particular medium was the result of some public demand or commission. This being so, it is tempting to attribute the late piano music to pressures exerted by the Société Nationale. The society was certainly well known for the premium it placed on chamber music, and there is no doubt that the Piano Quintet of 1879 was occasioned by its policies. It is much less clear why this work was followed by such determined efforts to rehabilitate the solo instrument. D'Indy's explanation is that Franck felt discontented with the state of the repertory as it appeared to him in or around 1880. He recalls how the composer once told a group of students how much he wished to enrich this repertory with a few new and substantial compositions. At this point, however, d'Indy breaks off to use Franck as a stick by which to beat the enemies of classicism. Holding up Beethoven as the exemplar beyond whom nobody had advanced, he goes on to attack piano literature as sterile and decadent, claiming that all quality had been lost in the struggle for more technique. With the best will in the world, assertions such as these cannot be left to go unchallenged. After all, Mendelssohn had written his *Variations Sérieuses* precisely on account of his dissatisfaction with the prevailing standards of pianism—and that was in 1841. Even earlier, Schumann had been obliged to found his 'League of David' to combat the philistines.

His C major Fantasy, op. 17, might easily have been seized upon as a major post-Beethovenian contribution. The Liszt sonata was just as clearly another. And what about the extraordinary experiments of D'Indy's own countryman, Alkan? It is quite misleading to have suggested that the repertory was in a dilapidated condition. What seems more probable is that Franck wanted to turn public attention away from the loftier Wagnerian ideals—to which he never became entirely acclimatized—towards those smaller and less pretentious genres which had failed to maintain their early popularity. That he was only partly successful in achieving this object may be attributed, not so much to any clumsiness of execution on his part, but to the die-hard conservatism of audiences.

The first of the new works, the sonorous *Prélude, Choral et Fugue*, was not, as might be supposed, based on Mendelssohn's excellent examples of the form. On the contrary, Franck's intention was simply to write a prelude and fugue in the style of Bach, and it was only after beginning the composition that he discovered that something was missing. The weak link, he estimated, occurred between the end of the fast-moving first section and the commencement of the fugue. A slower episode needed to be interposed at this juncture for the majesty of the counterpoint to make its full effect. Naturally enough, the suggestion came to him of making this middle section a chorale. The whole scheme would thus retain its unity, while being given added power and depth. Anyone encountering this most impressive of all Franck's keyboard works for the first time is bound to be struck by the richness and density of its figuration, in particular the arpeggios among which the opening B minor theme lies embedded. The syncopated rhythm, with its accent on the second of each group of eight notes, is a subtle enough stroke with which to have begun. Close examination of this passage will reveal the immense individuality of Franck's pianism. The intrusion of chords of the third into the arpeggio makes for greater plangency, while the almost unnoticeable addition of the semibreve in bar 2 has the effect of lending further support to the figure. Even the choice of key—the same as Liszt used for his resonant-sounding sonata—seems significant. After the preludial flourishes, the work settles down to express a sadder and more Brahmsian theme, first announced in octave chords high up in the treble. This is interrupted by a tentative, falling motif, tonal to begin with but soon becoming semi-tonal. When we proceed further into the second and third movements, we realize that this fragmentary motif is recalled to form the link leading to the Choral, and from there to the Fugue. The idiomatic character of the writing in this opening moderato movement is astonishing. It is this that renders Gabriel Pierné's orchestral transcription so ineffective.[1]

One of Franck's boldest inventions was to have cast the *poco piu lento* in the exceedingly remote key of E flat. Assuming the over-all tonality to be B minor, this represents a transition to the sharpened mediant major. Yet another contrast is achieved by presenting the Choral in severely diatonic terms. The conflict between chromaticism and its opposite thus becomes the driving force of the whole work. Among the pianistic novelties of this movement, none has gained the composer more publicity than his habit of spreading the main chords over four octaves, with the notes of the melody obtained by crossing the left hand over the right. Inexperienced

Ex. 15

Cesar Franck: 2nd Movement - "Prélude, Choral et Fugue"

performers have complained that this causes discomfort, but few would question the sumptuousness of the sounds produced. Franck's famous stretch (reputedly an octave and a fourth) probably came to his rescue here, leaving pianists with smaller hands to bewail their limitations. An interesting indication of the cyclical character of the *Prélude, Choral et Fugue* can be discovered in the manner in which the falling transitional motif is interspersed between the statements of the chorale, and is even made to provide the first part of the fugue subject. As with many a work by Beethoven, everything is more closely related than it seems. When the last movement is reached, the tonality returns from E flat minor to the original B minor. The Fugue, which is in four parts, is given a conventional exposition, after which it merges with the more romantic texture Franck chose for the surface of the work. Near the conclusion, it joins with the theme of the Choral to furnish a brilliant peroration. Possibly the most disappointing section of the composition is its coda. Buoyant though it sounds in performance, one cannot help feeling that it reverts to an archaic

[1] As Norman Demuth has pointed out, the transcription of the *Prélude Aria et Final* made by Vittorio Gui is a far more convincing exercise, if only because this second work is so much *less* adroit in its pianism.

type of sensationalism. As Ralph Wood once said in quite a different connection: 'How effective—but how second-rate!'.[1] Apart from this single lapse, the work stands as a monument to the composer's skill and integrity.

Notwithstanding the attributes we have attached to it, the *Prélude, Choral et Fugue* proved too experimental for Franck's contemporaries. The form which it took laid it open to criticism from purists and those jealous of the composer's authority. Saint-Saëns at once set out to probe the work's deficiencies, relying on his triumphant malice to shake the faith of its advocates. 'The chorale is not a chorale, and the fugue not a fugue' was his gleeful conclusion. (As Gervase Hughes has amusingly commented, he could hardly have denied Franck the right to call his first movement a prelude.) Worse still, this expert pianist—whom Liszt once ranked as his only surviving rival—found the whole thing 'uncouth and tiresome to play'. As to his first charges, it cannot be denied that the chorale is punctuated by recitative-like material and the fugue permitted to trail off without completion. But one can easily put too fine a point on these distinctions. What Franck does with each of his forms goes a long way towards justifying the liberties he took. If one thinks of his work as a kind of sequel to the late Beethoven sonatas, then its inconsistencies are not without precedent. Like them, it poses special difficulties of interpretation, arising partly out of the fusion of a multiplicity of forms. It is hardly enough to state that such spiritual reveries are unsuited to the piano. What is more to the point is that they presuppose a revaluation of the player's technique. To approach them in the romantic spirit enshrined by Anton Rubinstein and his colleagues would be altogether wrong. They demand full dedication to the musical values they raise, and are liable to be distorted by over-emphasis. As Alfred Cortot has bravely said in connection with Franck's work: 'One disproportionate outburst of feeling, and the ideal curve that encompasses the whole piece is spoilt.'[2] This 'ideal curve' is of the highest importance in all the composer's piano works. It should receive precedence over questions of *rubato* and

[1] The observation was made about the Vieuxtemps-like passages in the Sibelius Violin Concerto. As with Franck's work, it contains glimpses of a false and discredited tradition. (cf. *Sibelius—a symposium*, ed. Gerald Abraham. Lindsay Drummond, 1947.) Apropos the coda to the *Prélude, Choral et Fugue*, is it not the case that Debussy parodied this when writing his *Dr Gradus ad Parnassum*?

[2] See *French Piano Music* Vol. I. trans. Hilda Andrews. O.U.P. 1932. This book contains the complete text of Cortot's essay on the piano music, and is recommended for its analyses of the works under discussion.

expression. Above all, Franck's music needs to be played with due
acknowledgement of its rapt quality. Thus approached, it yields a
calm beauty only to be found in the *arioso* styles of an earlier
epoch.

Mlle Marie Poitevin is renowned for having launched the new
work on 25 January 1885, and there was to be a gap of more than
three years before the composer heard its successor, the recondite
Prélude, Aria et Final, given a similar send-off. This second essay
is often thought to be musically, if not pianistically, superior to the
first; though it is difficult to see why this should be so. It begins
with an andante in old rondo form, and is much more homophonic
than might have been supposed. The key changes in its first few
pages are too proliferous to give the listener much time in which
to catch his breath, and it is a relief to move on to the straight-
forwardness of the Aria. Unlike the episode of this type in
Schumann's F sharp minor sonata, it is encased between an
introduction and an epilogue. Professor Demuth considers it to
have been influenced by Gounod, and it is true that there is a
suggestion of sentimentality. Its main theme recurs in the finale,
where it is made to soar above a rippling accompaniment. The
rondo form of the prelude is also recalled for this last movement,
the climax of which is reached by augmentation. Reasons for the
work's neglect are not too hard to seek. Repetition plays an excessive part in it, and the passage-work is very reflective of organ
textures. These are imitated quite blatantly in the numerous
pedal-points and tenth chords. On the credit side, however, there
is much to be said in favour of the grand, inspired melodies which
go to make up the later sections of the triptych. It should be confessed, too, that the intricacy of the part-writing frequently offsets
the chordal bias. Dedicated to Mme Bordes-Pène, who was unfortunately stricken with paralysis only two years after giving it its
première, it was first heard at a Société Nationale concert on 12
May 1888. Public reaction was not particularly gratifying, M.
Boutarel regarding the work as 'long and tedious' and his colleague
Julien Torchet complaining of a lack of novelty. The first of these
judgements is one that posterity seems determined to uphold.

Occupying a place between Franck's efforts at rejuvenating the
piano was the second of the composer's concertante works involving the orchestra. The *Variations Symphoniques* was in one
sense inspired by *Les Djinns*, since it was in order to reward the
pianist Louis Diémer for his playing at the Châtelet concert that
it came to be written. The affection in which it is held throughout
the world should scarcely require an explanation, for it is a lively
and brilliantly organized composition. Franck had always been
attracted to the principle of theme and variations, usually seeking

to give it an original twist by harnessing it to some other, contrasting form. He did this to remarkable effect in his *Prélude, Fugue et Variation* for organ. The new work proved no exception to the rule in that its object was to assimilate the variation idea to a ground plan which Tovey once described as 'a finely and freely organized fantasia'. It begins, like so many of the composer's works, with a brief antithetical dialogue. A biting allegro theme, delivered in unison by the strings, is countered by a series of drooping 'dimuendo' phrases from the piano. Neither of these constitutes the raw material out of which the variations come to be fashioned, and it finally becomes clear that there is a 'double subject', the second part of which is still to follow. Allowing for the composer's more pathetic sensibility, the mood of this opening section is not unlike that displayed in Beethoven's Fourth Piano Concerto. The complete separation of soloist and orchestra suggests another point of resemblance. Once the atmosphere has been established, the way is paved for a dramatic conflict which reproduces itself on a number of different levels. First of all, however, the second part of the variation theme needs to be presented, and this turns out to be a simple, graceful tune couched in the rhythm of a sicilienne. Heard initially on pizzicato strings (rather reminiscent, incidentally, of the slow movement of the D minor Symphony), it is properly announced by the soloist in a succession of rich chords. The interest attaching to this theme lies more than anything in its harmony, a domain over which Franck continued to exercise the greatest skill. After it has been stated, a path is left open for the development of all these ideas in the six variations and finale to follow.

The first of these departs from the harmonic and rhythmic scheme hardly at all. It is again conducted by the piano in opposition to the strings, with a touch of woodwind colour at the very end. There are no clear breaks between the variations, which exemplify the principles of *enchaînée* or *attaquer de suite* which are to be found in later scores such as those by Poulenc. In Variation II, the melody is re-enthroned by cellos and violas, while the double-basses provide a pedal support. Decorative arabesques are performed by the piano, and horns and woodwind once more add their distinctive timbres. Variation III is one of the more fanciful episodes, exhibiting a rich vein of *jeu perlé* at the keyboard. By comparison, the orchestra's role remains discreet and sketchy. It is only with the fourth variation that we encounter a revival of some of the material first stated in the work's introduction. The ebullient string motif of the opening bars is now worked into the texture, which from this point on takes considerable rhythmic liberties. The same motif is combined with other ingredients to

serve as the basis for Variation V. As in *Les Djinns*, Franck makes
no attempt to play down a long and numinous interlude giving
vent to the more rarified emotions. Hints of this appear at the
beginning of Variation VI, which first of all presents the theme in
the major. Its latter part consists of an exploitation of the piano's
falling motif in an extended reverie. The finale, rather in the
manner of the coda to the first movement of Schumann's Piano
Concerto, derives its impetus from a prolonged trill. It turns out
to be fast and gay, with an inspired *dolce ma marcato* theme,
closely related to the original sicilienne-like subject, but cunningly
speeded-up in a duple rhythm. As if to complement this, the
dramatic opening string figure is recast in the form of a light-
hearted waltz whose cross-accents provide yet another instance of
the composer's slick ingenuity. The piano writing in this finale is
scintillating throughout. It effectively refutes those who would reject Franck's claim to be considered a pianist-composer of the first
rank. A closely-spaced canon rounds off what by this time has
become a charming divertissement.

The première of the *Variations Symphoniques* took place, without any great elation or rejoicing, on 1 May 1886. Suggestions that
it might meet with a chequered passage arose out of the second
performance it received the following January. By that time,
Franck's pupils had decided to honour their teacher by arranging
a festival of his works at the Cirque d'Hiver, the intention being
partly to shame the 'pompiers'. The way things worked out, however, it was Franck himself who suffered most of the embarrassment. Planned under the baton of the ageing Pasdeloup, the
concert was divided into two parts—the first consisting of *Le
Chasseur Maudit*, the *Variations Symphoniques* and an excerpt from
Ruth; and the second of the 'Marche' and 'Air de Ballet' from
Hulda, along with the Third and Eighth Beatitudes. The idea was
that Pasdeloup should conduct the opening half of the programme,
and Franck the closing half. As usual, it was discovered on the day
of the performance that the orchestra had been insufficiently
rehearsed. This would not have mattered so much had there been
no work for soloist included, but the presence of such a rhythmically
tricky composition as the *Variations* should have alerted the
organizers to the possibility of disaster. All went reasonably
smoothly up to the finale, at which point the leader made a wrong
start, throwing the piano hopelessly out of alignment with the
other instruments. Such a humiliating occurrence had not
happened before when any of Franck's works was being performed, and an inquest revealed that Pasdeloup's senile gesturing
had probably been somewhat to blame. The truth is that he no
longer possessed much of a claim to being France's greatest con-

ductor. For one thing, he was already very old, and for another he had developed a nervous phobia concerning his rivals, Colonne and Lamoureux, each of whom was making a strenuous bid to take over the title. After this débâcle, it was not to be wondered that Franck came to the rostrum to direct his half of the programme amid an atmosphere of gossip and jeers. That he himself was probably too wrapt up in contemplation to worry about his conducting did not conduce to any improvement from among the players. The end of this brief festival was accordingly no less inglorious than its beginning.

Considering what a careful man Franck was, it seems hardly credible that so many of his compositions provoked a disturbance in the concert-hall. Many of these upsets stemmed from the composer's unwillingness to subject his musicians to a rigid discipline. A little more tyranny and ambition in his character, while they would probably have deprived him of his reputation for saintliness, would doubtless have equipped him with far greater control over the forces of his destiny. Not only was he too easily satisfied with the interpretations made of his work, but he signally lacked the drive to bring about any improvements. It may be surmised that, like a number of facile executants, he was a hopelessly poor judge of another's rendering. To that extent, the praise which he inevitably bestowed on his more struggling disciples was in all probability sincere. What Coquard once said about him—that 'he thought the most complicated things in music quite naturally'—will not be disputed. But his aesthetic equipment was very ill-balanced all the same. Precisely on account of this infatuation with what was difficult, Franck allowed himself to overlook matters of a general and critical kind. It was always much easier for him to rattle off a passage in double counterpoint than to stand back and take a long, cool glance at the questions of taste and style which his music raised. Moreover, it was not as if he were the inventor of a distinct musical philosophy of his own. As so many of his detractors have pointed out, he took his counterpoint from Bach, his pianism from Liszt, the nobility of his ideals from Beethoven and the uncertainties of his taste from the Second Empire. Such a hotchpotch of influences would have been hard to assimilate at the best of times. Unfortunately, Franck made no real attempt to reconcile them, preferring to sink himself in the pedantries of the music-teacher and the false pieties commissioned by his opposite numbers in the church. Regarded as an artist, he stood at the furthest possible remove from his successor Debussy, to whom every musical problem was first and last a problem in aesthetics. Franck was a 'musician's musician'—with all the strengths and limitations implied by the term.

IX

Elijah in his glory

Unlike the disturbances which threatened his other music, that which beset the Piano Quintet of 1879 was personal. Having made no attempt to return to chamber music until conditions were more receptive, Franck took heart from the stipulations of the Société Nationale by attempting a work in the most difficult of all its forms. Whether he was conscious of having broken a forty year silence, no one can tell. What is certain is that he invested in the Quintet the full range of knowledge and passion which he had brought with him to his present age of fifty-seven. The most aggravated of all his compositions, it follows the tradition of the Trios in its confidence and breadth, while going completely beyond them in emotional expressiveness. Still clinging to the cyclical principle, it makes use of a complex network of recurrent motifs, aspiring to be the composer's most advanced formal experiment. Homer Ulrich has drawn attention to the strictness with which Franck approached his task:

> In so far as economy of thematic resources is concerned, few works are so tightly-knit. The cyclical principle is carried to its utmost limits. One theme, the cyclical theme of the entire composition, appears in various guises throughout the work: as second theme and coda theme of the first movement, in the development section of the slow movement, and as the theme of the finale's extended coda—each time appropriately altered in tempo and considerably modified rhythmically. That theme, playing so important a part in providing inner unity between the contrasting, shifting sections of the various movements of the Quintet, is in turn derived from one of the cyclical themes of the F sharp minor Trio of 1840.[1]

[1] This passage may be contrasted with Norbert Dufourcq's remark that the work is '. . . une furieuse melée que Franck nous incite a suivre, et il nous tient haletants en présence de ses difficultés personelles'.

Such deliberate narrowing of resources might have seemed
suspiciously like a sign of impotence. But of all the words that
might be used to characterize this impetuous work, that is the
least relevant. Some listeners have attacked it as a 'sport'—a sort
of 'poème de l'extase' among chamber offerings. Others are easily
carried away by its beauties. Perhaps it is an indication of the
work's vitality that hardly anyone reacts to it with indifference.

As may be imagined, the Quintet did not prove easy to write.
As a matter of fact, it set its composer one of the stiffest creative
hurdles he had ever had to face. Demanding slow and steady concentration, it occupied him throughout most of the year 1878–9.
Certain features of the design stood out from the beginning as
eccentric. The most obvious of these was that the work was planned
in three and not four movements. The first makes use of an
introduction for strings alone, the descending steps of which provide the germinal idea on which the whole composition is based.
This habit of building entire works around a 'motto' theme
gradually took possession of the composer, as it is alleged to have
done with Beethoven and Tschaikovsky, leading him to view the
Violin Sonata and the D minor Symphony in the same light. Once
the Quintet's 'motto' has been stated, it is followed by a straightforward allegro in sonata form. Léon Vallas, in his biography of
the composer, expresses surprise that Franck should have given the
more dramatic subject to the string ensemble and its tender complementary theme to the piano, thus reversing the instruments'
natural propensities. However, it does not take long for the material
to be shared out among the various partners, the development
section providing ample scope for individualism. Very typical of
Franck is the pivotal *dolce con passione* theme with the repeated
flattened F which forms part of the second group of subjects. Its
unexpected pull towards a G natural gives it a characteristic yearning quality. Probably it was this initial movement which created
the stir among those of the composer's friends who were taken
aback by the work's eroticism. A slight lowering of the emotional
temperature takes place in the slow movement, though passion
and lyricism are by no means so glibly forsaken. A connecting
episode, deriving from what has gone before, leads to the finale
which, of all the various sections of the work, remains the most
concerted in style. Franck to a large extent abandoned the principle
of separate discourse in this movement, opting for a forceful
joining-up of reserves in the manner of the Brahms F minor
Quintet. Its bold cycle of keys led d'Indy to speculate on a possible
dramatic programme. Although the second and third movements
can be classified as a *lied* and *scherzo* respectively, it is actually the
case that all three movements are in sonata form. Next to the

Violin Sonata, this helps to make it the most tightly-unified of all the composer's chamber-works.

The rumpus which attended its première on 17 January 1880 was caused by Franck's having foolishly assigned the solo role to

Ex. 16

César Franck: 1st Movement - Piano Quintet.

Saint-Saëns. At least, it was assumed that his experience as a performer would be needed to launch it, and nothing intervened to correct the assumption. Unhappily, it was chiefly owing to the great man's skill as a sight-reader that trouble was encountered, for it gradually dawned on the more astute members of the audience that what the pianist was playing was both new and alarming to him. It was not that he made any noticeable mistakes of execution. Rather, the content of the work seemed to be impinging on his sensibilities for the first time, causing him to experience a mild attack of nausea. When the performance was over, the unsuspecting Franck went up to offer his congratulations, at the same time making over the dedication of the new Quintet to his friend. This was altogether too much for the scowling Saint-Saëns, who stamped noisily off the platform leaving the manuscript still standing on the piano. Such an ill-mannered gesture could hardly have failed to communicate itself to the persons sharing the stage.

Even so, Franck's pupils did not appear to be aware of it, and it fell to one of Pleyel's assistants to retrieve the offending document from the waste-paper basket into which it was eventually plunged. No one seems to have recorded Franck's own comments—if indeed he ever made any—but he must surely have been hurt by the cruelty of the rebuff. That he did not choose to forgive it is suggested by his decision to alter the proposed dedication, substituting his pupil de Bréville's name for that of the disrespectful miscreant. (This course was in all probability made easier for him by the outbreak of quarrelling at the Société Nationale which followed hard upon the heels of the première.) What is sometimes overlooked about this whole affair is that several other people who were present showed signs of emulating Saint-Saëns's sentiments, if not his bad behaviour.[1] Loyal friends of the composer like Charles Bordes later confessed how uncomfortable the music had made them feel, while the performance is said to have brought a blush to the cheeks of no less an amorist than Liszt. Perhaps the most amusing comment on the evening's entertainment was that made by Delaborde, who simply said: 'Le Père Franck me ravage.' Final proof of the Quintet's power to shock had to await the verdict of the composer's wife. She, at any rate, was left in no doubt as to the unholiness of her husband's affections, and it may well have been the special knowledge which Saint-Saëns had of the matter that led him to express such a sour view. We shall reserve the story of the two men's cupidity for a later chapter.

The second of the last great chamber-works proved less glum and contaminating. Like Chausson's *Poème*—which it pre-dated by ten years—it was inspired by the violin playing of Eugene Ysaÿe, whom Franck had first heard at the Vieuxtemps home in Paris around about 1877, and thereafter elsewhere. Cast in the form of a sonata, the new work fulfilled an ambition which had been permitted to languish for nearly thirty years. Students of the composer's early career will recall that it was in 1859 that Cosima Wagner had displayed her interest in Franck's songs. In responding to this interest, he had promised to write her a Violin Sonata, an undertaking that was somehow never begun. Now that he had been reminded of the beauty of this noble instrument, it was no hardship for him to set about reconsidering his intentions. The 1886 sonata was not dedicated to Cosima, however, but to the famous executant who had been Franck's fellow-countryman. During the autumn of that year, Ysaÿe had announced that he was getting married, and it came as a pleasant surprise to him

[1] e.g. Duparc's puzzling remark: 'Qu'avons-nous écrit a coté de cela?' Perhaps, however, he was only expressing his surprise that Franck had allowed himself such unusual freedom of feeling.

when Charles Bordes, who had been chosen to represent Franck at the wedding, handed over the manuscript of this sublime work. The composer had previously read it through with Mme Montigny-Rémaury back in Paris, and Bordes's gifted sister was at hand to advise on its performance. It was this last-named lady, as brilliant and short-lived a musician as her more creative brother, who partnered Ysaÿe at the piano when the virtuoso gave the music its first airing. Present at that memorable session were Théodore Radoux (the ex-bassoonist who had deprived Franck of the Directorship of the Liège Conservatoire back in 1870), Sylvan Dupuis, and the poet Jules Laforgue, who had just returned from Berlin where he had been acting as tutor to the Empress Augusta. At the public première, which took place in Brussels, the two artists met with the expected fiasco. This time it was caused by a failure in the lighting arrangements. By the end of the first movement, the hall had become so dim that it looked as if the concert would have to be abandoned. At the crucial moment, Ysaÿe struck the music-stand with his bow, and gallantly called out 'Allons! allons!' to his wilting partner. Plunged into darkness, the performers seized hold of their courage, racing through the rest of the work from memory. It was not often that Franck's music had been so adroitly saved from disaster.

The sonata has four sizeable movements, making it one of the bulkiest in the repertory. Its rhythms are not less subtle than those of the Quintet, though the mood is far more tranquil and refined. Franck originally intended the first movement to be played slowly, but on hearing Ysaÿe speed it up he declared himself in favour of the faster tempo. In the end, the designation *allegretto* was placed at the head of the score. Despite this, the quickest movement still continues to be the second, an exhilarating *tour-de-force* for the pianist in the key of D minor. Both these initial movements are in sonata form, with certain modifications. They are succeeded by an eloquent *recitativo quasi fantasia*, the function of which seems to be transitional; while to end Franck proffers a beautiful canonical *rondo* of an entirely new design. As with the Quintet, a single 'motto' theme asserts itself from the outset. Robert Jardillier, in his monograph on the composer's chamber music, has claimed that it develops out of a cell of three notes—a Gregorian *torculus* in the language of his analysis—but such an interpretation credits Franck with too theological a bias. What emerges as the first subject is actually a pregnant, undulating phrase of eight notes, highly improvisatory in character, which traces the outline of a dominant major ninth. It is tempting to suggest that it was of this theme that Proust was thinking when he wrote the famous passage in *Swann's Way* which begins:

At first the piano complained alone, like a bird deserted by its mate; the violin heard and answered it, as from a neighbouring tree. It was as at the first beginning of the world, as if there were not yet but these twain upon the earth, or rather in this world closed against all the rest, so fashioned by the logic of its creator that in it there should never be any but themselves; the world of this sonata.

An extra limb is added to this phrase in the succeeding bars, and this is subjected to recall in the movement ahead. One of the significant features of the exposition lies in its preoccupation with the interval of a third. As in the case of Chausson, this interval exerted a good deal of fascination for Franck. It posed the possibility of a rocking melodic figure—a kind of cybernetic oscillation—deriving its components from the notes of the common chord. The composer's favourite sequential devices were facilitated by its use.

Continuing our analysis, the second subject comprises another descending scale motif. It sounds fervent and expressive at the point where its G sharp gives way to a G natural. There is no real development section in this movement, a condition that parallels the first movement of the String Quartet.[1] Listeners will have no difficulty in relating the texture of the ensuing Allegro to such whirling ostinato-like structures as the B minor Scherzo of Chopin. Not so the violin's glorious cantilena, which bodies forth with all Franck's customary ardour. The minor mode also governs the mood of the Fantasia, which progresses in its centre of gravity from D to F sharp. Some of the material it exhibits is culled from the previous movement, other parts are new. The cadenzas and flourishes proclaim a debt to the baroque composers, but the harmony remains modern. This whole section leads without a break to the finale, a gentle Allegretto upon which most admirers of Franck would be happy to rest all their claims. The canon with which it begins is certainly a perfect example of the composer's craftsmanlike powers, while the principle of interchange between the instruments makes for a real element of flexibility. It must be seen as a tribute to Franck that no more splended epilogue can be found in French sonata literature, or indeed in that of any neighbouring country. Only the 'Regenlied' movement which brings to an end Brahms's G major Sonata, op. 78, offers itself as a serious competitor. Dissenting critics have nonetheless blamed the com-

---

[1] This is worth relating to Leland Hall's comment that 'the structure of his (Franck's) music is strangely inorganic. His material does not develop.' (*From Bach to Stravinsky*, ed., D. Ewen. W. Norton, N.Y. 1933.)

poser for having too great a bias towards the keyboard, arguing that the work's instrumental balance is precarious. Certainly there are times when the piano seems to be swamping the violin, but this cannot be said about the last movement, except possibly during the coda. What serves to distinguish this music from so much else that Franck wrote is its freedom from spiritual cant. Unburdened by any kind of programme, its melodies ripple like the water from a mountain spring.

Though not appreciated to the full at the time of its first performance, the A major sonata did more to publicize Franck's name —and incidentally the whole art of chamber music—than any other in his canon. Ysaÿe and Pugno became its regular champions, carrying it around the world as if it were a mascot for French culture. When the Piano Quintet had been played in Brussels, Gevaert had accosted Franck with the words: 'You have transformed chamber music and opened a new road for us!' If this proved to be a somewhat premature assertion, its truth was handsomely acknowledged in the success that now attached to the sonata. Through this single sonata people were led to interest themselves in the composer's other works, as well as in the chamber music of the entire French nation. Its fame spread to literature and art, as its many extra-musical associations testify. Apart from the use Proust made of it, there remains the vivid description contained in Camille Mauclair's novel, *The City of Light*, in which Ysaÿe and Chausson are pictured performing the work in Rodin's studio.[1] Another sculptor, Victor Rousseau, was inspired to carve his statue, *Ecstasy*, as a result of listening to it (the figures are vaguely lesbian and it would have mortified Mme Franck to think that her husband had helped to inspire them).[2] During the present century, the sonata continues to be a great favourite with performers and the public alike. Some of the charm attaching to its melodies is reproduced in a series of isolated songs which Franck wrote at about the same time. They include the smoothly-flowing 'Nocturne' (1884)—an invocation to the stars based on de Fourcaud's mystical poem—and the ever-popular 'La Procession' (1888). The latter *mélodie* is the composer's best-known con-

---

[1] Mauclair, it will be recalled, was one of Chausson's poets, and a trusted friend of the composer. In addition to his novel about life in Paris, he wrote a number of treatises on music, of which the best known are *La Religion de la Musique* (1909) and *Histoire de la Musique Européenne* (1914).

[2] The critic Martin Cooper notes another (and less explicit) parallel between Franck's music and the erotic-religious paintings of Bouguereau, one of the senior academicians of the day. (cf. *French Music from the Death of Berlioz to the Death of Fauré*, Oxford, 1951.)

tribution to the genre, and consists of a touching portrayal of the priest and his retinue trudging across the fields on Corpus Christi day.

To crown his efforts in the chamber music sector, Franck chose to embark on a fully-fledged String Quartet. Like Fauré and Brahms, he tended to regard this form with awe and superstition. Recognizing it as the confessional medium of the mature Beethoven, all three musicians postponed their initial skirmish until they were well past middle-age. Indeed, in the case of the two Frenchmen a solitary example of the genre is all that exists. This being so, we are justified in expecting a work of the highest quality. It must be conceded—even by his enemies—that Franck does not disappoint these expectations. His Quartet is the least vulnerable of all his compositions. Always a painstaking composer, the care which he took over this sacred enterprise—his swan-song in every important respect—may be gauged from the hushed comments of his disciple d'Indy, who feared to trespass on his privacy during the months of its gestation. His work bench littered with the scores of Bach, Schubert and Beethoven, Franck entered into a period of total dissociation, filling each day with his earnest entreaties of the muse. The fact that he was exceptionally slow to start may be taken as evidence of the solemnity which surrounded the venture. As if in imitation of the Bonn master's sketchbooks, he found himself making several versions of each theme. Though begun in the early months of 1889, it was the end of October before he was able to write *finis* to the first movement—an outsize creation that takes all of seventeen minutes to perform. The scherzo proved an easier proposition, being dashed off in a mere ten days. Most tedious of all to write was the Larghetto, a sovereign movement that none of the Viennese masters would have been ashamed to acknowledge. As for the finale, that depended on welding together a variety of themes from earlier sections of the work; so that despite its grandeur it did not present itself as an insuperable creative hurdle. Franck always found it within his powers to invent new tricks with old material, cynics having detected in this a motive prompting the composer to opt for the cyclical approach.

In its adoption of a generative phrase—running right through its four movements—the Quartet sticks to the principles already exemplified in the Quintet and the Violin Sonata. Where it differs is in the emphasis placed upon formal innovation. No critic has been able to improve on d'Indy's description of the first movement as 'sonata form inscribed within a *Lied*'. What this implies is the existence of two thematic tableaux. Beginning with a *poco lento* section (containing the famous falling third theme), the movement only announces its sonata connections at the transition from D major to D minor, when the tempo changes to an *allegro moderato*.

Since this initial section is too long to be considered an introduction, it has become the practice, following d'Indy, to refer to it as the *Lied*. Thus classified, it clears the way for an examination of the sonata episode, which exhibits two distinct subjects of its own.

Ex. 17

César Franck: 1st Movement - String Quartet

The second of these modulates into the relative major and not the dominant. Linking them is a figure that returns during the finale, where it forms the ascending fifth motif heard just after the main statement. As with the Violin Sonata, there appears to be an absence of development, its place being taken by a set of fugal variations based on the *Lied*. These involve a reversion to the slower tempo of the opening. The recapitulation consists of a straightforward repeat of the sonata allegro, but the coda to this extraordinary movement calls upon another brief reminiscence of the *Lied* theme. Complicated though it may sound, the form goes a long way towards justifying itself. Like Beethoven's *Grosse Fuge*, it strikes us as both profound and unique. How Franck came to think of it remains something of a mystery. The Scherzo Vivace which forms the second movement is conversely quite orthodox. Set in the key of F sharp minor, it renews its composer's preoccupation with mediant harmonies. Listeners may agree that its facetiousness achieves the effect of placing the Larghetto in bolder relief. Described by Norman Demuth as being equal to the slow movements of Beethoven, Schubert and Brahms, this next section is a really sublime intrusion. Its principal subject was a donnée for which Franck had to coax his imagination to the utmost. ('I have got it at last!' he cried out jubilantly to d'Indy, 'It is a most beautiful phrase.') An augmented version of this subject appears, according to the composer's custom, in the finale, while another tune briefly recalls the preceding Scherzo. The *lied* theme—that which began the entire work—is actually the first to recur in the Quartet's concluding movement, which is otherwise notable for the rare succession of keys through which it passes. Commencing in D major, it reaches out to such remote tonalities as D flat, E flat and B flat minor. First performed on 19 April 1890, this was the only one of Franck's compositions to have been greeted with unmixed applause. That it helped to establish him as the heir to the great romantics is suggested by the fact that Proust later commissioned a private performance of it in his bedroom at the Boulevard Haussmann.

Meantime, those sympathizers who were accustomed to regarding the composer more in the light of what Norman Suckling has called 'the Beethoven succession' had discovered fuel for their beliefs in the D minor Symphony (1888). As we know, Saint-Saëns had been anxiously cosseting his reputation as a symphonist at about the same time as Franck, and viewed in historical terms his was the prior claim. The Symphony in C minor, op. 78, which he had proudly presented at the St James's Hall, London, in May, 1886 was actually his third in order of composition. Though impressively scored, the work had failed to achieve the tragic grandeur at which the composer was aiming. The most French of all the great musicians, Saint-Saëns was as deficient in seriousness as he was over-endowed with the qualities of grace and refinement. Hence it was becoming apparent that he lacked the weight necessary for this most hallowed of roles. Gounod flattered his ego by continuing to refer to him as 'the French Beethoven', but by the early 1890s progressive thinkers had already decided that he was a spent force. Fortunately, Franck's turn was only just on the point of coming round. So that although the Symphony met with a puzzled response on its first appearance, it was not long before converts were being won. Both the strength and the weakness of his approach lay in the fact that he built directly out of his own interests, and out of the larger awareness he had of classical models. Unlike Saint-Saëns, he felt no compunction to think in specifically French terms, and there was no question of him having to exclude the Wagnerian influence. The result was that his work assumed something of that rootless quality often attributed to the more emancipated Russians. In common with Tschaikovsky, he had the job of reconciling a strongly personal style with a form that was foreign in its origins. Constant Lambert was particularly hard on Franck when he described the Symphony as 'a chimerical monster, a musical Minotaur that fortunately has had no progeny'. But one can appreciate what he was getting at. A less spiteful view was expressed by Wright Roberts at the time of the composer's centenary in 1922. Minimizing charges of disloyalty, he wrote:

> Quietly, at first half-consciously, Franck built up from the ground a structure of symphonic music in his adopted country. He built it mainly with German bricks, but they were the best available.

Those still inclined to withhold their praise should be reminded of Debussy's unsolicited commendation, and should be required to produce evidence of superior native attainments.

As with the Piano Quintet, the most striking feature of Franck's symphony is its departure from the usual four movement plan. In this case, the slow movement takes over the added function of a scherzo. Otherwise, there is little in the work's formal structure to account for the public's initial bafflement. Evidently, it was the style or instrumentation that provoked the notorious flood of abuse. The use of a cor anglais was one source of annoyance, even though there was a precedent in Haydn's 'Philosopher' Symphony (No. 22 in B flat) and in the early work of Saint-Saëns. Oddly enough there is no record of anyone having protested against the composer's decision to include a part for bass clarinet—an instrument still less common among contemporary symphony orchestras. Possibly the attitude which professionals took up towards Franck's handling of orchestral problems is best illustrated by the fact that neither Lamoureux nor any other conductor was anxious to be saddled with the task of giving the première. Even after being forced to fall back on the traditional Société des Concerts du Conservatoire, Franck found that few of the players were eager to be co-opted. When Jules Garcin reluctantly arranged for two performances of the work to be given on 17 and 24 February 1889, the rehearsals were accordingly viewed with a mixture of desultoriness and antipathy. Franck himself attended these, clutching his copy of the score in stubborn pride, accompanied by his pupils Louis de Serres and Pierre de Bréville. The Director of the Conservatoire, Ambroise Thomas, is alleged to have been present at the final run through, sitting bolt upright in his seat with an expression of polite disdain on his face. All this preliminary ill-will must have played its part in determining the reactions of the audience on the first evening. Any doubts that remained were broken down by the quips of jealous rivals. Gounod—with whom Franck had by this time developed a more distant relationship—unfortunately set the pattern for these by his mock-pedantic labelling of the Symphony as 'the affirmation of incompetence pushed to dogmatic lengths'.

Present-day critics intent on analysing the work have sometimes come up against an impasse with its first theme. This is the brooding D minor figure given out by the lower strings. Its likenesses to other well-known romantic fragments—including excerpts from *Die Walküre* and Liszt's *Les Préludes*—are sufficiently complete to have aroused a more than usual amount of scepticism.[1] Close inspection of this figure reveals that Franck's guilt does not lie so much in plagiarism as in the habit he developed of writing short

[1] Still more remarkable is the similarity of Franck's figure to the 'muss es sein' theme from the last Quartet of Beethoven. Correspondences between these two composers are explored in R. V. Dawson's article 'Beethoven & César Franck' (*Music and Letters*, Vol. XI No. 2, April, 1930.)

three-note phrases, any one of which could be taken to resemble the work of others. If he had laboured to invent longer and more individual melodies, he would never have laid himself open to such charges. As it happens, his besetting sin consisted of 'slithering' from one note to another in a series of inconclusive adumbrations. The Symphony is full of these quasi-thematic interruptions, just as it is also well stocked with tunes of a more juicy variety. The pity is that the joins are so badly concealed. Having begun with this amorphous phrase, Franck goes on to cap it with an answering figure on the violins. The mood has by this time established itself as grief-stricken, though traces of urgency can be detected in the violas' tremolo. Woodwinds enter within the next few bars, and the whole episode culminates in an Allegro which forms the first subject. Derived from the opening Lento, it surges forward with the pace and swagger of one of Liszt's Mephistophelean entreaties. However, it is not long before the tempo changes again, and we are back to another slow section in which the cantabile second subject makes its appearance. Played by the strings in the key of F, it glides chromatically into the famous 'Faith' motif—the *idée fixe* around which the whole symphony revolves. Commentators do not

Ex. 18

César Franck: 1st Movement - Symphony in D minor

find this an easy theme to justify. The note A—which is the new mediant and hence a weak index of tonality—occurs no less than eleven times in its first eight bars. Development proceeds conventionally enough, though further alterations of speed may serve to confirm the listener's original misgivings. A similar regularity attends the recapitulation, except for one or two unexpected modulations and a piling up of the 'Faith' theme in broader strokes towards the conclusion. Balancing its claims, this movement is more notable for its faults than its virtues. One cannot argue that it overdoes the principle of *demande et repose*, since we have it on Guy Ropartz's authority that Franck was actually trying to reproduce the ancient 'double' form.[1] But there is no doubt that it contains an

[1] The only comparable work to aim at reviving this form is the Symphony No. 2 by Henri Dutilleux (1959), first performed by the Boston Symphony Orchestra under Charles Munch. In it, a small orchestra—including harpsichord and celeste—is pitted against the usual full forces.

excessive number of pauses—suggested perhaps by the habit of switching from 'great' to 'swell' at the organ—and would have benefited from pruning.

The Allegretto which follows is a far happier example of the composer's genius. According to Louis de Serres, it was inspired by the thought of 'a procession of olden times'—though no one has yet ventured to propose a more detailed programme. Played at a lively pace, it can delight the most jaded palate. The introduction is allotted to *pizzicato* strings and harp, the main melody being taken up by the cor anglais. Demuth, somewhat curiously, assumes

Ex. 19

César Franck: Allegretto - Symphony in D minor

this to be the 'Faith' theme. His view does not have the authority of Grove's *Dictionary*, neither is it shared by John Manduell in his contribution to Robert Simpson's volume, *The Symphony: Haydn to Dvořák*. On purely circumstantial grounds, the first movement's big F major tune is surely the more likely candidate; particularly in view of its strident reappearance later on. This is not to deny that, considered as a melody, it is inferior to its competitor. The scherzo-like section which comprises the remainder of the slow movement maintains the high level of inspiration. It secures the attention with a graceful E flat major theme, in dotted rhythm, announced by two clarinets above a winding cello counterpoint. After the return of the cor anglais tune, the movement ends quietly. Further evidence of the work's melodic prodigality is furnished by the finale. Here we encounter joy bordering on vulgarity, the syncopation which results from tying over the last of the theme's four crotchets being a shade too explicit in its catchiness. Weak-beat accentuation is actually a mannerism the whole symphony does much to proclaim. It was possibly contracted from Schumann, whose 'Rhenish' Symphony offers a number of parallels. In the *dolce cantabile* theme in F sharp, which represents Franck's second subject, there is a mincing sentimentality equally redolent of the older Romantics. Flashbacks to the first and second movements help to give this finale its cyclical character, and Franck allows himself to be tempted into writing a massive fortissimo climax. Not every listener will find himself moved by the rhetoric of this ending, which in some ears has a tendency to screech. The building of sound upon sound can go only so far before destroying the tension which it has set out to create, and Franck does not seem aware of how patently his structure risks being toppled. Nevertheless, it is this last movement that has done most to win the Symphony its universal appeal.

Ex. 20

César Franck: Finale - Symphony in D minor

Allegro non troppo

Cellos and Bassoons

Though Frenchmen would be aggrieved to admit it, there is strong justification for the view that interest in this work has been keener in England than any other country.[1] At least, there was every sign of it being true at the time of both World Wars. Typical of the idolatry aroused by the 1914–18 conflict was the judgement expressed by Cecil Gray. Writing during the zenith of the hostilities, he found it possible to claim that:

> Franck's symphony is a great work. A new addition to the great chain of mountains, the legacy of the last two centuries, it stands somewhat apart from its fellows, but from the summit one can dimly discern through the veiling mists the faint shadowy beginnings of the new range, less austere and dignified, perhaps, but full of a mysterious and haunting loveliness.

Only a few years later, however, the same critic was to take up the cudgels for Sibelius, after which he returned to trounce Franck's symphony as 'the unapproachable model of everything that should be avoided in symphonic writing'. Such abrupt reversals of fashion have always been a source of pleasure and anxiety to the composer's admirers, and it is significant that they keep on recurring. Ronald Pearsall, who may be counted among Franck's most recent champions, has told us that:

> In that music conscious decade that followed the end of the last war, no symphony was greeted with more rapture than

[1] Possible reasons for the English sympathy towards Franck are debated in Ronald Pearsall's article 'The Serene Anxiety of César Franck' (*Music Review* Vol. 27, No. 2, May, 1966). The composer's combining of 'high moral purpose with a grain of melancholy' is one of the explanations offered.

César Franck's. This was particularly true in the provinces, and every season of the City of Birmingham Orchestra's programme was ornamented by at least one performance of the Franck symphony, as well as the ubiquitous *Symphonic Variations*. In the plebiscite concerts, where audiences sent in postcards to vote for a favourite concert, the Franck Symphony always had a huge following . . .

Yet once again the pendulum has started to move in the opposite direction, set in motion by the anti-romantic aesthetics of the early 1960s. It is a little too soon to say whether this will result in a complete stripping of Franck's popularity. The enthusiasm at present being shown for such latter-day transcendentalists as Messiaen and Barraqué suggests that all may not be lost.

Few major works of Franck remain to be discussed. The symphonic poem *Psyché*—which many people mistake for a cantata— is easily the most neglected of these.[1] Inspired by Georges's mythological interests, it was based on a literary sketch by Sicard and de Fourcaud. These authors took as their subject the Greek myth in which a young maiden, Psyché, is transported to the Garden of Love, there to meet with the son of Venus. Impelled by curiosity, she cannot resist gazing on the face of her lover, a crime for which she is made to suffer perpetual banishment. In the ending of the sketch, however, all is forgiven and the happy pair soar upwards in a new and glorious immortality. The work was planned in three sections and scored for orchestra and chorus. The principal characters do not have solo parts allotted to them, so that it does not pretend to be a miniature oratorio. Considered in the context of Franck's previous output, it could be said to have arisen out of a marriage between *Rédemption* and *Les Eolides*. Part I— entitled 'Sommeil de Psyché' and 'Psyché enlevée par les Zephyrs' —portrays the heroine asleep amid premonitions of bliss. Three melodies are chosen to express the nature of her dreams. These are particularly notable for the beauty of their string texture. Next comes a short episode depicting the flight of Psyché to unknown regions. The Zephyrs who accompany her on this trip must have struck the composer as so similar to his Aeolids that he was temporarily drained of inspiration, and it was Duparc who came to his rescue by suggesting that he borrowed a theme from the earlier work. The action of Part II takes place in 'Les Jardins d'Eros'. Psyché now reclines on a bed of flowers while strange voices mur-

---

[1] Perhaps it is precisely on account of the work's curious form that it has incurred this neglect. Better prospects might await it in purely orchestral guise, while Jean Babilée has even turned it into a ballet which he entitled *L'Amour et son amant*. It was produced in Paris in 1948.

mur to her of the delights of love. These auditory intruders (who consisted of sopranos, contraltos and divided tenors) also caution her against the perils of direct confrontation. The music then gives way to a passionate duet, created by the interlocking of two orchestral themes. This is by far the most audacious section of the work, both in tone and construction. Having failed to heed the warnings, Psyché is made to receive her punishment in the third tableau—beginning with the section entitled 'Le Châtiment'. Here the chief melody is sung by the sopranos, and this is followed by a long choral lament. When full expression has been given to suffering, the orchestra is allowed to join with the voices once more in pursuit of a grand 'Apothéose' in which the protagonists are eternally reunited.

Harmless though the story seems, it had the effect of dividing Franck's associates into two camps. The composer, armed with his customary naïvety, had assumed that his work was devoid of sensual overtones. He was backed up in this opinion by d'Indy, who went further and put a Christian construction on the whole thing. Félicité, on the other hand, detected in Eros's gentle tremors the symptoms of an orgiastic decline. She is also alleged to have disliked her husband's harmonic experiments. According to her granddaughter, Mme Chopy, Franck's wife actually mislaid her admission ticket to the first performance of *Psyché*—and was thus spared hearing the work she so much detested. Modern readers will hardly be deterred from interpreting this as a typical Freudian slip. Probably on account of their greater immersion in dialectics, many of the composer's friends went to extreme lengths to embrace a Platonic-religious explanation of his tone-poem. It must be remembered that at this time France was very much in the grip of a sedate Hellenism similar to that which Goldsworthy, Lowes, Dickinson and his followers later imported into England. Fauré's classical Requiem had appeared while Franck was working on his score. There was accordingly no shortage of argument about how far it was possible to go in reconciling the teachings of Socrates with those of Christ. Tiersot was the most prominent of those critics who saw Franck's work as a dialogue between the human soul and its ideal archetype, though Gaston Poulin went as far as to agree that the composer had 'held aloof from any carnal thoughts'. Neither of these interpretations gains much support from the text.[1] D'Indy's embellishments came later, having been

---

[1] Franck's version incidentally departed from the original myth to the extent of providing a happy ending. In the Greek story, Psyché's banishment remains permanent. Readers interested in a pictorial representation—roughly contemporary with Franck's account—are referred to the painting *Enlevement de Psyché* by the Nabi artist, Maurice Denis.

spurred on by his reading of Gustave Derepas's book. To the last-named commentator, Franck's symphonic poem appeared as an allegory of redemption. Present-day listeners would do best to make up their own minds on this tangled issue, the outcome of which can scarcely be expected to place them in moral jeopardy. Perhaps Julien Green was nearest the mark when, in his *Journal Intime*, he described *Psyché* in the following terms:

> C'est la musique d'une âme qui émigre vers les pays où le soleil ne brille qu'à travers la pluie et la brume; elle est heureuse, mais tristement, si l'on peut dire, et par le souvenir.*

Whether or not out of a desire to eliminate the corporeal, Franck at first proposed to make the singers invisible to the audience. It was only d'Indy's complaint about their inaudibility that caused him to change his mind.

The fact that he was required to subdue his amatorial instincts (he was still heard to murmur the words 'J'aime! j'aime!' quietly to himself when seated at the keyboard) did not prevent Franck from being increasingly content with his lot, especially during the days following the Quartet's good reception. 'At last people are beginning to understand me!' was his joyful exclamation on that occasion. Hard on the heels of the Salle Pleyel concert, another triumph awaited him at Tournai, where he participated in a recital given by the Ysaÿe Quartet. By then it was April 1890, and the composer had only six more months to live. The accident which hastened his death was one of those absurdly unpredictable affairs that so often determine the course of history, and invites comparison with that which befell the discoverer of radium. One evening in May, Franck was crossing the Pont Royal on his way to visit Paul Brand, the pianist in Ysaÿe's little group. Not looking where he was going he got in the path of a horse-omnibus and was struck a severe blow in the chest. At the time, the injury did not seem too serious, and the composer mistakenly continued on his way, spending an exhausting few hours playing the second piano part in his *Variations Symphoniques*. The months ahead were to reveal a general decline in his health, however, and he was to take the unusual course of excusing himself from further concerts, including the important revival of his Quartet arranged by the Société Nationale. By the autumn, complications had set in. A chill which he was unlucky enough to catch on 17 October quickly turned to pleurisy, with

---

* It is soulful music which propels us towards regions where the sun does not shine in such a way as to penetrate the rain and mist; it is blissful but, so to speak, sadly reminiscent.

the result that he was compelled to take to his bed. There he lingered for almost three weeks, rallying slightly on 7 November but suffering a fatal relapse on the following day. During the anxious phase of his illness, Franck slid into a semi-comatose condition, deliriously wrestling with a new fugue subject and lamenting the incompletion of his latest Magnificat.[1] The doctors who attended him (his cousins Féréol and Brissaud) said that he frequently begged to be released from his musical obsessions. Among his last words were cries of 'Mes enfants! mes pauvres enfants.' Whether these were intended to reflect a concern for his family or his band of pupils is not clear. In either case, it remains typical of the composer that his final thoughts were for those he was leaving behind.

Franck died at about five o'clock on the morning of 8 November. His funeral was held two days later, without giving d'Indy an opportunity to return from Valence, where he was engaged in preparing a concert. A memorial service was offered at Sainte-Clotilde, though the burial actually took place at Montrouge. Later on, the composer's remains were transferred to the cemetery at Montparnasse. Perhaps because he was piqued at not being able to attend the funeral, d'Indy quickly took it on himself to criticize the manner in which the whole operation had been conducted. It was chiefly he who invented the myth that all the major institutions combined to boycott Franck's interment. In fact they probably did not consider the occasion important enough to justify a conspiracy. It is true that the Ministry of Fine Arts neglected to send a representative, and Ambroise Thomas failed to put in an appearance on behalf of the Conservatoire. It should be remembered, however, that Thomas was eighty-four at the time, and the prospect of standing at the graveside on a bleak November day could not have struck him as alluring. The truth is that he did sense his responsibility, and dispatched a delegate in the shape of Delibes. Also present were Fauré, Bruneau, Cahen, Benoît, Widor, Guilmant, Joncières, Lalo and Augusta Holmès. The oration was delivered with great dignity and emotion by Chabrier. Speaking of the work done by his friend, he said:

Adieu, maître! In you we salute one of the greatest artists of the century, and also the incomparable teacher whose wonderful work has produced a whole generation of forceful musicians, believers and thinkers, armed at all points for hard-fought and prolonged conflicts. We salute also the upright and

[1] This already consisted of a collection of fifty-nine versicles—published after the composer's death under the title *L'Organiste*. They are uneven in merit, but add substantially to Franck's organ canon.

just man, so humane, so distinguished, whose counsels were sure, as his words were kind.

His sentiments were quietly endorsed by all who had come to pay tribute, except perhaps by Saint-Saëns, who had decided to issue his grudging respects before embarking on a trip to Egypt. Had he been told of Franck's praise for *Samson et Dalila*, his grief might have taken a more pronounced form. Fourteen years later an equally distinguished gathering formed in the square of Sainte-Clotilde to unveil the Lenoir monument. Speeches were heard from the heads of the Académie des Beaux-Arts and the Conservatoire. But by that time Franck's fame had become widely-spread, and his position in the annals of European music made immovably secure.

It was fitting that the composer's last works should have been for his beloved organ. The *Trois Chorals*, which he had written on vacation at Nemours during the previous summer, had been sketched out on an old piano, but the stops had been added on his return to Paris. 'Before I die,' Franck had been heard to murmur, 'I am going to write some organ chorales, just as Bach did, but with quite a different plan.' In the event, they turned out to be singularly complex and profound compositions which have done much to influence the shape of organ music in the present century. Despite their acknowledged debt to Bach, it is really of Beethoven that we are most reminded, for each aims at being a large essay in the variation form. The changes rung in No. 1 are principally tonal and ornamental. Beginning in E major, it moves through a wide range of keys in the space of a few pages, including incidentally the flattened sub-mediant. Decorations and inversions abound, but there is no lack of drama—as the joyous seventh section confirms. No. 2 in B minor differs in being a noble and grave passacaglia in which nothing is permitted to grow out of the theme. It is interrupted by a short cadenza-like interlude. Most popular of all is No. 3 in A minor, an unpretentious study in the principles of melodic progression. Reverting to a quasi-toccata style for the opening, Franck goes on to present the chorale as a majestic intrusion, punctuated by long, interrogatory silences. In the succeeding section, the mood becomes more lyrical, giving the impression that the composer is reluctant to abandon his improvisations. Finally, a tonal and thematic synthesis appears, the peroration coming quietly to rest on a *tierce de picardie*. Looking back, it is the gentle, pastoral manner that Franck was best fitted to celebrate, and it seems entirely appropriate that he should have chosen it for much of this last, great cycle. Critics will always find something to condemn in his organ music, just as they will in all else that he wrote. The 'pull-up' registration was enough to have given several of his

pieces a slightly stilted quality, while the composer's passion for
modulation has failed to endear him to a generation sickened by a
surfeit of harmonic colouring. But only a bigot would quibble at
the inspiration underlying his finest works, among which these
Chorals deserve an honourable place.

The state of mourning into which the circle fell on Franck's
death had the effect of bringing members closer together than they
had ever been before. As a composer, he had said all he had to say,
and it only remained for his work to be properly acclaimed. Considered as a teacher, however, his testing time was still to come,
since it was not until his pupils were made to stand on their own
feet that their training could meet with appraisal. We have not
sought to expound Franck's system of instruction for the simple
reason that he had none. This should not be taken to mean that he
relied entirely on inspiration to see him through, but it does suggest
how indifferent he was to what we should nowadays call method-
ology. Lekeu has confirmed that no textbooks ever came his way;
while students at the Conservatoire were sometimes amazed to discover that their professor was not even conversant with Bazin's
treatise on harmony—the prescribed vehicle of study. Basically,
Franck's aim was to avoid placing his students in any kind of
straight-jacket, holding that it was unforgivable to cramp individual
talent. Though by no means lax in his attitudes, he was one of those
rare teachers whose policy it was to refrain from moulding his
charges to the same image. As long as they submitted to a preliminary stage of discipline, his pupils were allowed to do much as they
liked. His normal inclination was to seek out the merit in a student's
work, and it was only if he sensed an underlying contempt for
learning that he would suddenly be led to assume a more forbidding
tone. All this implies that he was better suited to teaching advanced
musicians. The constant prodding required by the remainder was
perhaps outside the scope of his temperament. His tolerance shone
like a beacon amid the spluttering interdictions of his colleagues,
most of whom were so weighed down with rules and regulations
that they had difficulty in achieving the limited objectives of the
classroom, to say nothing of more exalted goals. In trying to account
for the special devotion which Franck inspired, it is necessary to
look beyond questions of procedure. The quality so many were to
remember was an abiding sense of affection, willingly bestowed on
all who came near. When he was waiting for a class to begin (and
he usually got there at eight o'clock, well ahead of most pupils),
Franck would as often as not wander over to another department
and inquire: 'Would any of you gentlemen care to come round to
my room and keep me company?' Such eagerness to mingle with
the rank and file must surely be accounted one of the composer's

prime assets as a teacher. In this sense, he was among the select band fitted to appreciate Pestalozzi's axiom that the cardinal principle of education is not instruction but love.

As we have already hinted, Franck was in some ways inhibited by his official position as professor of the organ. Both Vierne and Tournemire (two of his best organ students) used to claim that they learnt very little about that instrument from attending his classes. The jump in standard which they afterwards faced from Widor came as a painful shock to them. Even allowing for the fact that he was no virtuoso, Franck did much to spoil the quality of his instrumental teaching by the habit he contracted of pulling out the stops and insinuating himself over the pedals whilst his pupils were intent on practising. Most musicians are familiar with the kind of teacher who cannot resist the impulse to rush in and demonstrate. There is unfortunately enough evidence to convict Franck of this sin—at least whenever the purely manipulative aspects of technique were under discussion. Actually, out of the six hours per week that students were required to spend on the organ, five were devoted to improvisation, a discipline over which the composer preserved a less strict control. As a rule, he would not interfere with a pupil who was in the process of working out a theme, preferring to sit back and listen in silence. Now and again he would break in with a brief injunction, such as 'Return to the tonic' or the more predictable 'Modulate! modulate!' (D'Indy has frankly admitted that the composer was sometimes unaware of the extent to which his pupils' key-changes had occurred by misadventure!) In matters of harmony and counterpoint, Franck generally took a liberal stand. He would admonish those who could not write a proper fugue, but he never attempted to teach these subjects in a mechanical fashion. Expression was one of the key words in his vocabulary, and correctness without feeling won his pupils very few marks. In the early days of a student's apprenticeship, there would often be some stiff exercises (Paul de Wailly was put through a particularly gruelling régime), but later on the atmosphere became pleasant and permissive. The themes Franck chose for counterpoint were as often as not taken from standard liturgical sources, the *Dies Irae* or *Jesu Redemptor* providing him with likely material. To illustrate his other principles, he usually chose to ransack the works of Bach or Beethoven.

In view of the charges of formlessness which are sometimes brought against his own music, it is surprising what a strong emphasis Franck seems to have placed on architectural considerations. It is not so much that he was a stickler for the sonata pattern— indeed he was always trying to think of new ways by which to lend this pattern greater variety—but he did like to insist that a ground plan should be present in the student's mind before embarking on his composition. Refusal to obey this requirement aroused his anger, and there were times when the gentle *Pater Seraphicus* was transformed into an irate tyrant. Exceedingly few such episodes are known to have taken place, however, and they never lasted more than a couple of minutes. One definite fixation the composer had was over the question of tonality. Where possible he used to urge his students to draw up a map of the various tonal pathways available, and he sometimes expected this to be presented prior to commencing work. Present-day teachers are inclined to look askance at such a method, which smacks too readily of dogma. They should remember that in Franck's day there were plenty of musicians who saw nothing wrong in restricting themselves to a handful of keys, most of which had been drained of their colour properties by constant repetition. If it seems as if the composer had a tendency to exaggerate the attractions of modulation, we should do well to recall the words of Jacques Rivière, who said:

> La modulation, chez Franck, est elle-même une forme de la continuité; elle n'a jamais le souci de créer un contraste; mais elle s'emploie à marquer d'exactitude les passages; elle est comme une main qui s'ouvre llentement, comme l'insensible introduction à plus de lumiere, comme une clarté filtrant à travers plus d'espace.*

The advice which Pierre de Bréville received on this and other topics seems to have been sensible enough. According to his article in the Mercure de France, written in 1933, he was encouraged to avoid complication; to dispense with all doubtful tonalities; to keep his sections from being too long; and to adhere to a good, firm plan. There is surely nothing here that might confuse or mislead. Viewing Franck's teaching as a whole, it appears to have been aimed at fostering originality without sacrificing the broad pillars of tone and structure.

To arrive at his status as an educator, it is perhaps necessary to separate what he taught from the manner in which he taught it. Bigoted though the profession may have been, there were doubtless other teachers whose competence went beyond his own, and this fact may even have been recognized by his pupils. What must be understood is that these young men were not just bent on discovering a classroom trickster or a ringleader to help them in their

---

* In Franck, modulation is itself a form of continuity; it is never concerned with creating contrast; but it distinguishes passages exactly; it is like a hand that opens slowly, like the imperceptible presence of light, like brightness filtering through space.

fight against officialdom. On the contrary, what they demanded was a man equipped to administer the soothing qualities – sympathy, understanding, a sense of idealism. It was not chance that led so unquestioningly to the composer being called 'Father Franck'. This was the instinctive title to which he aspired, not in the way that a real parent does – for that would have implied a dourness born of responsibility – but according to the fashion of a benevolent, almost fictional, paterfamilias. It has become tedious to insist that Franck was above all a good man. What we are in danger of forgetting is how very rare this commodity has always been, and how instantly it tends to be recognized by those who prize it. The nineteenth century was guilty of setting too much store by goodness, our modern inclination being to exalt cleverness. If these qualities are construed as opposites—which they are surely not—there is a further temptation to regard men like Franck as simpleminded. But no one could have been more resolute in his convictions than the composer of *Les Béatitudes*, and none submitted himself more patiently to the claims of adversity. It has yet to be shown that these attitudes of his were mistaken. Charles Bordes once hinted that Franck may actually have been 'an invention of his pupils'; the implication being that they projected on to him all those qualities of which they were unable to find a suitable embodiment elsewhere. But this is to overlook the drawing power of the attributes which he *did* possess. As Norbert Dufourcq has reminded us, 'the seraphic appearance pre-supposed a combat which it is only too easy to forget'. No doubt it was their awareness of the composer's victory over his struggles that caused his disciples to pledge their long allegiance.

PART THREE

X

A gallery of eccentrics

The reputation which Franck won as a teacher had the effect of ensuring that an ever wider variety of students would seek to reach
the privacy of his circle. As time went by, however, the distinction
between private and public commitments became less strict, and
some of the composer's pupils were drawn from the larger classes
of his rivals. Guy Ropartz and Paul Vidal, for instance, were both
originally Massenet pupils, and so was the versatile Pierné. On the
other hand, men like Sylvio Lazzari and Paul de Wailly soon latched
on to Franck as their sole guide. A small group of the most determined pupils were taught in extra-mural fashion, in response to
some special request. Augusta Holmès and Guillaume Lekeu came
into this category. Still others imbibed something of the Franckist
spirit without giving up their jealously guarded independence.[1]
Considering that Franck spent the whole of his professional life
giving lessons, it would serve no purpose to make a list of every
student who ever attended a class taken by him. Such a list could
only interest an archivist or institutional historian. As with any
experienced professor, there were only a few among the hundreds
who crossed the composer's path whose personalities proved well
attuned to his, or whose gifts were such that they compelled treatment out of the ordinary. Since we have been occupied with the
more famous of the pupils up to this point, it is perhaps time we
turned to look at others about whom posterity has still not made
up her mind. Many of these are musicians who contributed little
to the circle's destiny, but who nevertheless did much to keep its
wider gyrations in constant motion.

[1] The most important of these 'outsiders' were probably Bruneau,
whose operatic activities kept him far too busy to maintain an academic
relationship, and Dukas, who remained loyal to his official teachers
except in the matter of offering his friendship.

One of the most senior persons to have come under Franck's care in the years following the founding of the new Republic was a daughter of the Irish army officer, Dalkeith Holmès. Augusta— for that was the imperial name she bore—was born in 1847, making her older even than d'Indy and Duparc. The reasons for her tardiness in entering upon a musical career may be sought first of all in her sex, then in the domestic encumbrances which she was obliged to renounce. Though it has been claimed that she was from mixed Celtic stock, most authorities place her as a probable offspring of the poet, Alfred de Vigny.[1] This scion of the romantic movement certainly took a strenuous interest in her upbringing, and even ended by attempting to make her his mistress. His hopes that the young girl might follow a literary path suffered a setback when she expressed her preference for piano lessons, and it was as an unusually beguiling prodigy that she made her artistic début. From the piano she passed rapidly to the voice, her singing being one of the most remarkable things about her. The novelist George Moore, who was completely infatuated by her, used to recall that Augusta's rendering of certain operatic arias had moved him beyond all other musical experiences. Dame Ethel Smyth—though presumably less prejudiced in her favour—was equally inclined to smother her with praise. As a first step towards her musical education, she attached herself to Lambert, the organist of the church at Versailles, where she and her widowed father had settled down. Alongside this spiritual penance, she submitted herself to the accumulated military influences inseparable from her position as a daughter of the regiment. Chief among these was the instruction given by Klosé, the bandmaster of the Artillerie de la Garde Imperiale, and sometime professor of the clarinet at the Paris Conservatoire. Transfixed between *le rouge et le noir*, Augusta evolved an unique and eclectic outlook, renowned for its bold masculinity.

Determined to reject the ties of family and hearth, she lost no further time in acquiring the experience—musical and otherwise— indispensable to her ambitions. In 1869, at the age of twenty-two, she set out on a pilgrimage to Bayreuth in the company of some distinctly emancipated revellers. Her self-appointed guide on this occasion was none other than the lascivious Mendès, whose recent marriage had in no way lessened his propensity for reacting to a new and pretty face. Piqued by his wife's attachment to Wagner, he was all too ready to be distracted by Augusta's charms, and it was probably during or after this expedition that they saw fit to become

[1] Vigny (1797–1863) was an idealist who believed in the isolation of the poet from society. He is best known today for his *Poèmes Antiques et Moderne*, his novel *Cinq-Mars*, and the drama he wrote on the life of Chatterton.

lovers. A child born of the affair later married the famous Henri Barbusse, author of the novel, *Le Feu*. Whether it was as a result of hearing *Das Rheingold*, or being subjected to Mendès's immoderate propaganda, it is a fact that from this time onward Augusta began to affect all the mannerisms of a trusted Wagnerite.[1] In the days leading up to the Franco-Prussian War, she ran a minor salon in the Rue Mansart, to which a good many writers, painters and musicians belonged. It was here that she was accustomed to play and sing amid the gaping frustration of her minions. One of these was Saint-Saëns. Despite having homosexual inclinations, he found himself compelled to lay siege, only to meet with vigorous discouragement. 'We were all in love with her,' wrote the irascible little man many years later, 'and any one of us would have been proud to have made her his wife.' The composer of *Samson et Dalila* penned two sonnets in praise of Augusta's beauty, one of which compared her to Astarte and the other (not quite so flatteringly, one would have thought!) to Sappho. Neither of these had the desired effect, and friendship was all they were fated to enjoy. Saint-Saëns was cruelly reminded of his passion in the days when Franck took over as Augusta's mentor, his behaviour during the première of the older man's Quintet being in all probability a reflection of the jealousy he continued to feel. Still other composers were distracted by this amiable termagant, whose appearance struck the respectable Rimsky-Korsakov as 'très decolletée'. It took her singing to subjugate d'Indy, but even he admitted, after hearing her version of the *Danse Macabre*, that he had fallen under her spell. The carefree outings she used to organize for her favourites —chiefly to the forest of Fontainebleau—were among the last forms of indulgence presided over by the Empire.

Though already the composer of numerous songs and smaller pieces, it was not until after the war that Augusta began taking the creative side of music really seriously. It was an astonishing vocation for a woman to profess, and the publicity it aroused was not all welcome. An opera entitled *Hero et Léandre* showed at once how obsessed she was with grand classical themes. Having a natural understanding of vocal effects, and remembering the training in bandsmanship which she had received at Versailles, she was able to combine her skills in an alternately lyrical and fulsome score. Though submitted to the Opéra Populaire, the work failed to achieve success, perhaps on account of the excess of confidence it assumed. Her setting of the Psalm 'In Exitu' met with no warmer a reception when it was played at one of the concerts of the Société

[1] It may have been the Germanic bias aroused by her liking for Wagner that caused Augusta to adopt the pseudonym Hermann Zenta, under which she launched many of her songs.

Philharmonique later in the same year. Not long afterwards she took the step of consulting Franck about the prospect of becoming his pupil. Their association began in 1875, when she was twenty-eight and he fifty-three. If members of the public saw in their Christian names hints of a mighty collision of wills, they were doomed to disappointment. By all inference, it was a timidly conventional relationship which they had, with no trace of impropriety on either side. Even so, there can be little doubt that Franck was passionately aroused by her, since it was the attention he lavished on his new charge that sparked off Félicité's first attack of punitiveness. The embarrassing ardour of the Quintet—which the composer wrote at the height of their work together—cannot be explained otherwise than by reference to his feeling for Augusta, which remained strong right up to the end of his life.[1] If further proof were needed, there is the testimony of Maurice Emmanuel and the curious remark (attributed by Vallas to another acquaintance) that their friendship served to refute any suggestion of mysticism on Franck's part. The alteration which the circle insisted on making to the dedications of the composer's *Trois Chorals* is also vaguely indicative of a need for suppression. Georges having submitted Augusta's name as one dedicatee, the pupils ruled it out in favour of Guilmant, Dubois and Gigout.

As evidence of the earnestness of her studies, and the single-mindedness with which she was determined to pursue her vocation, Augusta spent much of her time between 1877 and 1880 preparing for competitions. This habit was not unique among Franck pupils, as d'Indy proved when he won the City of Paris prize some years later, but the general inclination was otherwise. In Augusta's case, one can see that there were special circumstances leading her to make the effort. As a headstrong young woman, used to dominating those around her, she not unnaturally regarded this as the most concrete way of demonstrating her artistic superiority. Moreover, as she was not attached to any school or college, it was a matter of some urgency to her to establish a position from which to continue working. Entering into rivalry with men might have seemed quixotic, but at least she could be sure that any success she won would have the effect of quashing masculine prejudice. Her first attempt was directed at the same municipal award that was conferred on 'Le Chant de la Cloche'. Indeed, it may have been Augusta's record (and her subsequent presence on the jury) that helped to inspire d'Indy's entry. The cunning which she brought to her task is illustrated in her choice of subject—a programme-

[1] 'What is that music you are playing? I emphatically dislike it,' was Félicité's virago-like comment on the Quintet when Franck first played it through at their apartment in the Boulevard St Michel.

symphony entitled *Lutèce*. Classicists will recall that Lutetia was
the original Gallo-Roman name borne by the city in the time of
Julian, the word *Parisii* not being coined until the third century
A.D., Perhaps on account of this direct appeal to local pride,
Lutèce won second prize, bringing its composer her first intimations
of fame. The joint winners of the competition turned out to be
Théodore Dubois and Benjamin Godard, both indisputably
brilliant technicians. The former was ten years older than Augusta
and already an experienced contestant; the latter adept at displaying that rich vein of charm which was to lead to him being described
as 'a musical Alfred de Musset'. Augusta's symphony was given a
complete performance at Angers in November 1884. Meantime,
she did not hesitate to re-enter the competition the following year,
submitting her cantata 'Les Argonautes'. This time she was
disappointed at receiving only an honourable mention, all the
interest going to Duvernoy.

Throughout the 1880s Augusta's musical interests had a hard
time keeping pace with her political zeal. A fervent believer in the
rights of the Celtic peoples, she had never been indifferent to the
struggles going on in her native Ireland. Many of the songs she
sang were really 'Home Rule' ditties pointlessly transcribed into
French. A glimpse of Garibaldi which she had been lucky enough
to get as a young girl turned her into a similarly tenacious partisan
of Italian unity, the crusade for which had died down somewhat
since the removal of Napoleon III's troops in 1870. Now that
internal jealousies—chiefly between north and south—were
threatening to bring about another turning-point in the affairs
of that nation, a call for further support was being made. Augusta's
concern stemmed partly from a desire to resurrect the swash-
buckling forms of statesmanship which had prevailed among her
father's generation, and partly from the genuine pity she felt for
the poor and downtrodden of all countries. The year 1882 witnessed
the production of two of the composer's most nationalistic works.
In March, her symphonic study *Irlande* was heard at the Concerts
Populaires, while a companion piece entitled *Pologne* followed in
December. This last work took as its subject the historic rape of
Poland and the colourful legend of Thaddeus Kosciuszko. Six
years afterwards came *Ludus pro Patria*—a sanguinary ode to *la
gloire* that was recited with obvious gusto by the actor Mounet-
Sully. The libretto for this composition had been written by
Augusta herself, as proof of her literary skill and inventiveness.
But the climax to all this elaborate posturing did not come about
until the Paris Exhibition opened in 1889. At this event, her new
Ode Triomphale received a stupendous performance, the acoustics
of the Palais de l'Industrie being shattered by the roar from twelve

hundred patriotic throats. Celebrity hunters were just able to make out the figure of Saint-Saëns seated among the audience, his high-pitched falsetto drowned amid the cheers of his neighbours. At last it seemed as if Franck's pupil had discovered her métier, there in the city which had given her shelter.

The truth is, however, that Augusta's ambitions were too princely for her to be satisfied with the role of musician-laureate. Like her beloved Dante, in whose honour she wrote a *Hymne à la Paix* for the Florence festivities of 1890, she aimed to reach the highest pinnacle of artistic success, fashion notwithstanding. Her studies with Franck having come to an end, she now felt free to plunge into the composition of grand operas in the Wagnerian manner, hoping to achieve the sort of réclame reserved for the mighty few. Working to her own libretto, she spent the next five years putting the polishing touches to a four-act drama called *La Montagne Noire*. The subject concerned the fate of yet another enslaved people, the inhabitants of Montenegro. These proud hill-dwellers occupied a province in the Middle East, having been cruelly repressed by the Sultan of Turkey. Throughout the nineteenth century, they formed part of the Ottoman Empire, against whose tyranny they periodically rose up in protest. The story recounted in Augusta's opera is that of the two soldiers, Aslar and Mirko, who lead an expedition into Montenegrin country with the object of putting down a revolt. In the first act, the pair can be observed swearing brotherhood in the rhetorical language of the day:

> Je jure devant Dieu de t'aime comme un frère
> Dans la vie ou la mort, dans la paix ou la guerre
> Et de sauvegardes ton honneur de chrétien
> Fût-ce au prix de mon sang, ou fût-ce au prix du tien!*

Very soon, however, a woman comes between them. The slave, Yamina, hurls herself at Mirko's feet and begs his intercession. Predictably, he grants her request for freedom only to find himself bewitched by her charms, and the two elope into the mountains. Act II is a village scene in the interior, and offers many points of correspondence with Bizet's 'Carmen'. There is even a rival heroine in the person of Helena, who plays Micaela to Mirko's Don José. Meantime, the other brother, Aslar, has the job of hunting down the fugitives. When he catches up with them, Yamina wounds him with a knife. Mirko is taken aback by this

---

* I swear before God to love you as a brother in life or death, peace or war, and to protect your Christian honour at the cost of my blood or with the price of my people.

turn of events and renews his oath of loyalty to his brother, even though it is obvious that he is still under Yamina's spell. In the end, the dilemma is resolved by a Montenegrin raiding-party which invades the village, killing Aslar and leaving the guilty couple to ponder the moral of their actions.

The music of *La Montagne Noire* is very rhythmic and martial, and at times the sound of the orchestra threatens to drown all that is happening on the stage. It was Augusta's *faiblesse* that she could not resist the temptation to write virile, explosive sounds such as no other woman composer would have dared to make. A casual onlooker might be forgiven for supposing that she composed all her music in imitation of the last act of *Götterdämmerung*. As Julien Tiersot has said when discussing her relation to the Franck school:

> Elle fut, elle aussi, élève de César Franck. Il est vrai que sa musique ne se ressent guere de cette direction: elle est toute d'éclat extérieur, sonore, d'une coloration vive, parfois violente, avec une affectation de virilité: les formes en sont d'ailleurs toutes melodiques et la caractère symphonique y est peu prononce.*

Her concept of drama was no less impatient, and one obvious criticism of the opera is that too much violent action is permitted to take place in the early stages. Act I is in this sense quite relentless. The dances and choruses are also inclined to be over-generous in their excitement, leaving the listener nothing in the way of emotional reserves. On the other hand, the *serments* of the two brothers form well-spaced dramatic peaks, and the seductiveness of Yamina is skilfully brought out. Her *larghetto* is easily the most lyrical moment which the score has to offer, though it perhaps goes on for a shade too long. It is difficult to be precise about the models Augusta chose when writing this work. Certain scenes are unmistakably Wagnerian, but others recall the later work of Gounod, particularly his opera, *Le Tribut de Zamora*, which had appeared in 1881. Whether or not Franck's *Hulda* exercised an influence is more doubtful. *La Montagne Noire* was mounted at the Paris Opéra on 8 February 1895, but unfortunately ran for only eleven performances.[1]

[1] A critical notice of the première may be found in Vol. 21 of *Les Annales du Théâtre*, ed., by Felix Duquesnel (Berger-Levrault & Co., Paris, 1896).

* She also became a pupil of César Franck. It is true that her music did not impel her in this direction: it is all outward brilliance, sonority, bright colour, occasionally violent, with a penchant for masculinity: the forms are besides melodic and the symphonic character hardly pronounced.

The remainder of Augusta's life was a bitter disappointment, both creatively and in terms of personal relations. She managed to write two further operas—*Astarte* and *Lancelot de Lac*—but neither was successful in securing a performance.[1] Instead, she had to content herself with the good esteem of a number of prominent judges. Some of these were enormously impressed by her music, Mahler going as far as to link her name with Wagner's. The French symbolists also rallied to her cause, Mallarmé becoming a close friend and adviser. But Augusta was not the kind that waits patiently for acclaim. By the turn of the century, her talent had largely run to seed, and her beauty become a thing of the past. Driven to drink by the absence of her usual admirers, she eked out her last years at a small apartment near the Opéra, where she kept a roomful of tender souvenirs to remind her of what she had once held so dear. Callers were apt to find her clad in a tattered, red-flannel dressing-gown, the skirts of which trailed behind her like the glad-rags of some deposed queen. She died in 1903, at the comparatively early age of fifty-six, and was buried at the Saint-Louis cemetery, Versailles, where a monument was erected to her memory. It was unveiled on 13 July 1904, amid a tiny circle of friends. Her former lover Mendès attained greater longevity, but met with an equally depressing end, being run over by a train while taking a short cut across the line near his home at St Germain. It is most unlikely that Augusta's music will ever be subjected to large-scale revival. Its tones are too stirring, its mood too consistently climactic. If an explanation of her failure is demanded, it must be put down to the excesses of her over-artistic temperament, and perhaps to the prejudice shown by an exclusively masculine world. A survivor from a more truly romantic age, she would probably have found even less to celebrate in the cynical, jazzed-up 1920s, sympathetic though that period may have been towards the idea of womanly defiance. Her position in the Franck circle remains obscure and ultimately inexplicable.

Another victim of hyper-intensity was the Belgian prodigy, Guillaume Lekeu, who was actually the last of Franck's many pupils. An equally convinced apostle of Beethoven, Lekeu has become entangled in such a skein of legend that it is proving difficult to assess him at his true worth. His case is described by

[1] It is astonishing how fruitful the theme of Lancelot appeared to be to members of the Franck circle. In addition to Augusta Holmès's work, versions of the theme—either operatic or programmatic—can be attributed to Chausson, Sylvio Lazzari and others. If we extend it to include that other Arthurian figure, Merlin, there is Benoît's *Merlin*, *L'Enchanteur* and Chausson's *Viviane* to complete the picture. Ropartz, too, wrote a *Chasse de Prince Arthur*.

his biographer, O. G. Sonneck, as being 'more tragic than that of Schubert or Pergolesi'—strong words and sufficient to implant suspicions of exaggeration in anyone's mind. Yet no less a critic than Debussy considered him 'the only musician whom Beethoven really inspired', and he was the subject of similar testimonials from Dukas, Ysaÿe and Vallas. D'Indy, who had the job of superintending what remained of his career after Franck's death, tended to be more reserved in his judgement, allowing that the young man was no more than 'quasi-génial'. Whichever view of him we take, there can be no doubt that in Lekeu the Franck school discovered a white hope the like of which it had never encountered before. A knowledgeable chamber music authority at seventeen, he was dead at twenty-four, having left behind a total of sixty compositions. That many of these were bristling with promise, while others come down to us tantalizingly incomplete, only adds to the regret. Such a huge production all within the space of seven years entitles the composer to a place among the most prolific, if not the greatest, of musicians. Not merely a musical machine, Lekeu interests us in other ways too—most notably as a visionary critic and letter-writer. The range of his curiosity was exceptionally wide when one considers what limited time he was given to develop it. Like Franck himself, he was the possessor of a near-mystical sensibility, which in his case was accompanied by a good deal of inner certainty over standards. He was thus typically Franckist in the direction of his thoughts, while being much more self-generating in his insights. We do not have to agree with the extravagant estimates of his talent put forward by his admirers to feel maddened and cheated at not knowing how his career would have turned out.

Lekeu was born at Heusy, near Verviers, in 1870, so that his nationality was unquestionably Belgian. Notwithstanding this clue, the fact that his family moved to Poitiers in France when he was nine years of age meant that much the same doubt as had attended Franck's career was allowed to spring up. Philip Hale, one of the composer's strongest partisans, referred to him as 'the best representative of the young French school'— a judgement that had the effect of infuriating Belgian patriots. Jean Huré and others of the nationalist faction were accordingly moved to get their own back by claiming Lekeu as a 'separatist', even though it is on record that he could not speak a word of Flemish and disliked the whole idea of a minority culture. 'Is not a Belgian school of composers merely an illusion and a snare?' he wrote at the time of entering for the Belgian Prix de Rome in 1891. At any rate, he took care to avoid following his colleagues Paul Gilson and Edgar Tinel, who made a point of setting Flemish texts. It should be remembered that Lekeu's education propelled him very rapidly in the direction of a cosmopolitan outlook. He had excelled at classics, later doubling for a teacher of Latin and Greek at one of the French lycées, and responded quite naturally to the aesthetic currents of several nations. Moreover, his idolization of Beethoven and Wagner tends to remove any suspicion that he might have developed into a regional composer. The argument about his nationality is hence a thoroughly pointless one, sillier even than that which has raged over Franck. It is interesting that Lekeu was also good at science, his physics master being the first to notice the pronounced nature of his musical gifts. When he gained admission to the University of Paris, however, it was to study philosophy, a subject in which he graduated with honours and towards which he retained a permanent predilection.[1] According to Tissier, the evidence of his musical talent was not revealed until he reached the age of fourteen, making him a rather late-starter as prodigies go. His first interest was centred upon the violin, and he only began taking lessons in harmony and theory in 1885. The hard work he put in at these subjects made it easier for him to embrace the rigours that came later.

Meantime, he played the role of sophisticated bohemian, ultimately joining the throng at Mallarmé's receptions and seeking out the company of men of letters. One of these was the Mozart scholar, Théodore de Wyzewa, and it was he who dissuaded Lekeu from enrolling at the Paris Conservatoire. Instead, it was proposed that he should take lessons privately with the Prix de Rome winner, Gaston Vallin. For about three months Vallin accordingly taught Lekeu the higher flights of harmony, after which his friend Read secured him an introduction to Franck. The meeting did not turn out to be quite as momentous as they had hoped, the composer of *Les Béatitudes* taking an unexpectedly churlish line. Confiding to his other pupils that he did not really want to be bothered with a fresh disciple at this time of his life, Franck almost lost one of the most illustrious members of his band. Eventually, however, he yielded to pressure and suggested a series of lessons at what, for him, was quite an exorbitant fee. Being from a well-to-do family, Lekeu could hardly refuse, and it was not long before he began receiving his money's worth. Though widely separated by age, the two men soon came to find solace in each other's company, Franck gravitating to his customary stance of

[1] His entry to the university occurred in 1888, which was also the year in which he was first introduced to Franck. At this time, he was still undecided about what profession to follow, and it was only in his graduation year that he finally opted for music. Among the compositions he wrote as a freshman, a String Quartet, an Adagio for two violins and cello, and a Cello Sonata have been preserved.

parent-figure. Alexandre Tissier has claimed that they actually met for a mere twenty lessons, two a week for the space of a couple of months, though the evidence is that Lekeu began his association with the composer in the autumn of 1889 and was still under instruction at the time of Franck's death in the November of the following year. Thus it seems probable that a reasonably thorough spell of tuition was meted out. Unfortunately, the deaths of both men took place within such a short time of their reaching agreement that we have no sure way of confirming how deep their relationship went. The effect of Franck's passing may be gauged from the letter Lekeu wrote to Louis Kéfer, the Director of the Verviers Conservatoire, on 15 April 1891. In it he says:

> I was completely bewildered; I passed four or five days a week smoking and watching the implacable rain pour down and telling myself how wise it would be to jump out of the window.

This confession at once makes clear the binding nature of their friendship and the peculiarly depressive mood it helped to engender. Along with Chausson and Duparc, Lekeu partook generously of that dangerous fascination which Franck exuded, a fascination half-way between admiration and love. But as had been the case with these earlier disciples, there was enough in Lekeu's own temperament to account for the melancholy excesses to which he fell prone.

Not supplied with any textbook to assist him, the young musician's studies took the form of oral instruction in counterpoint. It was considered that he had learnt sufficient harmony from Vallin (and indeed the evidence of his early compositions tends to uphold this verdict) so that he was not obliged to produce the sort of exercises for which many of Franck's Conservatoire pupils were being prepared. Everything points to the fact that his work with Franck was pitched at an exceedingly high level. Judging from the prodigious fugues which appear so regularly in Lekeu's chamber-works, he must have submitted some surprising things to his master. For once in his life, Franck was confronted with a pupil whose skill at counterpoint came close to rivalling his own, or at least gave indications that it very soon would. The rules passed on were extremely simple, however, Franck insisting only that his pupil's work should sound well and should be strongly expressive. The latter requirement was something he need not have concerned himself about, for 'expressiveness' was the one undefaceable trademark by which Lekeu's compositions would come to be recognized. Indeed, it is hardly too much to say that it was he and not Alban Berg who did most to deserve the title of pioneer of that musical style which is the counterpart to Edouard

Munch's drawings and Strindberg's plays.[1] Later in his short life, Lekeu was to say that, facile as he was, it never took him less than six days to complete a fugue—an admission that serves to underline the rigour with which he approached the task. When, for example, he was set a particularly difficult subject during the first heat of the Belgian prize, his judges had to restrain him from apologizing for his efforts. Armed with such an impregnable technique, it is not to be wondered that Lekeu admired Franck more for his 'serious' works than for the programmatic excrescences which he had permitted himself. He is known to have thought *Rédemption* a colossal masterpiece, and he once described his feelings as 'frozen and bleeding' over the neglect of his master's unpublished works. An outspoken critic of his more famous seniors, this boy of twenty sneered at nullities like Ambroise Thomas; hated Bruneau for submitting to Zola's influence; and excoriated Massenet for lording it over Franck at the Conservatoire. In addition, he retained a strong, instinctive dislike of Magnard, into whose company he had been thrown during a German tour in 1889. It will be agreed that his personality was far more positive than that of the average Franck pupil.

If his antipathies strike us as powerful, it becomes difficult to find words by which to describe his enthusiasms. Like many others, he was aroused to a point of frenzy by Wagner's music. The story of his collapse during a performance of *Tristan* gains in credibility as one reads through his remarkable letters to Kéfer and to his mother. Sonneck has compared his sensibility with that of the poet Leopardi. Certainly, there is a similar piercing quality about their perceptions, each writing as if in the grip of a profound lamentation. There is a difference, however, in that Lekeu's sadness is constantly being interrupted by bursts of sanguine passion and exclamations of hero-worship. For all his pessimism, he cannot be considered an elegaic composer. Contrary to Hale's hasty conclusions, we do not find premonitions of death scattered throughout his correspondence. What does emerge is evidence of an ever-present struggle with inspiration, a continuous anguish in the expectation of failure. This mental condition seems to have been endemic among the Franckists, but one has the sense that Lekeu was reacting to his own demon and no one else's. Eyes always blazing and tongue quick to lash, he went around in a private creative universe, like a young Beethoven amid the

[1] The difference between Berg and Lekeu lies, of course, in the more pathological lengths to which the former carried his habits of expressionism. Though there are 'wails' and 'sighs' in Lekeu's music, these are more of an echo of the *Tristan* mentality; whereas in Berg they are deliberately horrifying.

courtiers. That he rarely took a step without clutching up his copy of the last Quartets serves to prove his powers of unconscious identification. 'I quiver still with the fever produced in me by this work' was his comment on the master's Fifteenth Quartet, and he proceeded to compare its effect to that which an operation for cataract might be expected to have upon a blind man. In his view, Beethoven's greatest contribution lay in the proof he had given that the String Quartet could be something more than the perfect formal exercise devised by Haydn and Mozart. His desire to emulate his idol was in reality nothing less than a desire to transcend the boundaries of form, making of music a vehicle for the extended repertory of emotions he had waiting to be expressed. As George Systermans has put it in his valuable article on the composer in Cobbett's *Encyclopaedia*:

> Lekeu intended to push to its furthest limits the romanticism of Beethoven's later years, and to give a preference to the lyrical expression of his inner emotions—passion, grief, ecstasy, despair—over considerations of form and style.

It is by means of the triumphant promulgation of these emotions that Lekeu's best work stands its chance of succeeding. Those who look to him to provide a high degree of unity and finish will be disappointed at what they hear.

The next step in his career was a crucial one, and it was as a result of d'Indy's prompt intervention that he was able to make it. The consequences of Franck's death—placed at a time when his ambitions were just on the point of flowering—had come to seem doubly painful to the still immature musician, so that what he needed at this stage was some new stimulus to take him out of himself. It is very much to d'Indy's credit that he grasped the responsibility for re-directing what could easily have amounted to a broken vocation. Urging the young man to set himself a goal and attain it, the future Director of the Schola hinted at the possibility of him winning the Belgian Prix de Rome. If he had brought it off, this could have been the means of securing wider recognition for his talents, and would in any case have assisted him to recover his poise. Unhappily, Lekeu did not possess the kind of smoothly-oiled talent that rises to the top in competitions. He was far too headstrong and self-willed. Nevertheless, he entered with a sense of dedication, and put up such a brilliant showing on the first round that he fully expected the prize would be his. The cantata *Andromède* which he submitted for the final was by a long way his most ambitious work to date. Whether the judges sensed his lack of aptitude for this larger genre, or were merely swayed by the usual academic considerations, they passed over Lekeu and slyly awarded the honour to a composer named Lebrun. This surprising outcome naturally became a source of anger and frustration with the proud competitor, and he did not hesitate to fire abuse in all directions. That the committee had thought reasonably highly of his efforts is proved by the fact that they were willing to offer him the second prize. No one had voted him the first prize, however, and that was enough to cause Lekeu's gorge to rise. Characteristically, he refused the mite of comfort offered, and removed himself from the scene. Very few of Franck's pupils managed to excel in competition with others, there being a good deal of prejudice shown towards them by juries. But in Lekeu's case, it remains doubtful whether his Franckist affiliations were the cause of his downfall. After all, Franck had been Belgian and Brussels was not Paris. It is more likely that the flaws in *Andromède* came to seem more serious with closer inspection.

The truth is that, although Kéfer gallantly performed this cantata at Verviers in 1892 and it was revived at Brussels some ten years after the composer's death, it cannot be put down as a masterpiece, or anything resembling one. The text by Jules Sauvenière gave Lekeu ample scope for dramatic representation, but like so many other Franck pupils his sense of drama was confined to inward situations. To make living figures out of godlike extraverts, as Perseus and Andromeda were obviously intended to be, proved quite beyond his powers. The stiffness with which they are portrayed is accordingly one of the crucial weaknesses in this otherwise competent work. Added to this, we must acknowledge a certain failure on Lekeu's part to sustain the quality of his inspiration. His temptation as a composer was always to go on at too great a length, hence depriving his work of the elements of shape and coherence. To this extent, the first part of the cantata is noticeably more intelligible than the remainder. Actually, three situations are depicted. The opening presents a religious scene in which the Ethiopians entreat their god Ammon to rid them of the monster which has been devastating the countryside. The deity replies that it will be necessary to sacrifice the maiden Andromeda by chaining her to a rock. In a previous phase of the myth Andromeda had flaunted her beauty before the tribe of Nereides, who are now in a position to witness the haughty virgin being dragged off amid cries of misery and supplication. During what follows Andromeda is portrayed alone with her grief, the Nereides periodically returning to mock her. Finally, in the third tableau, the hero Perseus arrives to free the victim and marry her in a burst of rejoicing. Aside from the marionette-like behaviour of the principals, the main drawback to the listener's enjoyment is likely to be the bombastic tone of the finale. Lekeu's failure to remain steady at this point suggests another of his typical shortcomings. Musically, the most appealing episode in the work is probably Andromeda's lament in Part II. Everything points to the fact that at this stage in his career Lekeu was rather infatuated by themes involving tragic splendour. He had earlier attempted an orchestral triptych based on Shakespeare's *Hamlet*—'une grosse machine' as he portentously described it—but the project fell through on completion of the second panel, partly as a result of the composer's absence of dramatic instinct. 'This character I feel neither old nor strong enough to depict,' he frankly confessed, 'the task requires a Beethoven.'

Much better suited to his talents were the two sonatas, one for piano and violin and the other for piano solo, which also date from the time of his coming of age. Regarding these impressive works, the latter is much less well known than the former. Perhaps this is because it is not really a sonata at all, being more of a five-movement suite. Relentlessly contrapuntal in style, it has not managed to attract the attention of pianists and occupies a somewhat similar position in Lekeu's canon to that of the *Prélude, Aria et Final* in Franck's. Actually, like most of the composer's pieces, it evokes a curious mixture of influences, first of all Bach and then Wagner. Not content with this, its creator placed at the head of his work a faintly morbid epigraph which reads:

> Comme une mère veille auprès de son enfant
> Elle a bercé de ses chansons ma mâle fièvre.
> La bonne fée, elle a ranimé de sa lèvre
> Ma lèvre, et refraichi pour moi, l'air étouffant.*

The lines are from George Vanor, and it is not hard to detect clear programmatic references in the ensuing music. Indeed, the 'bonne fée' theme is one that Lekeu re-employs in the second movement of his *Quatuor Inachevé*. This theme, however, does not make its complete appearance until quite late in the sonata, the dominant motifs being those of the 'mâle fièvre' and 'air étouffant'. Probably it is on account of the loosely cyclical fashion in which each of these fragments comes to be used that academic critics have been impelled to withhold the title of sonata. For among the five movements of the work, the first and last can easily be disposed of as a prelude and epilogue, respectively. The unity of the remaining movements is quite marked, in the purely thematic sense, but there are no suggestions of a sonata design. Rather, it is the fugal form that seems to predominate. The prelude is distinguished chiefly by its nobility of harmony, and for tentatively proposing the subject

* Like an old mother in the presence of her son, she quietens with songs my masculine agitation. The good fairy touches with her lips my lips, dispersing the suffocating air.

of the second movement's fugue. When it arrives this is worked out in the manner of an organ fantasia, more fugato than strict fugue with a plethora of canonical imitations. The mighty basso ostinato climax is, however, a literal re-statement of the corresponding section of the prelude. This in turn provides a new subject which is developed in the third movement. The chanson motif has by this time firmly asserted itself. Reverting to a very much slower tempo, the fourth movement continues the dour contrapuntal struggle and it is only with the epilogue that the mood becomes more consistently relaxed and joyful. Sonneck describes this ending as 'a calmness of the soul after the conflagration'. To progressive ears, it is perhaps apt to sound banal. A final verdict on the work is not easy to pronounce. Its thundering climaxes are more impressive than effective, and for all its bravura it is too taxing for the concert-hall.

By comparison, the G minor Violin Sonata presents a very different case; it must on any count be reckoned as Lekeu's finest completed composition. Commissioned by Ysaÿe, after his hearing of *Andromède*, it was written with an ardour and élan almost worthy of *Tristan*. As a matter of fact, many listeners may be inclined to view it as an attempt to transpose Wagner's *Liebestod* into chamber music terms. 'Je n'aime pas la musique jolie et non sentie' the composer was once overheard to say, and nothing which he wrote bears out this philosophy more than the present work. In three movements, the sonata begins, like most works belonging to the Franck school, with a slow introduction. Very quickly, however, the music gives way to a joyous *vivo con passione* theme in bold curves and clear accents. So far, originality seems to have been sacrificed to sheer brio. By choosing a pithy bridge-passage (to be repeated in the third movement in true cyclical fashion) and electing to make his second subject complementary to the first, Lekeu nevertheless shows himself able to follow through in tightly-knit sonata style. His chief failing, as far as this movement is concerned, can be traced to a certain indifference towards development. The composer was too inclined to look to sequence as a substitute for the genuine working-out of ideas, and like Liszt he was given to repeating the same figure at a variety of pitches. He tended to be at his best when a programme of some kind was at hand to urge him on. The sonata's *molto lento* movement is generally considered one of the high points of his inspiration, its beautifully controlled cantilena and unusual 7/8 rhythm combining to make it especially memorable. The form is a simple ABA, with the initial section constituting a calm, sad reverie and the interpolation a 'cramignon' or Walloon folk-song. The latter is one of the few concessions Lekeu ever made to his national idiom. It does not take him long to effect a return to his customary contrapuntal severity for the finale. Distinguished as it undoubtedly is, the Violin Sonata would have benefited by greater telescoping of its themes and a little less in the way of padding. It was played in Paris by Paul Viardot and Bertha Demanton in 1899, and in Boston by Karel Ondriček and Alice Cummings in 1902.

Meantime, its composer did not allow his critical faculties to remain idle. Though prevented from revisiting Bayreuth by his absorption with the Belgian contest, he was prompt in compensating for this by making a trip to Aix-la-Chappelle in October of 1892 to hear Schumann's little-known opera, *Paradise and the Peri*. It impressed him deeply, and he referred to it in his usual hyperbolic way as 'a sublime work of incomparable poetry'. He had himself begun an opera based on one of Alfred de Musset's comedies, but Franck had advised him to be wary of writing for the orchestra before he has mastered the small genres. The result was that *Barberine*—which he had started even before his luminous Bayreuth experience—never got much beyond the planning stage. It is impossible to feel sincere regret about this. Not only is it probable that the work's dramatic subtleties would have eluded the composer, but we cannot help reflecting that Musset's strained sophistication would not have found an echo in his thoughts. He was much better at catching the mood of the symbolist poets, making it open to speculation whether he would have gone on to become a *Lieder* composer had time permitted. As an amateur versifier, Lekeu wrote a considerable quantity of craftsmanlike poetry, most of it expressive of his richly-tormented *vie intérieure*. The images it proposes are generally related to sleep and death, its colours confined to the silver-grey spectrum made fashionable by Verlaine. A song-cycle based on his own 'poèmes' made its appearance in 1892, and consisted of three melodies—'Sur un tombe', 'Rondo' and 'Nocturne'. These do not suggest mastery of an essentially vocal style. On the contrary, they are not sufficiently separated from the piano's turgid harmonies. 'Rondo' is a catchy and spirited number, but the other two songs are brooding and sombre. 'Nocturne' was transcribed for orchestra, à la Duparc. Otherwise, there is little enough by which to compare the composers' talents as exponents of the *mélodie*. More interest might have attached itself to Lekeu's development as a literary artist, since his rhythmical experiments with blank-verse were clearly very *avant-garde* for the time.

During the last year of his life, the composer embarked on a new and still more frenetic venture with his Piano Quartet, a work that sadly remains incomplete. Opinions of the surviving portion tend to be uniformly glowing. Sonneck refers to it as 'a priceless torso', while the critic of the *Boston Journal* (it was performed in that city in its unfinished state by the Hoffmann Quartet in 1896) proclaimed that 'everywhere it breathes genius'. Had it been finished, it would probably have been the longest work of its kind in the repertory. Without doubt it would have ranked among the most intense in tone. By this time, Lekeu had fallen into the habit of expressing contempt for his previous compositions. The Violin Sonata—about which he had enthused so vigorously only a short while before—now seemed 'a penny toy' by the side of his latest undertaking. Furthermore, he went on record as saying that he did not any longer care whether the public understood what he was writing. Using an old Erard piano, the composer tirelessly thumped out his ideas from morning till night, confiding to a correspondent—'I am playing for a big stake'. In the same letter, dated 22 February 1893, he applied to himself the following lines which Baudelaire had written to Théodore de Banville:

> Vous avez empoigné les crins de la Déesse
> Avec un tel poignet, qu'on vous eût pris a voir
> Et cet air maîtrise et ce beau nonchaloir
> Pour un ruffian terrassant sa maîtresse.*

The first movement of the new work was bitter and questing in style, following no established pattern of form. Its two principal themes were unified in the composer's mind beforehand, which may account for the delay which he experienced in putting notes to paper. A significant bridge-passage connects these themes as in the Violin Sonata. Brief improvisations on the earlier lead to the development, and the recapitulation is marked by a double climax, the second steeper and craggier than the first. This whole movement—which was not completed until 16 July 1893—is directed to be played 'dans un emportement douloureux'. Only part of the succeeding nocturne was written by Lekeu, the rest being added by d'Indy after the composer's death. This second movement adopts a ternary form and is preceded by a reminiscence of the 'bonne fée' theme from the Piano Sonata. The mood at times recalls Tschaikovsky, especially in the sorrowful contours of the melody. Whether the Quartet would have run to one or two further movements is something we are left to ponder for ourselves.[1]

---

[1] Also left unfinished at Lekeu's death was his plan for writing a number of Piano Trios. One of these was completed in 1891, affording Franck mild satisfaction in its embryonic form.

* You have grasped the hair of the goddess with such strength, and with the fine air of indifference of a master towards his mistress, a villain striking his doxy, that you have been able to take full sight and possession of her.

The correspondence in which Lekeu engaged during the writing of this work is full of pungent declarations. While allowing himself an improved standard of workmanship, the composer constantly affirms his belief that the task of the creative artist is to master the intricacies of feeling. In a letter to his mother, dated 17 February 1893, he insists that 'expressive chaos must also be harmonious' and goes on to expound the relationship between beauty and grief which, in retrospect, appears to be the key relationship exemplified in his music. It would be interesting to inquire further into the ramifications of Lekeu's aesthetic, particularly into the nature of its psychological undercoat. Speculative critics may care to examine the line of descent which runs from Poe through Baudelaire to Duparc, seeing Lekeu as the inheritor of a debased tradition of 'ordre et beauté'. Certainly there are similarities between Duparc's mystical strivings and that search for the ineffable which occurs in works like the Violin Sonata and the Quatuor Inachevé. Yet it would be misleading to imagine that Lekeu could ever have evolved into a religious *exalté*. One feels that there was another side to him which had its feet too firmly planted on the ground. Equally remote from his sensibility is the religious eroticism that went to compose Wagner's later 'persona'. For although he lived beyond the age at which one tends to fall in love, there is no evidence that Lekeu was plagued by affairs of the heart. Like Ravel, he contented himself with an exaggerated attachment to his mother, to whom he wrote in the midst of one separation: 'The future absolutely must re-unite us and I wish that my life might end as it began in the cradle of your love.' These are scarcely the words of a normal young man, being more suggestive of the Oedipal character of the analyst's case-book. One can imagine how inconsolable his parents must have been at the prospect of life without him.

The actual circumstances of his death are poignantly described by Paul Prist in his book *L'Enfant de génie de la musique contemporaine*. It seems that Lekeu ate some contaminated sherbet and came down with a fever which soon revealed itself as typhoid. He lingered for a number of days, ironically dying on the day after his twenty-fourth birthday. This was at Angers, to which his parents had moved during their son's student years, and which town had looked like providing him with the security he needed. D'Indy and other members of the circle were deeply shocked at the news, feeling that they had lost their most promising recruit. On 29 April a concert was organized at the Salle d'Harcourt in Paris under Vincent's direction, the programme consisting of the Violin Sonata, the song 'Sur un tombe', the posthumous *Fantaisie Symphonique* and a scene from *Andromède*. As a tribute to the composer's memory, it was a necessary and moving occasion. That it failed to ignite widespread enthusiasm was perhaps only to be expected. The task of building up Lekeu's reputation was typically protracted, and is still going on at the present time. Debussy was among the first to call attention to his case, arranging for a performance of the Quartet under the auspices of the Société Nationale in February 1896. It was a hearing of this truncated masterpiece that led Philip Hale to exclaim:

> Lekeu's voice was his own. His music is not like that of other men; he thought in his own way and his emotional eloquence in this Quartet is genuine and convincing . . . such music does not suffer when played after a noble work by Beethoven, but it makes a work like that of Dvořák's which followed unendurable.

Meantime, Stavenhagen and Berber had played the Violin Sonata in Munich, Berlin and Leipzig without winning any but the most patronizing response. 'Amateurish', 'sterile', 'vague'—these were some of the critical epithets the work drew in non-French speaking countries, probably out of a perverse sense of national pride.

Strangely enough, such esteem as did attach to Lekeu's compositions came about through the inclusion of his orchestral fragments in concerts given by d'Indy, Colonne and Chevillard. The Fantaisie—or to give it its full title the *Fantaisie sur deux airs populaires Angevins*—had been completed in November 1892.[1] The folk-songs upon which it was based (one jolly and the other ablaze with light) were allegedly noted down by the composer during a dinner he was enjoying with his bank-manager. Whistled strains made their way in from the street as they ate, and Guillaume lost no time in groping for his pencil. As may be imagined, d'Indy regarded his enthusiasm as commendable, finding the *fête populaire* which occurs at the beginning of the work particularly appealing. Others have complained of a certain dullness in Lekeu's choice. The fact is that neither of the two songs is especially hummable, and attention needs to be concentrated on what the composer was able to do in the way of combining them. The skill he displayed in adapting the melody of the first song to the rhythm of the second is one measure of his ingenuity. Another may be found in the manner in which he succeeded in varying the instrumentation. So many critics have deplored d'Indy's influence that it is a pleasure to be able to record a case where nothing but good ensued from his

---

[1] This work was also performed by Sir Henry Wood in London during 1903.

prescriptions, and it may be regretted that Lekeu did not benefit earlier from the assistance of Franck's principal henchman. Answering a letter of 26 June 1893, the ordinarily unapproachable Vincent offered his pupil a most valuable set of recommendations for overcoming depression. In particular, he urged the young man to get to know himself and his abilities; to allot a portion of his time to reading; and to induce one or more of his friends to advance their candid opinion of his work. The feeling of impotence, d'Indy wrote, was common to all creative artists, and was something to be endured rather than resisted. Through no fault of his own, this advice came too late to be of much use. Hence we shall never know for certain whether Lekeu would have risen to the achievements predicted for him or whether he would have plunged headlong into the abyss of unreason.

Holmès and Lekeu were each in their different ways concerned with pushing music to its outer limits of expression. Dynam-Victor Fumet—who represents the third in our gallery of eccentrics—had no such aim and wielded a far less cataclysmic influence on those around him. This is not to say that he was a conservative composer, or lacked the imprint of a distinctive mind. On the contrary, it is difficult to think of anyone, unless it is the weird Erik Satie, whose career sounded a more individual note. But Fumet was astonishing chiefly as a politico-religious freak, a kind of counterpart to the seedy insurgents depicted in Joseph Conrad's novels. His musical temper, though frequently prophetic, was not nearly as aggressive as the circumstances of his life might lead us to believe. Born at Toulouse in 1867, he was a year younger than his friend Satie and has not yet succeeded in arousing the same degree of interest. Unlikely as it may appear, he began his studies at the Paris Conservatoire by enrolling in Franck's organ class in 1885, also allowing himself to be taught composition by the sympathetic Guiraud. He withdrew from the Prix de Rome in 1886 after experiencing the usual bitter disappointments. Up to this time, he might have been taken for just another young aesthete escaping from the dreariness of a respectable professional career. What most of his teachers failed to see was the utopian inclusiveness of the lad's mind, which even at this stage was moving in realms generally reserved for the Gandhis and Lenins of this world. Politics form an interest with the majority of students, but the intensity of Fumet's convictions found no parallel among his comrades in the arts. The strength of these convictions may be judged from the fact that, young as he was, he had already become an associate of Kropotkin and Louise Michel and was contributing regularly to the anarchist journal, *La Revolté*. No theorist, he was willing to kill and be killed for his beliefs, spending much of his spare-time helping to manufacture bombs for the use of the party. On learning of this shocking activity, the Toulouse authorities took the understandable step of notifying the boy's Conservatoire teachers, at the same moment being fixed to withdraw his scholarship.

Being faced with such a difficult decision, the institution was at first loath to propose expulsion. Saint-Saëns and Reyer—neither of whom could have been accused of radicalism—considered that anything of that kind would be both foolish and precipitate. Indeed, they handsomely offered to testify to the young man's exceptional gifts. But without financial support there was nothing for it but to give up. Fumet's opportunity to join the Franck circle was consequently a thing of limited duration. It is true that César was generous to him in a number of ways, even to the point of securing him brief, part-time appointments following upon his removal from the Conservatoire. Their association had nevertheless reached a tenuous stage at the time of Franck's death only a few years later. Accepting the fact that he could well have been allowed to continue with his studies, it is still out of the question that Fumet would have developed into a loyal member of the band. His outlook was too experimental to have fitted in with the musical aspirations of the circle, while its moral tone would have struck him as depressingly orthodox. Not that he continued to exhibit the customary left-wing leanings towards agnosticism. Once he had got over his first flush of revolutionary ardour, he was on the contrary notable for the enthusiasm he invested in religion. Alchemy, spiritualism and the occult also came to figure as his province during the nineties, and he even went as far as to devise a cabbalistic religion of his own, based on the teachings of the great heretics. This phase of his life bears a curious resemblance to Satie's *Rose-Croix* period (1890–8), during which he came under the spell of the eccentric theologian, Sâr Peladan, and wrote his moving *Messe des Pauvres*. It should not be forgotten, either, that the English Pre-Raphaelites were just beginning to add to the climate of fetishism in France. Fumet's dabblings were in all probability a reflection of what he had learnt from these cults. The link with Satie was due to more prosaic circumstances, however, and can be traced to the fact that both composers were reduced to seeking a living in popular music.

Stanislas Fumet—in a memoir entitled *La Poesie à travers les arts* published in 1954—has claimed that it was his father who influenced Satie and not, as might have been considered more likely, the other way round. Unquestionably, it was Fumet who first occupied a position as pianist at the Chat Noir, the Montmartre night-club at which the famous shadow-plays were performed, making it possible that the claim is just, at least as far as it relates to the café-concert adventure. Both men were clearly attracted to the gay, flip styles in vogue in the cabarets and music-halls of the city, though it is prudent to recall William Austin's submission that the moving spirit behind both their enthusiasms could have been Chabrier. The tendency to experiment with chords of the seventh and ninth, and to engage in quasi-popular improvisation, is plainly apparent in the work of Franck's older friend. It can also be traced in the earliest compositions of Debussy, who had quit the Conservatoire for Rome in the same year as Fumet's entry to the institution. The composer's son nevertheless insists that it was Dynam-Victor's interest in dissonance that impelled Satie to write in the fashion of the *Sarabandes* and *Gnossiennes*. Priorities of this kind are notoriously difficult to establish with accuracy. For instance, part of the inspiration underlying the latter group of pieces undoubtedly came from the Exposition Universelle of 1889, the angular fourths, frequent grace-notes and modified scale progressions seeming to constitute obvious links with the *gamelang* style. But it is true that plenty of similarities exist between the work of Satie and Fumet, quite apart from their common preference for 'chansonnier' harmonies. A glance at their respective checklists shows that each wrote a sizeable number of religious works, and these help confirm that each was endeavouring to invent an unaffectedly archaic mode of expression. It is instructive, for example, to compare Satie's *Messe des Pauvres* with the two Masses which Fumet wrote in the year 1914; the *Messe Martiale* for four-part choir and organ and the *Messe du Christ Roi*, to which children's voices were added. The former composer's fondness for writing pieces in groups of three, in accordance with the idea of the Trinity, likewise recurs in the latter's *Triptyque Symphonique* (1913–14) and *Trois Ames* (1915). The last-named is a set of three orchestral tone-poems celebrating earth, fire and water, and proposes itself as a typical expression of Fumet's mystical interests.

Probably the reason why so little was heard of the composer during the period when Satie and Debussy were enjoying their greatest notoriety was that he had begun to suffer a marked creative lull. We know that Satie allowed himself to be caught up in the swirl of café society, not returning to his religious preoccupations until the very end of his life and then only from a safe distance. Fumet, on the other hand, seems to have undergone a long religious crisis following his escape from the Chat Noir, a crisis that culminated in attempted suicide. It was the Catholic theologian Léon Bloy who enabled him to recover his self-esteem, and from the middle of the 1890s onwards Fumet cast himself in the role of a subdued Catholic convert. Whether this acceptance of an orthodox religion contributed significantly to the neglect into which his musical interests had fallen is something that cannot easily be determined. Much of the evidence suggests that the composer was also going through a preliminary stage of the *Wanderlust*, thinking out ways of seeking his fortune abroad. The succeeding years in fact took him to South America, where he did a variety of casual jobs and indulged in long, Whitmanesque meditations. The seaports appealed to him very strongly, and it was at one of these that he met and married a simple Protestant girl whom he later converted to Catholicism. In due course, they returned to Europe, taking up residence at a tiny village in the Pyrenees to which they had been attracted by the ancient church. Fumet never renounced his enthusiasm for church music, and it was given scope for development when he got himself appointed choirmaster at the famous Oratorian College of Juilly in 1897. The stability which he derived from this appointment was enhanced by a transfer to the Parisian church of St Anne's in 1910, at which he continued as Maître de Chappelle for the last thirty-nine years of his life. It seems odd to think that he was still alive and at work after the Second World War, yet the fact is that many of his best works date from that period, in particular the impressive Requiem (1948).

There can be no doubt that Fumet, for all his anarchist zeal, was basically a kind and affectionate man. As with many another high-spirited individual, the violent moods of his youth gave way to a benign and tolerant old age, leaving him a rich and varied life to look back on. His career, viewed in its non-musical aspects, illustrates the typical intellectual's progress 'from toreador to sacred cow'. To attempt an assessment of his standing as a composer would be more difficult, and perhaps a little premature, for most of his works remain unpublished and are exceedingly elusive of access. Aside from the religious compositions, which aim at a simple purity and candour, he wrote a String Quartet and two Trios; six études and a collection of salon pieces for the piano; and a choicely imponderable array of rhapsodies for the orchestra. Included among the last-named are some dance-movements, like the *Tourbillon* (1942) and *Hiératique* (1943), and a number of visionary tone-poems with queer titles. It is tempting to recognize anticipations of Messiaen in such works as *Notre Mirage, Notre Douleur* (1920–30), *Le Sommeil d'Adam* (1935), and *La Prison Glorifée* (1943). That Fumet, too, was fascinated by a pantheistic explanation of the universe is suggested by his early *Messe des Oiseaux* for women's choir and organ (1928). The style displayed in most of these offerings has been described as 'anachronistic modernist'—which is only another way of saying that the composer was trying to adapt his zest for plainchant to the discoveries of the post-Wagnerian world. His love of chromatics marks him out as a faithful follower of both Franck and Wagner, yet there is a constant striving for concision in his music which cannot be attributed to either influence. It is more like the Satiean habit of *dépouillement*, but differs in not being quite so ruthless.

Clearly, not all of Franck's associates experienced the *avant-garde* urges of Fumet, but it is worth pointing out that he was not alone in his feelings. Compared with d'Indy's generation, the later pupils strike us as more audacious, not merely in their musical thinking, but in the stance which they adopted towards their art. This may be construed as a reaction against the stiff-necked attitudes prevalent during the earliest days of the Republic, when art and anarchy had not been encouraged to mix. The new spirit was what led eventually to the decadence of the *fin-de-siècle*—a phenomenon that found expression in music no less surely than in the sister arts. In one respect at least, Franck's last pupils were resolutely unlike those he had taught in his prime. They had grown up alongside the founders of the modern movement. Accordingly, they were influenced, not only by Wagnerian theories, but by the forces of symbolism and impressionism. It is no accident that Debussy became both the friend and classmate of many. The naturalistic outlook, so much reviled during the heyday of Zola and his followers, was again proving very much more widespread now that its tenets had become officially recognized. It would consequently be wrong to proceed on the assumption that those disciples who joined Franck in the final decade of his life behaved in an entirely similar fashion to their predecessors. By and large, they can be shown to have more in common with the musicians of our own day, especially in the attitude which they took up towards the question of artistic freedom. Personally sympathetic to Franck though they may have been, there was hardly one among them who did not move further away from Franckist principles than, let us say, Duparc or Castillon had done. We have already noticed how confidently Fumet was able to anticipate certain twentieth-century trends, and it may only have been Lekeu's early death which prevented him from playing a comparable role. It is true that Holmès remained an unabashed romantic, but she was older than the others and her pose had been an anachronism from the beginning. What finally distinguished the younger members of the circle was their tendency to outlive the ideas of their teacher.

A pupil who survived to witness the Second World War, and hence to avail himself of the modern musical temper, was the Austro-Italian composer, Sylvio Lazzari. One of the least conspicuous of Franck's little band, he invites comparison with d'Indy on account of his mountaineering background and obsession with folk-song, yet the two musicians could scarcely have been more unalike in their temperaments. A lanky and pliable Southerner, whose enormous height tended to distinguish him from any company with whom he threw in his lot, Lazzari was born at Bolzano (then known as Botzen) on the last day of 1857, and his childhood was spent amid unrelievedly provincial surroundings. Though evidently very musical, he was denied an artistic career, his parents insisting upon him going to the university to study law instead. This he was able to do at Innsbruck, where his gangling appearance and seafaring interests often caused him to be mistaken for a Breton sailor. A hard worker, both at his vocation and his hobbies, he managed to retain his hold on music while at the same time passing all of his law examinations. Assured of his doctorate, he even placed himself under a number of different masters in Munich and Vienna. These combined to equip him with such an efficient technical grounding that he had no difficulty in being admitted to the Paris Conservatoire in 1883. Before this, however, he was obliged to seek out his parents' consent to what was a costly switch in his ambitions. While awaiting their approval, he visited England—in further pursuit of his maritime fancies—and doubtless acquired a taste of that broader experience which his upbringing had withheld from him. On his return to France, it was Gounod who helped him to fulfil his musical intentions by pleading his case before the Conservatoire authorities. Always charitable in his sponsorship of the young, the composer of *Faust* was determined that such creative potential should not be allowed to go to waste.

Actually, he need hardly have worried himself on that score, since there was little enough that any academy could teach his protégé. Music came very easily indeed to Lazzari—so much so that he would already have been capable of making his way as a fully-fledged composer. It was only experience of the concert world that he lacked, and the presence in his class of such luminaries as Dukas and Debussy hinted that it might not be long before he completed his equipment. Unfortunately, a tactical sense was the one quality he never succeeded in acquiring, so that his works rarely made the impact they might have done. As far as fluency went, he had nothing to fear from the competition of his classmates, but somehow he failed to secure any of the attention which the public willingly bestowed upon them. Perhaps it was the case that, like Fauré and Guy Ropartz, he was a shade too facile to be arresting. More probably, it was his total unawareness of guile as a weapon that caused him to slip behind his contemporaries whenever prospects seemed about to open up. Since he was placed under Guiraud on entry to the Conservatoire, his meeting with Franck did not come about until later. When it took place, there was no suggestion of any deep involvement on either side. César certainly formed a high opinion of the young man's abilities, and one of the things that startled him into a 'shock of recognition' was the String Quartet which he was shown in 1888. This, it will be remembered, was more than two years before the great D major was due to appear. It says much for Lazzari's progressivism that he was able to answer the Société Nationale's call for a French tradition of chamber music with a promptness and imagination shown by few of his elders. Not content with a single work, he went on to write a Sonata for Violin and Piano in 1894. Unlike the Quartet, this was intended to emulate rather than anticipate the work of his teacher and must be judged in relation to Franck's famous A major Sonata. Ysaÿe and Pugno—both of whom maintained particularly cordial sentiments towards Lazzari and his ideas—were again responsible for championing it on the concert platform. This sonata, together with a Piano Trio dating from about the same time, brought the composer's name before a wider European public.

Like most musicians of his period, however, Lazzari found himself much less interested in the concert hall than in the opera house. His earliest stage work had been the music for a pantomime entitled *Lulu*, an entertainment which had been shown to the public in 1887. This earned the composer a brief vacation in his beloved Brittany, and it was while he was there that he decided on the subject of his first opera, *Armor*, a romance of the Round Table that recalls Chausson's troublesome score. In much the same fashion as his predecessor—though without a trace of the same crucifying effort—Lazzari used this venture as a means of exorcising the ghost of Wagner, with whose music he had become predictably infatuated. Its completion left him free to respond to other and more up-to-date currents. The opera was given its première at the Landestheater in Prague, on 7 November 1898, being thereafter revived at Hamburg in 1900 and Lyon in 1905. By far the most popular number turned out to be the Prélude, a delicate exercise in tonal values which was abstracted to form a concert-piece in its own right. As in the case of Wagner's expressive preambles, it contains a beautifully clear statement of the principal leit-motifs, the mysterious theme of the Korriganes being the first to be heard. This is followed by the sea motif, which rises gradually and impressively from the basses to take in woodwind and upper strings. Finally, everything gives way to a stirring announcement of the chevalier Armor's theme by the brass. The effect of the whole prelude is to create a mood which is at the same time sombre and compelling. It is a pity that the opera itself seems too derivative to merit inclusion in the modern repertory. Nevertheless, it was a useful work for Lazzari to have written, since it gave him valuable experience in working on a sizeable scale (there are three long acts built around a libretto by Jaubert) and a foretaste of the difficulties he would later run up against in *La Lépreuse*. It could also be said to have confirmed the composer in his preference for the *tragédie de la mer*.

The most ambitious of all Lazzari's works for the stage was unhappily the occasion of such bitter controversy that he had to wait more than ten years before seeing it performed. To the ordinary musician, an opera on the theme of leprosy might have seemed a thoroughly foolhardy project, and a ready-made vehicle for keeping people away from the box-office. But Lazzari was not an ordinary musician. He regarded it as a challenge to his moral idealism. The inspiration behind the work came from an article by the literary critic, Jules Lemaître, in praise of a poem which had recently appeared from the pen of Henri Bataille. This poem was really a species of ballad in which the hopeless love of a young man for a leper-woman is depicted. The phrases of the review which caught Lazzari's attention were those in which the critic singled out the tragic simplicity of the situation:

> . . . avoir découvert un poème plus naïf que les plus naïves ballades anonymes . . . avec des choses douces et tragiques, simples et éternelles comme si M. Henri Bataille était un inconnu chanteur de la Bretagne la plus légendaire.*

Having gone on to read Bataille's verses, the composer of *Armor* immediately set about getting permission to use them as the basis for a new opera. He had taken out naturalization in 1896, and once he had completed his score his intention was to have the work put on at the Opéra-Comique. At first, all went well, the opera being accepted without adverse comment. When it came to mounting it, however, dissident voices began to make themselves heard. Civic leaders complained that the subject was degrading and distasteful, while questions were eventually asked in the Chamber of Deputies. The upshot was that performance was withheld, and Lazzari himself embroiled in a series of discreditable encounters. The real motives behind the dispute are not easy to identify. Public outrage apart, there are some grounds for believing that other composers set to work to sabotage *La Lépreuse*; at any rate Lazzari became the victim of a certain amount of financial double-dealing.

*. . . to have discovered a poem more simple than the simplest anonymous ballads . . . with things sweet and tragic, elemental and eternal, as if M. Henri Bataille were some unknown, legendary Breton songster.

In cases of this kind, the public is often the best judge of whether or not to proceed. Unluckily for Lazzari, no opportunity was given for them to render their verdict, and he had to bide his time until the year 1912 before the authorities relented. By then society had grown more permissive, and some of the impact of the work was no doubt lessened. Certainly the warm response it secured at that late date could scarcely have compensated the composer for the disappointment he must have felt at its earlier rejection. The plot of *La Lépreuse* is indeed very simple. It tells the story of a young man named Ervoanik and his love for the beautiful Aliette. In Act I we are shown the hero seeking out his parents' permission to marry, only to learn from them that his beloved is actually the daughter of a leper. Shocked though he is at the news, it does little to weaken his attachment, which soon becomes a matter of acutest consternation to his parents. Matelinn, the boy's father, forbids the marriage in the most violent terms, while his mother Maria takes refuge in tears. Later on, she reconciles herself to the idea, and suggests to the couple that they should repair to a colony where they may obtain absolution. Throughout this act, Lazzari proves himself to be a master of characterization and atmosphere. The contrast between Matelinn's healthy, peasant home, and the terrible shadow which lurks over his son, could not have been more skilfully achieved. Moreover, the folk idiom in which so much of the music is couched seems the perfect vehicle for expressing the emotions of the drama. The song 'Rien ne peut me consoler' illustrates the composer's uncanny ability to extract the essence of a situation without running the risk of sentimentality.

Act II of the opera carries the audience into the house of Aliette and her mother, Tili. The last-named character is hideously diseased without realizing the legacy she has bequeathed to her daughter. Meanwhile, Aliette herself has an acute premonition of her fate, hoping only to ally herself with the faithful Ervoanik in a chaste and merciful companionship. The temptations of the situation prove too much, however, and the mother's loose talk is sufficient to shatter their resolve. In a melancholy berceuse— 'Ferme tes yeux tout doux!'—Aliette sings her beloved to sleep. When he awakes, she forces him to drink from a glass which she has pressed to her lips, ensuring that he shares in all that is to befall her. The action of Act III then concerns Ervoanik's discovery of his malaise, and his pitiable farewell to Matelinn and Maria. The lament which he sings on leaving home, just before seeking out the Pardon of Folgoat, is possibly Lazzari's finest operatic moment. 'Voyez ces gens qui vous regardent,' he sighs, 'Ils pleurent, puis petit à petit ils m'oublièrent; mais vous, ma mère, vous pleurez toujours . . .' The ending of the opera is equally moving, if a trifle too stagey in conception. To witness the two lovers forsaking the world to enter 'la maison blanche'— where misery alone awaits them—is to re-invite some of that histrionic agony which accompanies Sidney Carton's famous

Ex. 21

Sylvio Lazzari: Alliette's Lullaby from Act II "La Lépreuse"

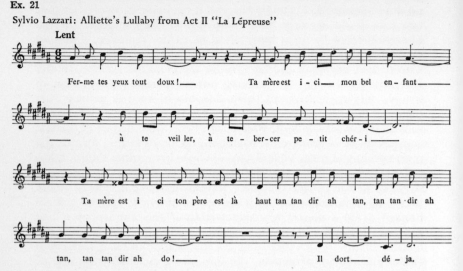

speech from *A Tale of Two Cities*, and it is small wonder that audiences responded to the scene with relish. But it is worth emphasizing that several of the greatest contemporary musicians also expressed their liking. Arthur Honegger, for example, paid handsome tribute by saying:

> La musique de cet ouvrage est tout entière sentie, pensée, exprimée avec l'honnetête d'un artiste noble, pour qui l'art musical, même a la scène, reste la religion à servir . . . La scene pathétique entre la mère et le fils, au troisième acte, est certainement une des plus belles pages dont puisse s'en-orgueillir la musique dramatique francaise.*

Yet this was in 1943, only a year before Lazzari's death at the age of eighty-five, so that half a lifetime elapsed between the work's première and its ultimate critical acclaim.

* The music of this work is wholly and entirely feeling and thought, expressed with the sincerity of a noble artist, since in respect of the musical aesthetic, the drama itself remains the religion to be served . . . The pathetic scene between mother and son, in Act III, is surely one of the most beautiful, one of the most powerfully elated pages in French opera.

Difficulties of a less acrimonious nature continued to hamper the composer in his struggle towards success amid foreign operatic circles. The rarely-heard *Le Sauteriot*—which was based on an old Lithuanian legend—was created at Chicago in January 1918, moving on to New York a few months later and finally coming home to rest at the Opéra-Comique in 1920. The music of this opera maintains the high level set by *La Lépreuse*. Its neglect can be attributed to a very uneven libretto by the German poet, Keyserling. Though not as harrowing a story as its predecessor, it deals with the same theme of martyrdom, this time describing the ordeals of a young woman who offers up her life to the Virgin to save someone who has maltreated her. Another post-war theatrical venture of Lazzari's was the drama, *Melaenis*, which took the form of an adaptation of Louis Bouilhet's poem by Georges Spitzmuller. It was first given at Mulhouse in 1927, and as far as is known has never been put on in the capital. Far more of a stir attended the presentation at the Opéra of the sensational *La Tour de Feu* in 1928. This astonishing work gave full reign to the composer's obsession with the sea, and should be related to d'Indy's *L'Etranger* which it post-dated by a quarter of a century. The plot recounts the trials of a lighthouse-keeper off the coast of Cornwall, and the manner in which he wreaks vengeance on his fiancée and her lover. Briefly, the situation is that Yves, the hero, finds himself deserted by the fickle Naic, a country girl who has allowed herself to be carried away, Zerlina-fashion, by a visiting seigneur. When he learns that the ship in which they are travelling has to pass through his channel, he decides to mislead the crew into steering it off course. Covering up the light of his tower, Yves witnesses the craft splinter and plunge to the bottom of the ocean. Horrified by what his jealousy has caused him to do, the keeper turns up his furnace and immolates himself in his blazing tower. It is fascinating to recall that this was the first opera ever to make use of cinematic effects on the stage. One can imagine the response aroused by the concluding scene, especially among those older opera-goers to whom the sight of Brunnhilde riding into the flames had been the ultimate in spectacle.

As with his previous works, there was much in *La Tour de Feu* which proclaimed Lazzari's attachment to folk-song. The popular chorus in Act I of the opera fell back upon his customary Breton sources, while certain of the love lyrics betrayed a similar connection. This being the case, it has surprised many writers to discover what variety the composer was capable of in his orchestral and vocal compositions. A *Rapsodie Espagnole* reveals that he had no difficulty in following Lalo and Chabrier into other regions of Europe, while among the tone-poems which he left is a discreetly

impressionist portrait of the Adriatic. The solo player will find
enough of interest in the Fantasy for Violin and Orchestra, and in
the brilliant *Concertstück* for piano. Perhaps the composer's most
remarkable orchestral work, however, is the piece entitled *Effet de
Nuit* which he wrote in 1904. This was inspired by the fourth of
Verlaine's 'Eaux fortes'. The lines, it will be remembered, describe
a platoon of halberdiers crossing a murky, rain-sodden plain during
the dead of night, their pikes gleaming against the livid faces of
their prisoners.* Along with Mallarmé's 'Le Guignon', it is one of
the most terrifying poems in modern French literature. Lazzari's
treatment is as brief and pungent as the original, and must be put
down as a remarkable contribution to the genre created by his
countrymen Debussy and Ravel. Surprisingly, Verlaine made a
great appeal to this unsophisticated admirer of the sea and the
countryside. His interest in the art of the *mélodie* led him to set
more than fifty poems by Verlaine, Bataille, Maeterlinck and
Klingsor, comprising a treasury of song it would be criminal to
neglect. If present critics of French music have nothing more
worth while to do, they would be conferring an important benefit
on listeners by making better known the melodies of Lazzari and
Koechlin, two of the finest exponents of this form since the death
of Fauré.[1]

The remaining facts of this gifted man's career need not detain
us long. He composed a variety of other music in response to the
demands of literature, most notably a symphonic poem on the
theme of *Ophélie* and some incidental music for Goethe's *Faust*.
The writer, Emma Klingfield, assisted him to make a German
translation of *La Lépreuse*, and the opera was eventually mounted
in that country under the title, *Die Ausgestossene*. His interest in
chamber music waned a little after its auspicious beginning, but he
nevertheless managed to add to his corpus with a splendid Octet.
Otherwise, he is best remembered for a mammoth symphony
dating from the year 1907. It is pertinent to observe that this
shows several traces of Franck's influence. After he had fallen into
the habit of visiting the older man at his organ class in the Conservatoire, Lazzari began to look eagerly to him for advice of all
sorts. Franck refused to give him lessons in the strict sense of the
term, believing him to be too far advanced to require it. What he
did do, however, was to coach the young man in the general

---

[1] Readers wishing to sample the quality of Lazzari's songs might do
well to begin with such superior specimens as 'Les Yeux', 'Le Cavalier
d'Olmedo', 'Berceuse Triste' and 'Le Chien de Jean Nivelle'.

* Then, with three pale barefoot prisoners, two hundred and twenty-
five halberdiers were on the march, their pikes gleaming like harrow-
teeth against the slanting lances of the rain.

principles of composition, and it is these principles which are most in evidence in the latter's symphony. A truly cyclical work, it followed the pattern set by Franck's own D minor work by combining the Scherzo and Lento in one long movement. As we should expect, the orchestration is highly competent throughout, and many of the themes possess grace in addition to dramatic propriety. Lazzari's last years were spent in a beautiful villa which he occupied at Suresnes, overlooking the Bois de Boulogne. Here he was able to enjoy a quiet retreat from the world which had so ill-used his talents, while at the same time being privileged to take in the vast panorama of Paris which presented itself to his gaze. He died on the 11 June 1944, a few days after the Allied forces had disembarked on the beaches of Normandy.

XI

From disciple to missionary

Somewhere towards the end of the nineteenth century, French musicians succeeded in crossing that strait which separates the romantic from the modern period, and one mark of their transit is to be found in the inclination they showed to revise the institutional basis of their thought. To a certain extent, this reflected the need for new standards, for a set of guide rules by which to judge the more freakish experiments of the time, but it also signalled a desire for conservation, an impulse to re-explore those traditions of knowledge which had been handed down from earlier times. The setting up of the Schola Cantorum, six years after the death of César Franck, must be interpreted in the light of this situation, since the institution proved among the first to look both backwards and forwards in its search for a modified musical aesthetic. Though its fame was to stem from its associations with d'Indyism, it should be recognized that the driving force behind the Schola lay in its concern with the polyphonic masters and its determination to re-assert those choral values which other conservatories had neglected to the point of atrophy. It would be a mistake, for instance, to think that it began life as a bricks-and-mortar edifice devoted to the education of young musicians. Long before settling on that aim, the school's founders had sought refuge in a choral society from which the first sparks of the institutional idea were struck. This society was the brain-child of Charles Bordes, whose enthusiasm for the strict contrapuntal composers of the sixteenth century was one of the more heartening features of the scene at the time of Franck's unexpected departure.

Bordes had been born at Vouvray-sur-Loire in 1863, and he was still a young man on taking up his duties as organist and choirmaster of the church of Nogent-sur-Marne in the provinces. His success in this post owed much to the interest he took in early

music, and in particular to the researches into Basque folk lore for
which he became famous. It was his scholarly zeal that persuaded
the authorities to offer him a move to the capital, an opportunity
he lost no time in grasping. After spending only three years (1887–
90) at his first church, he was hence able to take his place as
musical helmsman of Saint-Gervais. From there he launched the
crusade that was to culminate in the establishment of the Schola,
and incidentally helped to confer a new dimension upon his
nation's musical life. At the beginning, progress was slow, since
few musicians or clerics had any but the most superficial notion
of what was at stake. In a sense, Bordes was fortunate in having
enlisted the support of his curé, de Bussy, without whose willingness to provide rehearsal time he would not have got very far. As
it turned out, the young choirmaster was also able to interest two
or three students from the Conservatoire, who gladly did a little
recruiting on his behalf. When he had summoned a nucleus of
choristers, he set about using his church as a venue for the promotion of such obscure masters as Josquin, Lassus, Vittoria and
Palestrina. It was with the Italian composers that Bordes discovered a profound kinship, and on 26 March 1891, he secured the
first of his many triumphs in attracting a large crowd to hear
Palestrina's Stabat Mater. The Miserere of Allegri was another
masterwork that began to appear on his programmes. Having
started with a mere twenty-five singers, the choir now exhibited
signs of growth, with the result that the maestro conceived the
idea of a split. One half of the group was henceforth conducted by
Tiersot, leaving the remainder under the control of their founder.
Later, d'Indy regularly deputised as assistant, giving some fifty
concerts in the space of a few short years. Bordes himself retained
the bulk of the work, however, and it was due to his energy that
the group eventually achieved immortality as the Chanteurs de
Saint-Gervais.

The next step was to create a proper organ of publicity capable
of spreading the society's aims. On the 6 June 1894, a meeting was
held at Saint-Gervais, at which a number of eminent musicians
were present. Notre Dame was represented by Perruchot, and
Saint Francois-Xavier by the Abbé Chappuy. This meeting was in
effect the beginning of the Schola, for during it the decision was
taken to establish what was laboriously described as La Société de
Propagande pour la Divulgation des Chefs-d'Oeuvres Religieux.
Naturally, the title was found to be too long, and it was duly
shortened to Schola Cantorum. An assembly was held in December
of the same year for the purpose of ratifying a constitution, but it
was two further years before the society could afford premises, and
even then great difficulties were encountered. Bordes jumped the

gun by negotiating for a site at the junction of the Rue Stanislas and the Boulevard Montparnasse, though at the time there were only thirty-seven francs and fifty centimes in the society's funds! As a result of calling on a number of subscribers—treating the project as if it were a campaign for one of the religious orders—the buildings were eventually commandeered, and courses in choral subjects were planned for the following October. A meagre ten pupils made up the school's first entry, but these rose to twenty-one by the commencement of the second year. Alexandre Guilmant took over the organ class which was added to the curriculum, leaving d'Indy to supervise new courses in counterpoint and composition. Meanwhile, Bordes himself became responsible for developing the vocal side. A commendable spirit of dedication soon communicated itself to staff and students, causing visits to Solesmes and other Gregorian centres to be made. Shortly afterwards, the faculty was joined by Edouard Risler, the distinguished pianist, and by the always versatile Guy Ropartz. Even at this point, however, setbacks tended to emerge. One of the most annoying was a change of incumbent at Saint-Gervais, for de Bussy's successor proved himself to be a man of brutally limited sympathies. (Among his more barbarous acts was to encourage the playing of Massenet's *Thaïs* during liturgical intermissions!) Yet none of this prevented the Chanteurs from continuing with their aims; neither was there any check on the publication of their journal, *La Tribune*.

Bordes's final coup was achieved by taking over the model church of Saint-Julien—which had been erected as part of the 1900 Exposition Universelle—and using it to give daily hearings of the old masters. These were given between the hours of three and six, with short breaks to mark the beginning and ending of each series. It is estimated that sixty thousand people attended, many of whom were impelled to make modest contributions to the cause. By means of their help, and a generous donation from the d'Indy family, the society was able to move its headquarters to the present building in the Rue Saint-Jacques. This was an historic locale in that it had once been occupied by a group of English Benedictine nuns. James II had even been buried near by, though his body had been missing since the time of the Revolution. Observers thought it apt that the Schola should have arisen on such warring ground, and no one could deny that a certain fitness hung over d'Indy's inaugural remarks. The effect of the move was to accelerate the Schola's progress towards becoming a large and powerful educational concern. A new concert hall, housing an organ and containing a seating capacity of five hundred, was built on the site of the old priory, and this enabled the staff to plan student recitals on a scale which would have been impossible before. Additional professors were appointed—including Louis de Serres for chamber music and ensemble—and the intake grew until it passed the hundred mark. By that time, much effort had been put into standardizing the curricula, so that a sense of the institution's separate identity was becoming clearly visible.

The aims and objects of the Schola were first laid down by d'Indy himself in his opening address as Director. His theme on that occasion was the need to view music as an art and not merely a craft. It was an earnest proclamation in which he indulged, but one that seemed long overdue in the light of France's persistently professional approach. What he was saying, in effect, was that the Schola did not intend to imitate other schools by flouting the aesthetic functions of music. It was not to be just another training ground for virtuosi or guild for music teachers. On the contrary, the emphasis would fall on intellectual considerations, with full recognition attaching to vision and design. Today, we are apt to think of d'Indy's system as just that—a collection of rules and nothing more. Yet his intention was to make it something much wider. For example, he was firm in his advocacy of historical studies—a fact which the Cours de Composition Musicale plainly corroborates—and not much support for the idea of specialization can be extracted from his writings. His artistic bias is discernible in the Schola's familial pretensions, which seem scarcely less pronounced then those of the Franck circle itself. Unlike the pupils at the Conservatoire, d'Indy's charges looked to the institution to provide spiritual nourishment. Disciples in all but name, they addressed their Director as 'Master' and not simply as administrative head. Fortified by his austere companionship, they needed no prompting to embrace the doctrine of art as the chief love of their lives. But there was still a distinction arising out of the different personality cult which emerged. Franck's peculiar virtues had sprung from humility, with the result that his pupils developed a reverent and self-effacing streak. By comparison, the ideals of d'Indyism were more militant, being an expression of the sterner moods to which its leader committed himself. Since it was also more prone to base itself on definite musical principles, the outlook at the Schola became the property of a less homogeneous group of followers. Martin Cooper has rightly drawn attention to the regional spread which attached to d'Indy's pupils, but it is no less true to say that they exhibited something of an internationalist appearance. At least, visitors from overseas helped to swell the ranks— both of the faculty and the student body—protecting the institution from that parochialism which had threatened its godparents.

Restrictions in force at the Conservatoire were constantly making it difficult for pupils of the wrong age or nationality to enter. The

Schola, on the contrary, dispensed with an age-limit, and made entry dependent only on an examination which applicants could sit in October of each year. Once admitted, a pupil found himself compelled to study a wide variety of subjects. For instance, vocal ensemble was incumbent on all students and not merely those who had forsaken instrumental training. Form and orchestration were also inescapable, while every string player was put through a special course in chamber music. Regular participation in concerts was encouraged, without any sanction being given to careerism. On successful completion of Part I, the student proceeded to the *deuxième degré* or *cours supérieur*. At the end of three years, he was granted a Diploma which came in three different classes, the terminology being *assez bien*, *bien* and *très bien*. (It will be recalled that Erik Satie, who passed out of the Schola in 1908, was among those to have been honoured by being placed in the last and highest category.) It was by means of these rigid standards that d'Indy was able to attract a varied and talented clientèle, a surprising number of whom found it a relief to be freed from the *prima donna* urges which other institutions had done so much to promote. By 1905, there were three hundred pupils enrolled at the school. This figure rose to four hundred in 1912 and five hundred in 1924. However, shortly before the second of these dates a number of calamities occurred which had the effect of depriving the institution of a portion of its leadership. The most stunning of these was the unexpected death of Bordes in November 1909, at the tragically early age of forty-six. When Guilmant followed him to the grave in March 1911, it looked as if fate had been unkind after all. Yet one cannot help feeling glad that it was not d'Indy who had been plucked from his pupils' midst, for nothing could then have saved the Schola from decay. As it turned out, the great man was to be spared for a further two decades, during which time his pre-eminence as a teacher, already unquestioned as a result of his assumption of the Directorship, went on to outstrip any that had been won by his rivals in other institutions, taking second place only to that which had been attained by Franck himself.

D'Indy, Bordes and Guilmant—these were the three pillars on whom the Schola had learned to rest. The passing of Guilmant was unfortunate, though hardly unexpected. He had been alive since 1837, and was by far the oldest of the triumvirate. A first-class organist, he had ranked among the successors of Benoist, yet his talents had remained those of a nineteenth-century musician. As a composer, he left a fair quantity of work for his own instrument, but will be better remembered for his scholarly *Ecole Classique de l'Orgue* and for the *Archives des Maîtres de l'Orgue* which he edited along with his colleague Pirro. The death of

Bordes, on the other hand, proved crippling to the imagination of all forward-looking minds. No one can say quite how he would have developed, for it is by no means sure that he would have confined himself to that species of composition called 'la fresque musicale'. Like the rich facets of his curiosity, his gifts were astonishingly varied. The humblest of prodigies, he had sought out the help of Franck when preparing that composer's Mass for Three Voices for a performance which was given in May 1890; though his original acquaintance with the master stretched back to those happy days at Quincy, when César had been immersed in the toddlings of his grandchildren and Bordes had presented himself as an eager boy of twenty. At that time, he was receiving lessons from the pianist Marmontel, without experiencing any ambition to become a virtuoso. What evidently attracted him to Franck was the spirit immanent in the great religious epics of the 1870s. It must be conceded straightaway, however, that Bordes never fell into the role of uncritical admirer. More of a purist in his approach to the choral heritage, the young man retained a sharp sense of his master's deficiencies, and he was not as inclined to hold his tongue as many of his fellow disciples. The portrait of Franck which he sketched in the *Courrier Musical* is hardly the most flattering to have been handed down to us. In it, the composer of *Rédemption* is revealed 'bellowing like a stag' at a group of novices, his 'expressive technique' hopelessly at variance with the spirit of the music.

Besieged by the volume of work he was made to undertake as conductor and administrator, Bordes rarely found himself free to indulge in composition. Yet the little he wrote thoroughly deserves to be rescued from obscurity. His thirty-three songs betray the influence of the symbolist movement, and may be thought of as the most advanced part of his production. They represent the obverse of the composer's antiquarian interests. Critics may have been led to expect traces of the Basque style to emerge in these melodies, but this does not prove to be the case. In choosing to set Verlaine rather than any of the folk-poets with whose work he was familiar, Bordes consciously ranged himself on the side of Fauré, Debussy and Chausson. His friend Tiersot refers to the spontaneity of expression and depth of tone which are apparent in many of the settings, at the same time deploring that they have not secured inclusion in the recitalist's repertory. As with Chausson, the songs were spread over the major part of their composer's career, spanning the years 1883 to 1908. Equally rarely heard in the concert hall are the brief orchestral works which Bordes found time to write. These do revert to an undisguised infatuation with the folk idiom, though of a somewhat more authentic kind than is evident in, say, Ravel. The Rhapsody on Basque Themes for piano and orchestra was composed at the behest of the Société Nationale, as was the Trumpet Fantasy which followed it. Both works are notable for their complex harmony and imaginative use of instrumental colour. In addition, there is a modest collection of chamber-works, including a *Basque Trio* and a *Suite Basque* for flute and string quartet. To complete the picture, choirs should not neglect to seek out Bordes's numerous motets, choruses and spiritual dialogues, of which the best is perhaps the moving 'Domine, puer mens jacet'. From the more scholarly angle, mention has already been made of the composer's editions for the French Ministry of Education, and his articles for La Tribune de Saint-Gervais. As important as either of these ventures was the Anthologie des Maîtres Religieux Primitifs which he produced in celebration of his polyphonic researches.

When all these things have been laid to his account, however, we are tempted to see Bordes's greatest achievement in still another light. This is the light shed by his unfinished opera, *Les Trois Vagues*, fragments of which lie open to inspection, the delight and despair of all musicians who examine them, at the Musée de l'Opéra in Paris. The idea for this amazing work came to the composer while he was on summer vacation in the little house at Bordagain, overlooking the bay of Saint-Jean-de-Luz, in the Basque country. It owed its inspiration to popular legend, though the story was largely self-generating. Sketches for the work—both musical and literary—first began to appear in 1892, and these seem to have given the composer an inordinate amount of trouble. Perhaps it was that he found it difficult to settle down to work in such a relaxed atmosphere, or else the constant interruptions caused him to lose heart. At all events, there was a period when the project looked like falling through. Gustav Samazeuilh, who knew the composer intimately and visited him in his white-cottaged retreat, implies that Bordes was not the most strenuous of workers outside of his official duties, that he was fond of toying with a score, 'à batons rompus', rather than really getting to grips with it. The fact is, however, that his health had never been good, and much of his life seems to have been spent warding off attacks of lethargy stemming from the surreptitious progress of his disease. Bordes nevertheless managed to complete enough of his opera to send specimens to his colleagues Kufferath and Guidé—the Directors of the Théâtre de la Monnaie—who were at once alert to its possibilities. A brief account of the plot should serve to explain their enthusiasm.

The work opens in the home of a Basque sandal-maker named Jean, who lives with his wife Maiten in a modest dwelling near the sea. In terms of geography, the setting is somewhere close to

Ciboure, that picturesque village on the waterfront which also happened to be the birthplace of Ravel. As the patient couple prepare to spend their evening together, it becomes apparent that all is not well between them. Jean has had a previous lover whose charms continue to torment him, while Maiten has already begun to vent her spite by behaving coldly. Gradually, we learn that Jean's inamorata was one of those hard, pixie-like creatures— part-woman and part-evil spirit—who can be found stalking the pages of romantic literature to such devastating effect. It has been suggested that Bordes based his characterization of her on Keats's *Lamia*. Whether or not this is so, the figure of Maya exhibits most of the cruel and implacable qualities we associate with that serpentine lady. The action of Act I is concerned to illustrate the power she wields over Jean, and presents her arriving at the cottage in the guise of an old friend. She is accompanied by a young pelota player named Gracien, who proposes making up a foursome to visit the village of Elizondo in the interior. There it appears that Maya's father—a dignified old gentleman called Récalt—plans to hold a fête to celebrate the feast of St Michel. At first, Maiten opposes the plan, suspecting that something evil is afoot. Jean, sensing his wife's anxieties, then assumes responsibility for refusing the invitation, hoping to banish all his old longings by a return to work. When evening falls, however, Maya returns on her own, cunningly waiting until Maiten has retired. As may be imagined, she immediately weakens Jean's resolve by her seductive entreaties, throwing her long arms round his neck and whispering into his ear. Still the young husband resists her, forcing her to leave his house. But while he prays for serenity, Maya returns in the form of a witch with sea-shells glistening from her hair. To his astonishment, she dances to a mysterious tune—haunting, sensual, ferocious. Step by step, he permits himself to be enslaved again, while she tells him of her power to control everything, even the ocean whose waves beat and roar on the distant surf. Her most terrifying weapons, she confides, are three: a Wave of Milk, a Wave of Tears and a Wave of Blood. These are the fates that will pursue Jean if he rejects her. With this threat she disappears in a cloud of sulphur and incense, leaving her victim gazing into the fading gleams of the fire. After a moment's hesitation, he rouses himself and plunges out into the night.

The setting of Act II is in the village of Elizondo in Haute Navarre. Here Jean has arrived in search of his enchantress, only to find himself caught up in the local festivities. A tall Gothic church marks the centre of the village, while the surrounding mountains are ringed with tiny farms. Standing in the main square is an inn at which Maya and Gracien are preparing to put up. The latter is due to take part in the pelota championships which are to form an important feature of the celebrations. It should be explained, perhaps, that pelota is a Basque game, not unlike badminton, in which an object is struck against a wall by a curious, elliptical-shaped racket. Jean decides to challenge Gracien at this sport, which is to be judged by Récalt. On the morning of the fête, all is bustle and activity. The clergy wind solemnly through the streets, attired in their cassocks and surplices, while the village band strikes up with flute and tambourine. Nearer the arena, horses parade nobly and the players make their appearance dressed in red and blue berets. Once the mayor and his colleagues have seated themselves, a flag showing the slaying of the dragon is unfurled and the main event permitted to begin. In the course of the play, Jean unwittingly intercepts a glance from Maya which he realizes was meant for Gracien, with the result that the two men become enemies. The game over, the defeated Jean is left to sit and bemoan his lot amid the unhurried setting of the sun. As the sky darkens and the angelus softly tolls, he spies Maya and Gracien standing on high ground overlooking the fountain, their silhouettes locked in a passionate embrace. At this confirmation of his fears all he can do is bury his face in his hands and despair. One of the supreme moments of this second act lies in the song of loneliness which Jean is then made to sing. It is not long before a desire for action possesses him however, and things are quick to reach a violent dénouement. Jumping up to accost the pair, Jean grasps Gracien by the shoulders intending to wring the truth out of him, but only succeeds in pushing him backwards over the masonry and he falls to his death. Before dying, Gracien manages to signal his forgiveness, an act that cannot but add to the despair of his antagonist. While Jean ponders what to do next, two caribinieri arrest him and carry him off to jail. In the meantime, Maiten, who has formed a shrewd idea as to her husband's whereabouts, has made her way to the village, and the curtain falls on her as she waits to be admitted to his presence.

An interval now occurs before we proceed to Act III, which takes place alongside a fishing village near Zarauz. There, amid treacherous waters and in sight of the rock of Guetaria, Jean and Maiten have elected to make a more humble life for themselves following upon the former's release from prison. Dawn breaks over the sea, and the husband prepares to man his boats. As he goes to move away, his bedraggled wife pleads with him to stay at home, arguing that some catastrophe is bound to befall him. She has had a dream in which Jean is overcome by three terrible waves, and she recounts to him in vivid detail what she believes will happen. Unnerved though he is by her prophecies, Jean will not desist from embarking on his day's work. This leaves Maiten with no alternative but to accompany him, and she thereupon resolves that when the waves appear she will fling herself in their path hoping her sacrifice will propitiate whoever has threatened them. In his portrayal of this scene, Bordes goes far towards adopting the Wagnerian leit-motif technique, using a theme of renunciation to symbolize the renewal of love which takes place. United by their pledge once more, the husband and wife make out to sea where they are immediately assaulted by an enormous white wave. As it continually seeks to submerge their craft, the couple are horrified to hear a chorus of *lamias* singing eerily in the background, like the sirens in Homer's *Odyssey*. Surviving this ordeal, they are next confronted by a curious mirage, the colours of which deepen from a pale violet to a rich, umbrageous purple. This too is accompanied by voices, but not those of the sirens. Instead, reminiscences of the final quarrel between Jean and Gracien are heard, with the dead sportsman's voice rising in anguish:

Jean, pourquoi m'avoir tué? . . . J'avais droit à la vie, j'étais jeune, j'aimais. Je t'aimais tant . . .

Strange wails and lamentations surround his entreaties, only to pass gradually into silence. Jean and Maiten are now compelled to face the last of their trials, and they go forward to meet death in a spirit of fearless heroism. It appears in the guise of a hideous, broiling tempest which reddens the sea all around them, hurling their boat upside down and flinging them stranded and inanimate on the rock of Guetaria. As the sun's bright disc emerges once more, casting a natural glow on the ocean's surface, their forms can be seen laced together in a last, blissful embrace, while the morning fishermen chant quietly in peroration.

Even from such a cursory outline of the opera's plot, it becomes obvious that Bordes had invented the trappings of a great masterpiece. How sad it is to have to report that so little in the way of music was composed to put flesh on his skeleton. That the entire work was nearing completion in the composer's head seems certain from the accounts left by various friends. Samazeuilh had felt quite convinced that the work was all but finished—especially after listening to Bordes's evocative playing of excerpts from it at the piano—and was staggered to discover that the score had scarcely been added to during the final phase of the composer's life. He and d'Indy were among those most deeply upset at the paucity of the surviving sketches. Guy Ropartz and Raoul Laparra, who were also staunch admirers, were so aggrieved that they could not let the matter rest there, and set about getting permission from Bordes's brother Lucien to attempt a reconstruction of the opera. This permission was readily granted, but the task turned out to be far more arduous than any of them had supposed. It was not just a matter of filling in the stage-directions or transferring the instrumentation from the piano to the orchestra. Large tracts of the second and third acts appeared to be missing, and there were few guide lines to show how they had been conceived. In the end, the editors were faced with much the same problem as confronted Elgar's admirers when they looked into the prospect of salvaging that composer's Third Symphony. They could proceed, but only at the cost of so much conjecture as to forfeit any right to the composer's name. No one wanted to risk tarnishing Bordes's reputation in this fashion, and the decision was reluctantly taken to abandon the project. In December 1923, fourteen years after the composer's death, d'Indy accordingly asked for signatories to a document—which may still be seen at the Musée de l'Opéra—testifying that every effort had been made to reconstruct the work, but that expert opinion was against going on with it. The document bears the names of Paul Dukas, André Hallays, Paul Vidal, Pierre de Bréville, Gustav Samazeuilh, Pierre Lalo and d'Indy himself.

Looking back on *Les Trois Vagues* from a distance of over half a century, we cannot doubt that it promised a new dimension in French opera, one that was only partially filled by such masterpieces as *Pelléas et Mélisande* and *Ariane et Barbebleue*. Whether Bordes would have been able to give greater reign to the sensuous element than is displayed in either of these fine but reticent works is something we hardly have any right to debate. But of all the various post-Wagnerian composers who were assembled in Paris at the turn of the century, none was better fitted to supplement the ideals of Bayreuth with those specifically Latin qualities of warmth and passion which Nietzsche had ended by exalting. Unlike most other expressions of the Gallic spirit, *Les Trois Vagues* can claim to have been a truly meridional work, an exercise in sensation as much as cognition. The second act's tableau would have been as lively and colourful as anything by Bizet, while in the sublime mysteries of the third act listeners would surely have been treated to an experience quite beyond the range of the composer of *Carmen*. To attempt an evaluation of the finished sketches would be pointless, seeing that they would have to be judged in isolation. One can only draw attention to the psychological subtlety of the scenes between Jean and Maiten in the first act; the meditative character of the soliloquies in which the former indulges at moments of conscience; the deft employment of popular tunes to buttress the dramatic events at Elizondo; and the extraordinary serenity of the choral writing at the very end of the opera. These, and other felicitous touches too numerous to mention, establish beyond dispute the fact that the composer would have moved on, had he been spared for a few more years, to become something quite different from the musical Francis of Assisi for which so many of his contemporaries mistook him.

If this reluctant disciple of Franck did not altogether escape from the dilemma of trying to pursue two careers at once, the later d'Indy differed in refusing to acknowledge the dilemma's existence, mustering all his superior energy to the task of becoming a complete musician. Triumphantly successful as a teacher, he was able to look back on a formidable list of compositions and expressed not the slightest intention of breaking off his commitments as an artist. What we do observe during his Schola years, however, is a perceptible scaling down of creative effort, a moderating of his former expense of vision. This should not be taken to imply that composing finally became a mere pastime with him. On the contrary, his output over the period 1900–31 would have delighted many a less prolific figure. What concerns us is really a question of scope. Whereas in the 1880s and 1890s d'Indy kept aiming at the most imperious goals—*Fervaal* and the orchestral works were typical preoccupations—his instinct in later years was to build with smaller bricks, relying on the piano and chamber ensemble to provide him with much of his stimulus. There were, of course, a number of monumental works to come, among which *L'Etranger* and *La Légende de Saint-Christophe* are clearly of the utmost importance, but the former had been begun prior to the flowering of the Schola while the latter spread itself out over a fairly manageable expanse. These things apart, one cannot help feeling that the composer's pedagogical experiences led him further and further away from the idea of size for its own sake. Indeed, it is tempting to note a parallel between this aspect of d'Indy's development and the change which overtook Franck at about the same age. Both composers began austerely, wrote a succession of epic works in middle age, then reverted in their sixties to a philosophy that was much less blatantly agog. In this context, it is instructive to think of the younger man's Piano Sonata and Sextet as attempts to recapture the mood which had attached to his teacher's *Prélude, Choral et Fugue* and String Quartet.

Notwithstanding these similarities, there can be no doubt that d'Indy remained the most facile, if not the most prodigious, of the Franckists. Like Hindemith in our own day, he acquired the knack of pitching into his daily stint in such a way as to make composition as easy as breathing, and almost as natural. This is emphatically not to suggest that he relapsed into a species of French *Gebrauchsmusik*. His famous loftiness of temper would never have permitted such a retraction. Nor could it be claimed that he was unalive to the part inspiration must play in all creative endeavour. He was no Paul Valéry, sardonically throwing cold water on the visionary principle. It was simply the case that he refused to await the promptings of his daemon; he considered it less morbid and more practical to get on with the job unaided. Some may be inclined to point to a paradox here. Certainly it is easy to laugh at the picture of a stern and unyielding administrator flogging his students into activity at the same time as he is expatiating on the theme of 'ars longa, vita brevis'. But the paradox is more apparent than real, as anyone who has ever written a page of serious music will be bound to recognize. It is only latter-day thinking which is disposed to equate inspiration with languor, originality with an absence of models. Benjamin Britten, in a piece of advice he once offered to young musicians, insisted that it was folly to spend too much time worrying about originality; which he explained as a *post facto* quality more to be deduced from a score than to be invoked beforehand. Had he been invited to give an opinion on the subject, d'Indy would surely have upheld this conclusion. If the final verdict on his own work is inclined to stress a certain lack of individuality, it should be attributed, not so much to the element of objectivity in his theories, as to an unfortunate bleakness of temperament over which he had little control.

Before we go on to consider the whittling down process by which the composer sought to accommodate himself to the later ideals of his teacher, it is necessary to single out some of the highlights which continued to attach to his theatrical career. *Fervaal*, as we have seen, had won him rather more than a modest round of applause—though perhaps not in his own country. The second major opera which he was to write bid fair to unburden him of this limitation. *L'Etranger*, which the composer first presented at Brussels in January 1903 and then at the Paris Opéra eleven months later, is possibly the most gripping of all d'Indy's stage works. Not explicitly *verismo* in style, it nevertheless strikes a far more realistic note than *Fervaal* and is less obviously a product of the new Jerusalem. Its subject is yet again concerned with what Ruskin once called 'the wild, fantastic, various, tameless unity of the sea'. This makes the work a kind of prototype towards which Lazzari and others were to look in the years ahead.[1] Less harrowing than *La Tour de Feu* or the ill-fated *Les Trois Vagues*, the opera is somewhat more compact in tone than might have been thought advisable, lending

[1] In terms of strict chronology, the earliest modern opera to aim at reproducing natural phenomena on this scale was Bruneau's *L'Ouragan* (1901), which attempted to represent a hurricane on the stage. It could not have influenced d'Indy's work, which had been envisaged earlier, but might well have acted as a precedent for later composers.

its composer little scope for variety of dramatic tension. Yet Pierre Lalo was impelled to describe the storm scene as the finest in the entire repertory, an opinion which has been echoed recently by the critic, Robert Pitrou. A scarcely less glowing tribute was elicited from Debussy, whose suite, *La Mer*, may have owed something to his presence at the Théâtre de la Monnaie for the première. This evocative triptych—a classic of twentieth-century music—was begun only six months after hearing *L'Etranger*, which is referred to in *Monsieur Croche* as a work of 'perfect balance' and 'unforgettable beauty'. Such compliments from a member of the *avant-garde* may seem strange, for it is well known that d'Indy hated the music of his younger contemporaries. Curiously enough, however, there was a certain affinity between him and Debussy which it is not easy to pin down. It lay, perhaps, in the constant natural piety which they shared. In any case, the delicate mixture of realism and symbolism to be found in this opera must have made an ample appeal to the creator of *Pelléas* and *La Damoiselle Elue*.

Ex. 22

Vincent d' Indy: Chanson populaire from "L' Étranger"

The story of *L'Etranger* is not in the least complex, it having none of the twists and turns we ascribe to the average opera plot. Action tends to be subordinate to theme at all points, with the result that the drowning scene at the end of Act II aspires to be the work's single dramatic peak. Occupying a mere two hours in place of the usual four, it commends itself by being much shorter than d'Indy's other operas. Its characterization is relatively simple and clear-cut; so much so that its symbolism can easily be mistaken for allegory. The events all take place at a fishing village—evidently a favourite

locale for French composers—wherein a young girl called Vita (an
obvious enough symbolic touch) is making up her mind to marry.
Her likeliest suitor is one André, a Customs Officer whose job it is
to hunt down smugglers. Quite unexpectedly, a Stranger enters the
village, sporting a striking emerald ring. His good manners and
exquisite appearance do little to attract him to the populace, who
are not given to admiring foreigners and who remain deeply suspicious of his intentions. Vita, however, shows herself to be less
prejudiced. In a candid gesture of friendship, she asks the Stranger
for his name, only to find herself gently rebuffed:

> Je n'en ai pas. Je suis celui qui rêve,
> Je suis celui qui aime.

It is obvious from this that her visitor is in the grip of a mission;
he is a mystic whose tasks place him above all earthly temptation.
No less obviously, Vita discovers that she is in love with him, and
cannot bear to see him go. With the greatest restraint they discuss
their respective roles, the Stranger confessing how much more
difficult it has become for him to renounce human passion. He tells
her that his ring was taken from the prow of Lazarus's ship, and is
the means by which he is able to control the sea around him. Vita
clearly does not believe this, and when the Stranger parts with his
talisman—he presses it on her as a sign that he can no longer fulfil
the terms of his mission—she recklessly throws it among the waves.
Meanwhile, André has returned in a blaze of conceit, having roun-
ded up the smugglers and won himself a modest promotion. Hopefully, he proposes to Vita only to find himself rejected. On the
following Sunday, the Stranger elects to depart. As he makes his
way to the quay, he observes that a storm is brewing and that one
of the fishing boats is in trouble. Since none of the villagers shows
courage enough to attempt a rescue, the Stranger is left to battle
his way to the wreck alone, Realizing the peril in which he is placing himself, Vita cannot refrain from leaping into the breach and
sharing his bravery. But the rope breaks and both are swallowed up
by the sea.

Considered as a subject, *L'Etranger* exhibits some of the flavour
of an Ibsen tragedy. The comparison does not seem at all far-
fetched when we take account of how popular the Norwegian's
plays were in Paris during this time. We know that Delius, who
lived in the Latin Quarter from 1888 to 1896, had been among his
keenest champions, and Henri Duparc was another. It is difficult
to credit d'Indy with the same sensitivity to newer literary currents
as these progressive artists displayed, but he could well have had
his attention tactfully drawn to them. Of course, one should not
push the case too far. There is a supernatural element to *L'Etranger*

that serves to place it in a different category from any of the 'problem plays' of the social realists. Yet it is worth asking ourselves whether the composer was necessarily as contemptuous of present-day mores as his detractors have claimed. Signs of modernism appear just as clearly in the stage-setting and production, particularly in the placing of the villagers for the final De Profundis. Beyond this, it goes without saying that traces of the composer's old affiliations remain. The work's tonal scheme hinges on Franck-ist principles, each character having an appointed key in which to sing. Vita, for instance, clings to a pure F major, while her fiancé André expresses himself in the more cloying vehicle of B flat. Moreover, a specific tonality is attached to each act—A major being the choice for Act I and F major for Act II. Scarcely more elusive are the occasional Wagnerian influences, this time more reminiscent of *The Flying Dutchman* than the later music-dramas. Like many followers of Wagner, d'Indy adopted the habit of writing his own libretti, and one of the chief weaknesses of 'L'Etranger' centres upon this fact. Gifted with only the stiffest and most old-fashioned kind of literary talent, his verse exudes none of that subtle, aromatic quality we find in the best French writers. The entire scenario of this opera consequently lacks buoyancy, and has the effect of dampening down rather than heightening the realism. Debussy's comments aside, the response which the score drew was very mixed. Camille Bellaigue continued to assert his hostility by referring to it as distinctly 'un-French'. On the other hand, Jean Marnold was quick to praise the magnificent polyphony it exhibited. This last quality d'Indy achieved with diatonic as much as chromatic tactics—another point of contrast with the earlier *Fervaal*. Best of all, perhaps, was the generous appraisal to which Fauré committed himself. As Professor of Composition at the Conservatoire, his word was beginning to count for something among the young, and it is wholly to his credit that he did not allow any institutional rivalry to curb his enthusiasm.

The other *magnum opus* by which d'Indy celebrated his survival into the modern age was the Second Symphony, his most impressive contribution to the genre and a work that was first heard in 1904. This was the year during which musical feuding in the capital aspired to reach a climax, the great occasion for dispute being the refusal of the Prix de Rome to Ravel. As a Schola official, d'Indy was not directly implicated in the quarrel, which took place largely within the precincts of the Conservatoire. But it is worth recalling the artistic climate in which his late works were made to appear. By this time, both Debussy and Ravel had pressed their impact on the public, and the temper of the critics was swinging away from classicism and romanticism towards an altogether novel conception of music, a conception based more on aural values and the sense of chordal movement. This was precisely the sector which d'Indy had failed to explore, many students having complained of the Schola's indifference towards training in harmony. Worse still, the new composers were unashamed in their ignorance of form— one of the principal bastions in that institution's creed. The upshot was that a bitter schism arose, separating those at the Rue Saint-Jacques from the bulk of their juniors elsewhere. It seems curious that d'Indy himself should have devoted so much spleen to harrying the minor revolutionaries, while stoutly maintaining his admiration for Debussy. One suspects that it was their callowness and irreverence to which he was really objecting, their purely musical shortcomings being nothing more than a secondary source of outrage. This conclusion is reinforced by noting the cold war which the composer was later to wage on the members of 'Les Six', whose neo-classical aims seemed a good deal nearer, on the surface, to his own. The gulf which separated him from these over-sprightly individuals—and it almost seems like an abyss to the contemporary historian—probably lay in the infinitely greater scholarship to which he could pretend, and in that moral inflexibility which he invariably imputed to his art.

It will be evident from what we have said that the merits of the B flat Symphony were not such as to have impinged on all and sundry. They would have been best appreciated by men like Franck and Chausson, neither of whom had remained alive to hear the work. Judged by the canons of the impressionists, it was music of the old-fashioned kind that d'Indy had written, and as such there could be no question of it getting a rousing reception. Looked at in the light of other standards, however, the symphony contained a great deal that was open to discussion. Dedicated to his friend Paul Dukas—whose determination to remain steady may have proved a valuable source of consolation—the work spans four long movements and aims at a Beethovenian nobility of utterance. There are two motto themes, each of which appears in the introduction, and these display something of the cellular, tonally-ambiguous quality we associate with the Franck school. Also reminiscent of Franck is the juggling that constantly takes place with the interval of a third. As is usually the case in a classical symphony, the first and second subjects strive to achieve contrast, the former being slow and insidious while the latter seeks firmer definition by being presented on flutes and clarinets in a livelier tempo. This second melody must be taken to represent d'Indy's ideal—it is clear, luminous and morally symbolic. In the finale, there is an attempt to combine the two themes in a dignified chorale, which then becomes the basis of the work's grandiose conclusion. Much of this first movement suffers from a corresponding heaviness of tone, the overloaded orchestration which the composer had earlier seen fit to renounce here returning to plague him. By comparison, the second movement appears less smudged, its attractive harp and woodwind exchanges helping to lighten the texture. After this comes a typically d'Indyesque folk-interlude, not altogether devoid of charm, which leads on to the finale, in which a variety of stated material is reviewed and epitomized. Several commentators have likened this resumé to Beethoven's recitative intrusion towards the end of the Ninth Symphony, though the effect is probably nearer to Roussel in cogency and organizational vigour. What remains d'Indy's own is the extraordinary control of rhythmic accentuation which he displays.

As with so many later works this symphony is remarkable chiefly for its astute handling of a number of different time-signatures. Over and over again the music passes smoothly and imperceptibly from four to five—sometimes even to seven—beats in the bar. The fluency with which the composer accomplishes such transitions must certainly be reckoned one of his principal assets—he is perhaps the supreme exponent of suppleness in the orchestral field. Contrapuntally, too, the flow is enhanced by an unobtrusive assurance in the handling of parts, while the generous use of augmented triads, reminding us yet again of the Franckist legacy, serves to create harmonic impetus of a kind few other composers could have maintained so adroitly. Despite these indications, it is a fact that d'Indy never developed into a major power in the symphony stakes. His busy career as an administrator forced him to put off further excursions into the genre until the outbreak of the First World War, when he foolishly permitted himself to be carried away by the idea of a programme-symphony depicting the conflict. This *Sinfonia Brevis*—subtitled 'De Bello Gallico'—is one of the composer's more embarrassing failures. In view of its crudities of intention, it could hardly have been anything else. Like Beethoven's *Battle of Vittoria*, it represents a completely unexpected reversal of ambition, containing all manner of noises-off and absurd patriotic salutes. The first movement re-enacts the approach to the Marne, while the Scherzo simulates the marching feet of the Allied army. In the Andante, French styles of music are exalted over what the composer would by now have described as 'Boche art'. Finally, the work proclaims the end of hostilities in a windy and portentous last movement. Written between the years 1916–18, it did not really pretend to be a symphony as much as a symphonic poem. Coming from the man who had privately chided Franck for his pictorialness, the whole venture had an element of farce about it and would have been much better dropped.

His feelings about Nature usually brought out the best in d'Indy, just as his patriotic excesses generally gave rise to the worst. It is therefore pleasant to report that in the years leading up to the Great War he was able to write a few pastoral sketches from which the quality of bombast is happily absent. Among these works, the neglected *Jour d'Eté à la Montagne* (1905) merits every considera- tion. Moving much nearer to the impressionist ideal, d'Indy treated this trilogy as a study in tone-painting.[1] Particularly fine is its first section—entitled 'Aurore'—which conjures up the sharp scent of pine as it floats across the mountainous Cévennes, recalling a region far less alive to the tramping of human feet than any in Respighi's famous poem. Indeed, the mood captured in these three enchanting nature-portraits comes very close to that celebrated in the earlier *Symphonie Cévenole*. The year in which they were com- pleted took the composer on a brief tour of the United States, where he had the honour of conducting the Boston Symphony Orchestra in a programme of music by Franck and other fellow-countrymen. On his return, he was alarmed to discover that his wife Isabelle had been taken sick and was dying. Stoical though he was, d'Indy never entirely recovered from her passing, Léon Vallas recounting how he once heard the composer playing the 'bien-aimée' theme from his *Souvenirs* (1906) 'avec une émotion prèsque sanglotante'. Only his dearest friends knew what he suffered in the loss of his ideal companion, the woman who had demanded so little of him and yet had thrown herself so willingly into each and every one of his quixotic musical adventures. The following year saw the appearance of the notorious Franck biography upon which we have already pronounced sentence. Ridiculously complimentary, its best parts are those which set out to analyse the composer's chamber music. Especially worth preserving is the section on the String Quartet (pages 182–97 in the Dover edition). The commentaries on the religious works are less valuable, being marred by excessive com- parisons with the Italian primitives. Scarcely any attention is paid to Franck as a writer of symphonic poems, and there are a number of minor inaccuracies relating to the early works. All things con- sidered, however, the book performed a useful function in spread- ing knowledge of the composer and his works, and is still regarded as an indispensable tool by later biographers.

By 1907 d'Indy had regained his composure sufficiently to think

---

[1] It may be interesting to remind the reader that d'Indy was an excellent amateur topographical artist, this being another of his numer- ous accomplishments. Some very good specimens of his work are repro- duced in his friend Canteloube's short biography. It appears that much of the time he spent in the Cévennes was taken up with drawing and sketching.

about resuming work. The first fruit of his labours was a gigantic Piano Sonata which remains as unplayed today as it did in the composer's own day. Wilfully erudite in structure, it must be accounted a system-built undertaking and one that did as much as any other composition to type its author as a possible forerunner of the dodecaphonists. Not that it contains much that is destructive of tonality, the comparison suggesting itself chiefly through a certain organizational rigidity which seeks to pervade each movement, especially the first. Beginning in E minor, it plunges straightaway into the most enormous variation cycle in which there are four linked statements of the theme. Variation I follows a ternary plan and is tranquil in the manner of the late Beethoven. Then comes Variation II which imparts a strangely dolorous mood more reminiscent of the French post-romantics. The bridge-passage used to link the different parts of the theme achieves prominence in Variation III, while Variation IV concludes by converting its material into the rich tonic major. Next to intrude itself is a Scherzo with two trios, the second of which goes on to form a brief coda. The finale is then allowed to appear, after the pianist has been permitted a long bravura introduction. Most of the material of this third movement is new, whereas the Scherzo and its companions had been derived, in good cyclical fashion, from what had gone before. Reasons for the work's neglect may be traced to the difficulty of the last movement's figuration. Melodies are announced by the upper fingers leaving the thumb and first finger to cope with some tricky accompanying thirds. Meanwhile, the left hand engages in the standard Franckist broken octaves, this time requiring a frightening power of agility. Anyone wishing to get to grips with d'Indy as a writer for the pianoforte might be better advised to forego this sonata in favour of the earlier *Tableaux de Voyage*, a delightful set of thirteen impressions begun during a tour of the Black Forest and Austrian Tyrol which the composer had embarked upon in 1889. They invite comparison with Schumann's *Waldscenen* and deserve to be permanently restored to the repertory.[1]

Two years after writing the Piano Sonata, d'Indy found himself warding off the opprobriums of a further musical faction—the newly established Société Musicale Indépendante. This venture had received the backing of Fauré, Schmitt and Koechlin, and was notable for the encouragement it was extending to Ravel. Though not specifically intended to replace the Société Nationale, there could be no doubt of the newcomer's tactics. Its members, many of

[1] For an excellent and very full analysis of these sound-portraits, the reader is referred to pp. 148–57 of Eric Blom's book, *Classics, Major and Minor* (Dent, 1958). The essay is entitled 'Vincent d'Indy's Enigma'.

whom were youthful iconoclasts, were apt to refer to d'Indy's cherished organization by a choice variety of names, the kindest of which was 'cette vieille dame'. The truth is that internationalism had got into the air, and the names of men like Stravinsky and Casella were now being preferred to those of most French men. Needless to say, such names tended to fall like hot coals from the lips of the older generation, who had to be content with prophesying an apocalypse. D'Indy presented himself as a splendid target in all this, since he was the one composer over fifty who could always be relied upon to snarl when baited. As far back as 1906 he had been lampooned in an article printed by the *Mercure Musical* over the signature of Emile Vuillermoz, the real author having turned out to be that incorrigible old mischief-maker, Henri Gauthier-Villars, otherwise known as 'Willy'. The chief complaints had been levelled at the composer's fetishism over form and indiscriminate musical catholicism. Made to retreat somewhat from his position of eminence, d'Indy continued to preach a stern dogma at the Schola while perversely consecrating his beloved Beethoven —that oldest of all musical Bolsheviks—in a new and scholarly biography. He began work on this last project in 1911, while recovering from an attack of pleurisy. On his return to circulation, his rival Fauré helped to patch things up by offering him a chair at the Conservatoire.

La Légende de Saint-Christophe—the last of the composer's three operas—was started as early as 1908, but the war was well under way before he had reached the final page. Described in a letter to Pierre de Bréville as 'un drame anti-juif', it arose out of his racial animadversions, which had been greatly stimulated by the Dreyfus affair.[1] Anyone looking at the opera today is likely to be nauseated by the pathological array of hates which it displays. The story rests on a legend by Jacques de Voragine, and has more connection with the medieval mystery play than with the modern theatre. Divided into nine tableaux, it recounts the trials of the giant Auferus, who is intent on offering his services to the world's most powerful monarch. His earliest encounters are with the Queen of Pleasure, the King of Gold and the Prince of Evil, all of whom prove to be usurpers who cannot imbue him with the idealism he desires. At the conclusion of Act I, Auferus has reached a preliminary stage of illumination by having his attention drawn to the King of Heaven. There follows a brief symphonic prologue, after which the giant renews his quest at the Vatican, where the Pope

[1] The letter is actually dated 30 September 1903, d'Indy having planned his opera some five years before starting work on it. The writing took him six summers (spent at Faugs) between 1908 and 1915 and the work was not performed in its entirety until 1920.

tells him to await a sign. This will take the form of a white rose
flowering in the midst of the forest. Going on his way once more,
Auferus next meets up with a hermit who instructs him in the
virtues of Faith, Hope and Charity. Later, while bearing a child
across a ford, the wanderer recognizes his sign and realizes that the
being he holds in his arms is none other than the infant Jesus. The
act ends with him being baptised St Christopher. Moving to the
conclusion of the opera, we see Christophe (as he is now called)
delivered into the clutches of his enemies again, being subjected to a variety of temptations. The King and the Prince come to
torment him, while the Pleasure Queen attempts to seduce him in
his cell. Though tortured and reviled, he resists all their efforts to
unconvert him and is executed as a martyr. The shedding of his
blood then becomes a source of general purification, the curtain
being made to fall on a scene of prayer and repentance.

Ex. 23

Vincent d' Indy: O Crux ave, Spes unica from "La Légende de Saint Christophe"

To understand the variety of innuendo which d'Indy sought to
put across in this pantomime, it is first of all necessary to realize
how many of the scenes are concerned with disillusionment. The
false prophets who are made to surround each of his evil figures—
sometimes disguised as fashionable artists, at other times as
scientists or freethinkers—can be identified with the composer's
enemies in such a degree that one is left in no doubt as to the venom
that lay at the back of it all. Along with Mozart's *Die Zauberflöte*—
though with heroes and villains in changed places—the work can be
considered a complex topical allegory. The question of what range
of models d'Indy followed is one that has never been entirely
cleared up. Doubtless, he allowed himself to be inspired by Wagner
as far as the polemics went, but may have taken the Passion play
as his prototype in the matter of staging. Norman Demuth is
probably right in thinking that *La Légende de Saint Christophe* was
the composer's lifework, artistically speaking. If he did not spend

more time on it than on many another project, at least he made it understood that nothing he had done was of greater importance to him. The walls of his study—otherwise kept strictly bare—were decorated with images of the Christopher story, and it is quite likely that he regarded his version of it as a kind of latter-day religious proclamation. The gospel according to St Vincent was too strong for most stomachs, however, and it is hardly to be wondered that the work met with such a gritty response from the public. Its chances of survival on the stage are now remote, though parts of it could reasonably hope for rehabilitation on the concert-platform. In one sense, this is a pity, for what the opera achieved, in a purely technical context, was the synthesis of several independent genres. Drama, singing, fairy-tale, satire—all these have a part to play in what ends by becoming a sort of religious spectacle. To remove any of these elements would be to destroy the work's unity. Nevertheless, the composer himself became the first to present a cut version, and it only remains to see whether others will follow suit.

Meanwhile, we have said little about the theoretical benefits which d'Indy was helping to confer on his art. His famous *Cours de Composition Musicale* was altogether to comprise four hefty volumes, only two of which appeared during their author's lifetime. Edited by Auguste Seriéyx from the lectures which the composer had been giving at the Schola, Books I and II had been published in 1903 and 1909 respectively. They constitute a magisterial survey of the ground an ordinary student was expected to cover in the course of his musical education. The important fact serving to distinguish them from other comprehensive textbooks can be traced to the sounder historical method they evince. Beginning with the period A.D. 300, the first volume goes on to trace the rise of the monodic phase as a genuinely significant epoch rather than the Dark Age it was usually shown to be. Similarly close attention is then given to the period of Palestrina and his contemporaries. At the commencement of the second volume, the reader is introduced to the baroque composers and only gradually is he permitted a glimpse of the music of a later day. Though there is a brief discussion of *Pélleas* and other modern masterpieces, the chronology ceases towards the end of the nineteenth century. Within the various historical divisions, d'Indy offers a succinct review of the main musical styles and forms. This is presented chiefly in Book II, the earlier volume being taken up with a study of the fundamentals—matters like rhythm, melody, harmony, tonality and expression. What the composer has to say about these basic concepts is often rather dry, though it is surprising how much musicological information on points of notation and interpretation he is able to impart.

Modes, ornaments, symbols, fashions of barring—all these are explained with impeccable learning. His exposition of the classical forms is likewise a model for aspiring teachers. Here he draws many examples from Bach—in particular from *The Musical Offering*—and these assist in building up clear pictures of the Fugue, the Suite, the Variation, the Ricercar and many other species of composition. After Bach's time, the exemplars tend to be Beethoven and Franck, with the latter's *Prélude, Choral et Fugue* coming in for frequent quotation.

Looking back on the *Cours* today, it is possible to find clear evidence of d'Indy's prejudices. For example, he greatly exaggerates the importance of the cyclical method, which obsessed him to a larger extent than it did Franck. It would be invidious to suggest that he is inclined to overrate Beethoven, but the impression given of his stature in relation to that of, say, Mozart is quite misleading. Like many scholars of his age, d'Indy saw only the Dresden china aspects of the eighteenth century's greatest genius, and his comments often add up to something like an unconscious slander. He would have been totally incapable of responding to the libertarian sentiments expressed in a work like *Cosi*. His attitude to Beethoven, on the other hand, verged on idolatry and marked a notable stride forward in that movement which was to end in the paeans of Tovey and J. W. N. Sullivan. Indeed, his analyses of the piano sonatas in the *Cours* occasionally remind one of the Edinburgh professor's brilliant essays. They are not, however, as systematic or complete, having more in common from that point of view with the briefer critiques of pianists like Edwin Fischer. On the whole, d'Indy tended to regard the sonata as a genre on its own, quite distinct from the concerto and the symphony. This led him to explore the early literature for forerunners, eventually causing him to champion such an obscure master as Wilhelm Friedrich Rust (1739–96). It was over his editing of this composer's sonatas that he finally came to blows with Saint-Saëns, who had doubtless been waiting for an excuse to challenge him for a long time. Volume III of d'Indy's treatise did not appear until 1933, by which date the author was safely dead and buried. It contains a full account of the development of dramatic music, this term being made to cover such divisions as song, cantata and oratorio. This is the least technical of the three books, though hardly the least controversial. In it, the author divides opera into an Italian period (Monteverdi to Scarlatti); a German period (Weber to Wagner); and a French period (Lully to Méhul). Guy de Lioncourt brought the story up to date by issuing a fourth volume—resurrected from notes and conversations—in 1951.

Like Franck at the time of the Prussian War, d'Indy found his pupils deserting him in droves during the years 1914–18. Also like his old master, he was irritated at not being allowed to join up himself. Though well over sixty, he was still an upright figure of a man whose legs were stronger than many a soldier's. Rejected for active service, the composer fell prey to a spirit of frustrated aggression. Throughout the bombardment, he exhorted his staff and students to remain in the capital, hurling accusations of cowardice at those who opted for a more sensible course. Developing a restless streak, he would pace the boulevards night after night in search of any scrap of news from the front. It was while he was seated in a brasserie off the Boulevard Montparnasse that he accidentally encountered a slim and rather pretty young lady named Line Janson, whose father had been an N.C.O. with one of the artillery regiments. Despite their differences of age and social class, d'Indy and Line struck up a sympathetic friendship which, to everyone's amazement, ended by him marrying her. The consequences of his impetuosity were predictable, though not as painful as many had prophesied. Unlike Isabelle, the composer's second wife might have been described as chic and fluffy. She preferred the climate on the Côte d'Azur to the fogs and rains associated with the Ardèche. It was not long, therefore, before she managed to persuade her husband to build her a villa at Agay, where she strove to enjoy a comfortable and somewhat lightheaded social life. The only drawback to their plans arose from the fact that the family fortunes had not weathered the war years particularly well. Too much had been invested in the Schola and other musical causes, while increased taxation and economic depression threatened to account for what was left. The outcome was that, for the last decade of his life, d'Indy frequently came near to living beyond his income. It has been said that the composer saw in Line a reincarnation of the green-eyed American girl he had once fallen in love with at Biarritz, and whose story is told in his *Lied Maritime*. However that may be, the newly-married couple experienced no regrets, spending much of their time commuting between Paris and the Riviera, where they disported themselves giddily alongside the international set.

The effect which Line had on d'Indy's artistic philosophy is not difficult to pin down, though it is perhaps harder to evaluate. For one thing, she seems to have been responsible for dissipating much of the solemnity which still clung to his thinking, without necessarily convincing us that the change was all to the good. Probably her most beneficial act was to arouse the latent Mediterraneanism which had always lain at the back of the composer's sensibilities. Instead of charting the same old ground at Faugs each summer, he now began to turn his attention to the legends of the South, even-

tually adding to his canon with two thoroughly relaxed tone-
poems. The *Poème de Rivages* (1919–21) and *Diptyque Mediter-
ranéen* (1925–6) are to be admired on account of their brevity of design and soaring spirit. They are precisely the sort of works the

Ex. 24
Vincent d' Indy: Diptique Méditerranéen

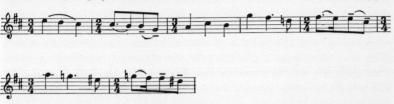

composer should have been writing at all stages of his career.
But even more effervescent was the operetta, *Le Rêve de Cyniras*,
which purported to carry lightheartedness to the point of levity.
This remarkable 'jeu d'esprit' belongs more to the school of Chabrier than to the Schola, and was an altogether unexpected project
for the composer to have embarked upon. D'Indy as a comic-opera
buffoon is admittedly a very partial portrait, and no one will be
accused of thinking him remiss to have neglected this line of effort.
Yet *Cyniras* reveals still another side to his character, one which
may have been born out of the satirical elements in *La Légende de
Saint Christophe*. On the surface, the work is a classical skit after
the fashion of Offenbach's *La Belle Hélène*. Beneath its façade of
humour, however, there lies a subtle commentary on the political
antics of the day, with the figure of Nestor intended to represent
Tiger Clemenceau and Menelaus the strait-laced Woodrow Wilson.
The whole venture falls into three acts and five tableaux. Unfortunately, no theatre would condescend to put it on during its first
few years of life, and when it finally reached the boards it was a
flop.

   The ultimate phase into which the composer now passed became
the most emancipated in his entire history. Not only did it point to
a marked simplification of style, but the whole effort of which he
was capable swung away from fustian forms towards a ripe and
fluent neo-classicism. Additional chamber-works sprang from his
pen in quick profusion, the G minor Quintet of 1924 being followed by a *Suite pour Cinq Instruments* in 1927 and an eminently
graceful Sextet in 1928. The String Quartet No. 3 made its appearance very shortly afterwards, crowning those the composer had
written in 1890 and 1897 respectively. Finally, two Trios—one for

piano and strings and the other featuring the clarinet—succeeded in bringing his production to a close. All these pieces for more intimate combinations were instigated by the Société Nationale. Meantime, administrative matters were handled with a comparable urgency of dispatch. Concerts and conferences were arranged all over France to celebrate the Schola's twenty-fifth anniversary, while the grinding polemics with 'Les Six' moved into a new dimension with a series of newspaper articles. On top of it all, d'Indy found time to continue his anti-Jewish harangues in terms that would have done credit to Hitler. He was indefatigable. Those who are old enough to have remembered him in person can testify that, even during his eightieth year, the composer was to be spotted pounding his way to work as the dawn broke each morning, with his astrakhan collar turned up to avoid the wind and a cigarette-holder permanently clenched between his teeth. When the moment came for him to stop, death caught him unawares. After completing a full day's work on his biography of Wagner, the composer suddenly complained of feeling unwell and within a few hours had passed beyond human strife. The date was 1 December 1931. Casting round for an epitaph for this brilliant but exasperating man, one is tempted to fall back on Pascal's dictum—'La Justice sans la force est impuissante'. Certainly there is no saying with which he could have concurred more enthusiastically. His mistake lay in refusing to see that even justice needs to be administered without tyranny.

Among those of Franck's pupils who preferred the classroom to the concert-hall, none did more for the movement—and has perhaps received less credit for having done so—than Joseph Guy Ropartz, with whose activities we shall be concerned in what remains of this chapter. D'Indy apart, he was the circle's most articulate educational spokesman and a musician who devoted an uniquely long life to the propagation of Franckist ideas. Where he differed from both d'Indy and Bordes was in the greater influence he brought to bear in the provinces, and in the purer reverence he displayed towards his master's principles, which he never compromised in the interests of a system of his own. Born at Guingamp, Côte-du-Nord, in 1864, he was not alone in his Breton affiliations, having much in common from that point of view with Lazzari. His family had been respected throughout Brittany for generations, and he grew up in an atmosphere of conscious regional pride. Indeed, his father—a distinguished scholar and advocate—was well known for his historical and archaeological researches, so that he was able to supplement his son's education with valuable tuition in local affairs. As a beginner, Ropartz studied at a variety of centres—at Rennes, where Fauré had held his first organ post, and

later at both Vannes and Angers.[1] During all this time, he did not
definitely make up his mind to become a musician. Literature
exercised an equally sharp fascination for him—especially the
writings of his fellow Bretons, so rich in legend and superstition.
In the end, however, he dutifully trod the same path as Coquard,
Duparc and Chausson in consenting to become a lawyer. Those who
knew him well nevertheless predicted that he would sometime
revert to one of his former loves, and it came as no surprise when he
ultimately presented himself at the Conservatoire in Paris. Here he
studied composition with Dubois and Massenet, neither of whom
made much impression on him. When it came to preparing for the
Prix de Rome, Ropartz forfeited his chances by transferring to the
unworldly organist of Sainte-Clotilde.

At this stage in Franck's career, his impact on the young was
not invariably staggering. Many pupils had contrived to wriggle
out from under the spell which he exerted, while others had no
particular difficulty in resisting it altogether. Ropartz reminds us of
the earliest generation of followers—the generation of Duparc and
d'Indy—in having straightaway pledged undying loyalty to his
teacher. It could truly be said of him, as it was much less accurately
remarked about them, that his whole life was dedicated to this
service. The manner in which he interpreted his mission was quite
individual. After quitting the Conservatoire, he felt no special urge
to remain in the capital and was never among those to have become
deeply enamoured by its attractions. Like all good missionaries, he
realized that his work lay in a centre more remote from the source
of the gospel. This centre proposed itself at Nancy, where he was
content to play a leading role for the first half of his working existence. As Director of the Conservatoire in that city, Ropartz went
far towards shaping its musical life—as well as the life of the surrounding regions—throughout the period 1894 to 1919. It was an
uphill task, shorn of the glamour which attached to work at the
Schola, but he performed it splendidly, rarely missing an opportunity to invite his Parisian friends to perform in the district and
constantly pressing his contacts in other parts of the country.
Bordes, it will be recalled, had helped to found branches of the
Schola at Avignon and Montpellier, so that a tiny network of institutions was already beginning to appear. Ropartz deserves full
credit for strengthening the peculiar alliances which were to spring
up between these various outposts. One of his most commendable
achievements was to ensure the goodwill of Eugene Ysaÿe—whom

[1] It is of interest to record that, in addition to the usual instruments,
Ropartz made use of his early musical education to learn the horn, the
bugle and the double-bass. His skill in instrumentation was to remain
prodigious.

he regarded as the century's greatest executant—and to see that he continued to plug the Franckist cause in programmes he was being asked to give all over the world. Another was to bring together representatives of Celtic music and imbue them with some of his own educational zeal. On any count, Ropartz proved to be a man whose services could never have been dispensed with.

Predictably, perhaps, the earliest works by this unselfish artist to reach a wider public were a series of *Scènes Bretonnes* in which the interest did not go much beyond native colour. Far more prophetic was his realization of Brizeux's poem *La Chasse du Prince Arthur*, which described the ringing sound of the hunt penetrating the forest at nightfall. A less incident-packed account of the legend than Chausson's witty *Viviane*, the work was just as effective in proclaiming its composer's skill at the mechanics of orchestration. The symphonic poem made an immediate appeal to Ropartz, and he fell into the Franckian habit of producing them in threes. Indeed, bulk could be said to have been the composer's strong suit even from the outset of his career. Surviving to write well over two hundred works, he achieved renown in almost all of the recognized forms— sacred and secular, intimate and spectacular. Among the highlights of his production should be reckoned five symphonies (one of them choral); the St Anne and St Odile Masses for choir and organ; a scene from Pierre Loti's *Pêcheur d'Islande* (1891); six String Quartets, three Violin Sonatas and a couple of Cello Sonatas; a full-scale opera entitled *Le Pays* (1910); and an austerely devout Requiem which first appeared just two years before the Second World War. One of the striking features of *Prince Arthur* lay in its clarity of outline. It represented a model symphonic study of the kind French composers were to make all their own. Beginning with a shimmering introduction, the work is propelled on its way by a

Ex. 25

Guy Ropartz: La Chasse du Prince Arthur.

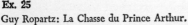

strong, grave theme emanating from the bass regions of the orchestra. This is amplified and punctuated by a series of majestic tuttis, and by a leaping, expressive kind of phraseology which helps to depict the chase itself. Horns and trombones join in the pursuit which subsequently rises to a furious pitch. Once the climax has been reached, however, calm is restored by a superbly pathetic melody from the violins, bordered by brief trumpet reprises, and the poem ends in a return to the opening tranquillity. Honegger was only one of the many musicians who never ceased to admire this fresh and exciting work.

But the *pièce-de-résistance* of Ropartz's Nancy years was unquestionably his opera, *Le Pays*, based on the novel, *L'Islandaise*, by Le Goffic. This was first mounted at the Opéra-Comique in August, 1913. Though the book from which it was adapted might fairly have been described as 'densely-packed', the opera itself proved almost unique in being concerned with only three characters. The chief among these is Tual, a young fisherman, who is shipwrecked on the island of Hrafuaga, after having witnessed the drowning of his companions. An islander named Jorgen shelters the survivor, giving his daughter Kaethe the job of attending to him. Tual and Kaethe fall in love and decide to remain together on the island to engage in a life of fur-trapping, and to raise a family of their own. Gradually, however, Tual's homesickness gets the better of his love, and he becomes obsessed with a desire to return to the mainland. Learning that a Breton schooner is passing nearby, the ex-fisherman cannot resist tearing himself away from his beloved and their still unborn child. Bluntly told, the story offers few points of sophistication. Placed in its geographical context, however, and viewed alongside Ropartz's uncannily apt music, it soon assumes the dimensions of a powerful lyric tragedy. There is a classical simplicity in the action of the drama, while its emotional undertones attain a remarkable concentration of force. One is made aware of these attributes from the outset, the work's sombre symphonic prelude going far towards creating the appropriate atmosphere. Listening to it, it is easy to imagine the piercing cries of the gulls as they dip and wheel near the island's shore, and the swirling movement of sea and sky. The hardness of life amid such surroundings has the effect of raising human passions to a special pitch of abnormality, and nothing extraneous is allowed to moderate their expression. Kaethe and Jorgen emerge as characters whose lives are both free and circumscribed after the fashion of Hardy's countrymen. Tual, on the other hand, may be considered a study in nostalgia—or more exactly in that feeling Welsh people describe as 'hiraeth'. Indeed, the whole opera is discreetly overlaid with a sense of 'parfum de terroir'.

It should not be imagined from this that Ropartz wrote music that was harsh or rugged. On the contrary, his was a most refined talent. A glance at the chamber-works should be enough to corroborate this fact, for few composers have contributed so much that

pleases by sheer delicacy of sound. Those who admire Poulenc's
arcadian *Concert Champêtre*, for example, will discover many of
its qualities in Ropartz's *Sérénade* of like origin. The combining
of strings with woodwind in the latter work could not have been

Ex. 26

Guy Ropartz: Sérénade Champêtre

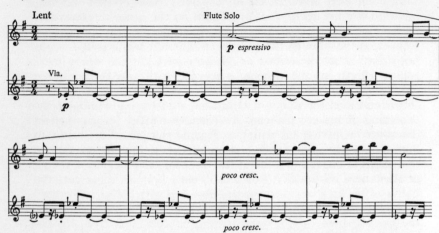

more gracefully achieved, and the inspiration is constantly on a
high level. What so impresses us about the composer's style is
precisely its quality of ventilation—something he could scarcely
have picked up from Franck. The violins are always dancing and
tripping in a tipsy, nautical fashion, surprising us with their frequent rests and sudden, wild harmonics. To look at the flute part
in this enchanting essay is to observe what a profound understanding Ropartz also had of the silkier tone values. Most of the skills
heard in the *Sérénade Champêtre* are reproduced in one of the
composer's best-known pieces for small ensemble—the *Prélude,
Marine et Chanson*. It should be sufficient to say of this divertissement that it suffers hardly at all from being heard alongside the
Sérénade of Roussel or the ravishing *Introduction and Allegro* by
Ravel. About the larger orchestral works, opinion has been more
divided. The symphonies, it goes without saying, are marvellously
competent works from every technical point of view. It is No. 3
which makes use of massed choirs, No. 4 being a cyclical, one-
movement composition very much more in the style of Franck. Of
the entire group, however, it is No. 6 which strives to do most
homage to the form. This strictly classical work is in four separate
movements, and is notable for its alert Scherzo and vividly rhythmic Breton finale. It was first performed by Charles Munch in

Paris during 1946, when its composer had reached the age of eighty-two. Tributes from his friends Louis Kornprobst and Fernand Lamy which appeared at about this time took the form of brief biographical studies, and a rare English appreciation was solicited from the pen of Rollo Myers.

Ropartz had been obliged to bide his time before being honoured as a composer, however, and historians will be forced to conclude that his work as a teacher aroused greater contemporary admiration. Certainly, he was imaginative as well as energetic in this capacity. Realizing that the line taken by d'Indy was liable to end in intransigeance, he never renounced the habit of tolerance which he had learned from his own teacher. 'On peut tout se permettre' was reputed to have been his motto throughout the forty-odd years he spent in the classroom, and he was acutely aware of the dangers of artistic suppression. In many respects, the stance he assumed was identical with that taken up by Franck, both teachers beginning with the assumption that any combination of notes was acceptable provided it gave rise to expressiveness. In a typically permissive statement of his creed, Ropartz once remarked:

> One will move us by his dissonances, another by his thought, another by his use of colour—it is enough to have something to say, a personality to express, and a total devotion to one's art.

No doubt he would have modified this position somewhat had he survived into the age of *musique concrète* and anti-art. But he is worth holding up as an example of benignity and liberalism, if only because so few of his colleagues confronted the revolutions of the early years of the century with anything but condemnation. Possibly the most valuable work he did in stemming musical prejudice arose out of the invitation he received in 1919 to head the conservatoire at Strasbourg. This city had lain under German annexation for forty-eight years, during which all French music had been unofficially banned. In accordance with the terms of the Treaty of Versailles, there was now an opportunity to re-establish French control once more. Ropartz took immediate advantage of the situation to accept the offer, becoming responsible for the Alsace premières of dozens of his countrymen's works. Quite characteristic of him was his decision to follow through by reversing the process—introducing the music of Alsatian composers on return visits to Paris.

Much of this forebearance which Ropartz displayed must be accounted a direct product of religious awe. More than any other pupil, he was the inheritor of Franck's sense of blessedness. D'Indy and Bordes were each sincerely religious men, but few will deny the former his bellicosity or the latter his sarcasm. The composer of *Le Pays* possessed the quality of grace in fuller measure than either. His sacred drama, *Le Mystère de Saint Nicholas* (1905), provides a good indication of how this quality impressed itself on his musical sensibilities, while his setting of the Psalms 'Super Flumina' and 'De Profundis' cannot be construed as other than a labour of love. The sight of Ropartz was in itself a reminder of the values which he attached to the faith—he was a proud, bearded figure who might have stepped straight out of the pages of the Old Testament. He and Charles Koechlin locked in conversation must have suggested a couple of prophets from Isaiah or Ecclesiastes, dispatched to cleanse musicians of their sins. By comparison, Franck—who had never had a day's legal training in his life—looked much more the comfortable, country solicitor. In fact, Ropartz had several other interests in common with members of the Franck-d'Indy circle. For one thing, he shared the regional obsessions which so few of them managed to escape. Chabrier had been acknowledged the singer of Auvergne, and d'Indy of that region around the Ardèche. Now other districts of France were beginning to find their voices. Ladmirault and Paul le Flem (the last-named a professor of counterpoint at the Schola) chose to champion the Breton cause in company with Ropartz, while de Séverac (another of d'Indy's lieutenants) set out to win acclaim with his *En Languedoc* and *Le Chant de la Terre*, both concerned to depict the province in which the Albigensians had flourished and died. One cannot very well argue that this movement was confined to France, for a similar spirit pervaded the English musical scene in the persons of Vaughan Williams, Holst and John Ireland. As usual, however, the Continent was a little ahead of its neighbour.

The death of Ropartz did not occur until 1955—by which time he had attained the gratifyingly Biblical span of ninety-one—but he had chosen to spend the years from 1934 onwards back in his beloved Brittany. His retirement from Strasbourg and d'Indy's sudden death in Paris were therefore two events that took place within a short time of each other. Together, they marked the end of an era as far as upholding the Franckist cause was concerned. There were still one or two prominent disciples active at this stage —Dukas, de Bréville and Tournemire among them. But the sands were rapidly running out. Dukas was struck down only a year or two after Paul de Wailly, neither of them surviving to witness the changes of the mid-1930s. Only another four years after that, Tournemire was found dead in the street at Arcachon, while his fellow organist, Pierné, had already preceded him to the tomb. Roussel, who might conceivably have helped to rehabilitate the reputations of several Franck followers, suffered a fatal heart

attack during 1937—that terribly gloomy year for French music
in which so many others, including Ravel, passed from the scene.
All these happenings serve to convey a picture of rapid dispersal,
such as often occurs when the founder or leader of a cult is unexpectedly removed. Yet it would be wrong to imply that the movement died out at the moment of d'Indy's death. Like the methodical
man he was, the composer of *Fervaal* left a will in which specific
provisions for the future of the Schola were included. In effect,
these were made necessary by the fact that the building itself had
been his property, and no one would have been entitled to continue
teaching there without a public enquiry. When this legal document
was read, it was learnt that Louis de Serres and Guy de Lioncourt
had been nominated to succeed to the Directorship. That is to say,
d'Indy had requested that a committee should be set up to decide
between the claims of these two disciples, and to apportion whatever other responsibilities might be involved in a continuation of
the institution's work.

Naturally enough, there ensued a squabble over the choice of
names, for the Schola was by this time an exceedingly large con-
servatory. It could boast among its fifty-four professors such people
as Roussel, Grovlez, Labey, Lejeune, Blanche Selva, Jane Bathori,
Samazeuilh, Abel Decaux and Louis Vierne. The privileged de
Serres, who was on a par with Ropartz in the matter of age, had
many points in his favour—not least among which were that he had
actually studied with Franck (d'Indy having introduced him to the
organ class in the middle of the 1880s) and had lived in close
proximity to Chausson and Fauré. As a person, he was inclined to
seem reserved and over-fastidious, but he had succeeded with his
Pièce Symphonique, based on an idea by Sully-Prudhomme, and
with a collection of *mélodies* which included the moderately popular
'Les Heures Claires'. De Lioncourt, on the other hand, could have
been mistaken for a religious bigot. Not born until 1885, he was a
much younger man whose teachers had included Saint-Saëns and
d'Indy himself. His interests continued to lie in plainchant and
polyphony, perhaps also in the liturgical drama of which he was so
formidable an exponent. His *Le Mystère de l'Emmanuel* (1924) had
marked him out as one of the resuscitators of this quiet and tenebrous art-form. Not surprisingly, perhaps, neither of these two
scholar-musicians commanded the total admiration of the faculty,
for neither could have been described as fully in tune with the spirit
of the age. When the committee for which d'Indy had given authority delivered its report, it accordingly exceeded its functions by
refusing to sanction the appointments he had desired. It even
ignored the recommendations of a delegation consisting of Gabriel
Pierné, Dukas, Guy Ropartz, Roussel and de Bréville, all of whom

resigned in consequence. Once the outcome was made known, de Serres and a number of his colleagues, including Labey and de Lioncourt, seceded from the Schola altogether and founded a new institution, the Ecole César Franck, which opened its doors at the Rue Jules-Chaplain on 5 January 1935. Thus a schism took place falsifying all hopes of future unity.

The events that followed are not of the utmost importance to our chronicle. When the dust had settled, and the combatants had been shown to their respective corners, it became apparent that there was not going to be any joining-up of resources. The tensions which had been permitted to fester beneath the surface of d'Indy's régime were such that, given an opportunity of this kind, it was inevitable that they would erupt with full force. Indeed, many considered it a good thing that they had been allowed to do so. As things turned out, the Schola was placed under the direction of Nestor Lejeune, continuing its role as an Ecole Supérieure de Musique and expanding its activities to cover the arts of drama, mime and dance. Its later directors have included the progressive Daniel-Lesur who, it will be recalled, was a fellow-conspirator with Messiaen and Jolivet amid the group which called itself 'La Jeune France'. At the time of writing, the institution lies under the control of Jacques Chailley, a former Professor of Musicology in the University of Paris and esteemed authority on the medieval period. It can count among its teachers such international figures as Alfred Loewenguth, Irma Kolassi, Pierre Pierlot and Jean Langlais. The Ecole César Franck has hardly flourished as handsomely. Headed by de Serres, it passed on his death in 1943 to the able hands of de Lioncourt, who did much to reinstate the ideals of the d'Indyists, if not those of Franck himself. In fact it is somewhat ironical that both institutions have devoted their efforts to canonizing the unseraphic Vincent, a salon having been dedicated to his memory at the Schola and a final volume of the Cours published in his honour by the Director of the Ecole. But, as anyone familiar with the French musical scene since mid-century will confirm, it was the Conservatoire that eventually re-established itself at the hub of the nation's artistic life, leaving all other academies to flounder enviously at the periphery. By the end of the 1950s, new comets like Pierre Boulez and Gilbert Amy were beginning to deposit their trail in the sky: a trail that was to lead, among other things, to a resurgence of dodecaphonism and a complete and pugnacious disavowal of the aesthetics of 'la belle époque'.

XII

Scholars and gentlemen

By ringing the changes on Franck's philosophy at the Schola, d'Indy and his colleagues moved steadily away from those shadowy realms at Sainte-Clotilde where the master had always felt himself to be most at home. But in the meantime many of the circle's system-free musicians had chosen to remain exiled within the church. Some of these merely went on labouring diligently on behalf of their teacher without wishing to modify what they had been taught. Others, armed with a bolder outlook, proceeded to occupy less saintly forms of habitation. Now that our task is drawing to a close, we must give closer attention to these secondary figures while at the same time adjudicating the claims of those discreet well-wishers, patiently disposed along the rim of the circle, whose presence had not been a necessity so much as an encouragement. We should do best to begin by listing the various old hands about whom we have so far said nothing. These men—and they include such veterans as Samuel Rousseau, Camille Benoît and Paul de Wailly—survived to pursue paths of their own, the direction of which was not necessarily indicated by indoctrination. Then, coming into an altogether different category, there is that select troop of organists who were taught by Franck, either at the Conservatoire or privately at Sainte-Clotilde, and who continued to pin their hopes to this instrument after his death. The young Pierné and Charles Tournemire clearly merit comment in this connection. Lastly, as members of the largest group so far unexamined, the names of Magnard, Dukas and de Bréville cry out for consideration. Our concluding chapter must therefore be an attempt to round up these independents and fellow-travellers, men who did not always strive to resemble their predecessors and whose interests are not to be sought in that work of codification which so urgently engaged the d'Indy faction. Whether they can be shown to have had much in common besides these facts is not easy to specify in advance. Perhaps we should be wisest to claim no more than that they all aspired to the ideals of the scholar gentleman.[1]

Casting our minds back to the circle's earliest days, several pupils then compelled gratitude by their willingness to become copyists and proof-readers. One of these was Samuel Rousseau, whose assistance on the score of *Ghisèle* was to prove so practical an aid. Rousseau is hardly an important figure in his own right, but merits recognition as one of his teacher's oldest and most trusted acquaintances. It is remarkable how much affection and respect he tended to elicit from the ageing Franck; perhaps on account of his having won the Prix de Rome in 1878. This was an achievement that no other pupil had been able to match—at least until Pierné equalled it four years later. Rousseau's birthplace is listed as Neuve-Maison, and the date of his entry into the world as 11 June 1853. While at the Conservatoire, his masters were Bazin and Franck, though he revealed himself to be such an early developer that it was only a short step before he outgrew the need for any guiding hand. In the same year as he set out for Italy, he had an opera, *Dianorah*, accepted at the Comique, a most unusual triumph for one who was technically still a student. Likewise, his *envois de Rome* were eagerly taken up in the capital's concert-halls. These consisted of three works—a *poème* on the myth of the Sabine women (1880); an oriental fable entitled *Kaddir* (1881); and an obligatory souvenir of the City of the Medicis, *La Florentine* (1882). Not content with such a rousing beginning to his career, Rousseau went on to capture the Paris municipal prize with yet another stage-work, *Merowig*, based on Georges Montorgueil's verses. This was played at the Trocadéro and secured the warmest acclaim. Among his later operatic ventures was a full-length study in German romantic legendry, *La Cloche du Rhin* (1898)—which hints at d'Indy's influence—and, much less ambitious in scope, a comedy called *Milia* which ended up on the stage of the Rue Favart in 1904. Unfortunately, these projects marked the finish of Rousseau as a composer, for he died in the following October—still a comparatively young man—leaving behind a barely completed lyric drama, *Léone*, which was presented six years after his death. It is a tale of revenge—or more properly vendetta—in the Italian fashion.

[1] What these ideals were can be best imagined from a glance at the virtues extolled by Montaigne several centuries earlier. Loyalty, sincerity, honesty and good faith were the qualities that went to compose his 'honnête homme', and they are very much those admired by the Franck circle. In certain cases, they were accompanied by a typically epicurean serenity.

Viewed in purely academic terms, there is a case for saying that Rousseau was Franck's most precocious pupil, but like so many prize-winning prodigies he had none of the vision and imagination required to satisfy posterity's examiners. His music is undeniably well-written, admirably suited to the voices and instruments it employs, and has a pleasing, surface charm. The final impression it leaves, however, is that of being tepidly sub-Gounod. If this seems unkind, it should be remembered that not many of Franck's pupils had it in them to imitate that efficient artist's smoothly-wrought cadences; indeed most of them suffered from a gawkiness which the years did little to dispel. What other traces of influence we can detect in Rousseau smack of Lalo rather than Franck. Certainly there is not much in the composer's training to account for the Southern spontaneity which occasionally breaks out in his music. Perhaps René Dumesnil has best summed up his particular skills and limitations when he defined his art as: 'plus facile que profonde, plus correcte que personelle, plus élégante que dramatique.' Bearing these strictures in mind, it could be said that Rousseau would have done better had he refrained from mortgaging so much of his time and ability to the theatre. He did write a quantity of chamber music, and also a few things for piano and solo voice. But the masses and motets which he contributed as part of his duties at Sainte-Clotilde—he was Maître de Chappelle there at the same time as Franck was occupying the grand organ—were perhaps the nearest approach he was able to make to the sort of music his teacher really revered. In particular, the *Messe de Paques*, the *Messe de Noël* and an orthodox but finely-worked Requiem stand to his credit as a church musician. Otherwise, one cannot help feeling that Rousseau's output serves to illustrate the failings of his age in much the same manner as that of Coquard, whose leanings towards a facile theatricalism he was fated to echo. Neither composer survived far enough into the twentieth century to adapt himself to the newer styles.

A far more diffident survivor from the vintage years was Benoît. Effete and detached, he does not really merit exhumation as a musician, but is interesting because his double career ran along quite unaccustomed tracks. Whatever we may think of him, it will hardly be maintained that he strove to put music first in his ambitions. Two years older than Rousseau, he grew up on the banks of the Loire, which may have been the reason why he was driven to take up the visual arts with what seems like greater propulsion. He became a pupil of Franck in 1872—the first year in which the composer attended to his duties at the Conservatoire—and can therefore be said to have moved freely among the circle's oldest members. Whether he himself deserves to be graced with the title of disciple remains something of a problem. Franck certainly liked him, but then he liked almost everyone who had the humility to settle down in his class. There is no evidence that he attempted to cultivate a deliberate friendship, and even if he had done so Benoît would probably have been too busy to respond. Aiming at a career in the museum service, he attached himself to the Louvre in 1888, rose to become Curator of Antiquities by 1895, and thereafter adjusted his musical aspirations to fit the conditions of his employment. His earliest compositions appeared by courtesy of the Société Nationale, while later on in his life he was given a certain amount of encouragement by the Schola Cantorum. It was the last-named institution which revived his *Eleison* for solo voices, chorus and orchestra in 1916. This work had originally been written in 1890, which year appears to have been the high watermark of the composer's promise. Unlike many who had placed security before self-expression, Benoît did not entirely renounce the practice of composition. He went on to contribute a symphonic poem entitled *Merlin l'enchanteur* which conscientiously attempted to repeat Chausson's modest success. An *Epithalame*, written for Anatole France's *Les Noces*, succeeded in bringing his name before a wider theatrical public, while some incidental music for a drama, *Les Corinthiennes*, had the further effect of unveiling his ancient history interests.

These belated spurts of activity convinced Benoît's friends that the composer had been mistaken in not applying himself more whole-heartedly to music from the outset. His own reaction seems to have been a twinge of regret coupled with an earnest desire to make up for lost time. An opera on the theme of Cleopatra—at which he worked enthusiastically following the armistice—was begun too late to yield him the sort of reward for which he now had cause to hope, and only the death scene ever seems to have been played. This made a powerful enough impression on those who heard it, its strength and beauty precipitating immediate tributes from both d'Indy and Samazeuilh. Also incomplete at the moment of the composer's passing—which took place in July 1923 —was a second *poème symphonique* provisionally entitled *La Nuit*. This is not nearly as original a work as Lazzari's essay in the same vein. Undoubtedly the main reason why Benôit failed to get the best out of himself as a creative artist was that he had too many irons in the fire. Not only did he continue to pay scrupulous attention to his duties at the Louvre, but he also aimed at a third reputation as a propagandist and critic. His sympathies in this last direction lay with Wagner more than Franck. The volume *Souvenirs* brought together his many translations from the work of the Bayreuth master, and it was a book that won a considerable readership. Deeply aroused by the world's great dramatists, Benoît had no hesitation in admitting Wagner to their company, seeing him as the lineal descendant of Shakespeare, Racine and Goethe. By devoting much care to the translation of the last-named author, he was able to add still further to his scholarly reputation while curtailing the dwindling time he had left for composition. A collection of his musical journalism appeared under the title *Musiciens, poètes et philosophes* in 1887, and he also gained renown for a Latin translation of Beethoven's *Elegischer Gesang*. Franck heartily disapproved of his pupil's critical activities, finding them too partisan in tone. D'Indy, on the contrary, found himself able to accommodate the writer's Germanic bias without loss to his ideals, and he accordingly offered him every encouragement.

If Benoît was a shade too complacent in his attitude to his art, Paul de Wailly erred on the side of earnestness. A native of Amiens, he was born in 1854 and was therefore pretty well a contemporary of Chausson. He too made the switch from law to music, commending himself to the singing-master, Romain Bussine, whose position in the Société Nationale gave him a certain standing in the musical world he would otherwise have lacked. It was Bussine who introduced the young man to Franck, to whom he thereafter showed a touching sense of loyalty almost without parallel among the circle's members. De Wailly was just twenty-seven when he began receiving lessons from his new teacher, and he responded with all the fervour of a mature student. As a musician, he had been largely self-taught up to that time, so that he really had far more to learn than most of his fellow-pupils. This may have been one reason why Franck meted out a firmer discipline to him than was customary. Only a pupil with de Wailly's dogged sense of tact and determination could have stayed the course he was set. In exchange for his labours, Franck helped him to an easy début through the auspices of the society, an event he celebrated with the cantata *Hylas, idylle antique* (1882). This dual tableau involved the collaboration of the poet Jean Lorrain, with whom Proust once attempted to fight a duel. Though he was to enjoy a long life, de Wailly never managed to capitalize on the successes of his master, nor did he succeed in persuading the public of their obligation to listen to his own music. He cannot be said to have lacked industry, for he wrote three symphonies, several sonatas, chamber music for five and eight instruments and a sizeable quantity of songs. Like Rousseau, he also contributed a volume of pieces for the harmonium, though this only made its appearance posthumously. The major creative effort of his life probably went into his four act oratorio *L'Apôtre*—a work of Christian piety that may be compared with Cahen's *Jean le Baptiste* and Franck's *Rédemption*. It is an indication of the time-lag that attended de Wailly's musical thinking that this principal fruit of his studies did not appear until 1924.

The claims of the foregoing composers can seem fanciful when set beside those of Franck's organ prodigies, among whom the formidable Gabriel Pierné occupies a central position.[1] One's first instinct is to rebel against the notion that this versatile artist need be classified as a church musician, yet that was precisely the capacity in which he started out and even continued for a good many years. Listeners are not always alive to the fact that it was he who succeeded Franck at the console of Sainte-Clotilde, a post he was proud to hold from 1890 to 1898. Up-to-date appreciations of his achievement are nowadays hard to encounter, for he was one of those unlucky musicians (Bruneau is another) whose fame could be said to have expired with their dying breaths. To his contemporaries, Pierné's star glittered in a dozen different spheres, and he was frequently held up as the model of how to succeed. Organist, conductor, composer—he fulfilled a succession of roles without apparent strain, while his ability to produce mammoth chunks of music remained undimmed to the very end of his life. How then can we account for today's sudden lowering of his stock? Is it that, like Ropartz, he wrote so much that the mind simply boggles at the idea of trying to comprehend it all? Or was it the case that he busied himself so unthinkingly with each and every genre that he somehow did not stop to make any his own? The truth does not readily correspond to either of these suggestions, and perhaps relates more to the public's unwillingness to be appealed to on more than one level at a time. For Pierné emulated Grieg and Sibelius in writing popular music simultaneously with his more serious works. Like them, he came up against resistance in his high-minded incarnations, only to find himself eagerly and sincerely adopted as a purveyor of 'bonnes-bouches'. Time has at least made amends to the Finnish composer in that his profundities have now outstripped his attempts at vulgarization. So far there has been no such reparation accorded to Pierné—possibly because the lines separating his various styles are murkier and less easy to draw.

The son of two professional musicians, this energetic Parisian had actually come from Metz, where his family were caught up in the Franco-Prussian War. Young Gabriel was only aged seven at

---

[1] Among the others, whom we shall scarcely have space to mention, it is worth noting Louis Vierne (1870–1937) whose organ symphonies were a harmonic continuation of Franck's work; the elderly Henri Dallier (1849–1934) who had come from Rheims and was to succeed Fauré at the Madeleine; and such lesser luminaries as the unfortunate Gaston Vallin, who destroyed everything he wrote, and Henri de Kunklemann.

the time of this tragedy, and hence not old enough to be launched on the road to musical acclaim. But it was not very long afterwards that he began clamouring for admission to the Conservatoire. His teachers, once he had settled down there, became Franck, Massenet and Lavignac. He collected prizes in all the subjects he was taught, being as industrious as he was gifted. (His lessons with Franck took place at seven o'clock each day!) It was with the cantata *Edith* that he secured the Rome award—not surprisingly, for it remains a solid and highly competent effort. The years the composer spent in Italy turned out to be the happiest of his life (unlike those Debussy forced himself to endure) and also among the most influential in shaping his taste. He was accordingly in no hurry to return home. What finally decided him to depart was the offer of an organ post at Saint-Sulpice, the clarinet-shaped towers of which were already becoming a familiar landmark to tourists. Pierné probably had no intention of anchoring himself to the church for life, however, more especially since he had been invited by Colonne to alternate as assistant conductor at that venerable musician's orchestral concerts. In the course of time, he went on to succeed his chief as director of these concerts, an honour he felt disinclined to relinquish until reaching his retirement in 1934. Meanwhile, he married into the family of Luc-Oliver Merson, the painter, and pursued a fairly calm metropolitan existence. His compositions—of which there were to be no fewer than nine operas, nine ballets, a clutch of oratorios and dozens of miscellaneous orchestral pieces—were mostly written while he was on vacation, as d'Indy's had been. The favourite resort in Pierné's case was Carantec. During the period leading up to the First World War, the composer produced a body of chamber music—including works for piano and woodwind instruments—and this tends to reveal his more serious side; a side that did not succeed in ousting his theatrical ambitions. Before commenting on the better known things he wrote, it might repay us to devote a few lines to the exploration of this youthful, idealistic phase in the artist's life.

Setting aside the album of fifteen piano pieces op. 5 (1883) and the various duos involving clarinet and bassoon, the first work of substance we come up against in the chamber field is perhaps the Violin Sonata, op. 36 (1900). Written in the same key as Brahms's third sonata, it offers music that is full of warmth and charm and includes an inventive section in 10/16 time. Harmonically, Pierné leads on from Franck with a richness that many of the master's organ pupils strove to share. His more advanced technique made it easy for him to write the sort of sequences this entailed, while his adventurous approach to instrumental values is sufficiently indicated by the fact that he was the first composer to use the saxophone

as a chamber instrument. Like his teacher, he also set a great deal
of store by a Piano Quintet (which appeared some years before that
of Fauré) of highly complex texture. This is a very fine work, well
worth reviving. Quite different from either of his compatriot's
essays, it is built around Basque melodies and exhibits a Zortzico
rhythm in its D flat second movement. The finale includes a typically Franckist reunion of themes. Some think that Pierné never
went beyond the achievements contained in this work, though others
are inclined to name the Piano Trio as the star of his chamber music
collection. The latter reverts once more to curious rhythmical
experiments, alternating a 3/8 with a 5/8 time signature. But easily
the most captivating of all the compositions this talented man wrote
in the intimate forms is his *Sonata da Camera* for piano, flute and
cello, op. 48. The unusual *mélange de timbres* is such that, given
Pierné's smooth accomplishment, nothing could have prevented the
work from being a delight. Conceived as a tribute to the flautist,
Louis Fleury, it begins with a fluid, expressive 'prélude', very
elegant yet spontaneous-sounding. This is followed by what is
possibly the best of the three movements—a melancholy 'sarabande' in which flute and cello engage in some beautifully fragmentary dialogues. The piano is then left to assume the chief role
in the 'final', though without doing anything to upset the delicate
instrumental balance. Listening to this graceful sonata, one can
appreciate why his friend Pirrou thought Pierné the keenest and
most whimsical sensibility of his time.

A cynic might have gone on to add that it was precisely this
ease of manner that did most to threaten the composer's integrity.
At any rate, signs of an increasing awareness of the market came to
appear in too many of his subsequent works. It is not so much that
they began to sound a false or artificial note, for naturalness was the
one quality he had a marvellous gift for simulating. Rather, an
impression of over-simplicity sought to assert itself. The songs—
including settings of Richepin and Klingsor—show what a dangerously facile talent Pierné possessed. Emotions were handled by him
almost as if they were counters in a game of roulette, and he could
switch from humour to tenderness and back again in an utterly
deceptive fashion. It is not altogether remarkable, therefore, that
each new work was quickly consigned to the realm of exhausted
pleasures. The price the composer was felt to pay for them seemed
too cheap. Looking at some of the religious compositions of the
same period, we can detect an analogous absence of struggle. The
Paysages Franciscains, for example, are limpid to the point of bore-
dom, fine though many of the episodes may claim to be from a
technical point of view. It is not so much Franck who is recalled
in their gentle transparencies as Massenet, the composer's other

teacher. One begins to get the feeling, too, that an Italian influence is being brought to bear—perhaps the clear Umbrian or Tuscan heritage absorbed during the Prix de Rome years. Pierné continued to work very hard at the sacred forms nevertheless. In 1907 he aroused enormous interest with his oratorio, *Les Enfants à Bethléem*, which had its première at Amsterdam. Gabriel Nigond was the author of the poem on which it was based. Its colourful tableaux depicting the coming of the Magi and the unveiling of the infant Jesus combined to give it much the sort of universal appeal that has since been conferred on Menotti's *Amahl and the Night Visitors*—though without benefit of television. An even better

Ex. 27

Gabriel Pierné: Les Enfants à Bethléem. - (Fugal motif).

example of the composer's power to please was provided in a second work, *Saint François d'Assise*, which was first heard at the Châtelet theatre in 1912.

Ex. 28

Gabriel Pierné: Gregorian theme from Saint Francois d' Assise

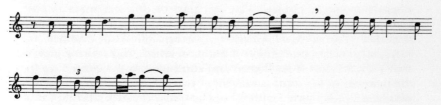

On the operatic front, much the same set of criticisms can be applied. *La Fille de Tabarin* (1901) was the earliest of the composer's successes in this sector, and one that benefited from the dramatic flair of Sardou. At least, this was the case as far as the box-office was concerned. From a less commercial standpoint, the work gained nothing from being touched-up to suit the audience's mood. A crude tale of adventure, it was rendered still cruder by the attentions of the dramatist, leaving poor Pierné to do the best he could with the music. The operas that followed were mostly to do with slightly *risqué* historical subjects, like the breathless *Sophie Arnould* which was created at the Opéra-Comique in 1927. To have por-trayed flirtations with love and death under the Directoire must have seemed an anti-climax to one who had begun his career under César Franck's solemn tutelage, but there is no evidence that the composer sensed any corruption of ambition. By that time, he had survived into an age of religious disbelief, and was responding to the post-war fever for *la gaieté*. One cannot help feeling that *Sophie* would have done even better as a silent film, with Norma Shearer and John Gilbert. *Fragonard* (1934), on the other hand—based on the life and loves of the eighteenth-century painter—had all the ingredients of a first-class musical comedy. The *trio des amants* in Act I aspires to some of the freshness of a rococo chanson, while the various duets—as, for example, between Frago and Guimard, or between Hubert Robert and the elusive *La Caissière*—are ex-pressly contrived to secure applause. Add to these the numerous *sonneries militaires*, included as a tribute to Soubise, and the luxuri-ant ball scene, and the whole comprises a brilliant and lively even-ing's entertainment. It was first performed at Porte Saint-Martin in the October following the composer's last season with the Con-certs Colonne. Among his many scores for the ballet, it is worth singling out that written in support of de Hellé's *Images* (1935) which a number of judges have compared to Debussy's *La Boîte à joujoux*. The earlier *Cydalise et le Chèvre-Pied* (1923) also suggests an affinity with the musician of *Syrinx* and *La Flûte de Pan*, though the comparison does not extend much beyond the choice of subject.

For all his Italianisms, there was something essentially Gallic about Pierné; he was a figure who could never have appeared any-where else but in France. The last part of this statement is one that can be applied no less accurately to an altogether different musician—the mystical Charles Tournemire. Also destined to succeed Franck as the tribune of Sainte-Clotilde, this retiring player took over the post from Pierné and continued in the church up to the moment of his death some forty years later.[1] A strict contem-porary of Louis Vierne, with whom he shared Franck's favours as a teacher, Tournemire lived his life in the service of God and the greater glories of the spirit. To many he almost seemed a resurrec-tion of his master, and it was true that no one had managed to imi-tate Franck's religious dissociations quite as poignantly. A native of Bordeaux, he came to Paris only to round off his studies, winning first prize for organ at the Conservatoire as a brilliant finishing stroke. Before this he had seen fit to place himself under Taudou

[1] The present incumbent is the blind organist, Jean Langlais, with whom Tournemire often undertook joint musical activities during the inter-war years.

for harmony and Franck for his solo instrument, later transferring
to Widor for the latter. The mechanics of organ-playing were not
what interested the young student, however, since what he really
wanted was to give expression to the profound ardours of the spirit
which he had discovered within. These soon made themselves felt
in his compositions, and though he showed no desire at all for
worldly recognition it nevertheless became obvious that in his
quieter way he would go on to be just as prolific as Pierné. It is sad
to have to record that he too developed a tendency to fall victim to
his own gifts, only these did not lead to over-facility as much as
over-complexity. Even today, when listeners have had several
decades in which to digest Tournemire's output, it is not uncommon to find him written off as a kind of organist's Alkan. This
is a great disservice to a man who wrote, not simply some of the
best organ music of the present century, but a magnificent treasury
of choral and orchestral works of a standard no nation can afford
to hold in contempt. When one also considers the affinities between
his style and that of the typical *avant-garde* figure of the 1930s—
especially as represented in 'La Jeune France'—it becomes all
the more vital that Tournemire should receive due recognition for
his efforts.

Of course, the composer's most formative period did not com-
mence until after Franck's death, by which time he had attached
himself to d'Indy for lessons. But evidence of the earlier teacher's
influence persisted in that preoccupation with vertical writing that
became so much a feature of his music. Throughout the sumptuous
Le Sang de la Sirène (1904), for solo voices, chorus and orchestra,
the harmony displays a characteristic richness that could only have
emanated from the Franckist *phalange*. This dramatic legend
incidentally won its composer the Grand Prix de la Ville de Paris,
and had the effect of broadening his scope so as to admit the inclusion of works for the stage. The two-act sacred drama to which
he gave the title *Chryséis* should be seen as a half-way house in this
process, which did not reach fulfilment until 1924, the year his
Les Dieux sont morts was mounted at the Opéra. A second contribution to the lyric theatre—the ill-fated *Nittetis*—has still failed to
secure performance. There can be no doubt, however, that Tournemire's nature was too introverted to remain long enthralled by the
stage. His dramas tended to be all of the mind and spirit. Much
more truly expressive of his interests are the assorted organ pieces
which lie scattered throughout his corpus, beginning with op. 2.
and ending with the *Petites Fleurs Musicales* of op. 66.[1] These often

[1] To these must be added the *Cinq Improvisations* (1961) which Maurice Duruflé transcribed from sound-recordings of Tournemire's playing
at Sainte-Clotilde. These are in two books and are issued by Durand & Co.

contain uncanny anticipations of Messiaen (whom Tournemire taught both privately and in his capacity as Professor of Chamber Music at the Conservatoire) and do much to proclaim a new musical language based on the idea of modal transposition. The two hundred and fifty-five pieces of the composer's *L'Orgue Mystique*, op. 55–7, for example, should be examined in close conjunction with his pupil's *Messe de la Pentecôte* and *Livre d'Orgue*. All three collections (Tournemire's is a complete set of offices for Sundays and festivals, including *entrées* and *offertoires*) enormously enlarge the resources available to the modern liturgical musician; especially in the direction of providing an iridescent screen of musico-religious symbols developed out of a combination of harmonic and monodic influences.

Mystical numerology seems to have been among the interests Franck unconsciously sought to promote, and the pupil who did most to transmit this interest to contemporary composers was undoubtedly Tournemire. A line of descent that links Franck's principle of the Trinity to Messiaen's ideal order would have to find room for works like the Triple Chorale, op. 41, of their intermediary. Tournemire's approach went far beyond his teacher's in that he did not allow it to rest exclusively on the notions of form and part-writing communicated to him. Like Messiaen, he experimented in his own fashion with new scales (some of which had been used independently by both Dukas and Debussy) and by means of the trick he exhibited of creating harmony through unit-addition. Much of the impression of variegation which his music suggests— and it is tempting to compare this to the effect achieved by stained-glass panelling—derives from its lavish adoption of augmented fourths, added sixths and other kaleidoscopic devices. Embedded in an underlay of plainchant—in which the tritone was *diabolus in musica*—such devices result in all manner of unexpected sounds, many of which seem to transport the listener across centuries of musical tradition in the space of a few seconds. Equally unlocalized is the composer's handling of other elements in his vocabulary. For instance, he proved himself to be an astute 'rhythmatician' —as may be demonstrated by a glance at the Sextet for piano and wind instruments which he wrote. His persistent rhythmic pedal-points again look forward to the 'isorhythms' of the exotic school, though they may also have stemmed from his deep immersion in the works of the ancient polyphonists. It is precisely these qualities of ambiguity which help to give Tournemire's style its distinguished twist, for otherwise it appears to have evolved naturally out of the Franck-d'Indy idiom. The rich colouring we associate with this idiom is certainly present in the composer's treatment of instruments, and we can detect it best in the eight symphonies with which he is credited. Their sonority and mobility place these among the finest specimens of the form ever to have been written in France, and one day they may 'kick off their tombstones' in the fashion that Mahler's and Bruckner's have done.

One of the most astonishing of Tournemire's orchestral works is the early *Les Combats de l'Idéal*, which is a trilogy on the theme of heroism. Each panel is given over to a particular kind of hero—the first to a seeker after knowledge; the second to an exponent of courtly love; and the third to a renowned spiritual veteran who could be described as the patron saint of the Franck circle. They are, respectively, Faust, Don Quixote and St Francis of Assisi. Only someone as unworldly as the composer would have possessed the temerity to bring these complex psychological figures into close juxtaposition. But Tournemire never had cause to feel ashamed of his idealism. His naïvety was so pure, and his faith so unbounded, that he almost succeeds in convincing us of how wise he had been in his choice. What these sketches lack, however, is just that profound regard for human foible that was present in each of their subjects. The result is that they exhibit no sharpness of touch, no genuine aptitude for dramatic characterisation. For all his crude materialism, Richard Strauss did better with the Knight of the Mournful Countenance, while the portrait of Faust hardly comes up to the standard set in Liszt's superb symphony. Purely descriptive music was not Tournemire's forte, though he did persevere with the idea to the extent of including a programme-symphony among his eight. This is the one known as *La Montagne* and reckoned as No. 5 in the series. Earlier on, too, he had attempted a version of the Tristan and Iseult legend along somewhat purer lines than Wagner's. Each of these works displays all the invention one could wish for, musically speaking, but neither adds anything to the composer's stature. His *Poème* for organ and orchestra finds him on surer ground, and there is enough in the Piano Trio and Piano Quartet to make us regret that so little chamber music flowed from his pen. Among Tournemire's remaining compositions, a handful of *mélodies* have been preserved which reveal a delicate sensibility obsessed with the possibilities of chromatic inflection. But the student will begin most profitably by returning to the organ works, especially if armed with Flor Peeters's useful guide.[1]

Each of the composers so far described acquired some, if not all, of his technique from Franck himself. This was not the case with Albéric Magnard, however, whose contacts were forged with d'Indy and Ropartz. From the former he received a strict training in every

[1] Entitled *L'Oeuvre d'orgue de Charles Tournemire* (Bruges, 1940), this belated tribute provides a brief analysis of each of the major works.

branch of musicianship, and from the latter the stimulus of a profound and lifelong friendship. The son of the editor of *Figaro*,
Magnard represents yet another of the circle's well-to-do members,
a man whose background lacked nothing in the way of social or
cultural amenities. That these did not inspire much gratitude in him
is a fact that must be attributed to his icy, choleric disposition.
Born in 1865, and brought up in a world of high finance and genteel
political debate, he made it obvious from the outset that he regarded
his home environment as a sham and a bore. Passionately devoted to
the life of reason, he much preferred to be left alone to enjoy his
Cartesian pleasures. So far the reader may feel reminded of
Chausson, but Magnard possessed little of that kindly dilettante's
sense of tolerance towards others, and nothing at all of his yearning
for the romantic aspects of existence. An altogether harder and more
saturnine individual, the composer of *Bérénice* was never able to
suffer fools gladly; and as almost all of his father's acquaintances
fell into that unhappy category he found scarcely anything in life
that amused him. Determined to have a musical career, despite the
rosy prospects that loomed in business or journalism, the young
ascetic entered the Conservatoire, as a student of Théodore Dubois.
But this was not until 1886. In the meantime, he indulged in a
number of those leisurely travels that only the sons of the rich
seem able to afford. A spell in England, spent at the Dominican
abbey of Ramsgate, enabled him to exchange his all too Proustian
milieu for one in which plain living and high thinking took the
place of conviviality. It is fascinating to imagine this spoilt Parisian,
much as he is portrayed in the Reverend d'Egon's letters to Gaston
Carraud, improvising moodily on his flute all day while the monks
went about their duties. Whether it was due to the habits of silence
which he thus acquired, or merely to temperamental obtuseness,
Magnard later adopted a pose at the Conservatoire that resulted in
the utmost docility. Dubois even claimed that he did not speak a
single word throughout the two years in which he attended for
lessons.

The musical interests which Magnard professed in his youth
were not quite as chilling as those to which he became attached in
later life. He began, like so many Franck disciples, by being an
ardent Wagnerian, a voyage to Bayreuth having constituted the
occasion for his enthusiasm. Even before that, however, he had
found solace in Chopin's dreamy and aristocratic art. What these
two composers taught him is not something that reveals itself at
first glance. It would be easy to account for his love of opera by
referring to the former influence, but the things Magnard admired
in the theatre were hardly the flamboyant machinations which had
aroused the instincts of his idol. Nor, despite his despairing out-

look, could he be said to have responded to the more melancholy strain in his Polish exemplar. Rather, he looked to Wagner to equip him with dramatic qualities of the sort which he could import into his more abstract compositions; while it was probably something of Chopin's fiery nationalist vigour that he hoped to transfer to his theatrical canon. Stage and study accordingly became, not the stereotyped antinomies they were for the average musician, but the means of fruitful creative interaction. When the young composer's tastes had extended a little further, it became apparent that they would include Gluck, Rameau and Beethoven. The zest for Franck's music owed itself chiefly to a hearing of the D minor Symphony, and one feels that it was helped along by Magnard's strong social convictions. That is to say, he was aroused to a point of indignation by the fact that so profound a work had been allowed to pass unsung by the critics. About the one point on which he saw eye to eye with Lekeu was that Franck was being made the victim of a most shameful neglect. The flattery heaped on Massenet and his school was a source of bitter feeling in both men. But Magnard had no need to ferret out his ideals from a corrupt musical situation; his artistic horizons were wide enough to have encompassed most of the time-honoured attitudes of dedication. There is no one whom he resembled more than his countryman Flaubert, whose ruthless pursuit of perfection was enacted all over again in the search for formal values to which he committed himself.

The earliest phase of his composing career—that which ended with the *Promenades* for piano—reveals both the strengths and weaknesses of Magnard's idealism. A *Suite dans le style ancien* demonstrates an anxious dependence on the teachings of the Franck school: its four movements all derive from a common thematic root. Likewise, the d'Indyesque First Symphony of 1890 turns out to be a work of the purest cyclic form, as short on material as it is long on development. Neither of these compositions was anything other than prentice stuff. The Quintet for piano and wind instruments which followed them is much better, and lays claim to a genre in which the composer was to invest heavily in the years ahead. But a Second Symphony had made its appearance within a very short time of the failure of the first (it had only one performance at Angers in 1893) and this marked a step forward in its relaxation and control. Instead of a monotonous polyphonic bombardment, the listener is relieved to be greeted with a second movement of surprising lightness and grace—a fetching *divertissement populaire* in fact. This, coupled with the robust finale, establishes the composer as more than a straight imitator of his seniors. At the same time as he was polishing his talent for the larger forms, Magnard took respite in a charming collection of piano miniatures depicting the various excursions available within the environs of Paris. These *Promenades*, as they were called, owe their title to the eighteenth number of Schumann's *Carnaval*; and in turn provided Poulenc with the heading for his unsuccessful parodies of 1924. They are all extremely attractive pieces and cover a geographical terrain which ranges from the Bois de Boulogne through St Cloud and Versailles to Rambouillet. Some of the scenes are evoked with impressionist delicacy ('Villebon', for example, employs carillon effects very much in the manner of Debussy or Moussorgsky), while others achieve a dainty neo-classicism which Auric and Francaix were later to strive for. The closing nuptial might also be related to

Ex. 29
Albéric Magnard: Trianon (from "Promenades").

Satie's hieratic art. Pianistically, they are neither complex nor difficult to play, though the repeated *ostinato* figures need a gentle touch.

Ex. 30
Albéric Magnard: Rambouillet (from "Promenades").

Anyone happening on Magnard through the medium of these unruffled sound-pictures may be dismayed to find how few comparable delights there are among his other compositions. It is almost as if the composer had decided to put away childish things immediately on reaching maturity. What we are offered in their place is a series of fairly dour chamber and orchestral works, enlivened here and there by distinct touches of clarity. This last quality is one that Magnard constantly strove to promote. It is what puts him apart from so many of the conscientious toilers of the period. The new-found earnestness which he acquired in the closing years of the century may well have been due to the death of his father; an event that occurred in 1894 and which prompted a solemn *Chant Funèbre* in commemoration. A thoroughly Beethovenian opus, this reminds us very much of the *Egmont* and *Leonora* overtures in its huge oppressiveness. Like several of Magnard's movements, it is built of two opposing themes, the first announced by the oboe and violins in a 3/2 rhythm and the second by trumpet and flute in a *pianissimo* 4/2. The lesser-known *Hymne à la Justice* which followed in 1902 seems to have been the product of a more affirmative phase, though it is improbable that the composer ever experienced much depth of conviction on the subject. At no time in his life did he seek to emulate Beethoven's noble sentiments towards humanity, and even his religious instincts had a tendency to wither. The pure tones of his chamber-works accordingly express the composer's ideals more sincerely than anything else one can point to in his art. His approach to the writing of these works was distinguished by its acute intensity. Despising lyricism, he chose to regard the medium as a challenge to his powers of dramatic fusion, using it to create what might be described as an internal theatre of forms. Fugue, sonata, variation, *Lied*—all occur with frequent regularity in his works for a limited combination, and their presence compensates for a certain harmonic and melodic slenderness which also seems characteristic. Tension is indeed the principle on which nearly all of Magnard's work proceeds, everything appearing to press urgently towards resolution. Landormy's term for it was 'violent meditation'—almost as much of a paradox as the 'serene anxiety' ascribed to Franck.

It is worth observing in this connection that an unusually large number of his movements are in sonata form, while the lighter rondo form is almost entirely in abeyance. The fugal style is to be found in the composer's Cello Sonata (1910)—an excellent work in which the piano is given rather too much prominence—and in his Piano Quintet (1894). Yet another example springs quickly to mind in the Third Symphony (1896) which might otherwise have earned the title 'Pastoral'. What is so typical about these intrusions is that they face up fully to the demands of the fugue as a form, abounding in stretti, canon, augmentation and all the other accepted devices. None of Franck's followers embraced his fondness for canon quite so eagerly as Magnard, who used it again and again to bind his compositions into the desired unity. Listeners may care to check that there is something resembling a complete, scholastic fugue in the finales of each of the Piano Trio (1909), the Violin Sonata (1901) and the Fourth Symphony (1911). Yet the first two of these works are by no stretch of imagination to be called academic; the Trio employs its fugue in the midst of a lively dance movement and the Sonata compensates for its austerities by throwing up a vividly poetic andante. In much the same fashion, the variation form can be accounted a fundamental force in the slow movements of the Second and Fourth Symphonies, as well as in the little-played *Hymne à Venus*. Instead of regarding the form as a succession of detached units, however, Magnard saw it as something continuous. The *Promenades* are about the only example of isolated variation technique in the composer's entire *oeuvre*. *Lied* forms occur often, as they do in both Franck and d'Indy, but more common still is the form of the *choral*. This can be traced in several of the symphonies, and also as a means of presenting the faith motif in the first of the operas. A patently borrowed technique relates, of course, to the cyclic habit which the composer chose to practise in so many of his works. This habit—instances of which are to be found in the Third Symphony, the Trio and the Violin Sonata—helps to substantiate the charge that Magnard was prone to over-develop his material.

If the chamber music virus sank deeply into the composer's bloodstream, the operatic germ came to affect him every bit as powerfully once he had moved on into the last phase of his career. It had first made its presence felt in the one-act *Yolande*, the première of which had taken place in Brussels during 1892. The second opera which he was to write—the tragic *Bérénice*—aimed at larger goals and perhaps remains Magnard's finest achievement. Loosely based on Racine's story, the work also harks back to Egyptian sources in a mixture of passion and classical simplicity. Performed in December 1911, the score was preceded by a lengthy statement of the composer's theatrical ideals, and these serve to shed ample illumination on what he was trying to do. In the first place, he was not endeavouring to present a spectacle of violence. Accepting the conventions of the great French tragedians, he struggled instead to depict a drama of conscience and love. It is significant that when Magnard wrote explaining the opera to his friend Paul Poujaud he fell back on the tale of the Princesse de Clèves to help him underline his points. Equipped with such a detached, almost omniscient, view of the events he was describing, it is hardly surprising that the composer was led to provide music of the most sober and restrained quality. As he himself put it in his account of the origin of Titus's declaration:

> J'ai employé la fugue dans la méditation de Titus, la douce harmonie du canon a l'octave dans toutes les effusions d'amour.*

Some commentators have seen this propensity for suggesting passion through the sternest of all musical forms as yet another proof of Magnard's epicene nature. The truth is, however, that he had not reached the stage, when he wrote this work, of fully comprehending the elements of sexual conflict. Having begun his life as a dedicated anti-feminist, he only gradually came to appreciate how much of the female character existed within his own make-up. Nevertheless, the opera rises magnificently to meet its obligations, particularly during the clamorous sacrificial scene in Act II and the marvellously compassionate *déploration* by which the abandoned Queen bids farewell.

Oddly enough, the style of *Bérénice* was not a matter which gave the composer great anxiety. Realising that Wagner's was the most up-to-date idiom of the day, he did not see anything shameful about appropriating it for his own stage works. Commenting on the reasons for taking this step, he wrote:

> Ma partition est ecrite dans le style Wagnérien. Dépourvu du génie necessaire pour créer une nouvelle forme lyrique, j'ai choisi parmi les styles existants celui qui convenait le mieux à mes goûts tout classiques, et ma culture musicale toute traditionelle. J'ai seulement cherché à me rapprocher le plus possible de la musique pure. . . . Il est possible que ma conception de la musique dramatique soit fausse. Je m'en excuse d'avance auprès de nos esthètes le plus autorisés.†

However complacent this may have seemed to his contemporaries, the policy Magnard chose to adopt had the merit of allowing him to concentrate more on the non-musical problems he was set. How much less energy he wasted, for example, than Chausson, whose fear of imitation led him to the brink of impotence. Today, when

---

* I have used fugue for Titus's meditation, the sweet harmony of canon at the octave for all his expressions of love.

† My score is written in the Wagnerian style. Deprived of the genius to create a new lyric form, I have chosen from among the existing styles that which best suits my purpose, rather than fall back on classical taste and my whole traditional musical culture. I have only looked for a tenable means of writing pure music . . . It is possible my view of opera is false. I can only excuse myself for not approaching more closely the outlook of the approved aesthetes.

we are less inclined to make a fuss over influences, the Wagnerisms in *Bérénice* appear hardly worthy of comment, while the efforts the composer put into shaping the libretto and determining the mood are likely to meet with the most appreciative response. Indeed, if the charges of plagiarism are pressed too far, one can always retort that what Magnard saw in Wagner was quite different from what the usual French admirer tended to see. He noted qualities of measure and design, of dramatic pace and balance, not at all the sort of things that had appealed to the more hot-headed composer. For this reason alone, he deserves respect rather than censure. In a sense, his view can be said to have anticipated the opinions of men like Ernest Newman and Hans Pfitzner. In its own day, however, *Bérénice* struck critics as too monotonous and derivative, and it ran for a mere eight performances. Probably many visitors to the theatre had come in the expectation of being ravished by music of the deliberately orgiastic kind, afterwards seeking to take out their disappointment on an unsuspecting composer and cast. If so, they were much to blame for their prejudices.

The last opera Magnard lived to complete was much less realistic than either of its predecessors, being more of the genre of *Fervaal* or *La Légende de Saint-Christophe*. Entitled *Guercoeur* after the name of its hero, it is an allegorical work in three acts with the first and third of these having their setting in Paradise. Act I shows us a group of divinities—Goodness, Beauty, Suffering and Truth—watching over the shades of dead warriors, among whom Guercoeur figures prominently. All the others are content to slumber in eternal peace, but he starts up and demands to be returned to earth where his beloved Giselle awaits him and where the cause of liberty still has need of his services. Goodness considers his request, but concludes that it would be dangerous to grant it. The attitude of Suffering is more subtle, however, and she takes it upon herself to release the young man from his bondage. (It is symptomatic that each of Magnard's deities is a woman!) The scene of Act II is accordingly a hillside in Tuscany near which Guercoeur was born and grew up. As the hero awakes, a choir of Illusion beckons him to his self-appointed tasks. On reaching the village, he discovers with dismay that Giselle has given herself to his best friend, Heurtal, who has not only broken his word but has subverted his political ideals to the extent of becoming a dictator. Although heartbroken at this outcome, Guercoeur forgives all and throws himself into the job of securing restitution for his people. They refuse to recognize him, however, and he is killed defending his principles. At the opening of Act III we therefore encounter the disillusioned fighter once more entering the gates of Paradise, this time being welcomed by Truth, whose balm he had formerly declined to acknowledge. Regarded as a morality play, the work fitted in well with what the composer's friends knew of his philosophy. Its exaltation of pessimism was the exact counterpart of Magnard's sense of disenchantment. Considered more as an operatic vehicle, it still came across in a rather dismal fashion, the characterization seeming grotesque and prehistoric. Some of this feeling was purely temporal and reflected the fact that, though written before the war, the work did not get performed until 1931. When we consider how Ropartz was obliged to orchestrate two of the acts from memory, it is perhaps remarkable that it ever got performed at all.

The reason which lay behind these happenings relates, of course, to Magnard's sudden death at the hands of the German army in September 1914. Ensconced at his luxurious country house in the region of Baron-sur-Oise, the composer was working to complete the score of *Guercoeur* (excerpts from which had been played by Colonne as far back as 1910) when he was interrupted by news of the invasion. Sending his wife and family into the country, he elected to remain at his desk with the stubborn pride for which he had become notorious. Probably he was assisted in his decision by the reverence he felt for his wonderful collection of books and paintings, including first editions of Diderot and Chénier and originals by such favourite artists as Boucher and Corot. As a platoon of Uhlans entered his estate, the composer fired his revolver from an upper window of the house, causing the death of two soldiers. What happened next is still something of a mystery. Carraud inclines to the theory that Magnard used one of the remaining shells in his weapon to commit suicide; the composer's wife, on the other hand, insisted that the Germans must have gone in and finished him off. Either way, it is difficult to produce conclusive evidence, since the invaders immediately burnt down the house along with all its contents. Lost in the fire were all the surviving copies of *Yolande* and a large part of the recent work on *Guercoeur*.[1] The manuscripts of each of the composer's other works—with the single exception of the Fourth Symphony—were also among the casualties. Such a wasteful end to a brilliant career must seem expecially poignant. It invites us to ask whether it was really necessary. Certainly the gesture was a thoroughly useless one, and may have done more harm than good. But it was a sublime gesture nevertheless, and one that was entirely in keeping with Magnard's steadfast, irascible character. He would have been hurt, but not surprised, to learn that

[1] Particularly successful among Ropartz's restorations must be counted the vocal quartet with which the opera ends. Indeed, the whole of the last act is very fine, containing as it does much orchestral part writing of chamber proportions.

the enemy also went on to desecrate the church of Saint-Gervais (whose singers he had praised in several of his *Figaro* articles) by pounding it with artillery on Good Friday 1918, just four days after the death of that other great 'musicien francais', Claude Debussy.

Fastidiousness has always seemed so much a part of the French artistic temper that it ceases to astonish us. Yet this trait tells us little about those extremes of hesitation and circumspection to be observed in the personality of Paul Dukas, who is the next figure we must deal with. Cursed with Duparc's urge towards self-destructiveness, he was saved from that composer's fate only by his superior innate control. Limiting his legacy to a dozen works seemed like an unduly modest course to his friends, but the standards Dukas set himself were actually so high that we are equally at liberty to enquire whether or not he was being arrogant. For if anyone applied to himself the same canons as he used to measure Beethoven, Berlioz and Wagner, it was this dignified and scholarly descendant of the Strasbourg bourgeoisie. The son of a banker and a talented woman pianist, he personified the type of the rich, culti-vated Jew such as used to be portrayed in the novels of Gustav Freytag. His musical standing in France continues to be very high indeed; only a shade below that accorded to Debussy and Ravel. In Britain, we are slower to appreciate his merits, having failed to mark his centenary in 1965 with anything like the festiveness it warranted. As there is at present no book in English which is devoted entirely to the life and work of this important musician, it might seem impertinent to proceed by summing him up in a few short pages. But we are only concerned here with his presence among the Franck circle. He must seek his due at the hands of other critics, who it is hoped will grant him a prestige equal to that which he enjoys in his own country. Perhaps the most valuable statement that can be made in the absence of a full-length assess-ment is that Dukas's achievement spread itself over a variety of contrasting sectors—including writing, conducting and compo-sition. Though he was not equally successful in each of these sec-tors, he devoted an equal portion of his life to them and hence de-serves to be treated as a complex figure. Moreover, though his creative output was slight, this too covers an unexpectedly wide range of forms. To have written only a handful of works, yet to be remembered for one's contribution to opera, symphony, sym-phonic poem and sonata, is to have attained an almost unbelievable triumph.

Dukas's education began conventionally enough at the Lycée Charlemagne, and then at Turgot, after which he took piano and harmony lessons from Mathias and Dubois, respectively. In 1884, when he had been at the Conservatoire for three years, he graduated to the class of Guiraud and devoted himself more to composition. Unlike Debussy, whose friend and junior he was, he did not go on to win the Premier Prix de Rome, his cantata *Velléda* managing to finish up with only a second prize. He did, however, secure a first in fugue and counterpoint, subjects that were to prove more useful to him in the years to come. Just at the point when he had completed his apprenticeship, military service overtook the composer, making it impossible for him to enter fully into the various commitments he had planned. Several unpublished sketches—including an overture to *King Lear*—were hopefully dispatched to Pasdeloup from the city of Rouen, where the young man was patently longing to conclude his basic training, but none of these opened a path for him in the profession he had chosen to follow. It was left for another overture, the enterprising *Polyceute*, to perform this function in 1892. This was a clever and craftsmanlike essay, rather too obviously redolent of Franck and Wagner. One of its purposes was evidently to make plain the composer's mastery over the orchestra, an achievement nobody cared to deny him. His first sizeable work was the Symphony in C (1897), which straddled the gap between Chausson's (1890) and d'Indy's No. 2 (1904). A few months after giving birth to this colossus, Dukas added to his output with the popular symphonic poem *L'Apprenti-sorcier*. The symphony is in three movements instead of the usual four (a typically Franckist preference, or so it would appear) and is revered today chiefly for its andante, a lofty yet continuously varied intrusion which the composer never improved upon. The tone-poem naturally won more adherents for itself, and is still among those most often played both in Europe and in the United States. It is of some interest to point out that the former work was first conducted by Paul Vidal, yet another Franck pupil who made his mark as the chorus master of the Opéra. The latter, on the other hand, was directed by Dukas himself.

An analysis of the symphony would reveal many pointers to Franck's influence, not least of which would be the space accorded

Ex. 31

Paul Dukas: Symphony - (1st Movement).

mf

to the working out of its themes. Beginning with a sharp, Borodin-like summons in the tonic key of C, the opening allegro advances into a splayed, dreamy second subject in which the intervals are more widely distributed. The rhythm remains unequivocally 6/8 throughout. At what seems like the end of the exposition, a new stepwise theme is announced by the horns, and this proves to be the motto cry on which the whole symphony is based. Having commenced with such a full tableau, it was not to be expected that the development would be short. What follows, however, is really too exhaustive an argument, with much of the energy and allure being thrown away. When we reach the second movement, we find the tonality has shifted to the mediant minor. This movement appears to have two principal themes, one melancholy and the other clear and confiding, but very soon a third idea is presented which modulates rapidly into still more remote keys. The composer is then left to weave his way back to the starting point without seeming to be too factitious. Once this has been accomplished, the finale reverts to being another allegro—but this time more *spiritoso* than *fuoco*.

Ex. 32
Paul Dukas: Symphony - (Finale).

It makes much of a series of triplets derived from the first movement and leads ultimately to a stridently optimistic climax. A vigorous and well-executed work, the C major Symphony was perhaps a shade too starved of personal essence to have made its composer an immediate and lasting reputation. As with d'Indy's larger compositions, the lack of a welcoming sense of authorship was one of the handicaps it had to overcome. Such a criticism does not apply anything like as forcibly to *L'Apprenti-sorcier*, which fully deserves its world-wide appeal. The subject, of course, was taken from Goethe's ballad, and relates to the frightening pranks of a magician's assistant. A superbly orchestrated study, it stands as the perfect model of its composer's skill. To grasp the understanding of tone-values which he possessed, one only has to compare the comic-sinister uses to which the bassoon is put with

Ex. 33

Paul Dukas: L' Apprenti Sorcier

Assez lent

the remorseful strains of the viola episode, right at the end of the work, when the abject apprentice is made to grovel before his master. In each case, the chosen instrument is exactly the right one to have used to convey the desired sensation.

What Dukas managed to prove with this latest composition—which was an instant success wherever it was performed—was that he was certainly no sorcerer's apprentice himself. If anything, he had staked his claim to being the sorcerer. At all events, it was

Ex. 34
Paul Dukas: L' Apprenti Sorcier

through the medium of his tone-poem that he suddenly acquired the fame for which so many members of the circle had laboured in vain. Aside from the captivating nature of the story, what was it about this work that caused it to triumph so regularly? Quite possibly it was the full-blooded and somewhat un-French exhibitionism which it displayed. We have said that Dukas was a retiring and fastidious personality, but the lean grace and charm which had been the mainstay of so many previous French composers found no backing in his philosophy, which constantly sought to exploit the qualities of depth, solidity and brilliance. It is not for nothing that later commentators have referred to him as a kind of Gallic Richard Strauss. In a way, the two composers could not have been more unalike, since there is not a trace of common ground to be encountered in their attitudes to their art. Dukas generally shunned publicity and hated anything but the best; his contemporary, on the contrary, developed a talent for self-advancement and soon reached a point where he became more than satisfied with the second-rate. What has united them in the minds of critics from both their countries is the mutual fascination with brilliance which they evinced. Looking at the Frenchman's favourite sounds, we can see that they range, like Strauss's, from the delicate harp harmonics which pick their way through *Le Sorcier* with such suspenseful effect to the agile, blazing brass of the full orchestra. How much more unfortunate it is, therefore, that Dukas chose to ally himself with restraint when it came to writing for the largest and most exciting combinations. This time we can hardly say that his silence was due to Franckist inhibition or incompetence. It was rather a matter of arriving at the right sort of standards, assuaging that proud Jewish sensibility which drove deeper and deeper into the furthermost recesses of art until it discovered a place of harmony and repose.

Spurning fresh opportunities for acclaim in the orchestral sphere, Dukas puzzled his admirers by making his next advance with the aid of the piano. The two works which he wrote at the turn of the century—the monumental Sonata and the severe *Variations, Interlude et Final sur un thème de Rameau*—must have seemed museum pieces to a public nurtured on the elegant trifles of the post-romantics. Actually, they constituted the logical sequel to Franck's late triptyches and came to act as a significant portent to the d'Indyists. This did not prevent d'Indy himself from misinterpreting the Sonata, the earlier of the two works to be played and discussed, by thinking of it as a purely cyclical invention. In his Cours de Composition Musicale, the Schola's Director professed to detect common themes linking the four movements of Dukas's masterpiece; a conclusion that is specifically rejected by Cortot, one of the work's prime exponents, and upheld by no other authority of eminence. The truth is that, although the Sonata owed much to the inspiration of Franck's essays, it cannot be put down as a direct imitation of them. Beethoven's influence was at least as pronounced in the composer's way of thinking, and he could well have followed the pattern set by op. 106 and 111. Professor Norman Demuth's judgement should be regarded as authoritative in this matter:

> Dukas may be said to be an honorary member of the great Franck tradition, for he subscribed to its ideals, although in principle only. His sonata in B flat minor is not *cyclique*, the somewhat sidelong reference to the first movement theme which appears very transitorily in the finale being hardly sufficient warrant for placing the work in that category.

As the professor goes on to admit, however, many of the Sonata's other themes are Franckist in shape and feel, if not in power of recurrence. The chromatic theme in common time beginning with the repeated E flat in the first movement, and that in 3/4 time commencing with a B natural in the second movement, are ready examples. Each has the characteristic see-saw procedures so beloved of

Ex. 35
Paul Dukas: Piano Sonata - (1st Movement).

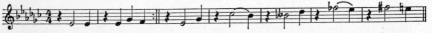

the master. Some critics might be inclined to go further and point to traces of Franck's pianism in the texture of the writing. Here the figuration is more workmanlike than brilliant, with occasional bottlenecks caused by following the laws of part-writing wherever they happened to lead. The habit is one that César inadvertently strove to pass on. But for all its derivativeness, the Dukas sonata is a massive and important contribution to the medium; in the opinion of Louis Aguettant 'la plus belle depuis Beethoven'. A full analysis may be sought either in Cortot's book or in the historical study by Blanche Selva.

Ex. 36

Paul Dukas: Piano Sonata - (2nd Movement).

It may be of keener interest to English readers to devote some space to a consideration of the Rameau variations which, though less frequently played, add up to a work of even finer calibre. At the time they were written, the form must have seemed just as out of date as that of the Sonata. There had, of course, been many earlier sets of piano variations of unimpeachable quality—witness Beethoven's on a waltz of Diabelli or Brahms's magnificent series on a Handelian theme. But the French pianistic tradition was once more sparse in such things. Undoubtedly the best of the few models Dukas had at his disposal was Fauré's splendid Theme and Variations, op. 73, written only three years previously. This, however, was a shortish composition and its style had been enlivened by occasional seductive touches. By contrast, Dukas proposed to make no concessions whatever to the romantic spirit. The theme he chose was itself drawn from that great age of French classicism to which he never ceased to feel indebted, coming from the menuet of Rameau's fourth suite of 'pièces de clavecin'.[1] Its title—mystifyingly given as *Le Lardon*—was an indication of how the fingers of the harpsichordist were compelled to imitate those of a chef running strips of fat through a fowl, the tips of the one set having to penetrate the gaps left by the other. This subject is treated to twelve variations in all, including the finale, and they can be said to fall into three distinct groups. Variations I to VI are concerned chiefly with the possibilities of melodic decoration; numbers VII to X then proceed to outline the various rhythmic potentialities of the theme; lastly, there is a lead-up to the Interlude—an unexpectedly

[1] It will be recalled that Dukas was one of those who worked on the restoration of *Les Indes Galantes*. Like Debussy, he considered Rameau 'un homme d'un génie admirable et tout français'.

virtuoso affair—followed by a grandly conceived peroration. As d'Indy was the first to point out, the whole composition exploits the three principal aspects of variation technique—ornament, decoration and amplification. Players anxious to try their mettle at it should be warned that its texture offers no opportunities for display; though perhaps it is slightly more enticing in this respect than the Sonata. Despite the desire he showed to develop an expressive keyboard idiom, Dukas refused to permit himself the comforts of a 'bien-chanté' manner, and there is nothing in this long chain of episodes which deliberately sets out to flatter the ear. The most attractive variations are possibly the third and fourth, the former of which presents an idealized version of the theme in the bass while the latter exhibits a gently submerged version spread out between the hands. Otherwise, one cannot fail to admire the skill the composer invested in, for example, Variation VII, where he attempts to paint a lyrical halo around the theme without ever stating any of its material directly; or in Variation IX, in which a bright counterpoint is allowed to make its appearance in the right hand. The Interlude and its preceding link-variation engage much more freely in modulation, so that when the original subject returns in the finale it is with a glorious feeling of renascence. Both this and the Sonata were given their premières by the Schola's pianist, Edouard Risler.

Never content to go on re-working a genre in which he had triumphed, Dukas had already transferred his attention to another field while his piano pieces were awaiting their acclaim. The target upon which he now set his sights was opera—a predictable enough rise in the level of aspiration. The choice of subject was at first a matter that proved troubling. As scholarly as ever in his range of interests, he began by selecting a Hindu drama entitled *L'Abre de Science*, but soon put it aside in favour of Maeterlinck's far more compelling *Ariane et Barbe-bleue*. This *conte-lyrique* occupied the composer throughout the greater part of the new decade, eventually obtaining its first performance at the Opéra-Comique on 10 May 1907. That it remains the second finest of all French operas— yielding priority only to *Pelléas et Mélisande*—is a judgement that most informed critics would not hesitate to endorse. In any case, it is a work of the highest and rarest quality, able to compete with any of the choicest fruits of the twentieth-century theatre. As the story was not one that Maeterlinck had invented—being unlike *Pelléas* in this respect—it was no surprise to the composer to find that others had preceded him with operatic versions of it. Grétry's *Raoul Barbe-bleue* (1789), to a text by Semaine, and Offenbach's *Barbe-bleue* (1866), based on a libretto by Halévy and Meilhac, were the best-known of these. After Dukas had made his setting, various successors were also impelled to try their hands: Bartók's *Duke*

Bluebeard's Castle (1911), using an adaptation of the Maeterlinck version by Bela Balaźs, and Rezniček's *Ritter Blaubart* (1920), with book by Eulenberg, being the most famous. As was the case with several of his fellow authors, Maeterlinck had concocted his *conte* largely from traditional French sources, including the legend of Gilles de Retz and the fairy-tale by Perrault. In his account, the interest centres upon the freedom-loving Ariane, sixth wife of Bluebeard, who probes the chambers of her husband's lair in order to discover the secrets of his previous life. While in pursuit of her task, she encounters his treasure-house and other possessions and, most revealingly of all, the former wives whom he has enslaved. On behalf of these unfortunate women she sets out to achieve deliverance, but is compelled to recognize that they prefer servitude to liberty. It was to this defeatist drama—so real and yet at the same time symbolic—that Dukas had the job of attaching his music.

The first thing to be said about the score which he submitted is that it aims at being more symphonic than operatic. The chorus pretends to an important role, though few incentives are offered to the principal singers. As with Bartók's setting, which seems to consist of recitative continually trembling towards arioso, the real focus of attention rests with the orchestra. This body certainly becomes the chief instrument of modification as far as the work's numerous 'leit-motifs' are concerned.[1] Such motifs naturally proclaim Wagner's influence, but Messiaen is not alone in reminding us that the Franck touch expresses itself in the manner in which they respond to the principles of change and variation. Even more

Ex. 37

Paul Dukas: Ariane et Barbe-bleue - (Cinq Filles d' Orlamonde).

---

[1] Most affecting of these is the haunting song of the 'filles d'Orlamonde', which has a vaguely Greek or Hindu flavour, and which recurs expressively in Acts II and III.

reminiscent of that composer is the tenebrous sense of gloom which hangs over the entire opera, breaking up during the second act into explosive streaks of light. Regarded in terms of plot, nothing very much is allowed to happen in the work, which does not aspire to be a parade of cruelty. In Act I we are shown Barbe-bleue welcoming his new wife, the high-point of the act coming at the moment when she discovers the jewels. To depict this discovery, Dukas relies on an evocative use of the whole-tone scale and on frequent showers of augmented triads. It is fascinating to note, from a technical standpoint, how the composer manages to differentiate each of the treasures—amethysts being made the prerogative of the horns, sapphires of the oboes, and pearls of the strings, with the accompaniment of a harp glissando. The only hint of a blood motif—and this is a point on which Bartók and Dukas differ markedly—comes when the rubies are unveiled.[1] There can be no doubt that the composer chose his tonalities very carefully in this work: the B flat used to remind the listener of the rubies contrasting with the sharp keys that are otherwise given preference. Indeed, Dukas's fondness for the latter may be interpreted as yet another Franckist trait. Harmonically, his method is more direct than, for example, Debussy's in *Pelléas*. Both the sounds and their orchestral clothing relate rather to conventional practice, with only occasional audacities. A shift of scene occurs in Act II of the opera, during which Ariane is left to explore the dungeons on her own. As the light breaks on her grim quest, a beautiful 'hymne solennel à la lumière' is heard from below. Almost as stirring is the grave *prélude* which is then invoked to introduce Act III, in which Ariane confronts herself in a mirror and settles down to await the return of Barbe-bleue, who has been wounded in a peasant revolt. On his entry, the freed wives are assembled to walk before his gaze in a fit of trembling. But it is out of love and not fear that they tremble, and the opera ends by them all reverting to 'un esclavage familier'.

Although Dukas lived on until 1935, he wrote nothing further in this vein. Relapsing into an almost unbroken creative withdrawal, he managed to complete only one work of significance during the ensuing twenty-eight years. This was the *poème dansé* entitled *La Peri*, an exotic study for the orchestra which appears to have been influenced by the Venusberg music from *Tannhäuser*. It was danced by Trukhanova at the Paris Opéra in 1912. Much the same range of skills was present in this lightest and most delectable of

---

[1] It will be remembered that in Bartók's opera the whole castle is presented as being drenched in blood—it appears on the weapons of the torture-chamber, on the jewels and on the flowers. His setting is thus in closer accord with the popular understanding of the legend, though both works strove to make a topical comment on feminism.

the composer's offerings—the adroit use of solo stringed instruments to create a mood of ripeness, the sudden and pungent interruption of brass fanfares, the overall sumptuousness of sound that almost served to eclipse the gayer Russians. Beyond this, there was only the conscientious round of teaching activities to occupy him. From 1910 to 1913 he acted as Professor of Orchestration at the Conservatoire, going on from there to the Ecole Normale to take charge of composition. He was a good teacher, though a maddeningly indifferent conductor. In the meantime, he continued to produce punctilious editions of the classics, including Beethoven and Scarlatti, and was inspired to write short pieces in memory of Debussy (*La Plainte au loin du Faune*, 1921) and Ronsard (a song to commemorate the quatercentenary of 1924). His music criticism, begun during the nine years when he wrote for *La Revue Hebdomadaire*, persisted with essays for the *Gazette des Beaux Arts* and *Quotidien*. Finally, he became the proud recipient of a number of honours conferred by his fellow-countrymen, ranging from a post in the Inspectorate to a seat at the *Académie*, where he filled the place formerly occupied by Bruneau. Throughout all these years of journeying towards a central position in the musical establishment, Dukas was somehow never able to recover the full flow of his genius. Whether it was that he became hypercritical, like Duparc, or merely found it increasingly difficult to decide on what idiom to adopt, we shall always regret this gifted man's decline. As Romain Rolland has said of him, he conveyed the impression of being a successor to d'Indy, with even greater promise attaching to his compositions. That the promise remained unfulfilled is our tragedy as well as his.

In the event, the musician who succeeded d'Indy as president of the Société Nationale, and who perhaps did most to ensure the further perpetuation of Franck's name, was Pierre Onfroy de Bréville. It is worth remarking at this stage that only three of the master's pupils survived beyond the Second World War, and none of these is alive today. They were Fumet, Ropartz and de Bréville. Of this trio, the first was too eccentric to have shouldered the burden of his teacher's mission; and was in any case out of sympathy with some of its aims. The second, though wholly committed in his sympathies, was unable to exert the necessary internal influence in the capital, having spent the greater part of his working life in the provinces. Only de Bréville possessed both the facilities and the inclination to do what was required, and he did it to the best of his ability. A more reserved personality than either of his two friends, he had decided limitations as a propagandist. The victim of a certain aloofness that went with his temperament, de Bréville was rarely to be found amid the limelight, preferring to labour conscientiously behind the scenes. In this habit he proclaimed himself a true follower of his master. Born at Bar-le-duc in 1861, he had been raised in a climate of solemn respectability, and the ideals which he had been made to serve propelled him in the direction of a quiet but determined patriotism. For this reason, his parents urged him to take up a diplomatic career, but this was something he declined to do. Instead, he applied himself to the usual studies in jurisprudence. At the same time, neither he nor his family saw anything harmful in his attaching himself to Dubois for harmony lessons. Around 1885 we find the young student slaking his curiosity by eavesdropping on Franck's organ class at the Conservatoire. What appealed to him about the ideas he heard discussed there was the support they gave for the notion of a French tradition of chamber music. The establishing of such a tradition quickly became a lifelong goal to which de Bréville pledged himself, doing his bit as an artist as well as an advocate. During the ensuing fifty years or so, he played an exceedingly active part in the musical activities of the capital, re-emerging again after the holocaust of 1939–45.

The first compositions to be weighed against this public-spirited artist's name were not chamber-works, however, but works for the stage. Despite all his enthusiasm, he was decidedly late in following up his intentions with respect to the former sector. It is tempting to think that the inspiration to write in the smaller forms—as opposed to merely championing them—sprang from the work he put in as a teacher of ensemble at the Conservatoire during the Kaiser's war. However that may be, his initial period as a creative artist was marked by fairly conventional ambitions, some of them even traceable to Massenet's example. The overture to Maeterlinck's *La Princesse Maleine* (1892) was followed quite naturally by incidental music for the same playwright's *Sept Princesses* (1895). Both works are characterized by a slightly sentimental *fraîcheur* that recalls Chausson rather than Franck. A similar sort of charm and reticence may be found in the composer's *scène lyrique*, entitled *Sainte Rose de Lima*, based on verses by Felix Naquet. This eclogue for solo voice, female choir and orchestra offers what is perhaps the earliest hint of a Franckist bias. At least, one is inclined to draw up some such guide-rule when explaining the dramatic works. In the instrumental field, an *Introduction, Fugue et Final* (1888) had already proved that Franck's beloved ternary principle was imposing itself on his style. A *Fantaisie*, also written for the keyboard, helped to confirm the link. But the fusion of exotic with academic elements did not necessarily portend badly for de Bréville, who showed how cleverly he could assimilate the two influences. A glance at such later works as the piano suite *Stamboul* (1894–5, with the addition of a final movement in 1913), and the setting of Leconte de Lisle's poem, *La Tête de Kenwarch* for baritone and orchestra, should be sufficient to indicate with what individual mastery the composer set about reinvigorating the tradition of French orientalism. This tradition, it will be remembered, harked back to David's *Le Désert* and Franck's *Ruth*. The contributions of de Bréville bridge the gap between these works and the bolder canvases of Ravel and Roussel.

As a striking addition to the literature of the piano, the suite *Stamboul* is worth the attention of any aspiring executant. Cast in four medium-sized movements, the work seeks to paint a portrait of what was once the holy city of Byzantium; the emphasis dividing itself among the city's various locations. The opening *Lento*, which moves rapidly on into an *Andante*, conjures up 'Les Muezzins' summoning the congregation to worship from atop the cathedral's minarets. (It should be explained, perhaps, that St Sophia was a Christian church long before it became a Turkish mosque.) To follow comes a movement entitled 'Le Phanar'—marked *assez animé pas trop vite*—which is actually a mandra dance typically performed by the inhabitants of the Greek quarter. 'Eyoub'— which is the next of the four—invites the listener to visit the lower end of the Golden Horn, region of the ancient tombs; while to end he is transported back to 'Galata', the noisy and exciting business centre of the city. Easily the most remarkable of the innovations de Bréville introduced into this vivid tetralogy are the special rhythmic inflections that recur on page after page. These amount to no tiresome pastiche—as Saint-Saëns's similar intrusions were likely to be—but represent the genuine article, communicated to the composer by his friend Astik Hamamdjian, a scholarly Armenian musician who happened to be living at Ortakeui during the period of his visit. They can be seen in the alternating $3/8+2/8+3/8$ pattern of the last movements *un peu plus lent* section; and in the comparable $9/4$ (made up of $c+2+3$) of the 'Eyoub' movement. The Greek dance also attempts to convey an unstylized, authentic rhythm, this time a quick $7/16$. Such peculiarities make the work extremely taxing to the pianist—though no more so than the post-1950 compositions ossifying in many a modern publisher's catalogue. Melodically, interest also attaches to the varied scale patterns displayed in the suite, the co-existence of B flat and C sharp in the scales of the third movement being especially notable. But what should do most to commend *Stamboul* to present-day virtuosi (it is too rugged for the average amateur) is the rare fluency of the writing. The flow of bars 64–116 of 'Les Muezzins', and the flying octaves of 'Galata', help to make it a sheer joy to play.

The year in which this inventive work first made its appearance also happened to be that in which the Schola Cantorum threw open its doors at the Rue Stanislas. Before very long, de Bréville's services were in demand at the new institution, and it was he who helped to pioneer the teaching of counterpoint. From 1898 to 1902 the composer put in a vast amount of his time coaching young men

Ex. 38

Pierre de Bréville: Suite Stamboul.

and women in this difficult art, a role that was later handed over to Roussel. In his capacity as a teacher, de Bréville wielded a highly beneficent influence, seeming to uphold d'Indy's dogmatic principles without giving rise to the slightest antagonism. Not quite as permissive in his outlook as Ropartz, he was nevertheless kindly and charitable in all his dealings, and several generations of pupils owed their balanced training to his habits of good sense. Much the same habits underlay the music he wrote during these years, everything being distinguished by a supple adjustment of the rules to the dictates of conscience. That he could adapt himself to all manner of styles is confirmed by an examination of the composer's *Portraits de Maîtres*, a set of light-hearted parodies for the piano, the last of which doffs its hat in the direction of Franck himself. As for de Bréville's own tastes, they continued to draw him more and more towards what could be called a superior salon manner. The *mélodie* held an enormous fascination for him as it did for so many of his fellow Franckists. In the entire course of his career—which in this regard spanned the period between Franck's *Nocturne* (1884) and Poulenc's *Calligrammes* (1948)—he wrote more than a hundred songs, many of which remain unpublished to this day. The best of them are equal to the general run of Fauré's effusions, and palpably better than any but a few of his teacher's. It is the opinion of a number of judges that de Bréville's finest moments can be found among these intimate trifles. Outstanding in his production are 'Bernadette', 'La Forêt Charmée', 'Une Jeune Fille Parle', 'La Petite Ilse', 'Berceuse' and 'Le Furet'. But the enthusiast would do well to take account of the various collections, especially the two books of Rondels from Charles d'Orléans and the four vocal sonatinas to words by Jean Moréas.

Every composer strives to crown his early career with at least one major work of art, and in de Bréville's case this effort went into his opera *Eros Vainqueur*, first produced at Brussels in 1910. The tribulations he endured over this quite innocuous composition— the title was probably responsible for sparking off a good deal of the opposition it aroused—are now apt to seem a matter of ancient history. But to the artist himself they must have had a permanently crippling effect—at least as far as his theatrical ambitions went. The idea for the work evidently sprang from the author of the book on which it was based—the decadent Jean Lorrain. It was he, it will be recalled, who had provided de Wailly with the inspiration for his cantata, *Hylas, idylle antique*. Choosing de Bréville for his new collaborator was a stroke of genius for which he can hardly be allowed conscious credit. When the score was finished, Lorrain and Albert Carré, the conductor, met to discuss the possibility of a performance, and the former stood amazed while his musician friend exclaimed: 'Mais c'est de la grande musique! Allez à l'Opéra!' But it did not prove quite so easy to mount. The inimitable Claire Croiza was eventually invoked to create the role of Eros, a part she relinquished in favour of Jane Bathori at a semi-private audition at the Vieux Colombier in 1918. From there the work went on to secure a concert performance at the Schola in 1922, but did not reach the stage of the Opéra-Comique for a further ten years after that. By this time, de Bréville had understandably become somewhat embittered, directing that there should be no more attempts to meddle with the opera until after his death. In our present age of sexual enlightenment it is difficult to acknowledge that the work could have presented any more embarrassment to its producers than, let us say, Franck's *Psyché*, which it very much resembles in places. Decorum is a fickle master, however, and luck seems to have been against de Bréville from the beginning. The plot itself involved very little action—perhaps this was a contributory factor—and merely unfolded the adventures and ultimate death of the Princess Argine, who permitted herself to fall in love with Eros. As in Franck's symphonic poem, the interest lay more with the creation of a sensuous yet pure atmosphere of yearning.

The failure of *Eros Vainqueur* (which incidentally had good enough notices in respect of its Théâtre de la Monnaie début) decided its composer against continuing with a career in the opera-house. Once the war intervened, he did not hesitate to throw all his efforts into the abstract forms, particularly those he was helping to teach at the Conservatoire. Among the many new compositions he wrote for chamber ensemble, the Violin Sonata in C sharp minor of 1918 stands out as triumphant. Writing many years later, d'Indy was to claim this as one of the finest French chamber-works produced since the conflict, and it is a judgement that still applies. Inspired directly by the circumstances of war, it was dedicated to the memory of Lieut Gervais Cazes, a friend who met his death in action. The first movement is an energetic Allegro, heavily packed with themes and a shade too overloaded in its development. Military references first appear in the Scherzando, an odd movement which exhibits de Bréville's favourite 9/16 rhythm once again. The lament comes in the Adagio which forms the third of the work's four movements, being based on a theme from one of the composer's songs—the sombre 'Héros, je vous salue' of Henri de Régnier. At this point, death strikes the hero down, and the sounds of a passing bell are heard. Predictably, the fourth movement then goes on to celebrate victory in a martial conclusion. First played by Enesco and Blanche Selva at a concert organized by the Société Nationale, the work made a profound and lasting impression on a people who had just been delivered from their enemies. The remaining chamber-works fall into two categories: those written in the 1920s, and the final group dating from after the Second World War. Amid the earlier, attention should be paid to the excellent though not very dramatic *Poème Dramatique* for cello and piano (1924), which reproduces a Beethovenian conflict between the *das bittende* (pleading) element and its *das widerstrebende* (resisting) opposite. It was first performed by Gérard Hekking and Jean Gentil on 24 January 1925. Afterwards came a refined Oboe Sonatina, and a second Violin Sonata (1927) which is served up in five linked movements and makes use of the rondeau form. This is altogether more sprightly and flowing than its serious predecessor.

Alongside the upsurge of interest in chamber music went a like determination to persevere with the piano as a creative medium. Having devised an orchestral version of *Stamboul* (extremely competent, but hardly as effective as the original), de Bréville now turned his attention to producing a fully-fledged Piano Sonata. There are not many specimens of this genre in French music, the nation's pianists preferring to charm their listeners with highly coloured *préludes* and *fantaisies* instead. Other than the Dukas sonata, upon which we have already commented, it would be difficult to point to a better example than that written by de Bréville in 1923. An immensely solid yet digestible work, it not only looks

back to Dukas's sturdy edifice but forward to the ingratiating but
still firmly-wrought sonatas of Dutilleux and Tony Aubin. Norman
Demuth sees it as forming the apex of the Franck tradition, and an
analysis of the texture of the *très lent* (♪ = 70) section, or the passage marked 'violent' with a 6/4 crotchet accompaniment, would go
a long way towards substantiating his claim. More lyrical than

Ex. 39
Pierre de Bréville: Piano Sonata.

Ex. 40
Pierre de Bréville: Piano Sonata.

Stamboul, the work is a beautiful illustration of de Bréville's gift for
cantabile writing, and abounds in subtle ornamentation of the kind
made famous by Couperin and his followers. The melodies often
emanate from the bass register of the keyboard (the whole sonata
opens, rather like Roussel's F sharp minor Suite, in the lower
depths) and move on to invite more and more complex decorative
treatment, strung out between the hands. The two succeeding
sonatas belong to the last phase of the composer's life, and represent
his third and fourth additions for violin and piano. Begun at the

outbreak of World War Two, No. 3 is cast in the key of C major and is notable for having a first movement in free variation form. Its fellow is in E minor, being much shorter and posing a link between the Andante and the Finale. The only other sonata which de Bréville left is for the viola, a highly chromatic work with a touchingly simple intermezzo in its midst. Remaining to his credit as a chamber musician are two Trios, one for strings and the other for oboe, clarinet and bassoon. Each of these deserves the luxury of an occasional performance.

Hardly anything more needs to be said about this second longest living of Franck's disciples (he died in 1949 at the age of eighty-eight, Ropartz soldiering on for a further six years to become the sole survivor). The series of articles which he wrote on his master —appearing under the title 'Les Fioretti de César Franck'—were published in the *Mercure de France,* a periodical to which de Bréville became music critic, in 1935 and 1938. They furnish us with some of the most life-like sketches of Franck at work in church and classroom, stressing the great man's punctual habits, bizarre attire, and lost, faraway look. The brief survey entitled 'L'Oeuvre Dramatique de César Franck' gained inclusion in a history of the French lyric theatre, and takes its place alongside the other studies of the subject by Destranges and van de Borren. The only other souvenirs of the association reside in the few liturgical works which de Bréville found time to write, the two motets and four *a cappella* choruses, the best of which is the harmonically audacious 'Cèdres du Liban'. Intelligently and individually conceived, they are all the same unmistakable products of the school in which their composer was reared, having much of the sweet saintliness of Franck's own *Béatitudes.* Looking at de Bréville purely as an artist, he at no time presented what a recent writer on music has termed 'the naked face of genius'. What he possessed was an abundance of carefully harvested aptitudes, which he used to create a most attractive and refined body of music. In this characteristic he resembled Ropartz and many another excellent but unspectacular musician. As Martin Cooper has pointed out, France has been singularly fortunate in throwing up figures of de Bréville's stamp— they tend to recur in every generation. They do not force themselves on our attention in the grand manner reserved for the Verdis and the Tschaikowskis of this world. But their work proves on examination to have qualities of truth and scrupulousness that are no less necessary to the cultural health of a nation. It was one of Franck's great merits that he perceived this fact, and made due allowance for it in all that he preached and taught.

Envoi

The commanding position which French music seeks to occupy in the modern world—and few commentators would question its supremacy over most other European schools—makes it imperative that we conclude our study by relating what we have learnt of the Franck tradition to the scene as it arranges itself today. To propose that this should take the form of anything beyond a simple outline would be to sanction the addition of another mass of material. It might seem tidier therefore—as well as less tiring to the reader—if we were to content ourselves with a few brief pointers. Above all, we must strive to present some assessment of the achievements of the circle as a whole, and some estimate of the current status of its members. The last obligation is crucial, if only because without it we shall be unable to indicate which composers stand in greatest need of reviving. Perhaps this is also the time to remind ourselves of the questions we posed at the outset of the book, especially those relating to the extreme singularity of the Franckist inheritance. Defining the exact nature of this inheritance continues to be a problem, but one which it must be our firm duty to resolve. Such a definition as we may propose need not lead to further commentary. The case for Franck's influence on modern musicians—and one is thinking here of traditionalists like Honegger and Dutilleux rather than of the *gamelang* masters—is one that musicologists can be left to prosecute. His power of reaching out into the twentieth-century world rests more securely with the example he set. Our summary should therefore seek to underline the lessons to be deduced from the circle's struggle, particularly as these apply to the serious artist cast adrift in a smug and decadent society. If we can learn anything useful from these lessons, it will go a long way towards justifying the pains we have taken. Another of our obligations must be to point out how the circle accommodated itself to the larger vision of French culture, what its place is likely to be in the nation's hall of remembrance.

Let us begin by inquiring what it was precisely that Franck and his followers achieved. Only a blind worshipper would claim that they added substantially to the world's stock of great music, so that their achievement can scarcely be regarded as purely artistic. Not that this should be taken to imply a devaluation of the few master-pieces which appeared. Works like Duparc's *L'Invitation au Voyage*, d'Indy's *Symphonie Cévenole*, Chausson's *Poème* and Franck's own Violin Sonata do not need the testimony of any critic. They can subsist handsomely on their merits. But if we separate music out into its various genres we can see at once that perfection is dependent on the exigencies of form. Without there being a symphony to envisage, Beethoven could hardly have written his famous *Pastoral*. His precursors are accordingly entitled to share in his glory. In the same way, the failure of Franck and his pupils to furnish us with an array of epic works must be set against the circle's admitted reputation for innovation. Clearly there were certain forms in which its members did not excel. It is difficult, for instance, to think that they contributed much to the ballet, despite its being an ancient national form much in need of revival. But one only has to look at the variety of forms in which they did interest themselves to recognize the full value of their efforts. How much does the *mélodie*—and hence its great practitioners from Debussy to Poulenc—owe to the sufferings of Duparc? Would there have been a String Quartet by Ravel without the one written by César Franck a dozen years earlier? Is it true that Roussel would have become such a classic symphonist if he had not been preceded in this ambition by d'Indy, Chausson and Dukas? These are the sort of questions historians should ask if they wish to encourage a just estimate of the circle's achievements. Moreover, they should be prepared to acknowledge the truths contained in their answers. In the meantime, it is necessary to return the argument to its larger context by asserting that without the Franckists' determination to discover new forms of expression, and to revive others which had lain dormant, the nation would have had to wait considerably longer for its aural revolution.

Invited to specify the group's boldest discovery, we should have to plump for the cyclic form. This device recurs like a trademark in almost every large-scale work by the composer and his pupils. Time has tended to decry its importance—as perhaps it is doing with the sonata principle itself—and one can hardly blame d'Indy and his friends for not sensing its transitoriness. The danger today is that we might be inclined to underestimate the number of good compositions it inspired. It may be that the musicians of Debussy's generation felt no need for such supports.[1] But then they were far more likely to be men of genius, artists who could afford to dispense with all system-built aids. For less richly endowed figures—a Chausson, say, or a Lekeu—the setting up of the drawing-board conferred inestimable preliminary advantages without which they might never have overcome their effusiveness. Anyway, is there not something commendable in the Franckists' determination to regard music as shape in addition to sound? Coming just when it did, their proclamation had a most salutary effect, not simply on those musicians who had allowed themselves to become enraptured by Wagner's endless *melos*, but also on their erstwhile colleagues in lighter sectors of the profession. For what it emphasized was that music was a discipline—an art that partook of precisely those elements of *logos* which had distinguished the Greek forms of culture many centuries earlier; forms that France had always professed to admire but had rarely stooped to imitate. In this light, Franck's influence was not so much Nordic and foreign as designed to promote a more proper obedience to the Gallic heritage. If there is one overriding merit to be attributed to the school of composers fathered by Franck, it is that they clung tenaciously to their conception of the artist as a superior individual, a prophet in the midst of his people. Unquestionably, their failures were being constantly re-enacted. But—and this is much more to the point—they were also being sporadically redeemed. Much of this idealism sprang from a purely technical appreciation of the virtues of form.

It was inevitable that dedication to these sober virtues would result in less attention being paid to melody and rhythm. The typical Franckist melody is slender in range and brief in duration. Franck himself was by no means bereft of inspiration, as works like the Symphony and Quartet confirm. But he rarely developed his ideas as continuously as Berlioz had done. Few of his melodies depart from the stock eight-bar formula, and those that do can be broken down into short, blocked-off units of either two or four measures each. When he attempted something bolder—as in his various *pièces héroïques*—he usually fell into the trap of obviousness, not to mention vulgarity. Only in his last Chorales do we get an inkling of how he might have used his insidious progressions to better effect. The urge to modulate played havoc with the composer's power to invent a true melody, forcing him to press on the leading note with a tiresome and predictable insistence. When left to mark time in a key, he would frequently commit the obverse

[1] Against this view, it might be argued that even Debussy was forced to return to the symphonic form for *La Mer*; many of his last works betray a similar acceptance of classical ways.

fault by doubling back too hurriedly to the tonic. Yet if Franck cannot be classed as a natural melodist, he was assuredly a very individual one. Phraseology rather than distance was his strong suit. Tiny slivers of notes remain firmly in the head—the Piano Quintet is full of them—and these almost convince the listener that a tune need not have a distinct outline in order to be believable. Though relieved of his master's worst vices, d'Indy also failed to excel in this elusive sphere. Ungifted with any very personal powers of expression, he was tempted to relapse into a banal and over-cautious system of tone-building. Chausson, on the contrary, exhibited the warmest lyrical talent, even though it did not always protect him from his technical inadequacies. Critics might be inclined to offer the same judgement on Duparc, who nevertheless managed to write one or two extremely long and controlled melodies in his better songs. In the last resort, however, none of these men had it in him to master what was involved, and all were a shade too contemptuous of the easeful attractions. By disdaining the comic-opera skills of their predecessors, it appears that they renounced one of the basic weapons in the composer's armoury—his power to charm and delight.

Perhaps there is more to be said on behalf of the circle's metrical innovations, though such praise as we bestow cannot always be extended to Franck himself. In most of the master's own works the possibilities of rhythmic subtlety are circumscribed by his fondness for the usual 3/8 or 6/8 movement. We hardly ever find him playing off three against four, or five against eight, as Fauré and the early Debussy loved to do. What he does display is a regular use of syncopation, achieved in common time by placing the accent on the second or fourth beat. This habit has not worn too well with the years, possibly on account of the pervasiveness of the jazz influence. (Humming the big tune in the last movement of the D minor Symphony, there is a temptation to speed it up in a jog-trot American style!) Probably this weak-beat accentuation is what has contributed most to the circle's reputation for spinelessness. Otherwise, one imagines that Franck derived many of his metrical notions from Beethoven, and critics of that master's lumpish habits of 'marching-and-halting' may be distressed to find them duplicated in the work of his admirer. Where Franck really lets us down is in his inability to evolve a clear-cut, masculine rhythm which can also bear the full burden of his musical thought in the manner that Beethoven's does throughout the Andante of the Seventh Symphony. Taking the circle as a whole, it was d'Indy who did most to restore rhythm to its properly appointed place. His control over ebb and flow was not something he had learnt from the Bonn master; it stemmed from a variety of polyphonic sources, hardly any of which were known to Franck. To examine the chant 'O crux ave, spes unica' from the opera, *La Légende de Saint-Christophe*—especially at the point where Sathanael trembles and the chorus begins 'O Sainte Croix, toi, notre unique espérance'—is to be reminded of what French music had lost in the way of serene and diastolic movement since baroque times. Many of the younger pupils imitated d'Indy and Bordes in their exploitation of these older patterns, though often without the same degree of skill. Perhaps the essence of their contribution lay in the power they captured of combining rhythmic tension with strict command over the forces of counterpoint.

Another, and more extraordinary, aspect of the circle's teachings consisted of the idea that harmony could be made to convey a sense of chiaroscuro. This at least was a discovery for which Franck should retain the credit. It is widely accepted that poetry can simulate gradations of light and dark by juxtaposing vowel sounds of the right substance and gravity. The older Italian masters were acutely aware of the need for such changes, as may be inferred from a study of the *Purgatorio* or *Paradiso* of Dante. That modern men of letters are not less sensitive is suggested by the presence of 'schools of light' like that of Mallarmé, and by the charred, sooty flavour which seems to cling to the verses of poets like Laforgue and T. S. Eliot. Quite recently, Professor Harry Levin of Harvard University has catalogued the various 'images of blackness' to be found in American writers from Poe to Melville.[1] By comparison, French art—and this applies to painting as well as literature—has appeared to stress the element of tonal contrast, frequently endeavouring to present deliberate fluctuations of luminosity. One only has to look at Manet's sumptuous blacks and greys, and compare them with the flakes of light a canvas by Matisse or Dufy will fling off. A similar sort of opposition is demonstrable in poetry by bringing one of Baudelaire's funeral visions into relation with, let us say, Valéry's 'Le Cimetière Marin'. In the cases of Manet and Baudelaire, their radiant darkness was perhaps the result of Spanish and German influences—the former owing much to his awareness of Goya's 'maja dolorosa' style and the latter to his absorption with Wagner's Venusberg. Up to the time at which Franck appeared, hardly any of this sophisticated play with colours had left its mark on the musical tradition. It is true that certain harmonic piquancies in the work of Couperin and his followers may be taken to signify their responsiveness to shading. But these are a far cry from the astonishing eruptions of brightness and

[1] See his book *The Power of Blackness* (Faber, 1958) for a full account.

dimness that we perceive in Debussy and Ravel. Without impugning the originality of either of these composers, it must be said that the real spur to their discoveries came with César Franck's impasto-like treatment of harmony.

The best method of coming to terms with this principle of *synaesthesia* is to work one's way through the fresco, *Les Béatitudes*. We have already devoted much space to identifying the various key-colour associations that appear in the work. But other and sometimes fresher experiments occur in the compositions of selected disciples. Duparc is clearly an interesting case to consider in this connection, since his setting of two of Baudelaire's poems seems to have been undertaken with more than a hint of the principle in mind. One may recall the sombre chords used to evoke the grotto at the opening of 'La Vie Antérieure', or the brilliant illusion of light that precedes the voice's entry in 'L'Invitation au Voyage'. D'Indy also resorts to the device in parts of 'L'Etranger' and so does Lekeu, in less blatant fashion, at the high-points of some of his chamber-works. That the idea did not spread to the entire circle—as happened with the notion of cyclic form—should be attributed more to variations of sensibility than to any technical failure. It was to the pantheistic or mystical composer that the idea really appealed, and it is impossible to believe it exercised much fascination for the more down-to-earth pupils. We should regard it as symptomatic that there hardly appears to be a trace of its use in such practical, workaday musicians as Coquard and Rousseau. Likewise, Augusta Holmès—despite all her romantic airs—was much too worldly to have been inveigled into employing it in her compositions; while the frigid Magnard would probably have sneered at its emotional connotations. Yet the chiaroscuro idea has proved vastly more important for modern music than any of Franck's pupils could possibly have realized. During the second half of the twentieth century, it has become commonplace for composers to build their works exclusively around some sound-colour equation.[1] Messiaen's *Les Couleurs de la Cité Céleste* is a significant product of the new trend, and no one listening to the work could fail to be convinced of its deliberate 'dérèglement de tous les sens'. No doubt Franck would have deplored the absence of form which is a characteristic of such music, but he could hardly have missed recognizing himself as one of its unconscious progenitors.

Turning now to the reputations of specific pupils, it appears obvious that mastery can show no correlation with acclaim. On the

[1] The most obvious case is, of course, that of Alexander Scriabin (1871–1915) who actually wanted a 'colour-organ' introduced into the orchestra.

contrary, it almost seems as if the weaker members of the circle had successfully conspired to overthrow the stronger. D'Indy, Ropartz and Lazzari were all three prodigiously equipped for the job of being composers—yet how many of them have received a fraction of their due in the matter? Duparc, on the other hand, could only manage to write a mere sixteen songs—many of them at bitter cost to his health and psychological equilibrium—but has virtually secured admission to the pantheon wherein rest Fauré and Debussy. To take a different series of examples, Pierné, Rousseau and Holmès were all prize-winners of one sort or another, fabulously gifted in the mechanics of their art. Despite the juries they succeeded in pleasing, their work scarcely survives today. Against this must be set the fact that Chausson, whose limitations weighed on him like a sackful of lead, is not only played but much admired. What can be the moral of such a chronicle? That facility does not pay? That personality interests us more than proficiency? Perhaps it would be truer to say that art relates only indirectly to skill, a conclusion d'Indy and his friends would have been willing enough to acknowledge in private but rarely stopped to confirm in public. Certainly the Franck circle offers triumphant vindication of the theory that genius is likely to have feet which, if they do not hastily revert to clay, are at any rate big and clumsy. But to uphold this opinion should not be sufficient to close the issue. After all, talent deserves its share of fame no less than genius. When one thinks of the fine legacy bequeathed by the more fluent members of Franck's little band, it seems almost criminal that so few people wish to be availed of its riches. Are we, for instance, to forego all further opportunities of hearing a work as noble as d'Indy's 'L'Etranger', or as brilliant as de Bréville's *Eros Vainqueur*? Can we really afford to neglect the chamber music of Castillon and Guy Ropartz, or the songs of Bordes and Lazzari? Only a bigot could possibly answer in the affirmative.

Just as irresponsible as our neglect of their music is the lack of comprehension we display towards the purposes of these brave and tireless men. Superficially, it might seem as if they were all slaves to some swarming interior vision that led them to turn the dagger inwards on their talents. To believe this would be to confess our naïvety in the face of the situation they confronted, for the difficulties with which they grappled were often quite beyond the possibility of outward solution. Inevitably the enormous gulf which existed between the setting up of their works and the withering reception which society was waiting to accord them had the effect of driving the Franckists towards a much greater degree of monasticism than would otherwise have been the case. The climate in which they moved was one that posed insoluble dilemmas of ambition and acquiescence, of sincerity and dissimulation, of communication and estrangement. All this seems plain enough to the detached historian, but strains the ordinary listener's capacity for vicariousness. Attending a concert of works by some of the more industrious of the circle's members, it becomes hard to say how much their industry was a stratagem against the pitfalls of despair. In this sense, it is tempting to draw a parallel between men like d'Indy and Ropartz and their literary counterparts in Victorian England. Naturally energetic and civic-minded, and always with the sounds of duty ringing in their ears, these different artistic cohorts responded to much the same range of commitments. 'Moral earnestness' was a catchphrase to which they would both have pledged their allegiance. Going even beyond this, however, they shared in that awareness of spiritual and cultural breakdown that has since become a favourite spectacle to intellectuals of the present age. If French musicians were free of the 'honest doubt' which so regularly returned to plague Englishmen of Tennyson's stamp, they were nonetheless afflicted by a similar feeling that everything for which they had toiled and struggled might in the end turn out a mirage. Only time can tell whether these fears and misgivings were justified.

Mention of the Victorians can lead us to make yet another useful comparison. This relates to what the English Pre-Raphaelites would have recognized as a religion of beauty. Of such a faith there are numerous indications amid the Franck circle. We have already observed how d'Indy was accustomed to deriving his analogies from the works of the Italian primitives. Bordes was likewise deeply infatuated with the aesthetics of the Quattrocento, which he would as often as not transplant to nineteenth-century France. Each of these men was in a sense reacting unfavourably against the substitution of noise for beauty which had become so much a feature of the period in which they were living. The average Franckist's attitude to Meyerbeer was precisely that which a visual puritan like Holman Hunt might have been expected to take up towards Rubens. In both cases, what was being demanded was something like a return to absolute standards, however antique these threatened to be. The comparison may be pushed to its logical conclusion by stating that what the Schola really objected to in the teachings of the Conservatoire was exactly that dreaded academic flatulence which the Brotherhood had detected in the precepts of the R.A., Professor Quentin Bell, in his illuminating Slade lectures on the nineteenth-century artists, has pointed to the singularly divided character of the period which followed the Industrial Revolution, arguing that its standards of excellence were different from any that had preceded it:

It was an age of aesthetic fragmentation. There was a schism between groups of artists so that we find two or more completely alien aesthetic principles at work within a society and these of so violently antagonistic a nature that the most assured judgement of one age can be entirely reversed by its successor; i.e. a situation in which good art is good in a different way to that in which bad art is bad. Thus in the seventeenth century a bad French artist would have been an inferior Poussin, in the nineteenth century a bad French artist was *not* an inferior Cézanne.

Naturally, one cannot speak in quite the same terms for the other arts, but if we substitute the names of Couperin for Poussin and, say, d'Indy for Cézanne, we can certainly arrive at a better understanding of the plight of music during the earlier years of the Third Republic.

This brings us to the sternest charge ever to have been directed against Franck and his associates—namely, that they hung too closely together in their musical aims, forfeiting that rich eclecticism which went into the making of such freelance musicians as Busoni and Casella. It is instructive in this respect to compare the achievements of the Franck circle with those which accrued to Fauré and his pupils at the Conservatoire. Both groups of artists sought to escape from the tired orthodoxies of the day, but there is a certain uniformity of tone about the former group that sets it apart and makes it seem almost dull. With all their leanings towards the stage, the Franckists can be accused of having invested too heavily in the more noble, self-sacrificing type of subject, of which Chausson's *Arthus* may be taken as typical. By contrast, the Conservatoire alumni went out of their way to choose highly daring themes—witness Schmitt's setting of Wilde's *Salome* in 1907 and Caplet's ballet on Poe's *Masque of the Red Death* which appeared a couple of years later. Of course, it was not only the thrills of decadence that members of the circle failed to explore. With a few honourable exceptions, they proved equally unalive to that sunny vein of gaiety which had been so brilliantly exploited by Bizet; and for that matter to the naturalism foreshadowed in Charpentier's *Louise*. One or two dates might help to fill out the picture at this point. The year in which Bordes welcomed his first contingent of students at the Schola also happened to be that in which Mahler set out for Vienna—two events that offered conflicting testimonies concerning the direction European music was subsequently to take. From another point of view, we may think it worth reflecting that Guy Ropartz and Louis de Serres were actually born in the same year as the more worldly Richard Strauss. Neither of these men was content to remain a mere epigone of Franck, but it is equally certain that neither went forward to greet the new age with quite the freedom shown by his German contemporary. Indeed, the twelve-tone revolution appeared to pass them both by with an elusiveness similar to that which had been displayed earlier by the various expressionist cults.

These facts alone serve to rebut the slander that Franck's pupils hastened to seek protection from across the Rhine as soon as he was pronounced dead. The myth that French musicians of the nineties permitted themselves to be crushed beneath the Teutonic heel is one that need hardly detain anyone today. It should be sufficient to state that it was only Wagner who had ever aspired to wield this kind of influence; and his strategies existed independently of, and frequently in opposition to, those of Franck. Certainly there is nothing in the idea that men like Strauss and Mahler conspired to take over the role vacated by their predecessor. As tastemakers they made even less impact than Brahms, whose music had always been cordially detested in Paris. To argue that the outcome of Franck's work was a strengthening of the Germanic strain in French music is accordingly to perpetuate a dangerous half-truth. In fact his sympathies were not more German than those of Berlioz, who had earlier described himself as 'un musicien aux trois-quarts allemand'; or d'Indy, who was to prove far more of a Lucifer among the angels. In any case, there can be nothing discreditable in the receptiveness which France had shown in the presence of the foreigner. As a nation she had always been particularly hospitable to aliens. From one perspective at least, it could be said that the entire history of music in Paris has consisted of a succession of willing capitulations—first of all to the Italians, then to the Germans, and ultimately to the Russians. There are even some who think the city is on the point of handing over the baton to the Americans. The point is that none of these conquests has really imperilled the native Muse—least of all that provided by the Germans. Contrary to what many critics have had us believe, Wagner's influence was amazingly fructifying. How else are we to describe the process that led to such ripe fruits as *Pénélope* and *Ariane*? To speak, as one musicologist has recently done, about Franck's aims having been conducted 'in an atmosphere which by nature was opposed to them' is therefore somewhat misleading. If such statements were intended to point up the French musician's resistance to systematization, they are all very well; but they scarcely take account of the voracity with which the nation has traditionally devoured its immigrants.

That the lessons which Franck had to teach could have been learnt more rapidly and efficiently is a point that will not be contested. When we consider how impervious to his entreaties the country was during the Empire, we need not be surprised that the composer so quickly assumed the look of an interloper. What we forget is that the bias of the reactionaries at that time was not so much anti-German—after all, it was they who had crowned Meyerbeer—as anti-musical. César would thus have been accorded the same chilly reception whichever part of the world he had come from. Later on, when the taste for heroics had been replaced by something more edifying, Frenchmen gradually lifted their gaze to take in some of those influences which they had missed rather than resisted while Louis had been alive. Among these we may count Beethoven's much the most profound and far-reaching. Franck merely had the effect of re-inforcing what was evidently to become a classical revival; he imparted no mysterious essence of his own. That is at least true of the content of his teaching. The example he conveyed is perhaps a different matter, for here there was scope for a new kind of imitativeness based on moral rather than musical grounds. To suggest that morality had played no part in determining musical fashions up to this time would be to risk another dubious generalization. But it is obvious that very few of Franck's forerunners had been able to imbue their pupils with the saintly spirit of dedication which he dispensed. The significance of this spirit should be sought, not so much in any changes of character it helped to implant in the men who placed themselves under his direction, but in the finer qualities of workmanship it was responsible for injecting into their compositions. Such qualities could only have arisen in a climate of absolute trust and self-reliance. Writing of this last virtue, Emerson once exclaimed:

> Oh what is Heaven but the fellowship
> Of minds that each can stand against the world
> By its own meek and incorruptible will?

Most Europeans—including perhaps Franck himself—might have preferred a grander vision of paradise, but few could have found happier words to describe the feelings of those loyal and defence-less disciples as they formed themselves around the hermit of Sainte-Clotilde just one hundred years ago today.

SELECT BIBLIOGRAPHY

Given such a wide field to cover, I cannot do more than present a brief but representative selection of material. Readers wishing for additional items on Franck will discover further bibliographies in Vallas, Kunel, Dufourcq, Buenzod and Gallois. The only attempt to provide a complete index of writings on the Belgian composer is contained in Kunel, but that does not go beyond 1942. Buenzod is the most useful supplement for the period 1942–66. For d'Indy, there is Vallas's 2-volume study, which gives ample documentation concerning work done before 1950, but which offers no guide to the articles occasioned by the centenary. A *plaquette* edited by Jean Naert and published in 1952 brings together most of the worthwhile papers written for that event. A good bibliographical guide to Chausson appears in the Barricelli-Weinstein volume, full details of which are included in the pages that follow. A *numéro spéciale* of the journal *La Revue Musicale* was devoted to this composer in December 1925, and another to Dukas in June 1936. As for the remaining figures belonging to the circle, no specific advice can be given. Very few of them have been honoured by separate studies, at least of book length, and there are some who seem to have elicited nothing apart from passing commentaries in the larger historical surveys.

Ackere, J. van: *Le Troisième Age d'Or de la Musique Française.* Paris; Max Eschig, 1966.
Aguettant, L.: *La Musique de Piano.* Paris; Albin Michel, 1954.
Aubin, T.: 'Lazzari.' *Comoedia.* 24 June 1943.
Aubry, G. J.: *French Music Today.* (Trans. Edwin Evans) London; Routledge, Kegan Paul, 1926.
Austin, W.: *Music in the Twentieth-Century.* London; Dent, 1967.

Baldensperger, F.: 'César Franck, l'artiste et son oeuvre.' Paris; *Editions du Courrier Musical,* 15 May 1901.
Barricelli, J.-P. and Weinstein, L.: *Ernest Chausson.* Norman. University of Oklahoma Press, 1955.

Bellaigue, C.: *Paroles et Musiques*. Paris; Perrin, 1925.
Benoît, C.: 'César Franck.' Paris; *La Revue Bleue*, 1890.
'César Franck.' Paris; *La Revue et Gazette Musical*, 1890.
Berlioz, H.: *Memoirs*. (Trans., Rachel and Eleanor Holmes. Ed. Ernest Newman.) New York; Knopf, 1932.
Bordes, C.: *Le Sentiment Réligieux dans la Musique d'Eglise de Franck*. Paris; Editions du Courrier Musical, 1 Nov. 1904.
Borgex, L.: *Vincent d'Indy, sa vie et son oeuvre*. Paris; Durand, 1913.
Borren, van de, C.: *L'Oeuvre Dramatique de César Franck*. Bruxelles; Schott, 1907.
Boschot, A.: *Chez les Musiciens* (2 vols). Paris; Librairie Plon, 1924.
Boucher, M.: *L'Ecole de César Franck*. Paris; 1917.
Bréville, P. de: 'Ernest Chausson.' Paris; *Mercure de France*, Sept. 1899.
'Les Fioretti de César Franck.' Paris; *Mercure de France*, Sept. 1935/Jan. 1936/July 1937/Jan. 1938.
Buenzod, E.: *César Franck*. Editions Seghers, 1967.

Calvocoressi, M. D.: *Musician's Gallery*. London; Dent, 1933.
Canteloube, J.: *Vincent d'Indy*. Paris; Laurens, 1951.
Cardus, N.: *Ten Composers*. London; Cape, 1945 (rev. edn., 1958).
Carraud, G.: *La Vie, l'Oeuvre et la Mort d'Albéric Magnard*. Paris; Rouart-Lerolle, 1921.
Chausson, E.: *César Franck*. Paris; Le Passant, 1891.
'Fervaal'. Paris; *Mercure de France*, April, 1897.
'Correspondence inédite de C. Debussy et E. Chausson.' Paris; *La Revue Musicale*. Dec., 1925.
Closson, C.: *Les Origines Germaniques de César Franck*. Paris; S.I.M., 1913.
Cobbett.: *Cyclopaedic Survey of Chamber-Music*. London. O.U.P., new edn., 1962.
Coeuroy, A.: *La Musique Française Moderne*. Paris; 1942.
Collaer, P.: *La Musique Moderne* 1905–55. (Trans., Sally Abeles, Cleveland, 1961.)
Colling, A.: *César Franck ou le Concert Spirituel*. Paris; Julliard, 1951.
Cooper, M.: *French Music from the death of Berlioz to the death of Fauré*. London; O.U.P., 1951.
Coquard, A.: *César Franck*. Paris; Le Monde, 1904.
Cortot, A.: *French Piano Music*. (Trans., Hilda Andrews, O.U.P., 1932). Vol. I.
Courville, X. de: 'Souvenirs Homériques—V. d'Indy, auteur d'opérette.' Paris; *La Revue Musicale*, Jan., 1932.
'Vincent d'Indy.' Paris: *La Revue Musicale*. Aug.—Sept. 1937.
Crosten, W. L.: *French Grand Opera*. New York; Columbia University Press, 1948.

Davies, L.: *The Gallic Muse*. London; Dent, 1967.
Dawson, R. V.: 'Beethoven and César Franck.' London; *Music & Letters*. Vol. XI No. 2, April, 1930.
Dean, W.: *César Franck*. London; Novello.

Debay, V.: 'César Franck.' Paris; *Editions du Courrier Musical.* 15 Nov. and 1 Dec. 1900.
Debussy, C.: *M. Croche, anti-dilettante.* Paris; N.R.F., 1926. (Trans., Langland Davies; Dover Books, 1960).
Demuth, N.: *César Franck.* London; Dobson, 1949.
Vincent d'Indy: champion of classicism. London; Rockliff, 1951.
French Piano Music. London; Museum Press, 1959.
Derepas, G.: *César Franck.* Fischbacher, 1897.
Destranges, E.: *L'Oeuvre Lyrique de César Franck.* Fischbacher, 1896.
Dufourcq. N.: *César Franck.* Paris; La Colombe. 1949.
Autour de Coquard, César Franck et d'Indy. Paris; Editions du Courrier, 1952.
Dukas, P.: *Ecrits sur la Musique.* Paris; S.E.F., 1946.
Dumesnil, R. and Combarieu, J.: *Histoire de la Musique* Tome III. Paris; Colin, 1922 (rev. edn., 1955).
Dumesnil, R.: 'Sylvio Lazzari.' Paris; *Le Monde,* 28 June 1945.
'Alberic Magnard.' Paris; *Le Monde,* 2 and 3 Sept. 1945.
Un demi-siècle de musique française. Paris; Librairie de France, 1925.
La Musique Contemporaine en France. Paris; Colin, 1950.
Duparc, H.: *Lettres à Francis Jammes.* (Ed., G. Ferchault.) Paris; Mercure de France, 1944.

Einstein, A.: *Music in the Romantic Era.* New York, Norton.
Emmanuel, M.: *César Franck, étude critique.* Paris; Laurens, 1930.
'La Musique de Piano de Dukas.' Paris. *La Revue Musicale,* May-June 1936.

Favre, G.: *Paul Dukas.* Paris; La Colombe, 1948.
Musiciens Français Modernes. Paris; 1953 and 1956.
Flem, P. le: 'Sylvio Lazzari.' Paris; *Paris-Midi.* 18 Aug. 1942.
Chausson et la musique pure. Paris; Euterpe, Sept. 1949.
Fumet, S.: *La Poésie à travers les arts.* Paris; 1954 (Trans. from his article in *Die Musik in Geschichte und Gegenwart.* Kassel, 1949).

Gallois, J.: *César Franck.* Paris; Editions du Seuil, 1966.
Ernest Chausson. Paris; Editions Seghers, 1967.
Gauthier-Villars, H. and Bréville, P. de: *'Fervaal'—étude critique et thématique.* Paris; Durand, 1904.
Gray, C.: *History of Music.* London; O.U.P., 1948.
Grout, D. J.: *Short History of Opera,* New York; Columbia University Press, 1947 (rev. edn., 1966).
Grove, Sir G.: *Dictionary of Music and Musicians.* London; Macmillan, 1954.

Hall, J. H.: *The Art Song.* Norman, University of Oklahoma Press, 1953.
Hallays, A.: 'Le Roi Arthus.' Paris; *Revue de Paris.* 15 Dec. 1903.
Harding, J.: *Saint-Saëns and his Circle.* London; Chapman & Hall, 1965.

Hervey, A.: *French Music of the Nineteenth Century*. London; Grant Richards, 1903.
Hill, E. B.: *Modern French Music*. Boston; 1924.
Honegger, A.: 'La Lepreuse.' Paris; *Comoedia*. 10 April 1943.
Horton, P.: *The Chamber-Music of César Franck*. London; O.U.P., Musical Pilgrim Series, 1943.

Indy, V. d': *César Franck*. Paris; Alcan, 1906. (Trans., Rosa Newmarch. London; Bodley Head, 1910. Re-issued Dover Books, 1965).
Cours de Composition Musicale. Paris; Durand, 4 vols. 1903, 1909, 1933, and 1951. (Ed., A. Sérieyx—vol. IV Ed., by Guy de Lioncourt.)
La Schola Cantorum, son histoire depuis sa fondation jusqu'en 1925. Paris; Editions de la Schola, 1927.
Beethoven. Paris; Collection Chantavoine aux Presses Universitaires, 1912.

Jardillier, A.: *La Musique de Chambre de César Franck*. Paris; Librairie Mellottee, 1929.
Jullien, A.: *Musiciens d'aujourd'hui*. Paris; 1892.

Kornprobst, L.: *J. Guy Ropartz*. Strasbourg; Wolf & Rouart, 1949.
Kunel, M.: *César Franck, l'homme et l'oeuvre*. Paris; Grasset, 1947.

Lalo, Pierre: *De Rameau à Ravel*. Paris; Albin Michel, 1947.
Lambert, C.: *Music Ho!* London; Faber, 1944 (rev. edn., 1967).
Lamy, F.: *J. Guy Ropartz, l'homme et l'oeuvre*. Paris; Durand, 1948.
Landormy, P.: *La Musique Française de Franck à Debussy*. Paris; Gallimard, 1944.
Lang, P. H.: *Music in Western Civilisation*. New York; Norton, 1942.
Laurent, A.: *Paul de Wailly, l'artiste, l'oeuvre*. Paris; 1933.
Paul de Wailly, le compositeur, l'artiste. Paris; 1940.
Lavignac, A.: *Voyage Artistique à Bayreuth*. Paris; Albin Michel, 1903.
Lioncourt, G.: 'La Mélodie de Vincent d'Indy: réponse à Léon Vallas.' Paris; *La Revue Musicale*. Oct., 1946.
Lockspeiser, E.: 'French Chamber Music' (in *Chamber Music*. Ed. Alec Robertson. London; Pelican Books, 1958).
Lorrain, M. G.: *Lekeu, sa correspondence, sa vie, et son oeuvre*. Liège; 1923.

Malherbe, H.: 'La Tour de Feu à l'Opera.' Paris; *Le Temps*, Jan. 1928.
Mauclair, C.: *La Réligion de la Musique*. Fischbacher, 1909.
Mellers, W.: *Man and his Music*. London; Barrie & Rockliff, 1962.
Mere, C.: 'La Tour de Feu.' Paris; *Excelsior*. Jan. 1928.
Moreau, C.: 'L'âme de Franck.' Paris; *Le Monde Musical*. 30 Oct. 1904.
Myers, R.: 'Guy Ropartz.' London; *The Listener*. 8 July 1948.

Northcote, S.: *The Songs of Henri Duparc*. London; Dobson, 1949.
Noske, F.: *La Mélodie Française de Berlioz à Duparc*. Paris; Presses Universitaires, 1954.

'The Solo Song outside German-speaking countries' (In *Anthology of Song*, Arno Folk Verlag, 1958. Oxford University Press.)

Oulmont, C.: *Musique de l'amour*. 2 vols. Paris; Desclee de Brouwer, 1936.

Painter, G.: *Marcel Proust*. 2 vols. London; Chatto & Windus, 1965.
Pearsall, R.: 'The Serene Anxiety of César Franck.' London; *Music Review* Vol 27. No. 2., May 1966.
Pitrou, R.: *De Gounod à Debussy*. Paris; Albin Michel, 1957.
Prist, P.: *Guillaume Lekeu*. Bruxelles, Lebeque, 1946.

Roberts, W.: 'César Franck.' London; *Music & Letters*, Vol. 3, No. 4, Oct. 1922.
Rodder, M.: *César Franck*. Turnhout, 1920.
Rolland, R.: *Musiciens d'aujourd'hui*. Hachette, 1922.
Ropartz, J. G.: 'César Franck.' Paris; *Revue Internationale du Musique*, June, 1898.
'Les Oeuvres Symphoniques de Dukas.' Paris. *La Revue Musicale*, May 1936.
Rostand, C.: *Les Chefs-d'Oeuvre du Piano*. Paris; Librairie Plon, 1952.
Roussel, A.: *Symphonie en si bémol de Vincent d'Indy*. Paris; Latinite, March 1930.

Saint-Saëns, C.: *Les Idées de Vincent d'Indy*. Paris; Lafitte, 1918.
Samazeuilh, G.: 'Ernest Chausson et "Le Roi Arthus".' Paris; *La Revue Musicale*, 15 Dec. 1903.
'Ernest Chausson.' Paris; *La Revue Musicale*, 1 Dec. 1925.
Paul Dukas. Paris; Durand, 1936.
Musiciens de mon temps. Paris; Renaissance du Livre, 1947.
Schneider, L.: 'La Mort d'Albéric Magnard.' Paris; *Le Temps*. 21 April 1931.
Schmitt, F.: 'Les Symphonies de Magnard.' Paris; *Le Temps*. 16 Nov. 1929.
Seitz, A.: 'La Génie de César Franck.' Paris; *Monde Musical*, 30 Oct. 1904.
Sere, O.: 'Musiciens français d'aujourd'hue.' Paris; *Mercure de France*, 1911.
Serieyx, A.: *Lettres de d'Indy, Duparc et Roussel*. Paris; Editions de Cervin, Lausanne, 1961.
Sonneck, O.: 'Guillaume Lekeu.' New York; *Musical Quarterly*, June 1919.
Stengel, R.: *Guillaume Lekeu 1870–1894*. Bruxelles; Editions de la Nouvelle Revue Belgique (n.d.).

Tiersot, J.: *Un Demi-siècle de Musique Française*. Paris; Alcan, 1918.
Tournemire, C.: *César Franck*. ed. Deligrave. Paris (n.d.).

Ulrich, H.: *Chamber Music*. New York; Columbia University Press, 2nd edn., 1967.

Vallas, L.: 'La Mélodie de V. d'Indy.' Paris; *La Revue Musicale*, Sept. 1946.
Vincent d'Indy (2 vols.). Paris; Albin Michel, 1946 and 1950.
'Lettres inédites de Saint-Saëns et d'Indy.' Paris; *La Revue Musicale*, Feb. 1947.
La Véritable Histoire de César Franck. Paris; Flammarion, 1955.
Vuillermoz, E.: 'Le Cas Lazzari.' Paris; *Candide*, May 1939.

Wailly, P. de: *César Franck*. Paris; 1922.

Ysaÿe, A.: *Eugene Ysaÿe, sa vie, son oeuvre, son influence*. Bruxelles; Editions de l'Ecran du Monde, 1949.

Zuckermann, E.: *The First Hundred Years of Wagner's 'Tristan and Isolde'*. New York; Columbia University Press, 1964.

INDEX